THE ROYAL SCHOOL OF NEEDLEWORK
Book of **Embroidery**

SEARCH PRESS

First published in 2018
Search Press Limited
Wellwood, North Farm Road,
Tunbridge Wells, Kent TN2 3DR

Reprinted 2018, 2019 (twice), 2020 (twice), 2021, 2023

Uses material previously published as
RSN Essential Stitch Guides: Bead Embroidery, by Shelley Cox 2013
RSN Essential Stitch Guides: Blackwork, by Becky Hogg 2010
RSN Essential Stitch Guides: Canvaswork, by Rachel Doyle 2013
RSN Essential Stitch Guides: Crewelwork, by Jacqui McDonald 2010
RSN Essential Stitch Guides: Goldwork, by Helen McCook 2012
RSN Essential Stitch Guides: Silk Shading, by Sarah Homfray 2011
RSN Essential Stitch Guides: Stumpwork, by Kate Sinton 2011
RSN Essential Stitch Guides: Whitework, by Lizzy Lansberry 2012

ISBN: 978-1-78221-606-3

SUPPLIERS
If you have any difficulty obtaining any of the materials
and equipment mentioned in this book, please visit the
Search Press website: www.searchpress.com

For more details about the work of the Royal School
of Needlework, including courses, tours, our Studio,
tutors and where some of our work can be seen, please
go to our website: www.royal-needlework.org.uk

THE ROYAL SCHOOL OF NEEDLEWORK
Book of **Embroidery**
A GUIDE TO ESSENTIAL STITCHES, TECHNIQUES AND PROJECTS

CONTENTS

See page 137.

See page 193.

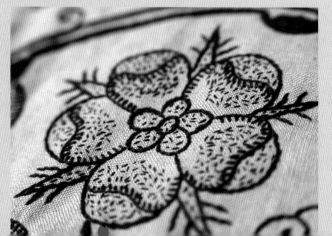

THE ROYAL SCHOOL OF NEEDLEWORK

Founded in 1872, the Royal School of Needlework (RSN) is the international centre of excellence for the art of hand embroidery. It is based at Hampton Court Palace in west London but also offers courses across the UK, in the USA and Japan. Today it is a thriving, dynamic centre of teaching and learning, and believes that hand embroidery is a vital art form that impacts on many aspects of our lives from clothes to ceremonial outfits, and from home furnishings to textile art.

To enable and encourage people to learn the skill of hand embroidery, the RSN offers courses from beginner to degree level. The wide range of short courses includes introductions to each of the stitch techniques the RSN uses, beginning with Introduction to Embroidery. The RSN's Certificate and Diploma in Technical Hand Embroidery offers students the opportunity to learn a range of techniques to a very high technical standard. The Future Tutors course is specifically designed for those pursuing a career in teaching technical hand embroidery. The RSN's BA (Hons) Degree course is the only UK degree course solely focused on hand embroidery and offers students opportunities to learn core stitch techniques, which they are then encouraged to apply in contemporary and conceptual directions. Graduates can go on to find careers in embroidery relating to fashion, couture and costume; to interiors and soft furnishings or in the area of textile art, including jewellery and millinery.

At its Hampton Court headquarters, the RSN welcomes people for all kind of events from private lessons to bespoke stitching holidays, intensive Certificate and Diploma studies, tours around our exhibitions, which comprise either pieces from our own textile collections or students' work, or study days looking at particular pieces or techniques from our Collection. Work by students and from the Collection also forms the core of a series of lectures and presentations available to those who cannot get to the RSN.

The RSN Collection of textiles comprises more than 2,000 pieces, all of which have been donated, because as a charity the RSN cannot afford to purchase additions. The pieces were given so that they would have a home for the future and to be used as a resource for students and researchers. The Collection comes from all over the world, illustrating many different techniques and approaches to stitch and embellishment.

The RSN Studio undertakes new commissions and conservation work for many different clients, including public institutions, places of worship, stately homes and private individuals, again illustrating the wide variety of roles embroidery can play, from altar frontals and vestments for churches to curtains, hangings and chair covers for homes and embroidered pictures as works of art.

Over the last few years the RSN has worked with a number of prestigious names including Sarah Burton OBE for Alexander McQueen, Vivienne Westwood's Studio for Red Carpet Green Dress, Patrick Grant's E Tautz, the late L'Wren Scott, Nicholas Oakwell Couture for the GREAT Britain Exhibition, the Jane Austen House Museum, Liberty London, the V&A Museum of Childhood and M&S and Oxfam for Shwopping.

About this book

This book brings together all the material from the RSN's bestselling *Essential Stitch Guide Series,* covering crewelwork, canvaswork, blackwork, silk shading, goldwork, stumpwork, whitework and bead embroidery. The books are written by RSN Graduate Apprentices who each spent three years at the RSN learning techniques and then applying them in the RSN studio, working on pieces from our collection or on customers' contemporary and historic pieces. All are also tutors on our courses.

Alongside the actual stitches and historic examples of the technique you will find a selection of works by the author and other RSN Apprentices and Students to show how a technique can be used in new ways. While the RSN uses traditional stitch techniques as its medium, we believe that they can be used to create very contemporary works to ensure hand embroidery is not just kept alive, but flourishes into the future. We hope these images will inspire you to explore and develop your own work. To ensure you have a comprehensive guide to creating your own embroidery, we have also added a new section on successfully mounting your work.

Above and top right

Hampton Court Palace, Surrey, home of the Royal School of Needlework.

BASIC MATERIALS & EQUIPMENT

As each type of embroidery covered in this book has its own thread, fabric and needle requirements, the specific tools needed are included within the relevant chapter. Here, I will introduce you to the tools and materials common to all types of embroidery. There are a few basic materials and pieces of equipment that you will need to achieve good results in your stitching, and also to keep you comfortable while working. After all, your time spent stitching should be relaxing and pleasurable, and if you are not comfortable your concentration span will be reduced and you will not be pleased with your results.

Frames

To keep an even tension on your work, you should always work in a frame. The type of frame you use will depend on the size of the piece you are working. A frame with a stand or clamp is generally the easiest to use as you will not have to hold the frame with one hand, while stitching with the other.

SLATE FRAMES AND TRESTLES

To get the best results you will need a slate frame. Although it is an expensive initial outlay, it is an indispensable investment for the serious embroiderer, as it allows you to control the tautness of the fabric in the frame and achieve better tension in your stitches.

Slate frames are made up of four lengths of wood (usually beech, as this is less likely to warp than other types of wood), two rollers with webbing attached and two stretchers with holes for pegs.

Slate frames come in various sizes. These refer to the length of the piece of webbing fixed to the roller, and your choice will depend on the size of the work you are creating. I recommend a frame 45cm (18in) or larger. It pays to spend time finding the centre of the webbing on each roller the first time you use your frame, as it will save time on future uses.

The top and bottom of the linen is first attached to the webbing on the rollers, and then the sides are laced with string. The pegs and strings are then tightened gradually to pull the linen taut in all four directions. You will need to remember to tighten the strings on a regular basis, but if you make it part of your routine every time you start stitching you will soon get into the habit. Framing up is covered in more detail on pages 16–19.

You will also need something to rest your frame on. Some frames come with their own stand. You can balance your frame between chair arms and a table, but at the Royal School of Needlework we use wooden trestles, which can be adjusted in height and angle. The distance between the two trestles is easily adjusted but will depend on the size of your frame. A slate frame of 60cm (24in) enables the average-size chair to fit comfortably between both trestles.

HOOP OR RING FRAMES

A ring frame is made up of two hoops between which you sandwich your canvas. These are great for smaller projects, but you must keep tightening the frame as it will slacken off quickly. Ring frames are available in a wide variety of sizes; for example, deep ring frames are more suited to canvaswork as narrow embroidery hoops do not grip the canvas as well. Ring frames with a dowel attached can be used with either a seat stand or a barrel clamp, which attaches to a table. These frames leave both hands free to stitch. An embroidery hoop is also useful for practising stitches or producing small samples. I keep one mounted with calico at all times in case I want to try out ideas. They are quick to set up, easy to transport and it takes just seconds to insert some fabric. You need to keep the fabric taut as a drum and will need a screwdriver to tighten the frame.

A 20cm (8in) or 25cm (10in) hoop is a good size. I prefer hoops with a deep frame, and it is beneficial to bind the frames with strips of calico or flattened bias binding so as not to bruise your fabric and to keep it from slipping. Be wary of leaving your fabric in the frame between stitching sessions as a ring mark will be visible and can be difficult to banish completely. Some frames come with a dowel, which leaves both your hands free to stitch. You have a choice to insert the dowel into either a seat or table clamp.

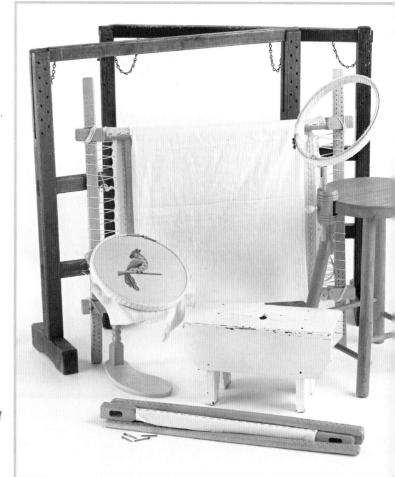

A selection of hoop frames, slate frames and trestles. A comfortable seat is also essential. Place your seat between two trestles and adjust the angle and height for your comfort. A footstool is useful, as are clamps for the ring frames. These additional items can make your working more comfortable and leave your hands free.

Other materials

In addition to your frame, fabric, needles and thread it will also be useful to have the following equipment.

String, **bracing needle**, **tape measure**, **buttonhole thread, cotton webbing tape**, **pins** and a **pincushion** These are used when framing up a slate frame.

Fabric scissors These are used for cutting soft fabrics, particularly the webbing tape.

General-purpose scissors If you are using canvas, bear in mind that this is quite a tough material, so do not use your best fabric scissors. Instead, use a large pair of paper scissors.

Embroidery scissors and **angled embroidery scissors** For the stitching you will need a pair of sharp embroidery scissors. Straight and bent scissors are both useful for cutting threads close to the canvas surface.

Thimble I always stitch with a thimble, but not everyone finds them useful.

Needle case This is useful for storing your needles safely in between projects.

Waterproof fineliner pens, **pencil**, **paper**, **tracing paper, pricker** and **ruler** These are used for creating and developing your design.

Screwdriver A screwdriver will help you tighten your ring frame.

Tweezers I like to have a pair of pointed and flat-ended tweezers in my sewing box. Both are helpful if you do have to unpick any stitches. Use them from both the front and back of the work to get every fibre out.

Mellor A mellor can be useful for laying down threads smoothly.

Waterproof marker pens and **machine thread** These materials are used when transferring your design.

Round-nose pliers A small pair of pliers is great for pulling stubborn needles through when weaving in on the back.

Shade card This is a useful tool to help when ordering materials for your project. Simply hold it next to your source photograph and pick the colour that matches best.

A **tape measure** This helps you to size up designs and judge if you have enough fabric.

Glass-headed pins These are vital to hold two pieces of fabric in position while you use your hands to stitch them together. I use the larger pins as they are stronger and last longer.

I use **watercolour paint** and size 0 to 000 **paintbrushes** to mark the design on my fabric.

Machine threads These are always handy and ideal to use when you want to produce a plumb line to ensure you place your design at the desired angle.

Acid-free **tissue paper** is used to cover and protect the areas you are not currently stitching.

A **magnifying glass** can make all the difference to the standard and neatness of your work.

Pounce This powder is made of ground charcoal or ground cuttlefish bone or a mixture of both. It is used to transfer your design, and you can make your own at home with a pestle and mortar.

A **baby brush** is useful to gently remove pounce after transferring your design and for removing fibres.

A **pencil** is used to mark distances or draw directional lines to help you stitch.

DESIGN

Inspiration

FINDING INSPIRATION

Copying a piece is great for learning the fundamentals, but I consider embroidery to be very personal and your work should reflect that and represent your own tastes and ideas. We will each be inspired by different subjects and inspiration can be found literally everywhere. Once you learn how to look, a whole new world will open up to you.

How often do you really look at something? I mean really look; not just take a photograph and move on. There is so much stimulus in the world today that we turn our minds off to most of it. I want to teach you to learn to look all over again. There are potential subjects in everyday objects, so do not ignore the seemingly banal and the mundane. After all, they only seem so because you see them every day.

USING PHOTOGRAPHS

Inspiration can often come from photographs. The light source is fixed, elements do not move and the colours are often good quality. Do not just blindly trace the elements as they are in the photograph. Use the photograph as your initial inspiration and make a composition from it. Here are some guidelines and thoughts for you to bear in mind:

- Do you need to put everything in your design that is in the photograph? There might be another flower hiding behind a leaf, for example. Do you want this flower in your design?
- Odd numbers are more satisfying to the eye than even numbers, so try putting three or five elements in, rather than two or four.
- Be aware of using photographs that are taken in a studio. They are often lit from many angles and this will give you unusual shadows. Photographs taken outside will usually have just one light source, that of the sun, giving you one set of shadows.

Tip

Look for the good in everything! Try looking at your washing machine. Forget it is a washing machine and look at the shapes it creates; a circle inside a rectangle. It is probably painted white, but does it look completely white? Are there shadows creating different tones?

Tip

If you are not confident with drawing, trace all of the elements for your design on to a piece of paper. You can then cut the elements out and arrange them on another piece of paper. Experiment with rearranging them until you find a composition you like.

This leaf had fallen in my back garden. Autumnal leaves come in an inspiring array of colours and shapes. You could arrange the leaves to make a design, overlap them or just embroider a part of one.

Materials for design

When coming up with a design, the most important 'material' is inspiration! A **pencil** is used to sketch my initial ideas. A **fine-nibbed pen** with permanent ink, **sketchpad**, **tracing paper**, **colouring pencils** and **ruler** are equally vital. Access to a **lightbox** and **photocopier** are useful, but not essential.

Note

It will take practice to work out which techniques will suit what subject matter, so have a go at the pieces in this book, and once you are confident with the stitching, return to this section to begin looking for new subjects. Here are some everyday things in which to find inspiration: tree bark, flowers, fruit, vegetables, ceramics, fabric folds, ornaments.

Coming up with a design

Don't panic! All you have to do is create a few outlines of shapes in which to practise different stitches. Start with something small and easy, and have a go at stitching it. Next time you will be more adventurous and want to progress to something slightly larger and more detailed.

If you are not used to producing your own design, lay a piece of tracing paper over individual drawings and trace the elements you like, then cut them out and arrange them in a pleasing layout. Remember the sketches underneath can still move, so as the design starts to take shape, you may prefer these elements to lie at a different angle or face a different way. Simply adjust to your liking, add another sheet of tracing paper and retrace. Start with a basic idea and build on its strengths. You may be surprised how different the finished embroidery looks from your initial ideas.

Once you are happy with the basic design layout, spend some time refining by retracing the design once more. Ensure that all of the lines are smooth, any stems you have included taper rather than bulge or narrow along their length, leaf tips have nice crisp points, all of the curves are enhanced and so forth.

The final step is to add detail and colour to your design. Before doing so, you may wish to photocopy your design several times so that you can try out different combinations. When colouring in, use only one pencil to shade each area, using it lightly in the hand for the lighter areas of your design and applying more pressure to those areas in shade. You may want to view different combinations of wools together to see which colours complement each other (see also page 15).

(see also page 15).

Tips
To help to create a well-balanced design consider the following:
- Placement of the design on the fabric: do you want it offset or central?
- The shapes of elements within the design: do the shapes reflect and enhance each other?
- The placement of shapes within the design: would you like them to grow over each other, be nearly touching or be well spaced?
- The balance of negative space within the design: think about the negative space as you plan your layout, leaving no obvious spaces or gaps as you distribute motifs.

Jacobean sampler
This monochrome piece shows how using different shades and tints of the same colour can produce a very effective and powerful design. English 20th century. (RSN Collection)

13

Composition

The placement or view of the subject can be as important as the subject itself. It is easy to get caught up in a pretty flower, for example, and forget about what is happening around it, but this can make or break a finished piece of embroidery.

Of course, if you are stitching simply for the beauty of an object (see *Poppy* on page 194 or the apples on page 94 for example), you might think there are no decisions to make: just place the subject in the middle of the fabric and start stitching. However, consider focusing in on the most interesting area, or mounting the finished piece in an oval or other unusually shaped frame. How about placing the embroidery off-centre as I have done in *Autumn Leaves* on page 199? The leaves are about to drop to the ground, indicated by the space left below them.

Can you add something to the background to enhance the piece? *Highland Cow* (see page 208) is a good example of this. Just a small amount of painting behind the cow suddenly places her in a snow-filled field in the middle of winter, and stops her being just a cow on a white background. The section on page 205 goes into more detail about painting your own background.

RULE OF THIRDS

This is a very old artistic technique that has its roots in mathematics, but all you need to understand is that the principle of this rule is to discourage placement of the main subject at the centre, thus preventing the picture from being divided into halves.

Split the image into thirds horizontally and vertically and place focal points of your design on or near the intersecting lines for a visually pleasing composition.

KEEPING THE EYE WITHIN THE PICTURE

To keep the eye from wandering out of the picture, keep all elements of the design pointing inwards and within the design area where possible, unless you are zooming in on a subject.

Endless Ocean
This design, used as part of the planning for the finished piece (see pages 178–180), shows how the rule of thirds can help you with your designs. Note how important elements of the design are near to the intersecting lines of the grid.

GROUNDING AN OBJECT

Depending on the subject, you might want to give your design an extra element to help put it in context. Take the silk-shaded pig below as an example. The pig needs something to stand on for it to make sense, in this case some tufts of grass. This is called grounding.

Pig
Small tufts of grass help to give a sense of realism and weight to the pig.
(Personal collection of Derek Watson)

NEGATIVE SPACE

The space around the design is as important as the design itself. Do not squash elements together; space out leaves and stems and balance the design as a whole. If an area of a photograph is a little confusing, make it clear by redrawing it or tracing and copying another element.

Think about the space around the edge of the design as well. Too close to the embroidery and it will look squashed; too much space and the embroidery will look lost.

Tip
Use two L-shaped pieces of card, as shown, to help you decide how much space around the embroidery will work best.

Using colour

Many antique tapestries appear to have subdued colours, but if you have the opportunity to view the back of the work you will see the vibrancy of the original colour – dyes were not as permanent in the past and many have faded over time. It is your choice whether you want to simulate the effects of time with muted colours, or create a more contemporary look to your design by using bright and colourful threads.

Using a range of dark to light tones in the colour families you choose will give greater depth to your design.

CHOOSING COLOURS THAT GO WELL TOGETHER

As in nature, all colours go together, and as long as you have an attractive combination of hues and tones, it will work. If you like it, use it. If not, don't! If you are not confident choosing colours you may benefit from using a colour wheel (see right) and choosing one of the following options:

- A *monochrome* design uses different tints, shades, and/or tones of only a single colour (see page 13 for an example).
- An *adjacent colour* design uses any three, four or five colours next to each other on the colour wheel.
- A *triadic colour* design has three colours, equally spaced around the colour circle.
- A *polychrome* design typically contains six different colours, equally spaced around the colour wheel. You can choose more but I would reserve this number of colours to larger projects. 'Poly' means 'many', and much like having lots of bright colours in the same outfit, it could look fantastic, but you have to wear it with confidence!

Note

- *Complementary colours lie directly across the colour wheel from one another.*
- *Split complementary colour designs use three colours: one key colour and the two either side of the complementary.*
- *Double complementary colour designs use four colours: two adjacent colours and both of their complementary colours.*

See pages 170–171 for more on colour.

FRAMING UP

Preparing a slate frame

Slate frames are made up of four wooden lengths – two rollers with webbing attached and two stretchers with holes for pegs or split pins. On first use, it is advisable to mark the centre of each of the rollers to ensure you insert your fabric squarely. In the following demonstration linen has been used, but simply substitute the fabric you want to use depending on the techniques you are working (see relevant chapters for fabric advice). If you wish to use a lighter fabric, such as silk, see page 218 for advice on securing a silk fabric to a calico background.

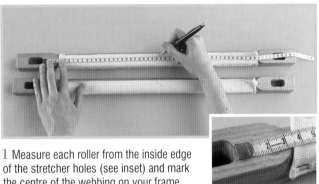

1 Measure each roller from the inside edge of the stretcher holes (see inset) and mark the centre of the webbing on your frame with a pencil.

2 Before mounting the fabric into the slate frame, you need to make sure that the right side of the fabric is facing upwards. With linen, the raised diagonal lines should run from bottom left to top right.

3 The top and bottom of the fabric should be attached to the rollers first. Fold the bottom edge of the linen along the grain of the fabric 1.5cm (½in) under itself as shown. Repeat on the top edge.

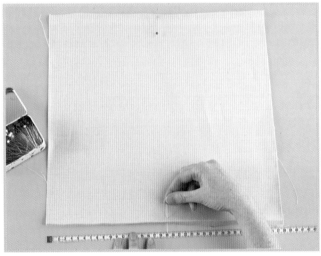

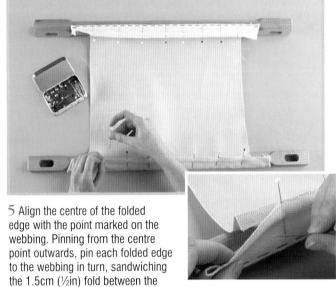

4 Measure along the crease to find the centre of the top folded edge and mark it with a pin. Using a second pin, follow the centre grain down to the bottom folded edge and mark this point with the pin. Use the line this creates between the two points to centre your work, as the fabric is not always truly cut on the grain.

5 Align the centre of the folded edge with the point marked on the webbing. Pinning from the centre point outwards, pin each folded edge to the webbing in turn, sandwiching the 1.5cm (½in) fold between the webbing and the back of the linen (see inset).

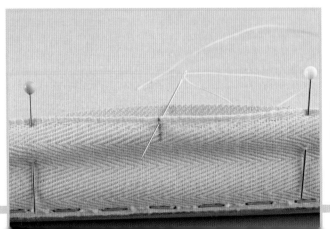

6 Thread a size 5 sharps needle with buttonhole thread and tie a knot in the end. Starting at the central point of the fabric, remove the pin and take your needle through the webbing to the front, hiding the knot between the webbing and the linen twill.

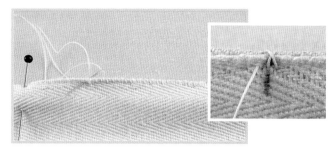

7 Stitching through the webbing and the linen, oversew a small cross to secure the knot (see inset). Use a strong tension to oversew the webbing to the linen with long-and-short stitches 3–5mm (¹⁄₁₆–¹⁄₈in) apart. Work to the left from the centre to ensure that the linen is secured smoothly and evenly, removing the pins as you go.

8 When you reach the edge of the linen twill, secure by stitching back along the oversewn edge in the other direction for 2.5cm (1in), then secure with two small stab stitches.

9 Cut the thread, then repeat from the centre to the right. Repeat the process on both sides of the other roller.

Tip
Before inserting the two stretchers, decide how far to roll in the rollers. This can enable you to sit closer to your work when stitching. As this is a small canvas on a small frame, I have turned the bottom roller over once.

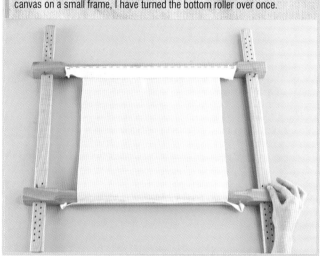

10 Insert the stretchers into each side of the rollers evenly and insert pegs or split pins into the evenly drilled holes to hold the rollers away from each other. Keep the fabric taut and gradually increase the distance between the pegs on alternate stretchers.

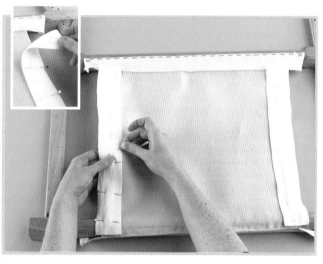

11 Roughly measure the distance between the rollers and cut two lengths of cotton webbing tape to the same length. Place each piece of cotton webbing tape on the side edges of the linen twill. Pin the tape into position, two-thirds over the linen and one-third off the linen (see inset) and fasten it to the linen with buttonhole thread and a basting stitch, a temporary stitch with large loops.

13 Leave a good length of string at each end before cutting and repeat on the other side.

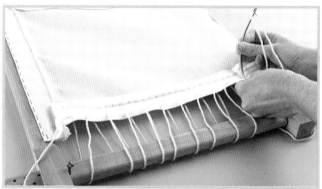

12 Thread your bracing needle with a ball of string and place the ball on the floor. Take the sharp end of the bracing needle down through the overhanging area of the cotton webbing tape and pull through a good length of string. Take the bracing needle underneath and up around the stretcher and back through the cotton tape at 2.5cm (1in) intervals.

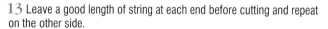
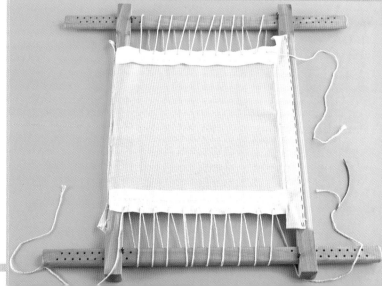

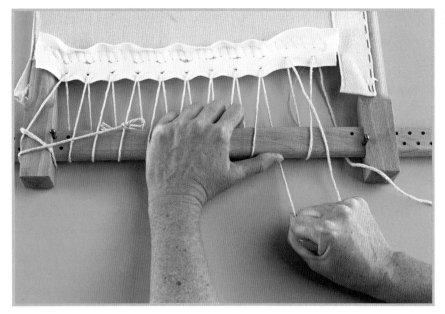

14 Starting from the centre of each of the attached cotton tape strings, pull each loop taut and hold it. Work to the side and secure the string with a slip knot, before working back to the other side. Work each side of the frame gradually to avoid pulling the fabric off-centre, loosening and retightening the knots gradually until the linen feels firm.

15 Finally, stand the base of the frame upright on the floor and use the sole of your foot to push down each end of the bottom roller. Move the pegs one by one to increase the distance between the pegs and tighten the fabric.

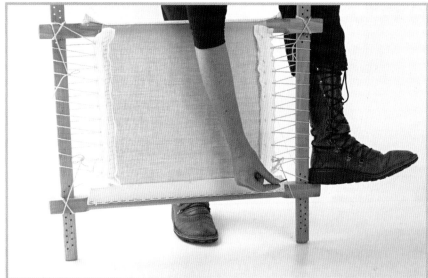

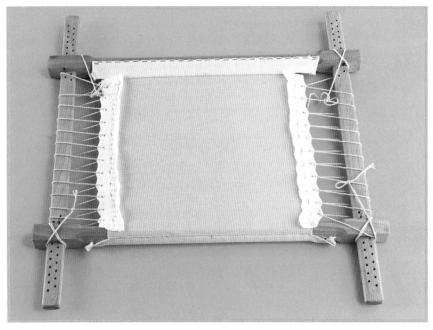

A tightened frame, ready for you to work your embroidery.

Preparing roller frames

This type of frame is a smaller version of a slate frame. Roller frames will not keep your fabric quite as taut as a slate frame, but they are portable and more readily available.

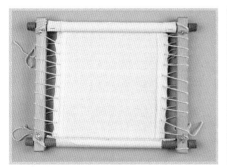 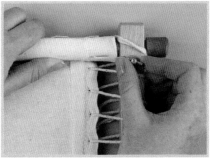 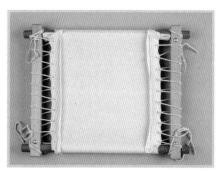

1 Follow steps 1–14 on pages 16–18 for preparing a slate frame, inserting the ends of the rollers into the ends of the stretcher. Turn the frame over.

2 Roll the bar up to tighten the fabric, then tighten the wingnuts to secure.

A prepared roller frame.

Preparing ring frames

Ring frames come in lots of sizes and are readily available, easy to frame up and portable. However, they do not keep the fabric very tight and so are best used for small projects.

1 Wrap bias binding around both rings individually, being careful to overlap the binding as you work. When you reach the end, trim the excess and secure it in place with a stitch or two. This will make the frame tighter, maintain fabric tension and reduce potential damage to the fabric.

2 Put the inner ring inside the outer ring and tighten the outer ring by twisting the screw until it is finger tight.

3 Remove the inner ring, then place the outer ring flat on the table. Place the fabric and backing fabric (if relevant) over the ring.

4 Lay the fabric flat, then press the inner ring into position, trapping the fabric layers.

5 Turn the frame over and use a screwdriver to tighten the frame.

A prepared ring frame.

TRANSFERRING A DESIGN

There are many different ways to transfer your design from paper to fabric. The method you choose will be dependent on certain factors, and these are explained here.

PRICK AND POUNCE

A traditional method of transferring a design, this was used by Michelangelo to transfer the design on to the roof of the Sistine Chapel, so it is certainly tried and tested! This method is particularly useful when you want to stitch on a dark fabric or an unusual surface.

Tip
Use white powder for dark fabrics, grey for light fabrics and black for mid-tone fabrics.

1 Copy the design on to a piece of tracing paper. Using a needle (size 9 is a good size), prick holes along the lines about 2mm (1/8in) apart from each other. Keep a towel underneath to protect your surface.

2 Place the tracing in position on your fabric and use pins to hold it in place, then rub pounce powder through the holes with a soft pad in firm circular movements.

3 Lift off the tracing paper carefully. Use a pencil or watercolour paint of similar colour to the colours in your design to join up the dots.

USING TISSUE PAPER

This is a good technique to use if you have thin lines as part of your design or you are not confident with your painting or drawing. I use this on designs that need to be very precise.

 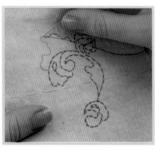  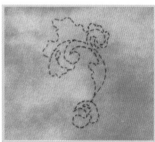

1 Trace the design on to a piece of tissue paper, then pin the tissue to your required fabric. Stitch running stitch in two lines across the tracing to secure it in place.

2 Using a cotton thread, stitch running stitch along all of the design lines through the tissue paper and the fabric.

3 When all the design lines are stitched, carefully rip the paper away so just the stitches are left. Remove these as you get to them with your embroidery stitches.

The transferred design.

USING A LIGHTBOX OR WINDOW

This is a quick, versatile method and great to use if you have a lightweight, light-coloured fabric.

1 Fasten the design to a window or lightbox with low-tack tape.

2 Place the required fabric over the top and tape this in place too.

3 Trace the design with a coloured drawing pencil.

USING A TRANSFER PEN

This is a modern invention and one worth knowing about. These pens are designed to be used on fabrics with some man-made content, such as polycotton. They do work on silk, but will not show up as much. The design often comes out thicker than the original, so it is not suitable for very delicate designs.

  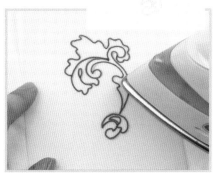

1 Trace your design on to tracing paper with a pencil (see inset), then turn the tracing paper over and use the transfer pen to trace the design on the back, leaving you with a reversed design.

2 Place it on to your required fabric in position, pen side down.

3 Iron with a hot iron for about ten seconds, making sure that you do not move the tracing paper while ironing.

POSITIONING THE DESIGN

To ensure you position the design appropriately, you may wish to use a tape measure to either centre it or offset it on the linen. If your design requires it to be positioned square on the fabric, creating a plumb line will help to achieve this.

1 To create a plumb line, insert a glass-headed pin into the top of your framed linen as shown. Position the pin with the sharp end pointing to the centre. Take another pin and follow the grain of the linen to the bottom (see inset). Insert the second pin into the linen, again positioning it with the sharp end pointing to the centre.

2 Take one reel of machine thread in a contrasting colour to the linen and wrap the thread around the top pin in a figure of eight. Unreel the thread and wrap it around the bottom pin. This creates a vertical plumb line to help you position your design. Some designs may require a horizontal line – or both a horizontal and vertical line, to create a cross.

3 Slide the tracing of your design under the plumb line. You should be able to use it to ensure the design is straight and gain the desired location on the fabric.

MOUNTING YOUR EMBROIDERY

Mounting will prolong the life of your embroidery, protect it from environmental damage, remove any creases or over-stretched areas in the fabric and display your work in an attractive manner.

Before removing from the frame

While the embroidery is still taut on the slate frame, use this opportunity to decide what size you would like the finished article to be. There are two initial options to think about: the traditional framing option and the contemporary framing option. For the traditional option, consider if you would like to mount your embroidery behind a mount card or slip window – this means making your piece slightly larger than the area to be seen. For the contemporary option, consider if you would like your embroidery mounted in front of mount card – this means making your piece the actual size you want to see.

The mounting process

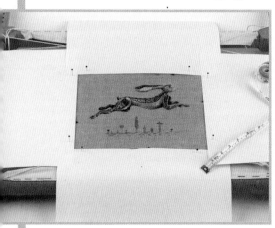

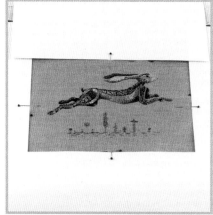

1 You will need to mask out the area you want to make your finished piece. I would advise applying pins on all four edges to start with, to ensure that you do not stray within 2.5cm (1in) of the embroidery. Include the extra allowance if you are opting for traditional framing. Mask the edges of your embroidery with four pieces of paper and adjust them until you are happy with the composition. Pin the paper pieces in place.

2 Measure the distance between the sheets of paper, make a note of the measurement and mark the corners with pins. Measure the distance between the pins and mark the centre of each side with a pin. You can now remove the corner pins – they are not vital.

3 Use a ruler, set square and mechanical pencil to mark the measurements accurately onto Museum Grade A mountboard. Ensure that the edges of the mountboard are clean and crisp, and not damaged, to ensure accuracy. Use the set square to check that your corners are square – even on brand new mountboard.

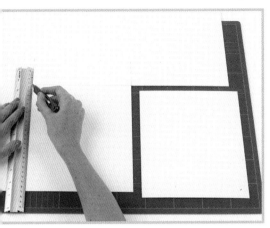

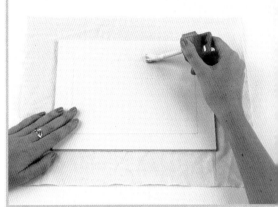

4 Place the mountboard over a cutting mat and place a safety ruler on the pencil line. Apply pressure to the safety ruler to keep it from moving. Use a sharp retractable knife to score the mountboard, using the safety ruler to give you a straight line. Keep the retractable knife upright, at a right angle to the board, and repeatedly score the card until you cut through it. If you are using 2mm (¹/₁₆in) card you will need to cut a second identical piece of card and glue them together; if using 4mm (³/₁₆in) you will only need one layer.

5 If you are gluing two 2mm (¹/₁₆in) thick pieces of card together, draw a box onto the back of one piece of card, 2.5cm (1in) in from each edge, and join the corner points with a diagonal line. Apply archival quality PVA glue along each of the drawn lines, then adhere the pieces of card together, ensuring they are correctly aligned. Weight them down with books while the glue is drying to ensure a strong join.

6 Cut a piece of calico 5cm (2in) larger all round than your piece of mountboard. Place the mountboard face down in the centre of the calico on a work table, so that you are viewing it landscape. Paste a line of glue on the back of the mountboard about 2.5cm (1in) from the top edge of the mountboard.

Tip
Avoid getting glue within 2.5cm (1in) of the edge of the board, as it can be hard work on the fingers trying to sew through dried glue. I draw on a box to ensure my spacing is even.

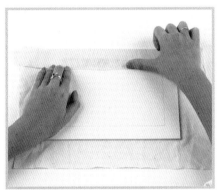

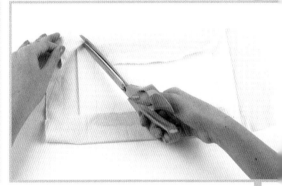

7 Fold the 5cm (2in) of calico above the mountboard onto the line of glue. Bring it down at the centre first and apply a little pressure as you work out towards each side. Smooth the glue downwards so that you keep it out of your 2.5cm (1in) margin.

Tip
If you stand up, you can pull the calico towards you and push the board away from you using your thigh.

8 Turn the mountboard around so that the glued edge is closest to you. Glue and fold as in steps 6 and 7 – this time you need to pull the calico as tight as possible; if you don't achieve taut calico, your embroidery could sag. To test it, before the glue dries, turn over the board and run your nail over the calico from one side to another to see if you could get it tighter.

9 Using a pair of sharp fabric scissors, cut away the corners of the fabric, otherwise when you fold the sides in, the fabric will be very bulky. Try to leave 5mm (¼in) of excess calico hanging over the corners of the board.

10 Position the mountboard and calico face down on the work table so that you are viewing it portrait. Paste a line of glue on the back of the mountboard, again keeping the glue about 2.5cm (1in) from the top edge and sides of the mountboard.

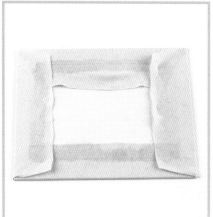

11 Fold the 5cm (2in) of calico above the mountboard down onto the line of glue, tucking in the 5mm (¼in) excess at the corners as you do so. Bring it down at the centre first and apply a little pressure as you work out towards the sides.

12 Turn the mountboard around so that the most recently glued area is closest to you. Repeat steps 10 and 11; this time you will need to pull the calico as tight as possible. Leave the glue to dry completely.

13 Measure each edge of your calico-covered mountboard and mark the centre with a sharp pencil. Break down your slate frame and remove your embroidery, leaving the marker pins in position.

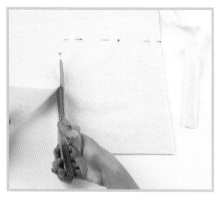

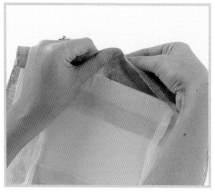

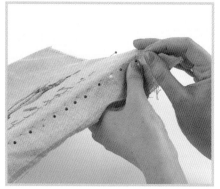

14 If your embroidery has a lot of texture on the back – especially if it is goldwork, stumpwork or appliqué – add a layer of bumpf, or curtain interlining, between your work and the covered board, to absorb any lumps. Simply mark out a piece of interlining to the same size as your mountboard and cut out.

15 Lay the calico-covered mountboard on your work table, face up, then place the layer of curtain interlining on top. You should have pins remaining in your embroidery that mark the centre of each side. Lay your embroidery face up over the covered mountboard so that pin markers match up with the pencil marks. Push the pins through the pencil marks and into the edge of the mountboard.

16 Starting in the centre and working outwards, work along one edge of the board, lining up the fabric grain with the card and holding it in place with pins. Look closely at the fabric to ascertain in which direction the fabric grain is most obvious, and start with that edge. Space the pins about 2cm (¾in) apart.

17 Repeat step 16 on the opposite side.

18 Repeat the process again on the two remaining sides.

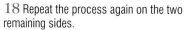

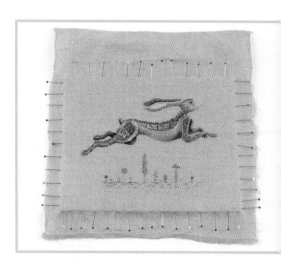

19 Stand back away from your work and review the position of the embroidery on the board. If you are not happy, now is the time to tweak it into a more favourable position. If you are happy with the general position on the board, you might want to return to the first edge you pinned, remove the pins one at a time and pull the fabric tighter over the mountboard before replacing each pin. Remember to start in the centre and work outwards again. Work around all four edges once more, removing the pins one at a time and pulling the fabric even tighter over the mountboard before replacing each pin. At this stage, you can increase the number of pins: pins should be positioned at regular 1cm (½in) intervals. If you have used interlining to absorb any lumps, cut away any excess on the back now.

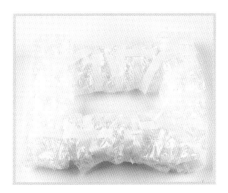
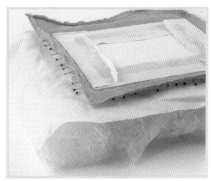

20 If you are mounting embroidery with any raised work on it, make yourself a bubble wrap window, then cover this with a layer of calico before placing your embroidery face-down on top. Trim the surrounding fabric down to 5cm (2in) all the way around the card.

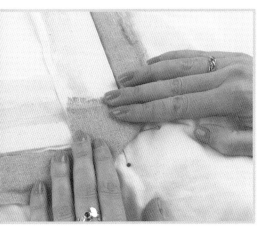
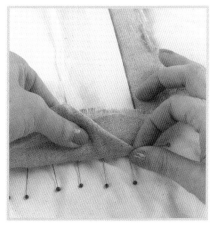
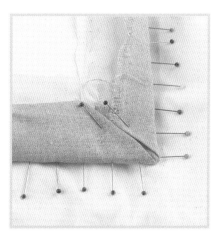

21 Start by neatly folding the corners. Fold the point of the fabric onto the mountboard squarely.

22 Keeping the fabric tucked into the fold, bring one edge of the fabric up at a 45° angle, then pin in place.

23 Repeat on the other side of the mitred corner, as shown.

24 Thread a curved needle with some buttonhole thread and tie a knot in the end. Fold the outer edge of the embroidered fabric onto the back of the mountboard. Cast on in the centre of one of the long sides, at least 1cm (½in) from the edge by taking the curved needle through the fabric and gripping the calico underneath.

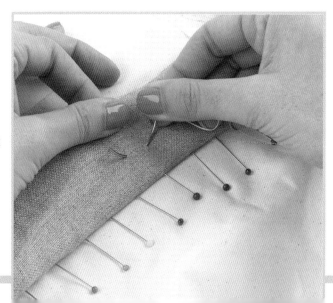

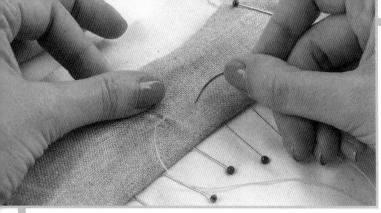

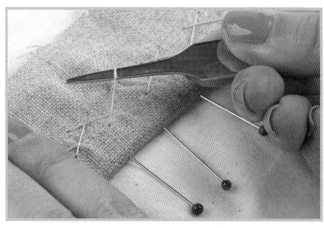

25 Pull the embroidered fabric tightly against the mountboard and hold in place through the calico with a herringbone stitch (see page 54). The herringbone stitch should travel in a straight line and be consistent in depth (about 1.5cm/½in). Also, try to keep the stitching at least 5mm (¼in) away from the edge. If you are right-handed, work from the centre to the right (remember that the curved needle will be pointing towards the left). However, if you are left-handed, you may find it easier to travel to the left; the curved needle will be pointing towards the right. It is vital that you keep pulling the embroidery fabric tight against the mountboard before applying it into position with the herringbone stitch. If not, the work will sag once the pins are removed. Ensure each herringbone stitch sits close to the previous one – this will ensure that all the fabric is held in place.

26 Continue to stitch a herringbone stitch as far as comfortably possible into the corner, remembering to pull the fabric against the mountboard. Go back to the beginning of the herringbone and pull up any slack on the buttonhole thread, using your mellor.

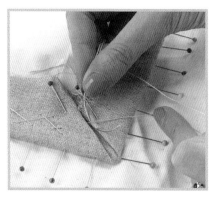

27 Bring your needle out through the very edge of the folded corner fabric.

28 Lay the buttonhole thread at 45° across the corner and take the needle in and out through the fold on the far side. Work a slipstitch towards the corner, alternating through the two folds. If you take your curved needle into the fold just behind where the thread is laying, your stitches will not be visible once the thread is pulled tight.

29 If you need to, use your mellor to arrange your fabric neatly and reduce bulk before you get to the end. Make your stitches smaller as you get towards the corner – this helps to keep tension. Aim to bring your needle out at the very tip of the corner on the far-side fold. Pull the thread tight, away from the point of the corner, and watch the slipstitch disappear. Take the needle back into the point of the near-side fold and bring it up in a position ready to start the herringbone stitch on the next side. Pull the thread through and it should disappear, leaving a nice, crisp corner without any stitches visible.

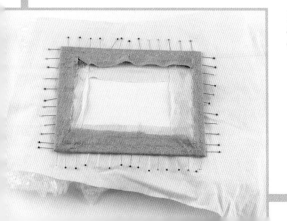

30 Continue to work a herringbone stitch along each side until you approach the next corner, then repeat steps 27–29.

31 Remove the pins and cut away the excess layers of fabric. Fold back the fabric at the corners and snip away a little beyond this, to reduce bulk.

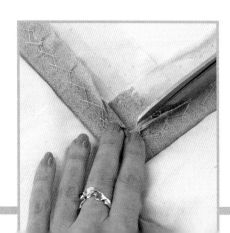

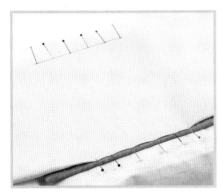

32 Cut out a piece of sateen almost double the size of the mountboard and iron out any creases. Lay face up over the back of your mounted embroidery and fold under the longest sides. Hold in place with pins, pulling and stretching as you pin. The sateen fold should be straight and parallel with the rest of the board. You may leave a 'recess' of up to 5mm (¼in), but there should be no herringbone stitch visible.

33 Fold under the remaining sides and, again, pin in place. Start by pinning in the corners, to keep the tension on the fabric, then pin along the sides, tucking any folded fabric under and out of sight.

34 Thread a curved needle with a length of buttonhole thread and cast on to the mounted fabric just under the sateen edge.

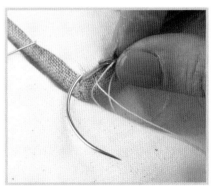

35 Bring the needle out in the mounted fabric in line with the sateen edge.

36 Lay the buttonhole thread over the sateen at 90° to the board edge. Take the needle through the crease, just behind where the buttonhole thread lies. Produce a slipstitch by working around the edge, alternating between the mounted fabric and the sateen to apply them to one another.

37 Keep the stitches equal in length. Keep corners crisp by always bringing the needle out of the point of the fabric being applied, and not the mounted fabric...

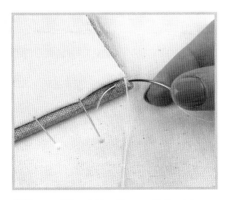

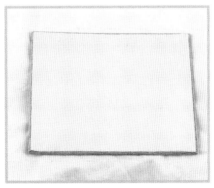

38 ... and then taking the needle back in line with the sateen fabric, to create a neat, square corner.

39 Finish off with two small holding stitches tucked under the sateen edge.

40 Ease out any pin marks on the edges of your embroidery using your mellor.

STARTING TO STITCH

Whether approaching a traditional or a contemporary design, one of the most basic and important principles of practising embroidery is understanding and planning the order in which your design should be worked.

These two pages list the most important key stitches in embroidery, and tell you where to find them within the book. I have split them into four types: essential stitches, filling stitches, outline stitches and surface stitches. In general, this is also the order in which you should work: create a holding stitch, then block in large areas of your design with filling stitches. Next, use outline stitches to frame the large areas, and finish off with any surface stitches you wish to use.

For specialist stitches relating to individual subjects, refer to the relevant chapter.

Essential stitches

These stitches are the most elementary and basic of all the stitches included in this book. The holding stitch (see page 39) is absolutely vital in making sure that your work remains safe and secure. There is nothing more disheartening than your carefully worked design coming apart, so always start and finish each thread you use with a holding stitch!

Stitch	Page
BACK STITCH	SEE PAGE 57
CHAIN STITCH	SEE PAGE 62
DETACHED CHAIN STITCH	SEE PAGE 71
DOUBLE RUNNING STITCH	SEE PAGE 138
FINISHING STITCH	SEE PAGE 39
HOLDING STITCH	SEE PAGE 39
RUNNING STITCH	SEE PAGE 57
SEEDING STITCH	SEE PAGE 49
SPLIT STITCH	SEE PAGE 58

Filling stitches

We usually work on the filling stitches first, but even these have an order of work, which of course depends on the design. If parts of the design look as if they are emerging from behind other areas, then stitch these areas first. For example; it is best to work the background before the foreground so that, when stitched, different elements of the design appear to be in layers growing over or in front of each other, which gives some perspective to your finished piece. Most importantly the neater and crisper edges will be visibly dominant in the foreground.

Stitch	Page
BLOCK SHADING	SEE PAGE 43
BUTTONHOLE STITCH	SEE PAGE 52
FISHBONE STITCH	SEE PAGE 54
HERRINGBONE STITCH	SEE PAGE 54
LEAF STITCH	SEE PAGE 52
LONG-AND-SHORT STITCH	SEE PAGE 42
PADDED SATIN STITCH	SEE PAGE 46
PADDED SATIN STITCH (SPLIT STITCH VARIATION)	SEE PAGE 331
SATIN STITCH	SEE PAGE 330
TRELLIS STITCH	SEE PAGE 44
TURNED SATIN STITCH	SEE PAGE 330

Outline stitches

The second step is to tidy up the edges. The idea is that outline stitches can be used to define shapes, cover any pencil or paint lines and hide your holding stitches or uneven stitched edges as well as adding a few details to bring the design alive. For example, trellis stitch (see page 44) is an ideal stitch to fill a large area quickly, but it does not naturally have a neat edge. If you stitch the trellis first, then surround it with another heavier stitch or an outline of your choice, all the uneven broken lines of the trellis will be hidden.

Stitch	Page
COUCHING	SEE PAGE 59
HEAVY CHAIN STITCH	SEE PAGE 63
PEKINESE STITCH	SEE PAGE 62
STEM STITCH	SEE PAGE 56

Heavy chain stitch, see page 63.

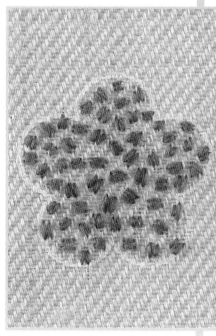

Seeding stitch, see page 49.

Fly stitch, see page 64.

Surface stitches

The third step is to finish off your work with a few surface stitches that will embellish, highlight and add texture to your design. These stitches are eye-catching and some can be built up into striking designs of their own.

Stitch	Page
BULLION KNOT	SEE PAGE 67
FEATHER STITCH	SEE PAGE 65
FLY STITCH	SEE PAGE 64
FRENCH KNOT	SEE PAGE 66
PISTIL STITCH	SEE PAGE 66
SKETCHED SATIN STITCH	SEE PAGE 139
WHIPPED WHEEL	SEE PAGE 69
WOVEN WHEEL	SEE PAGE 68

Long-and-short stitch, see page 42.   *Whipped wheel, see page 69.*

CREWELWORK

Tile in the Arts and Crafts style

This design, worked by Jacqui McDonald, includes examples of chain stitch, stem stitch, whipped stem stitch, split stitch, pearl stitch, back stitch, satin stitch and couching. It is typical of the style employed during the Arts and Crafts period.

Details from a polycolour crewelwork screen
See also page 32.

FROM THE AUTHOR

I imagine you have picked up this book as you have a love of art and colour. Perhaps you are an embroiderer already and want to learn more, or perhaps you are simply curious about the craft and want to try it out. This section of the book is intended to pass on the information I received from my tutors when I undertook a three-year apprenticeship at the Royal School of Needlework. Its aim is not to give you designs to copy and follow, but to show you how to perfect the stitches and provide examples of how these stitches can be used within your own designs. As such, this is the perfect introduction to free embroidery.

Before joining the RSN I worked for the National Trust and looked after many beautiful pieces within their collection. It was here that my interest in embroidery began. Beautiful inspiration was all around me, from ornately plastered ceilings to walls covered with tales in tapestry; furniture upholstered with wild foliage, beautiful twisting and turning leaves and flowers spreading and covering every inch of available space. The regimented holes of the canvas led me to believe the process was fairly easy and I was sure that I would enjoy stitching if I had a go. I soon took up canvaswork as a pastime and wondered if embroidery, allied with my conservation skills, could be a worthwhile career move.

Once at the RSN I realised that freestyle embroidery suited me better as I could be in command of where to bring up my needle and where exactly I felt each thread should be placed, so I took great pleasure in discovering Jacobean-style crewelwork.

As well as providing an invaluable stitch guide, I hope to encourage you to understand the basic principles of design and show you how to work your own designs confidently, building them from inspiration around you, and to spark a passion for this charming and traditional art form.

Jacqui McDonald

THE HISTORY OF CREWELWORK

Although it is commonly thought of as a woven tapestry, the Bayeux Tapestry is in fact the oldest surviving example of crewelwork. The illustrations on the piece tell the story of the events leading up to the Norman Conquest, and are embroidered on to the linen surface with a two-ply worsted wool. Laid stitches (see page 47) were used for the characters and scenery; couching (see page 59) for outlines and stem stitch (see page 56) to define detail and to render the lettering.

Worsted wools are thought to have originated in the farming village of Worstead in Norfolk. This native resource, most appropriate to the British climate, was manufactured into clothing and became one of Britain's most successful industries. To this day the inhabitants of Worstead continue the tradition of spinning, dyeing and weaving fleece from local sheep. Although primarily spun to produce woollen cloth, at some point it became popular to use this yarn to embroider. At first, monochrome motifs stitched in wool, with a small number of different stitches, such as stem and seeding, (see pages 56 and 49) were the most common, but embroidered curtains and bed hangings that resembled designs inspired by woodcut prints are known.

Foreign trade created by Elizabeth I, initially devised to bring back valuable spices, found a foothold in Northern India where English merchants picked up coffee in Mocha and cloth in Gujarat. Egyptian trade was found to be profitable as they too welcomed cotton cloth in exchange for silver, which reduced the drain on English silver, while the Persians provided a market for the English woollens. Inevitably some of these Indian and African fabrics made it back to Europe, where they were well received. Palampores and pintadoes, painted calicos that came to be known in England as chintz, were produced on the Coromandel coast of India and became very popular in the now-furnished households of Britain.

By the late seventeenth century, cheap, washable cotton cloth and luxurious woven silks were in huge demand and contributed to the changing fashions in Britain. Fine, beautiful fabrics encouraged less padding to be worn and instead more to be added to the furniture, which during the Tudor period had been fairly stark.

Furnishings obviously called for something a little more durable than clothing and designers began to create textile furnishings with easily accessible and more resilient materials such as dyed wools and heavy-duty linens; their designs inspired by the fashionable Tree of Life patterns found on the palampores.

After the Protestant Reformation there was little demand for ecclesiastic work, so it was more common to see embroidery used for secular and domestic objects. Crewel embroidery thus became more popular, and professional craftsmen, laden with pattern books, travelled the country redesigning the interiors of the wealthy; adorning country houses with cosy furnishings, panels, fire screens and bed hangings embroidered with exotic illustrations. The lady of the house would then embroider these patterns with colourful crewel wools.

Crewelwork reached its peak in popularity during the following Stuart period, after Elizabeth I died and James VI of Scotland acceded to the throne of the United Kingdom as King James I. Increasingly, amateur embroiderers took up needlework for pleasure and to furnish their own home, and it became the done thing for a young lady to accomplish.

> ## Note
> *King James I reigned between 1603 and 1625, when this highly decorative style was at the height of fashion. The Hebrew form of James is Jacob, and it is from this that the term Jacobean is drawn.*

Opposite:
Curtain with Jacobean crewelwork
Wool on linen with large stylised leaves, birds and squirrel. English 20th century.
(RSN Collection 1177)

Polycolour crewelwork screen
This framed and unglazed screen was worked in the late nineteenth century in England. English 19th century.
(RSN Collection)

TOOLS AND MATERIALS

THREADS

Crewel wool

Crewel embroidery is stitched in crewel wool, a fine two-ply worsted yarn made from the long fibres of a sheep's fleece. The word 'crewel' appears to be derived from the Old English word 'clew' for a ball of yarn. Variously spelled 'crule', 'crewle', 'croull' and 'croyl' it was pronounced as a monosyllable up until the fifteenth century. It became the two-syllabled 'cruel' and 'cruell' in the mid-sixteenth century and by the seventeenth century it had become the 'crewel' we use today.

I like to use Appleton crewel wools as they have such a good range of colours and a variety of shades within each range. Appleton have over four hundred different shades of colour available to purchase in either a skein, a length of 8m (8¾yd) or a hank, a length of 160m (175yd).

It is important to remember that wools are dyed in batches and each dye lot may not result in a colour identical to the next. For this reason, it is best to estimate the quantities needed in advance of starting the project, particularly if your project is especially large.

Skeins of crewel wool in a variety of colours.

NEEDLES

For such a common article, and possibly one of the world's best inventions, there is little known of the complete history of the needle. Some examples date as far back as the Stone Age. During the Bronze Age and the Iron Age, metal needles evolved for different jobs and for the most part have changed very little since. Of course brittle, rusty, iron needles were adequate to stitch fabrics and leather together crudely to make basic clothing, but fine, smooth needles must have been developed by the mediaeval period for the elaborate and detailed ecclesiastical embroidery of the period, known as Opus Anglicanum, and, of course, the Bayeux Tapestry.

Crewel

Crewel needles are sharper and more slender than chenille and tapestry needles, and they are ideal to use when stitching your linen into the frame as their smaller eye helps to keep the buttonhole thread in the needle.

These are also the best needles to use with crewel wool when aiming to achieve a smoother long-and-short stitch (see page 42) as they cut through the former threads more cleanly than chenille needles, which can leave a slight dip or hole in the stitch surface.

Chenille

The majority of the time, you will find a chenille needle the best to use and, unless noted, this is the needle you should use for the stitches in this book.

Chenille needles have sharp points that increase your accuracy, a large eye that makes them easy to thread and a wide shaft that parts the fabric sufficiently to allow the crewel wool to pass through with minimal shredding of the fibres.

Tapestry

These needles have nice wide eyes making them easy to thread, but their most useful attribute is their blunt point, which makes whipping and weaving easier: the blunt end will find its way between the yarns more smoothly. In my experience, a sharp needle always seems to head straight through the fibres you do not want to touch!

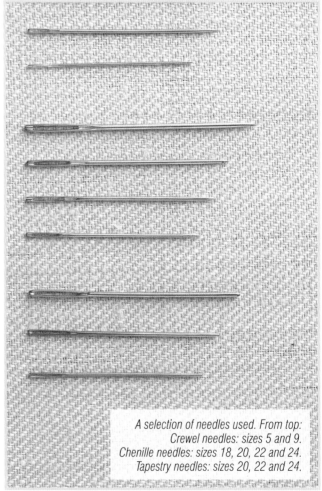

A selection of needles used. From top:
Crewel needles: sizes 5 and 9.
Chenille needles: sizes 18, 20, 22 and 24.
Tapestry needles: sizes 20, 22 and 24.

FABRIC

LINEN TWILL

Crewel embroidery has traditionally been stitched on heavy linen twill. Due to its durability and absorbency, this was readily available during the initial growth of crewelwork in England, where it was commonly used for warm and soft furnishings for the home.

Still in use today, linen twill is ideal to use for embroidery with crewel wools. Natural linen has some give, so when you bring the needle through the fabric, the grain of the fabric parts easily to allow the needle through. Helpfully, it also closes up again when you have finished pulling the yarn through.

Linen twill is made from the fibres of the flax plant, which is planted in the spring and harvested in late August. The plants are pulled out of the ground by the roots so as to take advantage of the fibres' full length. These long fibres are what gives the fabric its durability.

Pulled when the base of the stem has turned yellow, the flax is 'dew retted', a process whereby the flax is left on the ground for a month to allow the outer bark to rot down and dry. The seed heads are then removed and the stems are beaten to break down the outer bark. The fibres are then combed to remove all the short tow fibres leaving the long soft strands ready for spinning.

Different lengths of the long fibres are spun in different directions and are named either S- or Z-twist, depending on the way the fibres are twisted. Linen twill is woven using both folded S-twist and Z-twist threads in both the warp and the weft.

The shuttle carrying the weft horizontally back and forth on a hand loom travels at a lower speed than a shuttle on a modern industrial loom, therefore the best-quality linen twill is still produced on a loom by hand so as not to break the fibre.

The fabric is constructed by the shuttle passing over and under two warp threads alternately across the width of the fabric. This produces its characteristic diagonal grain lines on both faces of the fabric.

OTHER FABRICS

I am in favour of sticking to the customary fabric for my traditional designs in support of these small long-established industries, but I also like to try different fabrics for my more contemporary or experimental designs. If you are not going to use linen twill for crewel embroidery, you will need to find something heavy enough to support heavily stitched wool, like a denim or heavy sateen jean, or an upholstery fabric.

DESIGN STYLES

Traditional designs

Elizabeth I started an enduring fashion for formal flower gardens, and the explorers of the time, returning to Europe from Africa, Asia and the Americas, brought many exotic and beautiful plants with them. This encouraged a fashion in crewelwork, and traditional Jacobean embroideries are usually packed with foliage, flowers, fruit, animals and insects.

Although not for everyone, the traditional style makes a nice introduction to designing your own piece of work. It is relatively trouble free as there are no rules to abide by. The shapes you create do not have to look realistic. In fact, they do not even need to be in proportion or have any perspective. Similarly, the colours do not have to be true to life and you can randomly position each element wherever you like: next to something completely unrelated or even hanging in mid-air! You could dot several small motifs across your design or you could link them up to create a scene (see page 33).

Try to use large bold, twisting, turning leaves and curvaceous, flowing stems wrapped with parasitic tendrils as well as ripe swollen fruit or young spring buds all with movement as if actually still growing. You could include a juicy caterpillar or a timid snail, a beautiful butterfly or even a crazy mosquito! British wildlife such as stags, hares and squirrels would feel very at home in a Jacobean scene. Equally, you could choose a more unusual wild animal such as an elephant, lion or giraffe; or perhaps exotic birds – maybe even a mythical beast like a phoenix or unicorn.

Jacobean sampler

A crewelwork embroidery worked in traditional Jacobean style. English 20th century. (RSN Collection 402)

RSN collection piece

This detail, from a piece in the RSN collection, shows a small rabbit peacefully nibbling on a grassy hummock. English 20th century. (RSN Collection)

Crewelwork panel

Another piece from the RSN collection. This panel was originally part of a border, most likely from the bottom of a curtain. It is a perfect example of a split complementary colour design (see page 15). European 19th century. (RSN Collection 1172)

SYMBOLISM

The Elizabethans often included symbolism and secret messages in their gardens. If you would like to personalise your design, you might try including things with which you have an association.

For example, I have an apple and a pear tree in my garden; I love ladybirds, tortoises and rabbits and have a passion for handbags and chocolate; so those often spark ideas for designs. You might have something exotic in your garden, so try combining it with a favoured flower or a pet that you hold dear, and you already have a plan.

RSN collection piece

A very cheerful-looking stag adorns this detail from a traditional English example. English 20th century. (RSN Collection)

Contemporary designs

Choosing a more contemporary feel for your crewelwork might encourage your own style. Inspiration is all around you! Look more closely at the things you already like.

Objects you have in and around your home are a good source of inspiration; painted china, soft furnishings, holiday photographs, magazines. Printed fabrics, duvet covers, curtains and tablecloths, might have a shape or even just a colour that you didn't notice before. Garden plants, autumn leaves and sculpture are also good sources of inspiration for contemporary designs.

Leaf

Using bright and contrasting colours has given a classic Jacobean-style leaf a contemporary feel. English 20th century.

BEFORE YOU STITCH

Tip
Leave the paper sleeve on the skein. This will help to prevent the wool tangling.

Tip
Using short lengths, about the length of your forearm, will prevent the thread from being overworked and becoming threadbare. You will have to thread the needle more often, but it is all good practice.

Using crewel wool

Crewel wool is available in larger hanks or smaller skeins. Skeins have two ends. One will be around the outside and the other will be coming from the centre. When using yarn from a skein of crewel wool, it is possible to pull the wrong end and be left with a big ball of knotted yarn. To avoid this, start using your crewel wool from the inside.

Using a hank

A hank is a very large amount of wool, and unless prepared for use will easily become knotted. Cut the wool into a usable length, folding it in half with the loop at the top. Ask a friend to hold on to the loop while you divide the ends into three and plait it like hair. If nobody is at hand, you can use a door handle to hold the loop.

Remove the wool from the holder. Pull each strand from the loop end. A single strand will slide out easily, leaving the rest of the hank in a tidy plait, which allows you to cut the strand to the length required for your stitching.

1 Always pull the end of wool that is coming from the centre and you should avoid getting the skein tangled up in knots.

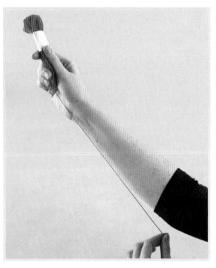

2 Cut a piece of crewel wool the length of your forearm (fingertip to elbow).

Threading the needle

Due to the fluffy nature of crewel wool, you may struggle to thread it on to a needle. Follow these easy steps for a fail-safe method.

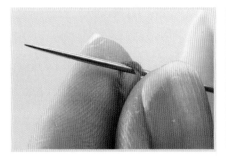

1 Fold one end of the cut yarn over the needle and pinch the folded yarn between your thumb and forefinger.

2 Keeping your grip on the folded yarn, slide out the needle. Turn the needle round and bring the eye of the needle over the folded end of the yarn.

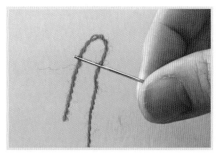

3 As you bring the needle down on to the wool, slowly release the tightness of your grip. The needle will slide between your thumb and forefinger and over the fold.

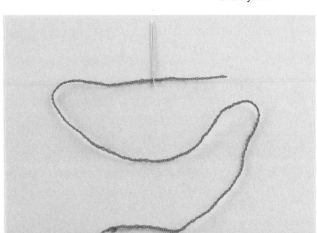

4 Pull the loop through the needle until the tail end of the yarn is also through, then tie a knot in the other end of the yarn by making a loop and pulling the end through.

STARTING TO STITCH

Holding stitch

Although rarely seen, this is your most important stitch. If you use these when starting and finishing each thread, you can be safe in the knowledge that all your hard work will be secure.

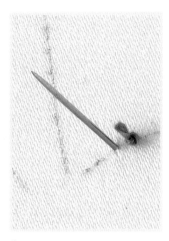

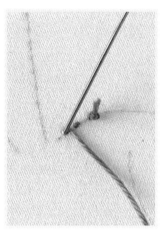

- Position the starting stitch so that it is close to where you will start sewing, and will be hidden under the subsequent stitching.
- Use these stitches to start and finish the embroideries throughout this book, unless the instructions specify otherwise.

1 Knot the end of the thread and take the thread down through the fabric from the top. Pull the thread through, then bring the needle up just behind the knot, either on the line or within the shape you are filling, so that it will lie under the subsequent stitching.

2 Pull the thread through, then make two tiny stitches close by.

3 Bring the needle up where you wish to start the first stitch and cut off the knot close to the fabric.

Finishing stitch

1 Working in an area that will subsequently be hidden beneath stitching, make two tiny stitches. Bring the thread through to the top of the fabric and cut it off close to the fabric.

RSN collection piece
A detail from a beautiful hanging. English 20th century.

CREWELWORK STITCH FINDER

Stitch	Type	Page
BACK STITCH	OUTLINE	SEE PAGE 57
BLOCK SHADING	FILLING	SEE PAGE 43
BRICK STITCH	FILLING	SEE PAGE 51
BULLION KNOT	SURFACE	SEE PAGE 67
BURDEN STITCH	FILLING	SEE PAGE 48
BUTTONHOLE STITCH	FILLING	SEE PAGE 52
CHAIN STITCH	OUTLINE	SEE PAGE 62
CLOSED HERRINGBONE STITCH	FILLING	SEE PAGE 55
CORAL STITCH	OUTLINE	SEE PAGE 58
COUCHING	OUTLINE	SEE PAGE 59
CRETAN STITCH	FILLING	SEE PAGE 49
DETACHED CHAIN STITCH	SURFACE	SEE PAGE 71
FEATHER STITCH	SURFACE	SEE PAGE 65
FISHBONE STITCH	FILLING	SEE PAGE 54
FLY STITCH	SURFACE	SEE PAGE 64
FRENCH KNOT	SURFACE	SEE PAGE 66
HEAVY CHAIN STITCH	OUTLINE	SEE PAGE 63
HERRINGBONE STITCH	FILLING	SEE PAGE 54
KNOTTED PEARL STITCH	OUTLINE	SEE PAGE 60
LAID STITCH	FILLING	SEE PAGE 47

Jacobean sampler
See also page 13.

Chintz Flower

Worked by Jacqui McDonald. This is shown in more detail on page 73, where the stitch choices and order in which they were worked is explained.

LEAF STITCH	FILLING	SEE PAGE 52
LONG-AND-SHORT STITCH	FILLING	SEE PAGE 42
PADDED SATIN STITCH	FILLING	SEE PAGE 46
PEARL STITCH	OUTLINE	SEE PAGE 60
PEKINESE STITCH	OUTLINE	SEE PAGE 62
PISTIL STITCH	SURFACE	SEE PAGE 66
QUAKER STITCH	OUTLINE	SEE PAGE 61
RAISED CHAIN BAND STITCH	OUTLINE	SEE PAGE 63
RAISED STEM BAND STITCH	FILLING	SEE PAGE 53
RUNNING STITCH	OUTLINE	SEE PAGE 57
SEEDING STITCH	FILLING	SEE PAGE 49
SLANTED SATIN STITCH	FILLING	SEE PAGE 46
SPLIT STITCH	OUTLINE	SEE PAGE 58
STEM STITCH	OUTLINE	SEE PAGE 56
TRELLIS STITCH	FILLING	SEE PAGE 44
TURKEY RUG STITCH	SURFACE	SEE PAGE 70
VAN DYKE STITCH	FILLING	SEE PAGE 50
WHIPPED WHEEL	SURFACE	SEE PAGE 69
WOVEN WHEEL	SURFACE	SEE PAGE 68

FILLING STITCHES

Long-and-short stitch

Because you can shade from light to dark and blend it seamlessly, long-and-short stitch is perfect to produce three-dimensional forms which can give a more realistic image.

Originally developed for ecclesiastical church work, the smooth colour blending created with long-and-short stitch could provide the iconic images of saints. The light and shade this stitch produces allowed the folds of robes to be represented, while the definition obtained produced realistic faces.

- Bringing the needle up and down in the fabric can leave behind trace fibres of wool. When doing so, make sure it is either within the design where stitches will later hide fibres, or well out of the way.
- Changing from a chenille needle to a finer crewel needle will produce a smoother stitch as the fine needle slices more cleanly through the previous rows of stitches.

> **Note**
>
> *The split stitch, although not seen, will act as a supporting wall and help to give your work a smooth outer edge.*

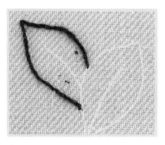

1 Starting from the rearmost element of your design (i.e. furthest in the background), work a split-stitch outline (see page 58).

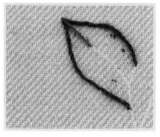

2 Bring the needle up in the centre of the design, then take the needle down over the split stitch. Draw the thread through to create the first stitch.

3 Work a few stitches to one side of the first stitch, taking each down over the outline. Vary the length of each stitch (this is what gives the stitch its name) to ensure a smooth surface.

4 Work the other side of your design in the same way, then thread another needle with a second colour. Continue working, alternating which colour you use.

Tip
To ensure a neat finish, angle the needle in and under the previous stitch.

5 As you work, gradually drop out the first colour and work exclusively in the second colour. Build up a small section on one side before swapping to the other as you work.

6 Switch to a crewel embroidery needle and bring it up to the surface by splitting the original stitch high in its length. Envisage lengthening the first stitch a little, and take the needle down at that point. If the shape happens to curve, just change the angle of your stitch slightly.

7 To build up the second row, split and lengthen all the other stitches of the first row in random heights along their length. Each stitch in the second row should be of a similar length and staggered at different depths across the area to be filled.

8 Introduce a third colour as you reach the ends of the first row, and gradually drop out the second colour by the time you start the third row. Remember to change the direction of the stitch when covering the split-stitch edges.

9 Complete the third row.

10 Introduce a new colour on each subsequent row, and work only up to the edge of your shape and not into any others.

11 Secure the thread by stitching small holding stitches (see page 39) in an area to be filled later. If there is no area to be filled later, secure the thread by weaving the needle through the heavy stitching on the back.

12 Work a split-stitch outline for any overlapping elements and complete them in the same way.

Tip
On more complex designs, you may find it helpful to add in directional lines to help guide your stitching.

Block shading

A bold filling stitch that is equally suitable for large and small areas. Gently blend shades of one colour or use more contrasting colours to produce bold stepped shading.

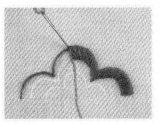

1 Work a split-stitch outline (see page 58).

2 Work a row of satin stitch (see page 46), working from the centre out and over the outline. Take the needle as close to the previous stitch as possible, and follow the shape carefully.

3 Change the colour of the thread and work another row. Start each stitch at the bottom and take the needle into the stitches above, splitting the thread.

4 Work another row in the same way, introducing a third colour and working into the stitches of the second row, splitting them.

Trellis stitch

This stitch fills large areas quickly, and is commonly used in traditional crewelwork.

- Starting in the centre and working outwards makes it easier to keep the stitches parallel throughout the shape.
- As an alternative, use the diagonal lines in the linen as a guide.

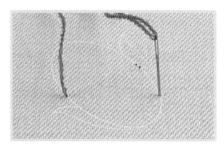

1 Bring the needle up on the marked line at the edge of the design, in the middle of the area you want to fill, and take it down on the line directly opposite.

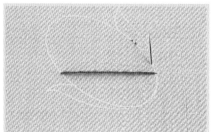

2 Pull the thread through so that the first stitch lies horizontally across the centre of the shape, then bring the needle up through the fabric further along the design.

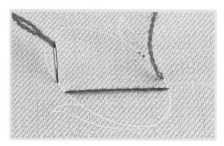

3 Take the thread down directly opposite, ensuring that the stitches are parallel.

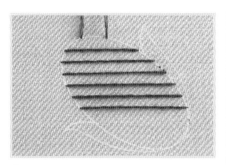

4 Continue to work the top half of the shape in the same way, by building up parallel lines. Be careful to space them evenly.

Tip
Lay the needle down when working to check the spacing.

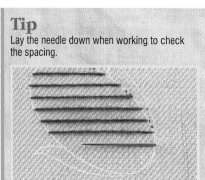

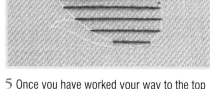

5 Once you have worked your way to the top of the shape, work the remainder in the same way, working downwards from the first stitch in the centre.

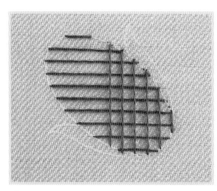

6 Again, starting from as near the centre of the design as your can, work parallel vertical stitches to one side.

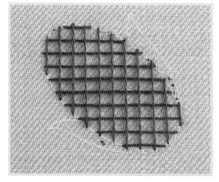

7 Work the other side in the same way and fasten off the thread on the marked line. You can hide the line later with an outline stitch.

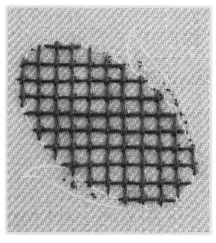

8 With a new thread, make small stitches over each intersection to secure your trellis.

Pomegranate

This piece shows a pomegranate, a common motif in Jacobean crewelwork. The design shows a number of filling stitches: the centre of the pomegranate has been worked in trellis stitch (see opposite), while the edges are worked in burden stitch (see page 48). The leaves are worked in satin stitch (see page 46).

Slanted satin stitch

Closely placed diagonal stitches are worked at the same angle over a split-stitch edge to produce a crisp finish with a smooth filling. Satin stitch is unsuitable for wide spaces, because long threads tend to gape when the fabric is released from tension, so when working larger spaces, divide them into smaller shapes first.

- Be sure to use the same colour thread for the stitch and the outline for a seamless finish.
- The satin stitch can be worked with a set angle or the angle can change with the sweeping curves of the shape.

 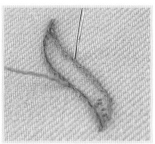  

1 Work a split-stitch outline (see page 58), then, starting in the middle of your shape, bring the needle up outside the outline.

2 Take the needle down opposite, angling the needle under the outside edge of the split stitch. This first stitch sets the slanted angle to which you will work.

3 Draw the thread through and bring it up slightly to the side of the previous stitch, then back down opposite.

4 Draw the thread through to create a stitch parallel to the first, then work stitches out to the end of the design in the same way, being careful to angle the needle in towards the previous stitch as you take it down through the fabric.

Note

Taking the needle down through the fabric at the side with the more acute angle helps you to keep the angle you set with the first stitch, and produces a smoother edge to the finished shape.

5 Return to the middle of the shape, bring the needle up on the other side of the shape and down into the acute angle: in this case it means working from the top to the bottom.

6 Continue to fill the shape and secure your thread to finish.

Padded satin stitch

To produce this stitch, successive layers of padding stitches that lie perpendicular to each previous layer are worked to produce a raised shape. Much like slanted satin stitch, stitches are then worked closely together and at the same angle.

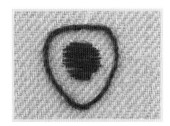 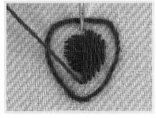  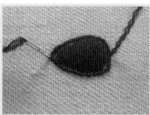

1 Work a split-stitch outline (see page 58), then work an area of horizontal laid stitch (see page 47) on the area you wish to be most highly padded.

2 Work a larger area of laid stitch perpendicular to the previous layer, covering it completely.

3 Continue adding layers of laid stitch, each at right angles to the previous one, gradually increasing the area covered on each layer.

4 Bring the needle up outside the split-stitch edge, then take it down directly opposite, angling the needle under the outside of the split stitch.

5 Bring the needle up slightly to the side of the previous stitch, then down directly opposite, angling the needle towards the previous stitch.

6 Work all the way to one side, wrapping the back and front in the process.

7 Work the other side in the same way to finish the area. Secure the thread.

This stitch is perfect for fruits and other rounded objects. This strawberry has a stalk made of bullion knots (see page 67).

Laid stitch

This was one of the main stitches used to fill the Bayeux Tapestry. It fills areas quickly without using up too much thread, as it covers the front with long stitches and uses short stitches on the back of the fabric.

• Lay the first stitch in the centre or widest part of the area to be filled. This will set the angle to follow and help to keep the stitches parallel to one another.

1 Bring the needle up on the outline of the shape you want to fill, and take it down directly opposite.

2 Pull the thread down through the hole and bring the needle up directly adjacent.

3 Take the thread back down directly opposite, adjacent to where you first brought the needle up.

4 Draw the thread through to create a parallel stitch, then start to work parallel stitches up and down across the shape. Partway along, introduce a second colour by laying in a single stitch then returning to the original colour for two stitches. Reverse the sequence (two of the new colour then one of the old), then continue with the new colour.

5 Continue in the same direction, adding new colours as you wish and following the sequence in step 4 to blend them in. Once the shape is filled, secure the thread to finish. If the outside of the shape looks a little uneven, do not panic. You can easily cover the edge later, using outline stitches.

Burden stitch

Burden stitch is often used for suggesting hummocky ground. It can be used quite densely by packing the stitches closely or less densely by spacing the stitches. This latter approach reveals more of the backing fabric.

Note
Working in this way keeps the thread on the back as discreet as possible, reducing the bulk and saving thread.

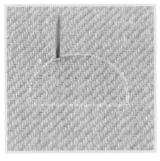   

1 Bring your needle up on the edge of the shape, then take it down through the fabric on the opposite side.

2 Leaving equal gaps, produce parallel horizontal stitches, alternating between working from right-to-left and left-to-right.

3 Starting in the centre, bring your needle up through the fabric just above one of the horizontal lines.

Note
To make this stitch easier to see, the blue thread has been fastened off and replaced with a new green thread.

   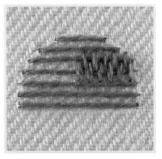

4 Take the needle back down just below the horizontal stitch two rows above. Draw the thread through and trap the middle horizontal stitch.

5 Bring your needle up just above and adjacent to the vertical stitch, then down just below the horizontal stitch two rows above. Work these two lines of vertical stitches alternately to one side.

 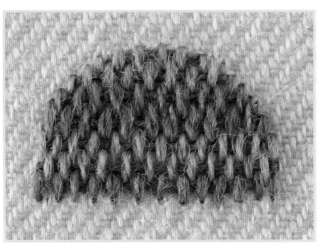

7 Work interlocking rows of vertical stitches over the other horizontal lines.

6 Work the two lines to the other side.

Seeding stitch

Small straight stitches are worked in random directions for this stitch. Varying the density of stitches you work over the area can produce effective shading – the more stitches, the darker the area.

- Try using several different colours for a mottled effect.
- Stitching densely creates a darker appearance; stitching sparsely a lighter appearance. Use this as your design requires.
- Working parallel pairs (see tip below right) makes the stitches easier to see from a distance: perfect for larger scale embroideries.

1 Working stitches in random directions, fill the area by making tiny straight stitches, each approximately 1mm long.

2 Pack the stitches closely together for a dense appearance at the edges.

Tip
Align the stitches randomly to improve the effect.

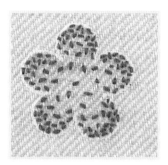

3 Spread the stitches out in the centre to create shading.

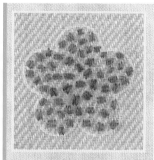

Tip
This example uses different colours, and the stitches are worked in parallel pairs. This makes them easier to see on larger designs and gives a different effect.

Cretan stitch

This stitch is a series of widely offset fly stitches. It is easily adapted to shapes of varying width, such as wide petals and leaves, or spaces that are too wide to be covered by a single band of stitching.

1 Draw a double stem line. Starting at the tip of your leaf shape, bring the needle up just outside the marked line.

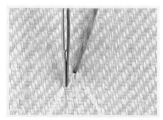

2 Take the needle down through the fabric on the line left of the protruding thread.

3 Draw the thread through to create a loop. Hold the loop and bring the thread up inside it from the back, on the left-hand stem line, then draw the thread through to tighten the loop against the needle.

4 Draw the needle and thread through, then take the needle down through the fabric on the outer marked line to the right of the first stitch.

5 Draw the thread down then through to create a loop. Hold the loop on the surface, and bring the needle up on the stem line on the right-hand side.

6 Tighten the loop on the needle, draw the thread through and take it down on the outer line on the left-hand side.

7 Continue to work down towards the base of the leaf by filling in alternate sides.

Van Dyke stitch

A row of equally spaced cross stitches is worked, with each woven on to the previous stitch. Once pulled taut, this produces a very attractive pattern that looks like a ladder with a central plaited vein. It is ideal for borders or leaf shapes.

- This stitch is not suited to being used as a closed stitch.
- Aim to keep a small even space between each stitch for an attractive finish.

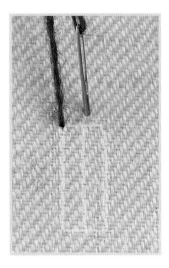

1 Draw a single central line the length of your shape. Bring the needle up through the left outer edge of the shape on the top of the marked line, then take the needle down just right and above the centre line.

2 Draw the thread through to produce a diagonal stitch just over halfway across the design.

3 Bring the needle up left of the centre line, and take it down on the right edge in line with the first stitch (see inset). Draw the thread through.

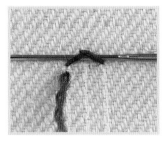

4 Bring the needle up on the left outer edge of the shape a little way along the marked line, then take the needle under the cross formed by the last stitch.

5 Draw through and pull on the thread to create tension before taking the needle down on the right edge in line with the up stitch.

6 Draw the needle through.

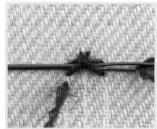

7 As you continue, take the needle only under the cross formed by the stitches made immediately previously, as shown.

8 Continue working the stitches towards the base of your design.

9 At the end, bring the needle up on the left of the central line.

10 Take the needle and thread through the final cross as before, then down on the right of the central line. Fasten off as normal to finish.

Brick stitch

Brick shading is an arrangement of stitches offset from one another to produce a shaded filling stitch. You may also like to try stitching small horizontal offset blocks of satin stitch, traditionally used to shade wide stems.

- To achieve uniform straight lines, it may help to draw horizontal lines onto your fabric with a pencil.
- By taking the needle down through the fabric in the hole previously created at the base of the stitch directly above, you will avoid any of the linen showing through.
- You can shade the shape by changing colour every other line.

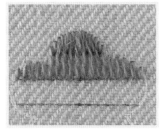 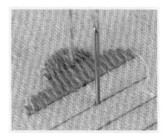 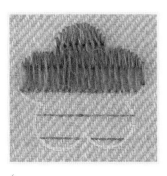

1 Draw parallel horizontal lines across the shape, then bring your needle up through the fabric on the second line from the top and take it down at the top edge of the shape to create a vertical stitch (this is a full-length stitch), then bring it up on the first line and take it down at the top edge (creating a half-length stitch).

2 Work alternate full- and half-length stitches along the top edge in parallel lines, without condensing to fit the shape.

3 The second line of vertical stitches should be worked in full-length stitches. Bring your needle up through the fabric at the base of each short stitch and down at the third line.

Note

The shorter stitches should fill the gaps between the longer stitches, so the top of the shape has an unbroken appearance.

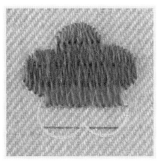  

4 Take your needle down through the fabric at the base of each short stitch and continue working horizontally across from one side to the other. Complete a second row of the same colour before changing shade for the third row.

5 By stitching two rows of each shade you will achieve alternating rows of blended and solid colour.

6 Work the final line with long-and-short stitches to the edge of the shape, exactly as you started (see step 1), then fasten off.

Buttonhole stitch

As the name suggests, this stitch was originally used to reinforce the slots cut for buttons. Also known as blanket stitch, it produces a neat outline of its own and can be worked with vertical threads or angled to fit a space. You can work the stitches more closely together for a denser appearance or slightly spread out for a less dense appearance.

- The outside edge of this stitch produces a clean, attractive outline of its own.
- Worked densely, a heavy look is produced. Worked openly, it produces a softer appearance.
- Tuck the needle in close to the last stitch on the inside edge, bringing the needle up wide on the outside edge to produce a curved shape. Keep the stitches parallel and an equal distance apart to fill a straight shape.

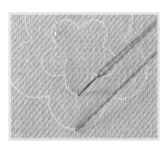 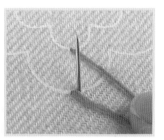 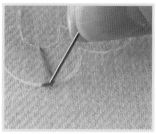 

1 Come up on the outside edge of the shape and take the needle down on the inside of the shape.

2 Assuming you are working left to right, hold the surface thread in a loop to the right, then bring the needle up on the outside edge, ensuring the needle is inside the loop.

3 Hold the needle in the fabric securely with your surface hand while you pull the thread from the underside to tighten the slack on the loop.

4 Pull the needle through and bring the thread up to the surface.

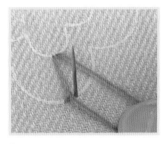  

5 For the next stitch, take the needle down through the fabric on the inside edge of the shape, slightly to the right of the first stitch. Again, leave a loop to the right and bring the needle up on the outside edge within the loop.

6 Tighten the slack while holding the needle in the fabric, then pull the needle through and bring the thread to the surface. Repeat these stitches until the shape is filled.

7 The final stitch needs a holding stitch on the outside edge to secure the last loop.

Leaf stitch

This stitch is a series of overlapping open diagonal stitches. It is easily adapted to forms of varying width, such as petals and leaves.

- Work from the base of your shape upwards.

1 Draw a double stem line. Starting at the base of your leaf bring your needle up through the fabric on one of the stem lines.

2 Take the needle to the opposite side of the leaf and take it down through the fabric on the line, creating a straight slanted stitch.

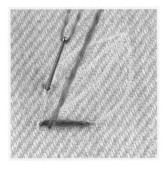

3 Do the same on the opposite side by bringing the needle up through the fabric on the other stem line just under the previous stitch and taking it down on the opposite side of the leaf.

4 Repeat the process, bringing the needle up just under the previous stitch and above the rest.

5 Continue by working up towards the tip of the leaf until the shape is filled.

This example has a stem-stitch outline (see page 56).

Raised stem band stitch

This is a neat stem stitch raised on a regular ladder foundation and is suitable for stems, outlines, leaves and borders. It produces a band that looks more padded in the centre than at the sides.

- Shading can be achieved by subtle changes of colour with each stem line.
- Using a contrasting colour for the ladder helps you to find the base stitches as the area becomes filled.

1 First produce a ladder of straight stitches an equal distance apart.

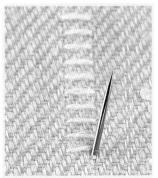

2 Using a contrasting colour thread, bring your needle up through the fabric at the bottom right-hand side of the straight-stitch ladder.

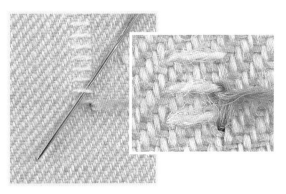

3 Draw the thread through, change your needle to a tapestry needle, then pass it under the second ladder stitch from the bottom and pull through the thread (see inset).

4 Pulling the tension to the right, pass the needle under the third ladder stitch from the bottom.

5 Continue to the top of the ladder and fasten off at the back.

6 Starting at the bottom, repeat the process to the left of the first vertical row using another shade of thread, if desired.

7 Repeat the process until you have filled your shape, changing the shade in each vertical row.

Fishbone stitch

Made up of alternate slanting stitches, this is typically used as a filling for small leaf shapes. It is worked open or closed from the tip downwards to the base.

• This is an ideal stitch for filling shapes such as petals and leaves. – or fish

  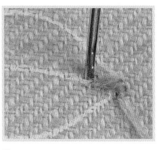 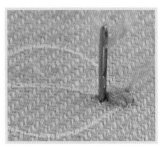

1 Bring the needle up through the fabric then back down to make a straight stitch at the start of the shape.

2 Bring the needle up at the outside edge of the shape, close to the straight stitch, then over the end of the straight stitch and down. Draw the thread through.

3 Bring the needle up on the opposite side of the shape, on the outside edge close to the stitch, then take it over the end of the previous stitch.

4 Draw the thread through, then bring it up on the opposite edge, adjacent to the earlier stitch, then down, covering the end of the previous stitch.

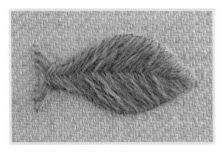 

5 Pull the thread through, and continue in the same way to the end of the shape.

This fish has been embellished with a fly stitch fin (see page 64), straight stitch lips and an eye made from a French knot (see page 66).

Herringbone stitch

Traditionally used to secure one fabric to another, if stitched evenly and neatly this stitch can provide an attractive embroidery border or filling stitch. Closed herringbone stitch is a denser version (see opposite).

• This stitch does not have a natural neat end unless your shape tapers away, so feel free to add some straight stitches to fill the shape.

  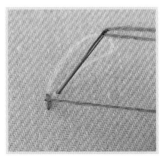

1 Bring the needle up at the edge of the shape, then down on the opposite side to create a diagonal stitch.

2 Bring the needle up a little way behind where you took it down.

3 Take the needle diagonally across the initial stitch, as shown, then down.

4 Pull the thread through, then bring the needle up behind where you took it down, and then across the previous stitch and down.

5 Continue in this way until the shape is filled.

Closed herringbone stitch

Closed herringbone stitch is
worked in the same way as
herringbone stitch (see opposite),
but with each stitch adjacent to
the previous one. This means that
the fabric is covered entirely.

RSN sampler

*This training sampler shows part of a set design which was worked by RSN Apprentices until 1951.
It featured four different design styles and this particular segment simulates a design style that was
popular during the Arts and Crafts Movement, a British design movement that flourished between
1880 and 1910. It relies mainly on outline stitches such as pearl stitch (see page 60) and couching
(see page 59) to define the pattern. English 20th century. (RSN Collection 402)*

OUTLINE STITCHES

Stem stitch

Stem stitch is the most well-known outline stitch. When used as a filling stitch, it is known as crewel stitch, and when the loop is held to the left instead of to the right, it is known as outline stitch. This stitch can be used as a solid filling stitch by working rows across a shape. It was heavily used during the Arts and Crafts period, when it became known as South Kensington stitch.

- Each twist of the stem stitch should lie in the direction of bottom left to top right.
- Hold the loop to the left if you are working stem stitch down your marked line.
- Hold the loop down if you are working along your marked line left to right.
- Hold the loop up if you are working along your marked line right to left.

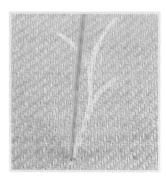

1 Push the needle up through the fabric at the base of your stem. Pull the needle and thread through to the surface.

2 Take the needle down through the fabric on the marked line at the length you wish the stitch to be (3–4mm/^{1}/$_8$in if using a single strand).

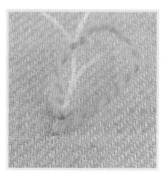

3 Pull the thread down through the fabric leaving a loop of thread on the front side of the fabric.

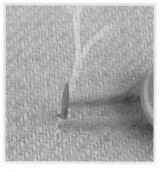

4 Hold the loop out of the way to the right as you bring the needle up to the surface. Bring the needle up on the line in the centre of this first stitch.

5 Leave the needle in the fabric while you tighten the slack on the loop against your needle.

6 Pull the needle and thread up through the fabric and make another stitch, equal in length to the first (see inset). When you bring the needle up again in the centre of the stitch this will also be the end of the previous stitch.

7 Continue along the marked line in the same way to finish your design.

56

Running stitch

Probably one of the easiest stitches, and possibly the first stitch you learned as a child. When embroidering on to loose fabric, out of a frame, several stitches can be 'run' on the needle at a time, but when embroidering on to taut fabric you will need to produce each stitch with two actions.

- Try to keep the stitches an even, uniform length.
- Running stitch is suitable for creating directional lines and filling.

  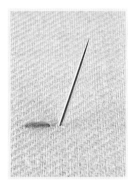 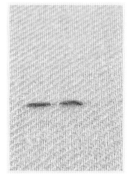 

1 Push the needle up through the fabric with your under hand. Pull through the needle and thread with your surface hand.

2 Decide on the length and direction of your stitch and take the needle down through the fabric at that point.

3 Leaving a gap between the first stitch and the next, once again push the needle up through the fabric with your under hand.

4 Pull the needle and thread through with your surface hand, and decide on the length of your stitch (usually an equal length to the previous). Take the needle down through the fabric at that point.

5 Continue in the desired direction, then make a finishing stitch (see page 39) and trim off the excess thread to finish.

Back stitch

Made up of small, equally sized stitches that cover the marked line without spaces, this stitch is frequently used as a foundation stitch for others. Try whipping it with a contrasting colour to produce a cord or weaving in and out under each stitch to produce a more decorative effect.

- Try to keep the stitch size even, unless the design requires otherwise.
- Try whipping or weaving with another colour to produce different effects.
- Use back stitch as the basis for Pekinese stitch (see page 62).

 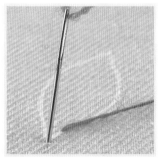  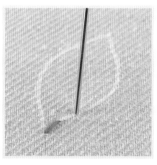

1 Push the needle up through the fabric with your under hand at the desired stitch length from the start of the marked line.

2 Draw the thread through with your surface hand, then insert the needle down through the fabric at the start of the marked line.

3 Pull the excess thread down to the underside.

4 Continue along the marked line, bringing the needle up at the desired stitch length from the first stitch.

5 Take the needle down into the fabric at the end of the previous stitch.

6 Complete the design in the same way, then finish off by making a finishing stitch and trimming the excess thread away.

Split stitch

This is a form of back stitch, but with the needle coming up to split the centre of the previous stitch rather than bypassing it, resulting in what looks like a mini chain stitch.

- This stitch is suitable for fine detail.
- Use it as a base for satin stitch (see page 46) or long-and-short stitch (see page 42) to produce a crisp and smooth outer edge.
- Try to keep stitches even.

1 Push the needle up through the fabric with your under hand. Pull through the needle and thread with your surface hand.

2 Decide on the length of your stitch and take the needle down through the fabric, on the line at the desired length.

3 Pull the wool through to the underside.

4 Push the needle up through the fabric in the centre of your first stitch, splitting the thread with the needle on the way up to the surface.

5 Each stitch should be equal in length to the first stitch but starting halfway back along the previous stitch. Continue along the marked line.

6 Pull the thread through to finish the second stitch. Start the third stitch at the end of the first, halfway along the second.

7 Finish the third stitch in the same way as before, then continue working along the design to the end.

Coral stitch

This is a stitch frequently found in seventeenth- and eighteenth-century English crewelwork. The stitches create a line with evenly spaced knots, and it is commonly used for outlines and tendrils in floral designs.

- To keep the coral stitch taut, hang on to the loop by pulling it in the direction of travel and release at the end of the action.
- To avoid wear on the thread, direct the needle's pull parallel to the fabric surface.
- Coral stitch tends to look more attractive when stitched with more than one thread in the needle.

1 Thread your needle with three strands of thread and bring the needle to the surface. Lay it along the marked line in the direction of travel.

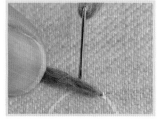

2 Hold on to the thread and take the needle down through the fabric on the outside of the marked line.

Note

The needle can be taken down through the fabric on the outside or the inside of the line, as long as you are consistent throughout.

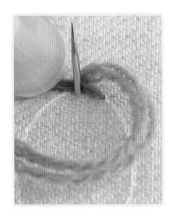  

3 Draw the thread through partway, to create a loop, then bring the needle back to the surface on the inside of the marked line and up through the loop.

4 Hold on to the needle and draw the thread through from the back to pull the loop tight.

5 Continue along the marked line, producing knots at equal intervals.

Couching

Originally used to apply gold threads to a background fabric, this works very well as an outline stitch.

- Avoid taking the couching thread up and down in the same hole.
- Couching works very well as an edging stitch.
- This is a very useful stitch to cover thick marked lines.

 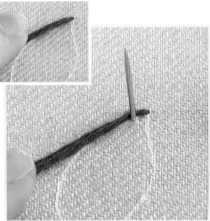 

1 Put several strands in a large chenille needle and bring to the surface at the start of the line to be couched. The number of strands in the needle will depend on the thickness you wish the couched line to be.

2 Lay the strands of thread on the surface along the line to be covered (see inset). Using another thread in a needle, bring the needle up through the fabric on the inside of the marked line.

3 Take it back down through the fabric on the outside of the line, ensuring that the small stitch traps the surface thread and holds it in the required position.

 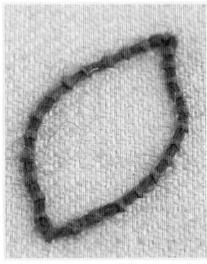

4 Continue couching small stitches over the length of surface thread at regular intervals.

5 At the end of the marked line, take both the surface thread and the couching thread back to the underside of the fabric and secure in the normal manner.

Pearl stitch

Pearl stitch is a decorative outline stitch made up of evenly spaced triangles, frequently used during the Arts and Crafts period when embroiderers had an enthusiasm for producing designs composed of various outline stitches.

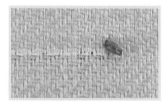

1 Thread the needle with three strands and bring it up through the fabric. Take it down above and slightly further along the marked line. Pull the thread through.

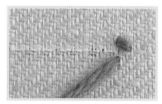

2 Bring the needle up directly below the point you took it down and draw the thread through.

3 Take the needle under the straight stitch created. Pull on the base of the slack loop to tighten the first stitch.

4 Take the needle through and draw the thread taut along the marked line.

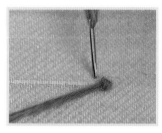

5 Take the needle down through the fabric above and slightly further along the line, parallel with the top of the first stitch.

6 Draw the thread through, then back up directly below where you took it down to make a second straight stitch.

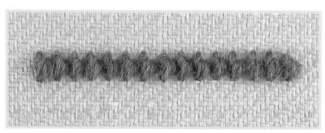

7 Take the needle through the second straight stitch, then repeat the method to the end of the marked line and secure in the usual way.

Knotted pearl stitch

This is a raised outline stitch. It is best used to give textural detail to your designs, as it emphasises shapes well when contrasted with flat stitches.

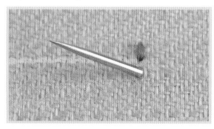

1 Thread your needle with one strand. Bring it up at the start of your line, then down directly above to make a straight stitch. Draw the thread through, then bring it up an equal distance below the line.

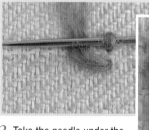

2 Take the needle under the straight stitch at the top and over the loop of the thread, then draw the thread through and down (see inset).

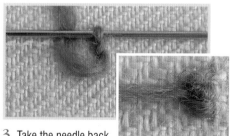

3 Take the needle back under the straight stitch at the top and over the loop of the thread again, then draw the thread through, back on itself to tighten, and across (see inset).

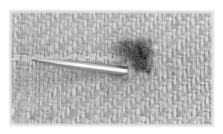

4 Take the needle down above and slightly further along the line. Draw the thread through and bring the needle up and an equal distance directly below the line.

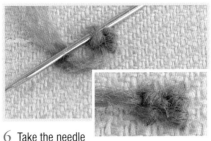

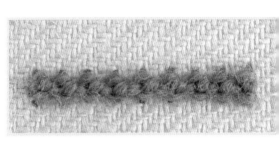

5 Take the needle through the new straight stitch and over the loop of the thread, then draw it through and down (see inset).

6 Take the needle once more through the new straight stitch and over the loop of the thread. Pull the thread through then back on itself to draw it taut, and finally back across (see inset).

7 Work along the painted line with the same method, and secure the thread in the usual way.

Quaker stitch

Quaker stitch is basically a stem stitch (see page 56) that has been combined with a split stitch (see page 58) to anchor the thread as it turns corners. It was specifically developed to produce clear and defined lettering on the Quaker Tapestry, a twentieth-century crewelwork piece that documents the history of Quakerism.

- To ensure that the finished work looks like a cord, do not pull the thread too hard.
- This is an ideal stitch to use for text in your work.

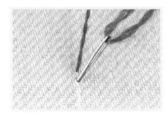

1 Bring your needle to the surface at the top of your marked line, then take the needle down through the fabric further along the marked line to make an initial stitch.

2 Bring the needle up again in the same hole as the initial stitch.

3 Push the needle down through the fabric one third longer than the first stitch. Draw the thread through, leaving a small loop on the left.

4 Keeping the loop on the left, bring the needle back to the surface, splitting the initial stitch in its centre.

Note
The loop must be on the left if you are working downwards and on the right if you are working upwards.

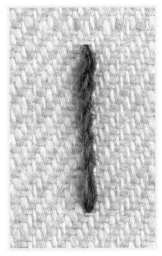

5 Pull through the slack on the loop with your under hand and draw the needle and thread to the surface.

6 Repeat from step 3, bringing the needle up two-thirds of the way through the previous stitch, and then continue along your marked line to the end.

Note
This stitch is worked as if it were a stem stitch (see page 56) as you take your needle down and a split stitch (see page 58) as you bring your needle up.

Pekinese stitch

An attractive embellishment to the back stitch (see page 57). In China it became known as the 'forbidden' stitch because workers produced whole embroideries using very small Pekinese stitch in very poor light, as a result of which it is said they became blind – another reason to have good lighting when you are stitching!

• Use the same colour thread as the back stitch to thicken an outline.

 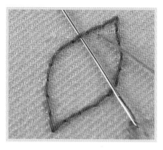 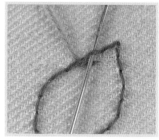 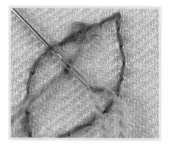

1 Work your shape in back stitch (see page 57), then bring your needle up through the fabric midway along one of the back stitches and pull the thread through.

2 Swap your needle for a tapestry needle and thread it upwards under the second back stitch.

3 Draw the thread through, then under the first back stitch and over the Pekinese thread.

4 Repeat by taking the needle and thread upwards under the third back stitch and downwards under the second back stitch.

5 Try to keep each loop of the Pekinese stitch equal in size by tightening each loop as it is produced, and continue along all the back stitches.

Chain stitch

This attractive stitch is one of the oldest of the decorative stitches and consists of a series of interlocking loops, each held in place by the next.

• To produce chequered chain stitch, use two different colour threads in the same needle and ensure that the needle only secures your chosen colour when you bring up the needle to anchor the chain. Like a magic trick, the unwanted colour will sink back below the fabric as you take the needle and thread back down.

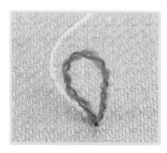   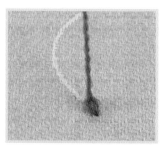

1 Bring your needle up and down in the same hole, leaving a large loop on the surface of the fabric.

2 Bring the needle up again at the point you wish to anchor your loop, making sure you bring the needle up inside the loop.

3 Hold the needle in the fabric with your surface hand while you use your underside hand to pull through the slack of the loop by tightening against the needle.

4 Bring the needle and thread all the way through to the surface.

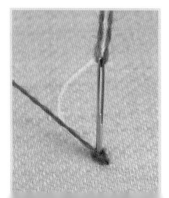 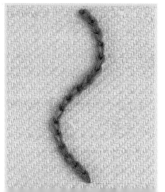

5 Continue with the second loop by taking the needle back through the first loop and the same hole in the fabric.

6 Continue along the design to the end, then secure the thread.

Heavy chain stitch

Heavy chain stitch produces a smooth, bold outline, rather like a braid, and is ideal for heavier outlines. Each chain is produced by threading the needle under previous loops and worked in the opposite direction from normal chain stitch.

1 Push the needle up through the fabric and pull it through at the start of your design, then take it down further along the marked line and pull it through.

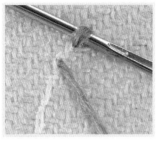

2 Bring the needle back up further down the line then take the needle under the first stitch as shown.

3 Draw the thread through and take the needle back down the same hole.

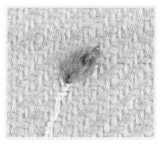

4 Take the needle down the hole, draw the thread through.

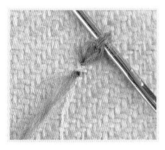

5 Push the needle back up one stitch length further down the line. Take the needle through the first stitch.

6 Take the needle back through the hole and draw the thread through.

7 Bring the needle back up further down the line, then pass it under the chains. Take the needle back down the hole and draw the thread through.

8 Continue along the design and finish in the usual way.

Raised chain band stitch

This is a decorative band worked on a foundation ladder stitch. Work one chain with the ladder showing or several chains to disguise and fill the base ladder.

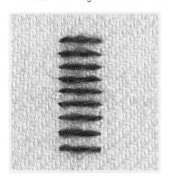

1 Start by stitching a ladder, bringing the needle up on alternate sides so as to make short stitches on the back.

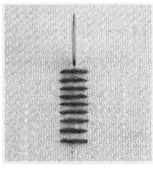

2 Thread a needle with another colour and bring the needle through at the top of the ladder in a central position.

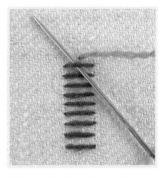

3 Draw the thread through and swap to a tapestry needle. Take the needle round and under the top straight stitch.

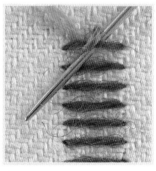

4 Draw the thread through and take it back down and under the straight stitch.
continued overleaf

63

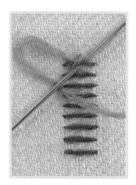  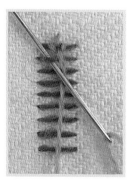 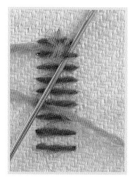 

5 This creates a loop. Take the loop under the needle.

6 Pull the thread through and down.

7 Take the needle up through the second straight stitch.

8 Take the thread through, then down and under the second straight stitch. Take the loop under the needle as before.

9 Repeat along the line to the bottom.

SURFACE STITCHES

Fly stitch

Fly stitch looks like a 'V' or a 'Y' depending on the length you make the holding stitch. Try varying the length of the stitches and the angle of the 'V' to achieve different looks.

 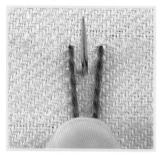 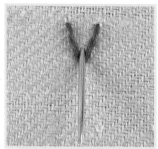 

1 Bring the needle and thread up through the fabric, then down to the left.

2 Pull the thread through, leaving a loop, and bring the needle up inside the loop, below and between the holes as shown.

3 Pull the slack through to tighten the loop against the needle.

4 Pull the thread through and take the needle down directly beneath the hole.

5 Pull through to complete the stitch, then secure.

Fly stitch can be used on its own, or to make designs. Varying the length of the arms or securing stitches, or the space between the arms, gives different effects.

Feather stitch

Feather stitch is often seen on smocking and Victorian crazy quilting. It is a decorative stitch that secures two pieces of fabric together and disguises the seam at the same time.

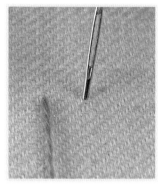 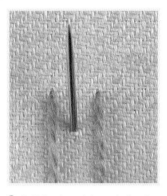 

1 Bring the needle and thread up through the fabric, then down to the right.

2 Pull the thread through, leaving a loop, and bring the needle up inside the loop, below and between the holes, as shown.

3 Tighten the loop against the needle, then pull the thread through and take the needle down to the right.

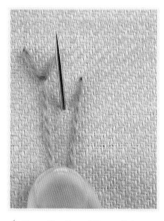 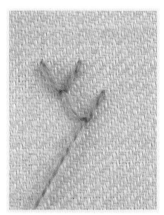 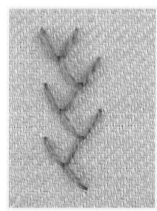

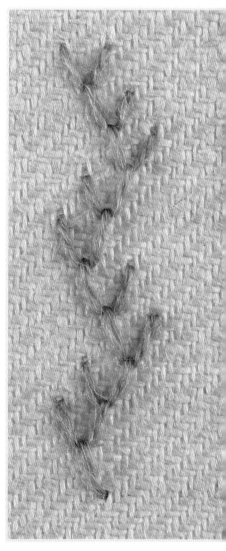

4 Draw the thread through to create a second loop, then bring the needle up below and between the holes.

5 Tighten the loop against the needle, then draw the thread through.

6 Continue as before, creating stitches to the left and right alternately.

Double feather stitch is worked in a similar way, but working two stitches in each direction every time.

French knot

• Use a single thread for a smaller knot.

Try producing different-size French knots by altering the number of threads in the needle and shade by combining different colour threads in the needle.

1 Thread your needle with two strands of thread to give a thick knot. Bring the needle up through the fabric where you want the French knot to sit.

2 Take the thread around the needle twice to form a spiral.

3 Place the needle into the fabric, near where it emerged.

4 Draw the knot down to where the needle enters the fabric.

5 Keeping the thread taut at all times, draw it through to complete the knot.

This bunch of grapes is made up of French knots with a stem stitch vine. Using two different shades of purple thread for the grapes gives a variegated effect.

Pistil stitch

Pistil stitch looks like a French knot on the end of a straight stitch, and that is why it is also known as a long-armed French knot. This stitch makes ideal flower stamens.

1 Bring the needle up through the fabric.

2 Hold the needle near the hole where the thread emerges, then take the thread around the needle twice to form a spiral.

3 Place the needle a short distance from the hole.

4 Holding the needle in place, draw the spiral down to the hole.

5 Keeping the thread taut, draw the needle and thread through to complete the pistil.

Pistil stitches have been used here as the antennae of this butterfly. Its wings are executed in whipped back stitch (see page 386) and it has a bullion knot body (see opposite).

Bullion knot

Bullion knots can be used singly to embellish designs or worked in groups to produce a filling stitch. Try producing different-size bullion knots by altering the number of threads in the needle.

1 Thread your needle with two strands to make a thick knot, then bring the needle up where you wish the bullion knot to start.

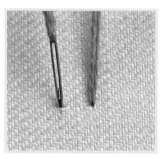

2 Take the needle back down where you wish the knot to end.

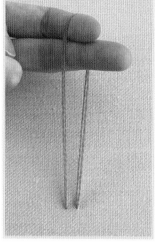

3 Draw the thread through, leaving a large loop, then bring the needle back up through the first hole.

4 Wrap the loop of thread a number of times round the needle.

5 Condense the spiral down the shaft of the needle and lay it down to check the knot reaches the end hole. Wrap or unwrap the spiral of thread to adjust the length to fit.

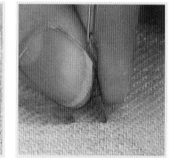

6 Pinch the spiral to hold it firm, then gently pull the needle through the spiral to make the loop smaller.

7 Place the needle in the loop to hold the spiral in place as shown.

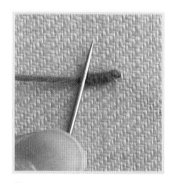

8 Ease the thread through to the back to pull the bullion knot into place.

9 Take the needle down the second hole and secure the yarn at the back.

Bullion knots can be used individually as motifs, or groups of them can be used as larger motifs, as shown here. Alternatively, larger groups can be used to fill areas of your design.

Woven wheel

Woven wheel creates a pretty stitch that looks like a small flower. Woven under and over an odd number of spokes, it produces a soft, smooth raised effect.

Note

This first stitch is made because it is essential that your wheel has an odd number of spokes.

1 Bring your needle up at the edge of your circle, then take it down a little way away in a clockwise direction.

2 Take the needle down and draw the thread through, leaving a small loop. Bring the needle back up at the centre of the circle and tighten the loop on it.

3 Take the needle down (as though finishing a fly stitch: see page 64), then bring it up a little way away clockwise.

4 Take the needle directly across the centre, and down under a spoke at the two o'clock position. Draw the thread through and bring it up a little way clockwise.

5 Take the needle across and down opposite, then make a small holding stitch (see page 39) in the centre of the spokes.

6 Bring the needle up slightly off-centre, between the spokes and above the holding stitch.

Note

To make this stitch easier to see, the yellow thread has been fastened off and replaced with a new blue thread.

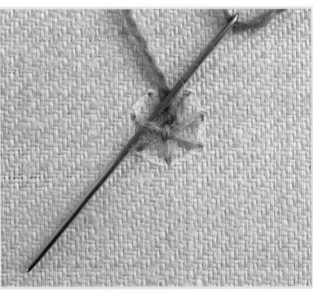

7 Change to a tapestry needle and, working anticlockwise, slip the thread over the adjacent spoke and under the next one. Keep the work tight against the centre.

8 Continue working in this way, weaving the thread over then under alternate spokes. Work outwards from the wheel's centre.

9 Continue working until the spokes are completely covered, then take the needle through to the back and secure the thread.

Whipped wheel

Also known as spider's wheel, this can be worked over an odd or even number of spokes and produces quite a raised stitch that adds an interesting ribbed texture.

1 Bring your needle up at the edge of your circle, then take it directly opposite.

2 Take the needle down and draw the thread through, then bring it back up two-thirds of the way around the circle.

3 Take the needle down directly across, then bring it back up roughly a third of the way around the circle.

4 Draw the thread across and down opposite, then make a small holding stitch in the centre.

5 Bring the thread up between two of the spokes, then swap to a tapestry needle.

6 Take the needle anticlockwise, over the first spoke adjacent, then clockwise, under the first spoke and also under the second spoke.

7 Draw the needle and thread through and pull the thread tight against the centre.

8 Take the needle over then under the second spoke, and also under the third spoke clockwise.

Note

To make this stitch easier to see, the dark thread has been fastened off and replaced with a new lighter thread.

9 Continue this sequence, taking the needle back over the previous spoke, then under the next two. Work all the way around the wheel until the spokes are completely covered. Secure the thread as normal.

Turkey rug stitch

Turkey rug stitch is also called Ghiordes knot. It is the same basic symmetrical arrangement used to produce a pile in Turkish and Persian carpet-making. The pile emerges from under the holding stitch that secures it through the base fabric.

- Using many shades of thread gives a different effect to using just one.
- There is no need to secure this stitch with an initial holding stitch.

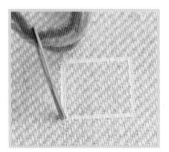

1 Thread your size 20 needle with three strands of thread and take it down through the fabric on the bottom left of your shape.

2 Pull the thread through, leaving a short tail. Bring the needle up a little way to the right.

3 Draw the thread through, then take it down a little way above where you first went down to make a holding stitch (see inset).

4 Bring the needle up beneath the stitch, then down to the right, leaving a loop.

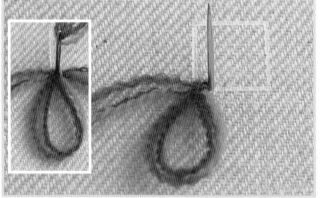

5 Bring the needle up to the right, then take it down in the space between the previous loop (see inset). Draw the thread through to create a holding stitch that traps the base of the loop, then bring the needle up a little way to the right.

6 Draw the thread through, then down to the right. Draw the thread through, leaving a loop the same size as the other. Create a holding stitch, as before, on the new loop (see inset).

7 Repeat the process to the end of the row, finishing on a holding stitch.

8 Start the next row directly above the last stitch and work to the left. Follow the previous instructions, but substitute the word 'right' for 'left'.

9 Work all the way to the top of the shape, alternating the direction of the rows as you work.

Note

Make sure that the loops are the same length as those on the first row.

10 At the end of the last row, bring the needle up under the final holding stitch.

11 Pull the thread through and remove the needle.

12 Use a pair of embroidery scissors to cut all of the loops.

13 Use the scissors to trim the yarn to length.

Detached chain stitch

Also known as lazy-daisy stitch, a detached chain stitch is a single chain secured using a holding stitch over the loop instead of another chain.

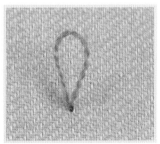

1 Take the needle up through the fabric where you wish the pointed tip of the shape to be.

2 Take the needle back down through the fabric, through the same hole, creating a loop on the surface. Hold the loop down to avold pullIng It through.

3 Decide what size you would like your lazy daisy to be and bring the needle up in the inside of the loop at this point.

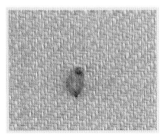

4 Leave your needle in the fabric and draw the thread through to tighten the loop against the needle.

5 Take the needle over the loop then down through the fabric to make a small holding stitch to secure it.

The flowerhead and leaves are made from lazy-daisy stitches, while the stalk is running stitch (see page 57).

BUILDING UP YOUR DESIGN

Now that you have learned all the stitches, I thought it might be interesting for you to read the thought processes I have gone through to produce the designs on the following pages.

Choosing stitches

Your design will need to be executed in crewel embroidery, so it is always good to come up with a plan of which particular stitches to use where. As I have mentioned before, designs evolve. You do not have to stick rigidly to the plan, and as my friends will tell you I am always changing my mind in the hope of improvement! The following tips will help you pick the best stitches for your design.

- Decide whether your design is more suited to a few select stitches or many different ones.
- Think about which areas of your design you would like to appear more solid.
- Similarly, work out which areas you would like to appear less densely stitched, and ask yourself whether you wish to see the background fabric through the stitches.
- Would you like texture? Which areas would you like flat and which areas would you like more raised?
- Remember that certain shapes lend themselves to certain stitches, as you will see on the following pages.

Good luck and get stitching!

RSN collection piece
A detail from a beautiful hanging. English 20th century.

Stitch order

The order in which you work stitches will differ with each design, as will how you plan to use stitches within them. Having used a coloured background fabric, I wanted a lot of the fabric to show through between the stitching and so become part of the design. This was achieved by working open stitches and leaving spaces between stitched areas.

The three colours used in the design have been distributed evenly throughout, based on a triadic colour combination, which uses three different coloured threads equally spaced around the colour wheel (see page 15). They provide a gentle and pleasing contrast to one another.

The overall design was divided up into areas to be worked from the back forward. The design is built up in layers to aid the illusion of perspective. Each area (or in this case petal) was filled with a filling or surface stitch before outlining to neaten the edges. Each subsequent petal looks as if it is in front of the last and its outline also helps to mask the base of the petal behind.

Working the design

Petals 1 and 2 The smallest petals at the back were filled using an open Cretan stitch (see page 49) in a pink thread, the marked line was then covered with a contrasting turquoise and pink Pekinese stitch (see page 62) to give it a soft, pretty outline.

Petals 3 and 4 The veins of these petals were simulated with shades of pink worked in raised chain bands (see page 63) that started wide and tapered as they met in the centre. Each petal was then heavily outlined in six threads of turquoise couched down (see page 59) with a few strands of purple. The thicker outline also helped to promote petals 3 and 4 into a more forward position than 1 and 2.

Petals 5 and 6 These two petals curved quite dramatically, and I wanted to be able to see the background fabric, so I needed to use an open stitch that could easily be manipulated to change angle and follow the curve. By dividing each petal into three lengthway sections, I narrowed the centre section. This made it easier to sweep a leaf stitch (see page 52) round the curves. It also widened the outline area enabling me to stitch a contrasting heavy border stitch. I chose a closed herringbone stitch (see page 55), as I was fairly sure I could sweep it around the curves and still keep a smooth outline.

Petal 7 This is the large central petal. With its very prominent position, it can afford more detail, embellishment and a good mix of colour. The main area was filled with pink seeding (see page 49) before the smaller internal petals were outlined in whipped back stitch (see page 386) in shades of purple. The main petal was then outlined in a heavy Quaker stitch (see page 61) in purple. The cord-like effect of Quaker stitch emphasises the prominence of the top layer. The central three small internal flowers were then embellished with a textural woven wheel (see page 68) in a contrasting turquoise colour.

Calyx/sepal 8 The calyx/sepal was outlined with split stitch (see page 58) before it was covered in a smooth long-and-short stitch (see page 42), shaded from light to dark turquoise. Finally, the stem was padded and covered with red satin stitch (see page 46).

Chintz Flower
The finished flower.

TREE OF LIFE

The Tree of Life represents one of the oldest spiritual symbols known to man. Symbolising the Tree of Life that grew in paradise, it represents the connection of heaven and earth, body and soul and the complete circle of life. References to the Tree of Life have been found throughout history in many ancient cultures spanning from Europe to the Orient.

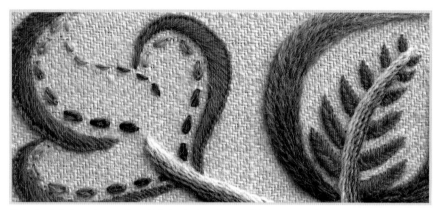

Detached chain and a running stitch in shades of green-blue were used to decorate the orange leaf and small herringbone leaves were inserted into the green-blue leaf. Blue and orange were used throughout the design, so that each leaf is embellished with touches of its opposite colour.

Acorns, worked in padded satin stitch (see page 46), are just about to drop from their bullion-knot cups. Notice in particular how the highlight colour is used on the acorns to emphasise their shiny texture.

The filling of the trunk of the tree is worked in raised stem band stitch (see page 53). Notice that each stitch is parallel and equal in length with those on either side. This is because the stitches are all woven onto a base ladder stitch which is equally spaced over the trunk and branches.

BIRD

Exotic birds, such as this characterful parrot, were widely used in the traditional style; some were realistic and others look quite made up! The mythical phoenix, usually seen rising from the ashes, was often used in embroideries to represent rebirth and new beginnings.

Long-and-short stitch in several shades and colours were blended to stitch the parrot's head plumage. A woven wheel was used to represent his eye and his beak was heavily padded before covering with a satin stitch. By keeping the stitches very close on the inside of the beak and spacing them widely on the outside it was possible to turn the angle dramatically. Finally, the face was textured with a filling of French knots.

The tail feathers consist of lengths of heavy chain stitch (see page 63). As they reach the ovals at the bottom they turn into rings of satin stitch that have been filled with pistil stitches (see page 66).

The body of the parrot was initially filled using a trellis stitch, as this covers a large area quickly. The trellis was then embellished with a few detached chain stitches. The parrot's wing was filled using a closed buttonhole stitch and rows of chain in different shades. Note how the closely worked stitches on the wing contrast with the sparser trellis on the body.

ANIMAL

Animals in crewelwork usually symbolise the basic instincts of human behaviour and were often used in traditional pieces to inject humour and interest. I have represented two people I know very well in this design, the lion is a soft and gentle, but powerful, character who is being taunted by the cheeky monkey.

The leaves of the palm have been stitched in a specific order to ensure that each leaf looks as if it is on top of another. Starting with the leaf furthest in the background and working towards the foreground, spaces were left to accommodate the monkey's hands and tail.
* To keep the leaf edges crisp and smooth, it is essential to stitch a split stitch outline before covering with satin stitch.*

Turkey rug (see page 70) and bullion knot (see page 67) surface stitches were used to embellish and add texture to the lion's head and tail.

The monkey was worked in slanted satin stitch (see page 46) in the same manner as the palm leaves, but the thicker areas of the body were padded with a few straight stitches under the satin stitch. Notice that the satin stitch also changes angle gently throughout. This ensured that none of the limbs ended up with long stitches that might gape, which is likely if the angle were fixed.

FLOWER

This Jacobean-inspired example uses large, bold leaves and curvaceous, flowing stems wrapped with parasitic tendrils. The young spring buds are imbued with movement, as if they are still growing. It is worked in monochrome red, with different tints and shades providing interest and contrast for a simple but eye-catching piece that allows the shapes to take centre stage.

The striking appearance of the main leaf has been achieved by combining a number of different padded and flat stitches: fishbone, herringbone, satin and padded satin. The main area has been left unfilled but was outlined in Pekinese stitch (see page 62).

Notice the negative space, an important point to bear in mind as you plan your layout. No gaping spaces or gaps have been left between the motifs, and good use of unstitched areas in the leaves and flowers helps to create a well-balanced design.

The ever-versatile back stitch (see page 57) has been used in many different ways in this embroidery. A plain back stitch is used to outline the herringbone stem of the right-hand flower. A single row of back stitch has been used to stitch the finer stems in a deep red colour before whipping in a contrasting shade (see page 386). The main stem is filled with several parallel rows of back stitch that were then whipped together. Finally, the hillock upon which the plant sits is a single row of back stitch with a contrasting colour woven in and out of each stitch.

CONTEMPORARY

The idea with this design was to make it more contemporary by keeping it fairly plain and using fewer stitches. You might dot several duplicates of this motif across the fabric at different angles to produce cushions or curtains.

Outline stitches do not necessarily have to be used to outline designs! The veins and stem of the leaf are all stitched in the same outline stitch, which finely spreads throughout the design. Several rows of the same split stitch have been used to fill the thicker end of the stem (see page 58).

Smaller leaves have been introduced into what would otherwise be a very smooth, dull shape, creating interest through the use of negative space. I have left them plain, without stitching, to contrast against the heavily stitched area of the leaf, so that they can be seen instantly from a distance in an interior scheme.

Four shades of green have been blended to produce this shaded leaf. After outlining the main leaf and all the inside leaves in split stitch, long-and-short stitch (see page 42) was used to fill it, starting from the tip and the outer edges in the darkest shade. As I worked into the centre and toward the base of the leaf, lighter tones were introduced.

CANVASWORK

Figs

*A canvas shaded piece worked in tent stitch (see page 124) with a cashmere
stitch (see page 102) background. Worked in crewel wool. 21st century.
(Rachel Doyle's personal collection)*

For more on this sample, see page 94.

Italian Bargello work
A sample piece of Florentine or Bargello work combining silk and wool. Italian, 17th/18th century. (RSN Collection)

For information about this design, see page 112.

FROM THE AUTHOR

Before I joined the Royal School of Needlework the only canvaswork pieces I had done were charted designs, followed closely and exactly, and always in tent stitch. During my three-year apprenticeship at the school I was introduced to canvas stitches and the possibilities of producing my own designs. Canvaswork is often overlooked as a creative embroidery technique. Try not to see the formal grid of the canvas as a restriction. Instead, look at it as you would any other background fabric – a space to fill with your embroidery. Similarly, do not assume that your canvaswork has to be worked in wool. Anything that will fit in the eye of a needle and through the holes of the canvas can be used – ribbon, silk, stranded cotton, metallic threads – and, of course, you can also apply embellishments to a piece such as beads and sequins. It is surprising how much detail you can put into a canvas piece, so almost any design can be adapted to this technique, be it a delicate landscape or a bold abstract design. There will always be a stitch to suit any surface or shape.

There are too many canvas stitches out there to illustrate in just one book, so I have chosen a broad cross-section of useful stitches to get you started. Hopefully these will be a starting point for your canvaswork and you will develop and add to what is illustrated here.

A good starting point is to sample some stitches. Explore this section and start with the ones to which you are drawn. They may inspire a design themselves. My piece *Swedish Boat Houses* (see page 93) was inspired by a sample of fern stitch. The strong vertical pattern married up perfectly to the texture of the houses.

The following pages will discuss the process of working a canvas piece, from choosing your canvas and picking a design to how to begin stitching it. There is then a stitch library from which to pick your stitches and throughout the chapter there are many canvas designs to provide you with inspiration. I hope this will give you the confidence to pick up a needle and realise the potential of this expressive technique.

Rachel Doyle

THE HISTORY OF CANVASWORK

Canvaswork is an embroidery technique using counted stitches on an openly woven base fabric. In the US the technique is called needlepoint. It is often incorrectly called tapestry work, which is actually a woven technique. Canvaswork was sometimes used to replicate tapestry and this may be the origin of the confusion of names.

It is difficult to say when the first canvas pieces were worked. It was used in a basic form on mediaeval vestments and furnishings, but it is really during the second half of the 16th century that canvaswork in its current form became a part of everyday life. All manner of domestic furnishings were covered in canvaswork, from wall hangings, and screens to the unusual 'table carpets' that were popular at the time. This work was more often than not stitched by amateur embroiderers at home, although some professional workshops did exist. The designs were often pictorial, heraldic, floral or simply geometric.

An important collection of canvaswork from this time was produced at Hardwick Hall in Derbyshire. Bess of Hardwick, the lady of the house, produced many embroideries together with Mary Queen of Scots, who was under house arrest at the hall. The embroideries are on permanent display at Hardwick Hall. The Oxburgh Hangings (*c.* 1570) are a series of canvaswork panels that were cut out and applied to a velvet background. Using small canvas 'slips' applied to another fabric was a technique that was widely used at the time to keep the drape of the fabric.

The Hatton Garden Hangings, now housed at the Victoria and Albert Museum in London, are another important example of canvaswork. These six large panels were originally mounted as stretched wall coverings and used to decorate a room as a cheaper alternative to tapestries. They date from around 1690, and were rediscovered in 1896 behind many layers of paper and paint in a house in Hatton Gardens. Professionally worked, they show classical columns surrounded by foliage, birds and animals. They include a variety of stitches including Hungarian (see page 112), rice (see page 122), eyelet (see page 99) and tent (see page 124).

As interior fashions changed so did the canvaswork. Table carpets became floor coverings and cushions became upholstered chairs and sofas. Many smaller canvas items such as book covers, shoes, pincushions and purses were also produced. However, by the end of the eighteenth century, there was a serious decline in canvaswork.

During the nineteenth century, canvaswork became once again a huge domestic pastime. At the start of the 1800s, charts for canvaswork designs started being produced in Berlin. The charts were handpainted on graph paper, with one square representing one intersection of canvas. Although expensive, these were an instant success. Wool from Saxony, spun in Gotha and dyed in Berlin was sold with these kits, giving them their name of Berlin wool work. These beautiful wools were available in a well-blended colour range alongside canvas made of silk spun around cotton.

Mr Wilks of Regent Street, London, a leading needlework supplier, began importing the patterns and wools in the 1830s and soon the popularity of Berlin wool work spread through the UK and then the rest of the world. By the middle of the century the patterns and even the wools were being produced in many countries, although the name was kept.

Figurative roundel with floral border

A canvas piece more reminiscent of a stumpwork design. The same designs were often used for different techniques. Canvaswork on linen worked in silk and wool; 18th century. (RSN Collection)

Industrialisation brought mass production of patterns and soon some 14,000 were readily and cheaply available. The delicate individual designs of the original Berlin wool work were soon lost to endless repeats of the same designs, stitched with harsh synthetically dyed wool from the 1850s onwards. The stitches used were always a tent or cross stitch. The only developments to the style were the introduction of beads and also plush work, which gave a sculptural effect.

The decline of Berlin wool work began in the 1870s. Designers such as William Morris turned away from the restrictions of canvas grids to more freeing surface embroidery techniques, such as crewelwork.

Canvas kits never quite went away and mass-produced designs were still available. In the 1920s the Royal School of Needlework began hand painting canvases, often based on historical designs. These canvases were usually for interiors such as cushions, screens and chair seats and would be worked by individuals at home.

Modern canvas kits are available in the form of a printed design with wools supplied. The unique interpretation of a design by the embroiderer is lost, and the huge variety of stitches available is reduced to simple tent stitch. However, there is a small but growing interest in reviving the individuality of pieces of work. Skilled embroiderers are creating new designs using a much wider variety of stitches to create contemporary pieces of art.

Canvaswork stitch sampler

A sampler of sixty-four 2.5cm (1in) squares stitched by Rachel Doyle. All are worked in the same colour crewel wool, but each is a different stitch. This piece shows the wide variety of texture that can be achieved with canvas stitches; 21st century. (Rachel Doyle's personal collection)

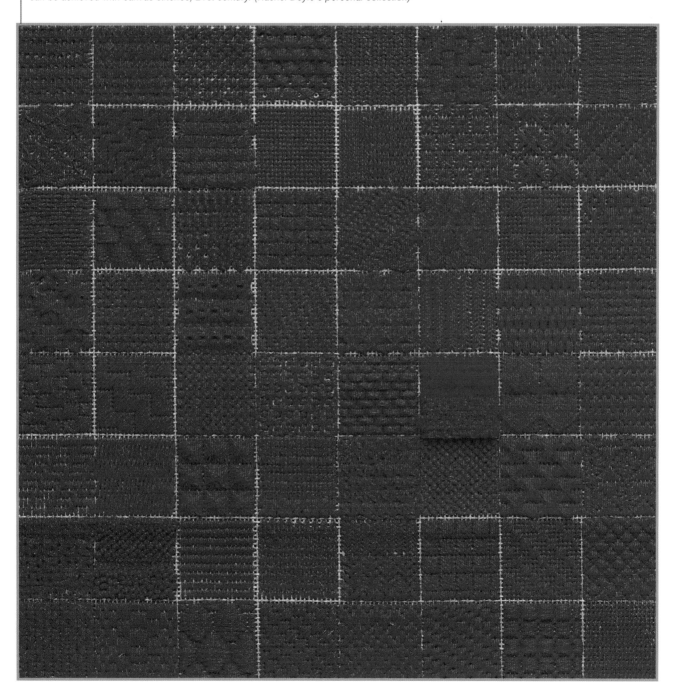

TOOLS AND MATERIALS

Canvas

The canvas is the foundation of your work and its structure, colour and scale should all be considered before starting.

SINGLE CANVAS

Canvas is a strong, even, openly woven fabric with clearly visible holes in it. Single or mono canvas is suitable for most projects and is woven with the same number of threads per inch in both warp and weft.

DOUBLE CANVAS

Double canvas is woven with pairs of threads in the warp and weft. These pairs of threads can be stitched over as one thread, or individually as two threads, giving you two scales of canvas in one fabric.

COLOURS

The majority of commercially available canvas kits are worked on white canvas, but for most projects I would recommend using a brown canvas called antique. The more neutral colour of antique canvas is far easier to cover with stitches than a bright white canvas. However, if you are working a project with a lot of light colours in it then the opposite would be true and a white canvas would be more forgiving to use.

SCALE

The threads per inch (TPI) of a canvas is important to consider. The higher the number, the finer the canvas. The finer the canvas, the more detail you will be able to put into your work. Conversely, the lower the TPI the quicker your piece will be to work. Students at the Royal School of Needlework generally work on 18TPI canvas for small designs. This is quite a fine canvas and allows a lot of detail to be put into the work.

A selection of white and antique canvas pieces. Always store your canvas rolled to prevent creases.

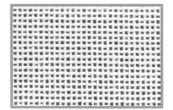

White 24TPI canvas – a very fine canvas.

Antique 18TPI canvas – a fairly fine canvas.

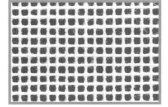

White 14TPI canvas – a medium-scale canvas.

Antique 10TPI canvas – an open canvas, unsuitable for very intricate designs.

Needles

Canvaswork is a counted technique and stitch placement is (for the most part) restricted by the holes of the canvas. Your needle should go through these holes and not pierce the fabric, so it is always best to use a blunt tapestry needle rather than a sharp embroidery needle. It is much easier to guide a blunt needle through the canvas than a sharp one, and you are also less likely to catch the thread of any previous stitches.

A sharp chenille needle should only be used when you want to pierce the threads of the canvas. This would only be for overstitched details once the majority of a piece is stitched.

The sizes of both tapestry and chenille needles are the same, and the smaller the number, the larger the needle. The larger the needle, the easier it is to work with. There are no rules as to the size of needle you use compared with the TPI of your canvas, but the threaded needle does need to pass through the holes smoothly. If you are forcing it through then it is too large and can widen the holes of the canvas. The easiest way to check is to thread the needle with the appropriate number of strands and make sure that it passes smoothly through the canvas holes.

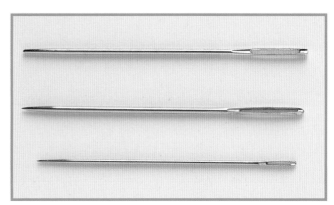

Top to bottom: tapestry needle, chenille needle, embroidery needle.

TAPESTRY NEEDLES

Tapestry needles have a blunt end and a long eye to ease threading. The eye is the widest part of the needle, so make sure that the complete needle passes through your canvas easily.

CHENILLE NEEDLES

Chenille needles look the same as a tapestry needle but with a sharp end. Again, compared with an embroidery needle they have a much longer eye for threading several strands through.

Threads

Within reason almost any thread can work on a canvas piece. The only restriction is fitting it through the eye of a needle and through the holes of the canvas. Usually several strands of thread will be used in the needle at once. These strands can all be of the same thread or different threads can be used at once. A single strand of metallic thread for instance might be combined with several crewel wool strands to give a subtle shimmer to an area. It is always a good idea to sample the threads you have chosen to see how many strands are needed to cover the canvas. Too few and you will have gaps, too many and the canvas can be distorted.

STRANDED COTTON

Stranded cotton is a strong, hardwearing thread. It is a great thread to use for canvaswork as it comes in a variety of colours and shades.

Stranded cotton is smooth and it will have a slight sheen to it when worked correctly. Always separate the strands of the cotton and ply them back together for the flattest possible finish.

SILK AND METALLIC THREADS

Fancy decorative threads will add interest to your canvaswork. Silk will give a great shine to your piece but it is a more delicate thread to use and it is not as strong as a stranded cotton.

Metallic threads are often very fine so it is a good idea to use them in the needle with another thread.

WOOL

Wool is a staple of canvaswork and like stranded cotton, it is also available in a wide variety of colours and shades.

Crewel wool is very fine so you will need to use several strands at once, while tapestry wool is fairly thick and can often be used with just a single thread. Wool is hardwearing and will have a smooth, matt texture to it when stitched.

CANVASWORK DESIGN

The majority of canvaswork done today is worked from a chart or on to a painted canvas, and designing your own canvas piece can seem like a daunting task. However, by sourcing your own design and choosing your own stitches you will create a much more expressive and individual piece. By working only from a drawn outline your stitching will be totally unique to you.

The original photograph and a slightly enlarged version (see above), made by scanning the photograph on to a computer then printing it out at a larger scale (see below).

Finding inspiration

The inspiration for a canvas design can come from anywhere. Using a photograph is the simplest method, or working from one of your own paintings or drawings. A good image to work from will have plenty of areas large enough to fit a few repeats of a canvas stitch pattern. A design with lots of different textures in it will allow you to experiment with different stitches.

Using your image

Once you have chosen your design, you will need to work out the best size to use it. Print out a few copies at different sizes if you have a digital version of the design; and use a photocopier to make larger and smaller copies of the design if you do not.

Place these side by side in size order and eliminate any that are too big (where the effect of the stitches will be lost) and too small (where the stitch patterns will be awkward to fit). When you have decided on the size you will work your design, make sure you also have a clear copy of your image at a size at which it is easy to see all the detail.

Creating a line drawing

To turn your image into a simple line drawing, you will now need to trace the design. Use a sharp pencil and a ruler for the outside edges and any straight lines in the design. Take care to make this tracing as accurate as possible.

1 Use a fine permanent marker to trace the main outlines. Try to aim for large block areas and do not get over-detailed.

2 Photocopy the tracing on to plain paper.

3 Use a permanent marker to go over the lines of the photocopy to make a final drawing.

Transferring your design to canvas

At this stage, the edge of the design is tacked on to the canvas and the design is drawn within this. The tacking stitches will be removed once the design is complete. Be careful not to go over the edges of your tacked outline when you mark the design as you do not want pen marks to show outside your stitched design.

1 Use a ruler to measure the outline of your design.

90

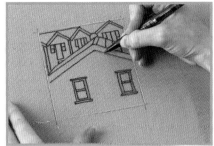

2 Thread a tapestry needle with a contrasting machine thread and use this to tack an outline on to the canvas.

3 Hold the final drawing behind the canvas and trace the main shapes only on to the canvas with a thick waterproof permanent marker. Do not trace the outline.

Picking colours for your design

Once the linework is complete, you will need to pick appropriate coloured threads for the design. One of the benefits of using stranded cotton and crewel wools for shaded designs is the range of colours available. Colour ranges are usually grouped together so it is easy to pick a range from dark to light for one colour.

THREADING A NEEDLE

The large eyes of tapestry needles are a huge benefit when threading them, but threading several strands at once can still be tricky. If it is a real struggle, try using a larger needle.

Always keep thread length short as it will soon become worn with the friction of going back and forth through the canvas. If the thread starts to look tired always start a new thread.

A shade card makes picking the exact colour you need for your design very simple.

1 Cut two 30cm (12in) lengths of crewel wool (or your chosen thread). You can use the first to help measure the second.

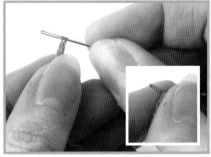

2 Fold both threads around the eye of the needle and pinch the wool over the needle to make a crease (see inset).

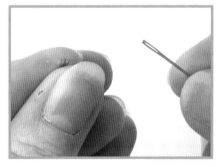

3 Pull the needle out carefully, keeping the creased wool pinched between your thumb and finger.

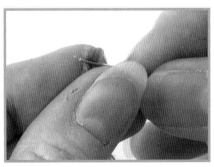

4 Place the eye of the needle over the crease. The wool should feed through easily.

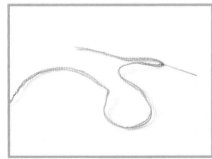

5 Knot the end. The wool is now ready for stitching.

Note

When working a large area in one colour, I find it speeds up the stitching if you thread up as many needles as possible with the same colour. These can be 'parked' in the webbing edge of your frame, ready to go.

STARTING AND FINISHING A THREAD

This is a very important part of canvaswork. A well-stitched piece can be ruined by bulky ends on the back, or loose ends poking through to the front. Threads should always be started and finished on the front. This does mean that you often have a lot of ends at the front of the work as you stitch, which can be distracting and messy to look at, but using this method will ensure you create the best possible finish to your work.

Note

Try to keep the knots and tail ends of each colour within the area stitched in that colour to avoid problems. If, for example, you left a tail end of black behind a white area, the thread at the back can cause a shadow on the front. Worse still, it could be pulled through to the front.

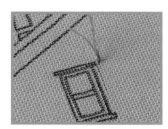 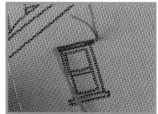  

1 Within the design area, but 2.5cm (1in) away from the part on which you are working, take the needle down through the front of the canvas. Draw the yarn through so that the knot sits on the front.

2 Bring the needle up inside the area you are working on, at the opposite end to the knot, and draw the yarn through.

3 Work towards the knot from the point you brought the needle up, catching the tail end of the yarn on the back as you work.

4 To finish the thread, take the needle up to the surface 2.5cm (1in) away from where you finished.

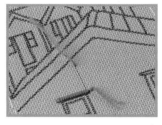 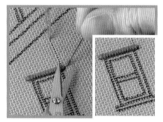 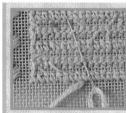

5 Use a pair of embroidery scissors to cut the thread, leaving a long tail within the design area. This will be cut off later, when you work this area of the design.

6 To remove a knot, pull the knot away from the fabric, then cut it. The end should spring back under the canvas, and because the tail was caught (in step 3), the stitching will stay secure (see inset).

Tip
Your last thread will have nowhere to be secured within the design (because it has all been worked), so turn the canvas over and thread the yarn through the backs of the other stitches. You may need to use pliers to help pull it through. Trim any excess.

Sampling your stitches

Refer to the stitch section (see pages 96–128) to find stitches that will suit your design. Once you have chosen your stitch – or stitches – and you have an idea about the sort of thread you would like to use, it is a good idea to test them out. It is important that the thickness of the thread is enough to cover the canvas. Generally, if the stitches within the pattern are horizontal or vertical and do not cross over, they will need more thread to cover the canvas fully. Diagonal stitches or crossed stitches use less thread.

TESTING YOUR THREAD AND STITCHES

Work an area of the pattern with your chosen thread. This need only be small, as you will soon see if the canvas is covered. If there is any canvas showing once you finish, add another strand of your thread. Be careful about using too many strands, as this can distort the canvas and the stitch.

Correct (left) and too few threads (right). Note the canvas surface is visible through the test area with too few threads.

HOW MANY TYPES OF STITCH?

The only limit to the number of stitches you use is the size of your design. Within this design each texture has its own stitch. The wooden panelling of the buildings all use vertical band stitches. The roofs are all tied stitches, and the doors and white wood panelling are all variations on a flat diagonal stitch.

This detail shows the stitches used in the window.

Swedish Boat Houses

Within this design each texture has its own stitch. The wooden panelling of all of the buildings is worked in vertical band stitches. The main house uses fern stitch (see page 107) to represent the wooden slats of the building. This raised stitch casts a shadow, giving the building a three-dimensional appearance.The smaller houses use straight gobelin stitch (see page 110). The roofs are all tied stitches, a couching stitch is used at the front and a tied gobelin stitch (see page 111) at the back. The doors and white wood panelling are all variations of the flat diagonal stitches cashmere (see page 102), Scotch (see page 123) and mosaic (see page 104).

Choosing stitches for your design

The choice of stitch in a canvas piece is integral to its success. But this does not mean that you have to choose a lot of stitches or very complicated stitches. Often fewer, simpler stitches work best. Think about the complete design when choosing stitches and do a bit of planning before you begin. Remember that the plan is not set in stone and will change and adapt as you stitch, but all the areas need to work with each other. The following are a few points to consider.

TEXTURE

Look carefully at the texture of what you are trying to represent on the canvas. Is it smooth, rough, even, uneven? Any stitches that lie flat on the canvas such as Byzantine stitch (see page 102) will give a smooth texture, while any stitches that cross over, such as Rhodes stitch (see page 122) will give a more raised appearance.

DEPTH

Again, any crossed stitches will give a raised appearance. The more they overlap, the greater height they will achieve. Think about what is in the foreground of the design, i.e. what is closest to the front. This will need to have the greatest height to it.

SCALE

The scale of a stitch is important in portraying the dimension of a piece. Larger stitches should be used in the foreground and smaller ones for objects that are further away. Consider how much of a pattern you can fit into the area you are stitching. If the pattern has a large repeat it will not be shown if it is put into a small area. Larger patterns need some space to show them off. Scale also plays a part when the design has small detailed areas: these can only be stitched with a small-scale pattern.

STITCHES FOR BACKGROUND AND FOREGROUND

If your design has a central object and a lot of space around it, think carefully about what stitch you will use for the background. There are two reasons for this. Firstly, you may want the background to stand out or fade away. Secondly, the speed at which a stitch can be worked is a big consideration in large areas. A slow stitch, such as tent stitch (see page 124), can take the enjoyment out of the piece if it takes a long time to complete.

The apple in the foreground uses fan stitch (see page 106), the only crossed stitch in the piece, as I wanted it to stand forward the most. The main direction of the stitch also slants from top left to bottom right, unlike all the other stitches in the design.

The next apple back in the midground uses a similar scale stitch to the red apple, but with a much flatter appearance, Scotch stitch (see page 123). The apple at the back uses a smaller variation of the same stitch to show that it is furthest away.

The background uses two different stitches. Both are flat diagonal stitches, but the one to the top of the design – Moorish stitch (see page 116) – is a smaller, more decorative stitch to give some perspective to the design. The larger stitch in the lower half is a larger variation of Scotch stitch: very quick to work and it has a less complex pattern to it.

Apples

This design uses only five stitches for the main areas – fan, Moorish and three variations of Scotch stitch (see pages 106, 116 and 123 respectively). All of them have a diagonal slant to give continuity throughout the piece, but they change in texture and scale to portray the depth of the design.

STITCH ORDER

The nature of working with canvas means that the positioning of stitches is determined by the threads and holes of the canvas. Because stitched areas should always sit next to other stitched areas and never overlap, an order of work must be established in order to create the smoothest possible outline to the shapes.

Unlike most embroidery techniques, in canvaswork you work the areas at the front of the design first and work backwards. With the example below, the bird is worked before the background as the bird is at the front. It is far easier to judge the edge of a solid area, such as the bird, than to judge the edge of a negative space, if the background was worked first.

The only exception to the rule is if there are any overstitched details in the design, such as the legs of the bird. These are much easier to site and stitch once the rest of the design is complete.

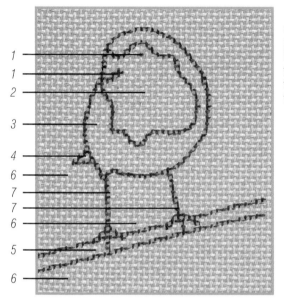

1 = 1
1 = 1
2
3
4
6
7
7
6
5
6

1 Draw your design on the canvas using a waterproof permanent black marker and identify the main areas. Number them in order from the front of the picture (i.e. the parts in the foreground) to the back.

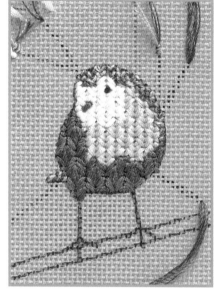

2 Work the foreground areas in order, referring to the number sequence you made earlier.

3 With the foreground in place, fill in the background stitches, and then the final details, such as the legs.

95

CANVASWORK STITCH FINDER

The following section of the book contains the instructions for a selection of stitches to introduce you to canvaswork. I have aimed to include a good variety of stitches to get any keen embroiderer started. Each stitch has written instructions, a set of diagrams and a square sample of the stitch. The contrasting area of stitches in each stitched sample demonstrates how you would work one 'row' of the repeated pattern before moving on to the next. The stitches are arranged in alphabetical order for ease of reference.

The diagrams for each stitch show how to work an individual stitch 'block' and then how these blocks fit together to make a repeat. For many of these stitches there is more than one stage to build up a block, and these stages are shown separately for clarity.

All the stitched examples were worked on 18TPI canvas and are photographed at the same scale, so you should be able to see how they compare with each other in size.

Before using any stitch in your work it is a good idea to sample it first on the same gauge canvas as your final piece. Seeing the stitch in scale will give you a good indication of how it will work within your design. Sampling also gives you the opportunity to make sure you are using enough strands to cover the canvas, as well as allowing you to work out how the stitch is counted, and how blocks fit together (see page 92).

Think of the illustrated stitches as a starting point. All of them can be adapted and rearranged to make new stitches. I have made some suggestions next to the stitches under 'variations' of how you could begin to make new patterns. Give these a try as well.

Note
The method for starting and finishing a thread is shown on page 92. Always use this method for the neatest results.

Horse Chestnut
A canvas stitch sampler with a wide variety of stitches in it. The leaf to the right uses a variation of Florentine stitch (see page 108) to show the direction of the veins. 20th century. (Personal collection of Jean Panter)

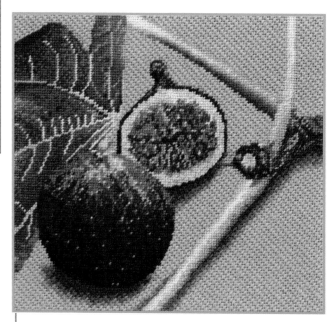

Figs
See also page 84.

STITCHES

WORKING STITCHES

When you work a stitch adjacent to another, work into the hole used by the previous stitch, rather than out of a hole that is in use. The latter approach will catch and damage the previous stitch, while the former will result in a smooth, clean appearance. This method is not possible for all areas of a design, but try to stick to it where possible.

RAISED STITCHES

All of the uppermost parts of the stitches in an area of cross stitches should point in the same direction (generally from bottom left to top right), as this gives a neat and tidy appearance. Compare the correctly worked area of upright double cross stitch on the left-hand side of the picture with the incorrectly worked area on the right-hand side.

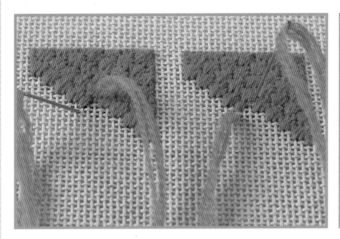

The area on the left-hand side of the picture is being worked incorrectly, as the thread emerges from an already-worked stitch. This will fray the yarn as you work, resulting in an untidy appearance and visible damage. On the right-hand side, you can see the needle being taken down in the correct place: any stray strands of yarn will be taken through to the back, keeping the front neat.

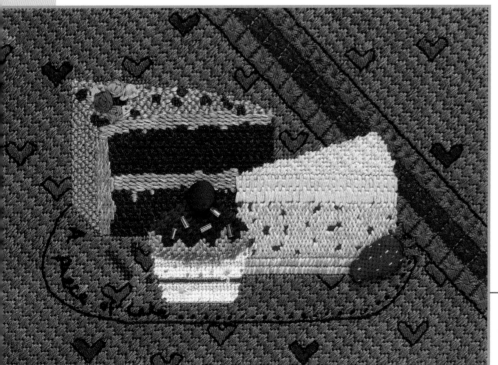

A Piece of Cake

A group of cakes with surface stitched details and applied elements. The strawberry is a tent stitched slip, cut out and applied. 21st century. (Personal collection of Sophie Long)

Algerian eye, variation

This stitch is worked across a square of four canvas threads by four canvas threads. Begin by working eight small stitches across a single intersection of the canvas. Next, work four diagonal stitches from the four corners into the centre. Take the needle down through the centre of the square for each of these. Finally work the two horizontal and two vertical stitches, again taking the needle into the centre of the square each time.

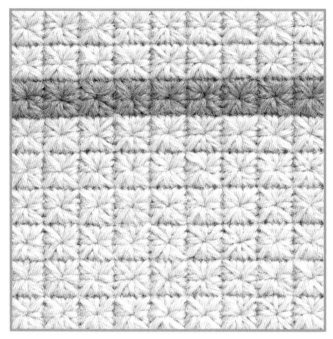

USES

This medium-sized stitch can be worked as a single decorative motif or as a block arranged in a grid as shown. It is a fairly flat stitch.

VARIATIONS

Instead of working the blocks as a grid, try working one vertical row and then beginning the second row two threads down, creating a half drop (see pineapple half drop stitch on page 120).

RELATED STITCHES

Algerian eye stitch is worked in a similar way, but without the initial eight small stitches. It therefore has just eight stitches in total, all taken into the centre of the square.

Eyelet stitch is again very similar, but has sixteen stitches all radiating out of the same central hole. This stitch creates more of an opening in the centre of the stitch.

Pineapple

This sampler of stitches uses eyelet and rococo stitches within the pineapple to give it texture. These are variations of Algerian eye and French stitch (see page 109). 21st century. (Personal collection of Becky Hogg)

Alternating cross

This stitch alternates a small cross with a larger cross, and the rows should interlock with each other. Begin the first row by working the small cross stitches, which cross a single intersection of the canvas and are spaced one canvas thread apart. Ensure the top thread of the cross is worked from bottom left to top right, then work back across the row, placing the larger cross stitches between. The larger stitches are three canvas threads high by one wide. Again ensure the top thread is always worked from bottom left to top right.

Begin working the next row by placing the small cross stitch underneath the larger cross of the previous row, then work back across the row, filling in the gaps with larger cross stitches.

USES

At this scale, alternating cross is a small flat stitch with a lightly textured appearance.

VARIATIONS

This stitch is usually worked in horizontal rows, but it can easily be turned and worked in vertical rows.

The size of this stitch can be doubled to make a larger pattern that will cover a greater area more quickly.

RELATED STITCHES

This stitch is also known as double cross stitch.

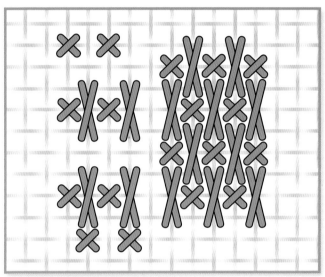

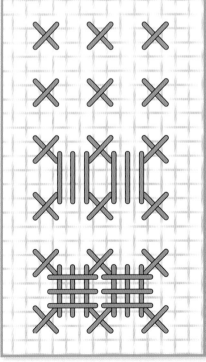

Barred square

The barred square part of this stitch is contained within a grid of small cross stitches.

Work the corner cross stitches to begin. These are each across two threads by two threads of canvas. Ensure the top thread of the cross is worked bottom left to top right. Leaving a space of two threads between the crosses, work two rows of cross stitches.

Work the three vertical bars of the barred square across four canvas threads, linking one row of crosses to the next. Next, work back across each square with the horizontal bars, again across four threads of the canvas. These horizontal bars should sit next to each other.

For subsequent rows, work a further row of cross stitches first, and then fill in with the barred squares.

USES

This is a medium-sized structured stitch with a padded appearance.

RELATED STITCHES

This stitch can be turned into woven square stitch by weaving the vertical bars of the square through the horizontal ones.

Broad cross

Each broad cross of this pattern is worked across six threads by six threads of the canvas, and the pattern is worked in horizontal rows. For the first row, work three long vertical stitches next to each other, each over six threads of the canvas. Bring the needle up two threads to the left and two threads down from the top of the leftmost vertical stitch. Take a horizontal bar six threads across from this point, then work two more bars directly beneath the first.

Begin the vertical bars of the second broad cross four threads across from the vertical bars of the previous broad cross. When working the horizontal bars, ensure that they meet in the same holes as the previous broad cross in the row.

The second row of broad crosses will slot into the gaps of the first. The easiest way to place the crosses of the next row is to make the centre vertical stitch of the cross first. Place this vertical stitch first, then work a bar either side. Finally, work the horizontal bars.

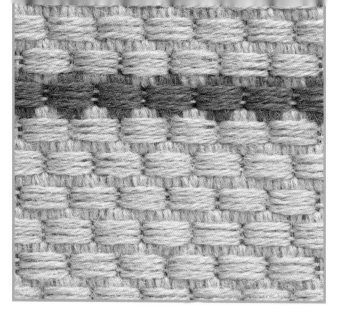

USES

This is a medium-sized raised stitch.

VARIATIONS

The bars of this stitch can be worked in the opposite order, i.e. place the horizontal bars first, then the vertical bars.

This stitch can be turned and worked in vertical rows.

RELATED STITCHES

Diagonal broad cross is the same stitch worked as diagonal stitches across five intersections of the canvas.

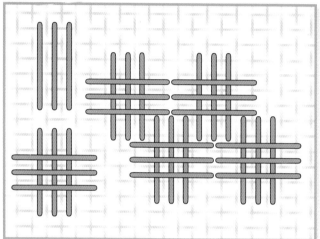

Broad cross pencil case

This pencil case was stitched using broad cross stitch. The canvas was worked as one rectangle of randomly coloured blocks. This was then made up into a pencil case. 21st century. (Rachel Doyle's personal collection)

Byzantine

This pattern is worked in long diagonal bands of the same sized stitch. Each stitch is worked from bottom left to top right across four intersections of the canvas, or four threads up and across.

Make five diagonal stitches in a vertical band. The stitch at the bottom of these will be the corner. Next, make four stitches horizontally across from the corner stitch. This will make five stitches in total for this row, the last stitch being the corner stitch.

Alternate between vertical and horizontal bands of stitches to make the stepped pattern. The second row can be worked above or below the first, fitting into the steps. The corner stitches of each row should meet.

USES

The repeat of this stitch is quite large, which means that it covers the canvas quite quickly. It is a flat stitch and very good for backgrounds.

VARIATIONS

The size of this stitch can be varied by working over more or fewer intersections of the canvas for each stitch.

The number of stitches in each step can also be increased or decreased.

RELATED STITCHES

By alternating each row of Byzantine stitch with a row of stepped tent stitch (see page 124) the pattern becomes Jacquard stitch.

Irregular Byzantine stitch can be worked by keeping the number of stitches in each step the same, but making the stitch length in each row of the pattern change: e.g. work a row of stitches across four by four canvas threads, then three by three, then two by two etc.

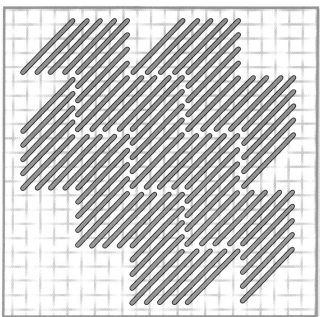

Cashmere, diagonal

Each rectangular cashmere block of this pattern is worked across two canvas threads by three. Make a tent stitch (see page 124) across one intersection of the canvas. Starting directly beneath this stitch, make a diagonal stitch across two intersections of canvas. Repeat to make a second stitch across two intersections of canvas. Finish off the rectangle with a second tent stitch at the bottom-right corner of the block. To work a diagonal row, continue the pattern with two longer stitches, then a tent stitch.

This pattern is worked in diagonal rows that lean from the top left-hand corner to the bottom right-hand corner. When working the next row to the right, the first tent stitch of each cashmere block should meet the top right-hand corner of the previous row's cashmere blocks.

USES

This is a flat stitch with a small pattern repeat. It is very good for backgrounds.

VARIATIONS

The cashmere block can be turned 90° and worked as a diagonal band with a shallow slant. The angle of the block itself can be reversed so that each stitch is made from the bottom right to the top left. The step pattern will then travel from bottom left to top right.

The cashmere block can be alternated with six tent stitches (see chequer stitch, opposite).

RELATED STITCHES

Straight cashmere stitch uses the complete cashmere block in straight horizontal and vertical rows. This pattern forms a straight grid of rectangles. Each block of this stitch can be alternately reversed (see reversed cushion on page 104).

Chain

This is worked as long straight rows that start at the top and are stitched down to the bottom of the design. The finished stitch resembles a chain, hence the name.

Begin by bringing the needle up through a hole of the canvas, and take it back down through the same hole, without pulling the thread tight, in order to leave a loose loop on the front of the canvas. Next, bring the needle up two canvas threads below the first part of the stitch and through the loose loop left on the canvas. Now the thread can be pulled tight. Repeat the stitch by taking the needle back down through the same hole it has just come up (through the first loop) and out again two threads below.

At the end of a row make a small vertical stitch over one canvas thread to hold the final loop in place. The second row of chain should be worked one thread across from the first.

USES

This is a small, flat stitch and useful for narrow shapes. It is also very slow to work, so only use it for small areas.

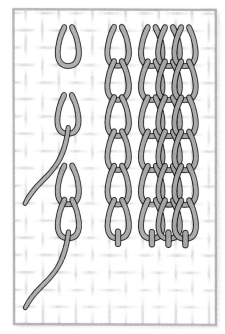

VARIATIONS

The length of the chain can vary, although the longer you make it the more likely it is that canvas will show. The second row can be started one canvas thread down, to give the design a half drop.

RELATED STITCHES

Detached chain stitch is a single chain loop held by a small vertical stitch (like the last stitch of a row). These can be worked as rows or as individual stitches.

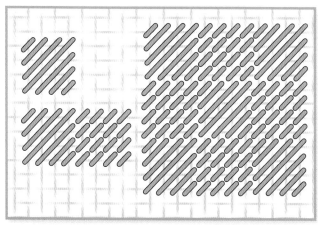

Chequer

This chequerboard stitch is made up of two alternating stitch blocks of tent stitch (see page 124) and cushion stitch (see page 104). The cushion stitch is made of seven diagonal stitches, covering a square of four by four canvas threads.

Begin with a tent stitch in the top left-hand corner, then make a stitch across two canvas intersections, then three, then four, then three, then two and finally another tent stitch. Directly next to this make a square of sixteen tent stitches (i.e. four by four).

Continue with these two blocks across a horizontal row. On the row below, place the tent stitch block under the cushion block and the cushion block under the tent block. Make sure all of the stitches angle from the bottom left to the top right.

USES

This is a flat stitch with a fairly large pattern repeat, which makes it good for large areas such as backgrounds. It is slower to work than other flat stitches due to the tent stitch.

VARIATIONS

This stitch can be worked with cashmere stitch (see opposite) in place of cushion stitch, in which case alternate with blocks of six tent stitches.

103

Cushion, crossed

The cushion-stitch block is made of seven diagonal stitches, covering a square of four by four canvas threads. Begin with a tent stitch (see page 124) in the top left-hand corner. Next, make a stitch across two canvas intersections, then three, then four, then three, then two and finally another tent stitch to complete the block.

With the cushion-stitch block in place, work the crossed part of the stitch. This is worked in the same way as half a cushion stitch block over the top of the first, but worked in the opposite direction. Begin with a long stitch across the centre of the block from top left to bottom right. Below and to the left of this long stitch, work another three stitches: the first across three canvas intersections, the second across two intersections and the third across a single intersection.

This crossed block can be repeated horizontally in rows or as an individual block.

USES

A flat stitch with a medium-sized pattern repeat, crossed cushion is good for more decorative backgrounds.

VARIATIONS

The cushion stitch block can be slanted in alternate directions (see cushion, reversed below), in which case the crossed stitches should also be alternated.

The size of the cushion block can be increased or decreased. When worked in three stitches over two by two canvas threads, the stitch is known as mosaic stitch. Blocks of differently sized crossed cushion stitch work well together.

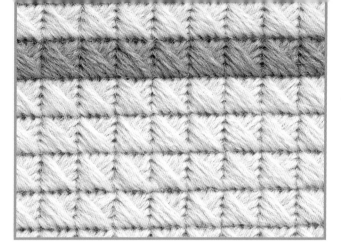

VARIATIONS

This stitch can be increased in size for a different effect.

RELATED STITCHES

This stitch is also known as Scotch or Scottish stitch.

When the stitch direction is the same for all of the blocks it is simply called cushion stitch.

When the cushion block is reduced to just three stitches, the stitch becomes reversed mosaic stitch.

Cushion, reversed

This version of cushion stitch is worked in straight rows. Each cushion block is made up of five diagonal stitches across a square of three by three canvas threads. Begin with a tent stitch (see page 124) in the top left-hand corner. Then make a stitch across two canvas intersections, then three, then two and finally make another tent stitch.

For the next block to the right, reverse the stitch direction: begin at the bottom left-hand side with a reversed tent stitch and work the other four stitches across to the top right-hand corner. The row below should mirror the row above.

USES

Reversed cushion is a slightly raised, structured stitch with a small pattern repeat. This adds a subtle texture to a piece.

Double linked cross

This stitch is made of two crossed blocks, linked together. Each pair is worked together. Make two cross stitches next to each other, each across two by two threads of the canvas. Make sure the top stitch of each runs from bottom left to top right. Next, make a vertical stitch across each. Finally make one long horizontal stitch across both crosses (i.e. across four canvas threads) to complete the block.

Work the blocks in horizontal rows. The row beneath should start two canvas threads across to give the pattern a bricked look.

USES

A small, raised stitch with a medium-sized pattern repeat. Great texture and very brick like, but slow to work.

VARIATIONS

The blocks can be worked vertically, and more blocks can be linked together. The pattern can also be worked in straight vertical rows, without the bricking.

RELATED STITCHES

This stitch is also called leviathan, linked or smyrna, linked.

Double straight cross

This stitch is made up of a large cross stitch held down by a smaller one. Make a horizontal stitch across four canvas threads, then make a vertical stitch of the same length across the middle of it. Next, make a diagonal stitch across the centre of this cross, covering two canvas intersections from top left to bottom right. Finally, make another diagonal stitch of the same length from bottom left to top right. Work the crosses in horizontal rows. The next stitch to the right should join at the right-hand edge of the previous cross.

The next row is worked below the first, two canvas threads down and across, so that the crosses fit into the gaps of the previous row. Make sure that the top stitch on all the crosses is always bottom left to top right.

USES

A great small bumpy, raised stitch, double straight cross can be worked as an individual stitch. It is good for creating a textured area.

RELATED STITCHES

This stitch is also known as star stitch.

Dutch

This crossed stitch is made up of an oblong cross stitch over a straight stitch. To start, make a vertical stitch over four threads of the canvas, then come down one thread and across two to the left of the top of this stitch. Make a diagonal stitch across four threads and down two threads of the canvas. Go up two canvas threads and make a diagonal stitch across four threads and down two. Work the pattern in horizontal rows so that the edges of the crosses touch.

The row below should fit into the gaps of the first, touching at the corners of the cross.

USES

A bumpy, raised, medium-sized stitch that is good for adding texture.

VARIATIONS

The vertical stitch can be worked last rather than first. The stitch can also be turned so that the rows are worked vertically.

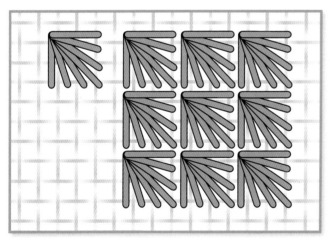

VARIATIONS

Try alternating the direction of the fan for each row, or alternating each fan within a row.

RELATED STITCHES

This stitch is also known as ray stitch.

Fan

This square stitch is worked across three by three canvas threads and is made up of seven stitches. Begin with a vertical straight stitch over three threads of canvas, working from bottom to top. Bring the needle out one thread across from the bottom of this stitch and take it into the same hole at the top. Repeat this 'fanning' around the square, each time taking the needle into the same hole. The pattern can be worked in vertical or horizontal bands. Make sure the seven stitches are always worked in the same order (i.e. the fan always follows the same direction).

USES

This is a fairly smooth small stitch. It is quite slow to work, but you can give direction to an area by angling the fan in the appropriate direction.

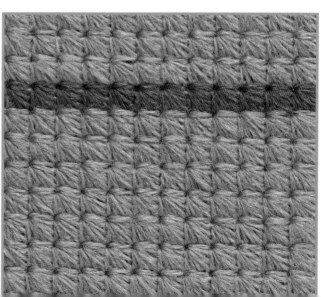

Fern

Fern stitch is an overlapping band stitch that is always worked in the same direction. Make a diagonal stitch across two intersections of the canvas from top left to bottom right. Take the needle under one thread of the canvas to the left and back to the surface. Make a second diagonal stitch across two intersections of the canvas, ending three canvas threads across from the start of the first stitch. Take the needle across the back of the stitch and out one thread underneath the first stitch. Repeat the two diagonal stitches, each one a canvas thread beneath the last.

The next vertical row is started from the top again and worked down, meeting the previous row at the edge.

USES

A very straight band stitch, fern is very good for clearly defined stripes.

VARIATIONS

The stitch can vary in length and angle. By making the diagonal stitch across three threads and down one, for example, the angle of the stitch can be made considerably shallower.

Alternate rows could be worked top to bottom then bottom to top for a different final appearance.

Fishbone, stepped

This stitch is made up of alternate rows of the same crossed stitch turned horizontally and vertically. Begin with a vertical straight stitch over four threads of the canvas. Cross this stitch at the bottom with a horizontal stitch across two threads of the canvas. Start the next long vertical stitch one thread up and across to the right from the first. Again cross it, with a horizontal stitch across two threads of the canvas. When enough vertical stitches have been worked, begin a horizontal row.

For the horizontal row below the first vertical row, make a horizontal stitch across four threads of the canvas, ending it at the bottom point of the last vertical stitch. Cross this stitch to the right-hand side of the horizontal stitch. Working down and across one canvas thread to the left at a time, work a row of horizontal stitches. Continue alternating between vertical and horizontal stitch rows.

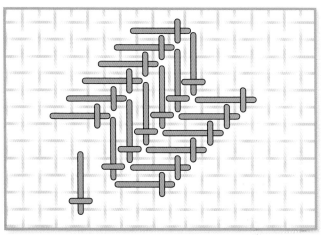

USES

A slightly raised band stitch, stepped fishbone is ideal for filling an area with a clear diagonal line.

VARIATIONS

The length of the long stitch can vary from row to row.

RELATED STITCHES

Horizontal fishbone stitch can be produced by working just the rows of horizontal fishbone stitches and joining them in diagonal rows.

107

Florentine

Florentine stitch is made up of a series of straight stitches of equal length, rising and falling in a pattern of steps.

In this example, each stitch is made over four threads of the canvas, and each step of the pattern is two threads of the canvas above or below the previous stitch. By varying the number of stitches at each step of the design a pattern of waves is produced. The pattern is set by the first complete wave of stitches. Each row above or below this then repeats the same design.

Generally one colour is used for one complete wave of the design. A varied use of colour is essential for this stitch.

USES

This stitch needs a large area to display its pattern.

VARIATIONS

The illustrated design is a very basic example of the stitch, which has endless variations.

RELATED STITCHES

This stitch is also known as flame stitch or Bargello work.

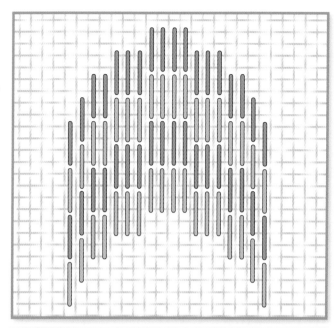

Horse Chestnut
See also page 96.

108

Flying cross

Flying cross stitch is a slightly elongated cross stitch, that is worked in diagonal rows. Each cross stitch is made across two by three threads of the canvas.

Making sure that the top stitch is worked from bottom left to top right, make one cross stitch, and then bring your needle up one canvas thread below the top right-hand corner of this stitch. Start your second cross from here. This and every following cross should start one canvas thread below the previous cross.

Work the second row directly beneath the first.

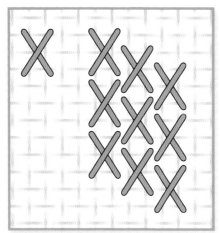

USES

This is a medium-sized stitch with a slightly raised effect that is useful for filling in large areas where some texture is required.

VARIATIONS

The crosses could be turned lengthways to give a shallower diagonal stripe.

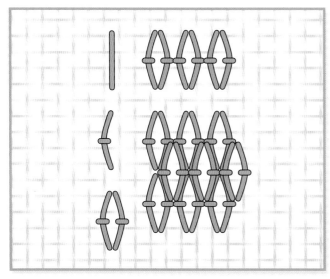

French

This stitch is worked over two by four threads of canvas. Make a vertical stitch over four threads of canvas, but do not pull it too tight. Bring the needle up to the left of the stitch, two threads down and one thread across. Make a horizontal holding stitch across one thread of the canvas, anchoring the long stitch to the left. Make a second vertical stitch in the same holes as the first. This time make a small stitch anchoring it to the right. Work a row of these stitches, beginning the stitch two canvas threads across each time.

For the second row, begin the vertical stitch in the same canvas hole as the small horizontal stitches of the row above. The pairs of stitches should fit into the spaces left by the previous row.

USES

This is a small, delicate and flat pattern that will fit into a small area. Note that French stitch can be quite slow to work.

VARIATIONS

The length of the vertical stitch can be increased, as long as it is across an even number of threads.

RELATED STITCHES

Rococo stitch is a slightly larger version of the same stitch. Work a French stitch, then make a third vertical stitch, again into the same two holes of the canvas, and anchor this just to the left of the first two stitches. Make a fourth vertical stitch and anchor this to the right.

Rococo stitch is worked in rows that slot into each other in exactly the same way as French stitch.

Gobelin, encroaching

This stitch is working in horizontal bands of slanted stitches. Start by making a row of stitches, each of which is worked over one by five threads of the canvas.

Begin the second row four threads below the first, and again make a row of stitches each over one thread by five threads, allowing for the encroachment of one thread between rows.

Always take the needle into the previous row, between stitches. Do not bring the needle out of the previous row as this can disturb the lay of the stitches. The rows of this stitch must be worked either from top to bottom or bottom to top in the area to be covered.

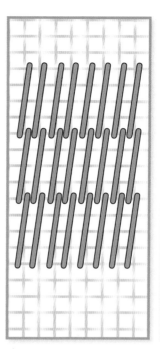

USES

The rows of this stitch are quite wide, making this a fairly large pattern. This makes encroaching gobelin good for quickly filling large areas.

VARIATIONS

The depth of this stitch can be altered, making a smaller, tighter band. The stitch depth can be altered within a row to create a more random texture.

RELATED STITCHES

The same stitch can be worked without the encroachment in a variation called slanted gobelin. Each following row is worked into the same holes at the bottom of the previous row.

Gobelin, straight

This is a straight stitch worked over a horizontal padding stitch. Start by making a padding stitch across the width of the area to be covered. Work back over this, adding vertical stitches across two threads of the canvas.

Start the padding of the second row two canvas threads below the first padding stitch. Work back across this, working each vertical stitch into the same hole of the previous row of stitches. Always take the needle down into the occupied canvas hole, not out of it.

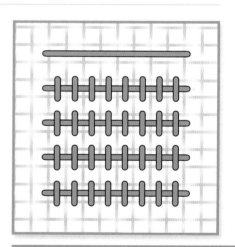

USES

This is a neat small stitch, with a slightly padded appearance. It is good for small striped areas.

VARIATIONS

The length of the straight stitches can be increased, in which case more rows of padding stitch are needed. If the stitch were across three threads of canvas, two rows of padding stitches would be laid first, for example.

This stitch can also be worked without the padding.

RELATED STITCHES

This stitch is also called upright gobelin.

Gobelin, tied

This stitch is made up of bands of slanted stitches held down (tied) in the centre.

To begin, make a slanted stitch across one by three canvas threads. Make a reversed tent stitch in the centre of this. Repeat across the row, always making the long stitch first and then crossing it.

On each following row, begin two threads down and make the long stitch so that it encroaches into the previous row, sharing the canvas hole with the reversed tent stitch. Always work the rows from top to bottom or bottom to top of an area.

USES

This is a very small and neat stitch that can give a delicate texture to small areas. Tied gobelin is very slow to work.

VARIATIONS

Try turning the stitch through 90° to work vertical bands.

RELATED STITCHES

This stitch is also known as knotted stitch.

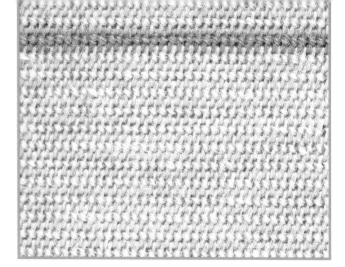

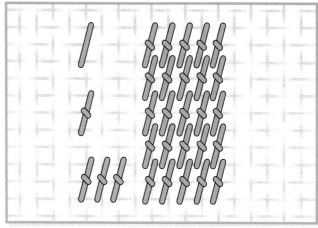

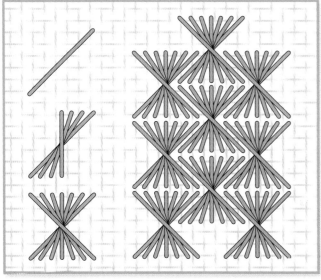

Half Rhodes

Each half Rhodes stitch is worked in a square of six by six canvas threads. Begin by making a long stitch across six diagonal intersections of the canvas, from bottom left to top right. Work the next and each following stitch from the bottom to the top, in order to keep an even tension on the stitch.

Bring the needle out one thread to the right from the bottom corner and take it up to one thread to the left of the top corner. Repeat the process for the third stitch. The fourth stitch should be vertical. Make three more stitches, so that the last stitch starts and ends in line with the first stitch.

Begin the second stitch six canvas threads below the first, so that the two stitches meet along their flat edges.

To begin the second vertical row to the right, begin three threads down and two threads in to the right of the lowest half Rhodes stitch. The hourglass shapes of the stitches should interlock together.

USES

This is a large, highly raised stitch that is fantastic for adding texture.

VARIATIONS

This stitch can be worked as a single motif as well as part of a pattern.

If the first and third rows of the pattern are worked without a gap between them, a diamond shape is left between the rows. This can be filled with a suitable motif, such as eyelet stitch (see page 99) or tent stitch (see page 124).

111

Hungarian grounding

This two-part wavy stitch is made up of vertical stitches of different lengths. For the first row, all the stitches are over four threads of canvas. Begin by making the first vertical stitch. Make the next stitch across one thread to the right and one thread up. Repeat for the third stitch. The fourth stitch is down one canvas thread. Repeat for the next stitch. Continue in this pattern for the width of the area.

For the second row, all the stitches are over two threads of canvas. Directly under the highest stitch in the first row make a stitch. Then make one to either side of this, again directly under the row above. Finally make a fourth stitch under the first of this group, to make a diamond.

With two canvas threads spacing between each, repeat the diamond pattern across the row.

Next, make a row like the first, mirroring it below the diamonds (note: the first and every following fourth long stitch should touch the previous row, containing the diamond between).

USES

This is a decorative flat stitch that works well for backgrounds.

VARIATIONS

Using different colours for the two parts of the stitch works well. The diamond part of the stitch can be worked as three stitches instead of four. Simply make the two centre stitches into one, across four threads.

RELATED STITCHES

Worked without the row of long stitches, the diamond part of the stitch (when worked as three stitches, instead of four) is Hungarian stitch. Work these with two canvas threads between each as shown, and on the following row fit the same stitches into the spaces left.

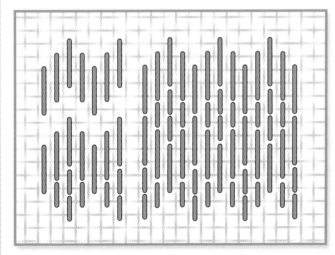

The Swamp

This design uses horizontal stitches to re-create the surface of the water. Multiple colours were mixed in the needle to give a painted look to the piece.
The grasses at the front were stitched over the surface of the canvaswork with a sharp needle. 21st century. (Personal collection of Paola Bianchi)

John

This stitch is made up of blocks of tent (see page 124) and reversed tent stitch with a long stitch separating them.

First work three tent stitches in a vertical line. To the left of these, work three reversed tent stitches to make a rectangular block.

Beneath this block make a stitch across two by one threads of canvas from top left to bottom right. Repeat this group in vertical rows.

USES

This is a small neat stitch with a slight texture.

VARIATIONS

Try beginning each vertical row one canvas thread higher each time. This will give a stepped effect.

RELATED STITCHES

Without the longer stitch to break up the blocks, this stitch becomes alternating tent.

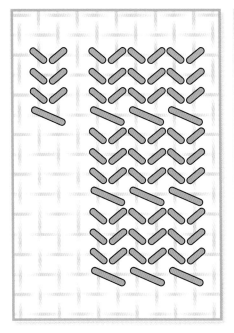
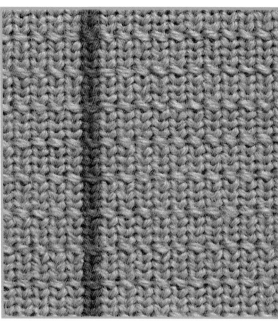

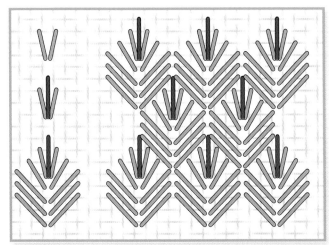

Leaf

Begin with a slanted stitch across one and down three canvas threads. Make a second slanted stitch to mirror the first, into the same hole. Beginning one thread above the previous stitches, make a straight stitch over four canvas threads and down into the same canvas hole as the previous two stitches.

Now work the right-hand side of the leaf. Come up one intersection down and across from the top end of the slanted stitch and take the needle down one canvas thread below the lower centre point of the leaf (the hole below the one shared by the first three stitches). Next, bring the needle up a further canvas intersection down and across from this stitch and make a stitch across three canvas intersections. Make two similar stitches below the first in the same way.

Work the left-hand side of the leaf in the same way in mirror image. Work in horizontal rows, fitting the next row into the spaces of the first. For positioning of the stitch it is easiest to work the rows top to bottom. Make sure that you tuck the ends of the stitches under the last stitch of the previous row.

USES

Leaf stitch creates a large stitch motif that can be worked alone or as a pattern. It is particularly good for large foliage and texture, as in Owl on page 114.

VARIATIONS

A vertical straight stitch can be worked across the centre of the leaf to give it a vein.

113

Owl

This piece shows off leaf stitch in the background by varying the colour of each leaf. 21st century. (Personal collection of Kate Haxell)

Icicles

The background of this piece uses diagonal stitches that have blended together effortlessly. 20th century. (Personal collection of Heather Lewis)

Maltese cross

The cross is worked in two overlapping parts. First, make a diagonal stitch from the bottom left-hand side to the top right-hand side across four and up eight canvas threads. Return to the bottom, one canvas thread across to the right, and take this stitch up to one thread to the left of the top corner. Next, make a third stitch; this one should be vertical across eight threads. Then make a fourth and fifth stitch following the pattern, ending up directly above and below the first stitch.

To make the second part of the cross, bring the needle up two threads across to the left and down two threads from the top left-hand corner. Make a diagonal stitch down to the right, ending two threads up and across from the lower corner of the first part of the cross. Return to the left, one thread down from the start of the previous stitch and take the thread across to one thread up from the previous stitch. Make a third horizontal stitch, then a fourth and fifth stitch following the pattern, so that the final stitch is from bottom left to top right.

Work the crosses in horizontal rows, so that their flat ends touch. The following rows fit into the spaces left, so that the centre top of the next cross meets the lower corner of the join of the crosses above.

USES

Maltese cross produces a very large raised motif that can be used alone or as part of a pattern. It is a fairly quick stitch to work and can be used in large areas where a very raised texture is needed.

Milanese

This stitch is worked in diagonal rows of triangular units. For the first unit, make a tent stitch across one canvas intersection. Below it make a stitch across two canvas intersections, then three, then four. Repeat this sequence of stitches over one, two, three and four canvas intersections in a diagonal row from top left to bottom right.

Work the next row of triangles in reverse, so that they fit into the gaps of the first row. The smallest stitch of one row should always be next to the largest stitch of the following row.

USES

Milanese stitch gives a flat, medium-sized pattern repeat that fills in quickly. It is good for backgrounds.

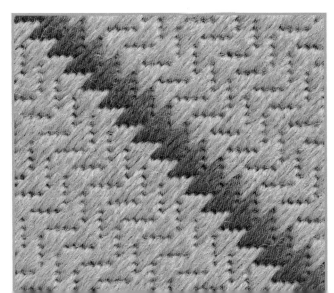

RELATED STITCHES

The triangles of this stitch can also be made with horizontal stitches across two, four, six and eight threads of the canvas to make straight Milanese stitch. This stitch has straight vertical bands of the pattern.

115

Moorish

This stitch is worked in diagonal rows and is very similar to Scotch stitch (see page 123).

To begin, a row of interlocking squares is worked. Make a tent stitch across one intersection of the canvas, then below it make successive stitches across two, three, two then one intersection again. Repeat these stitches to produce a diagonal pattern of interlocking squares across the area being worked.

Adjacent to the squares, work a row of tent stitches following the step of the squares. These should be three tent stitches up and three tent stitches across. Next, work back down the other side of the tent stitches, fitting the square pattern into the spaces. Repeat these two rows to continue the pattern.

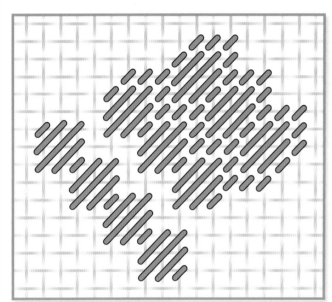

USES

This is slightly more textured version of Scotch stitch. It is good for backgrounds and filling areas quite quickly. The pattern gives a nice diagonal stripe.

RELATED STITCHES

Try working rows of cashmere stitch (see page 102) instead of Scotch stitch for the interlocking squares. Intersperse the rows with tent stitch as described above.

Norwich

This very large square stitch is worked across a section of canvas measuring nine threads by nine threads. Begin with a stitch from the bottom left-hand corner to the top right-hand corner across nine intersections of the canvas (1–2). Then make a stitch from the bottom right-hand corner to the top left-hand corner (3–4). Continue to follow the numbers on the stitch diagram to the right – you will make eighteen stitches in total. The final stitch (35–36), should be slipped under stitch 29–30 at the edge.

USES

This stitch can be worked as a single motif or as part of a block of the same stitch.

VARIATIONS

The same stitch can be worked across any square of an uneven number of threads. A combination of sizes in one area can work well.

RELATED STITCHES

This stitch is also known as waffle stitch.

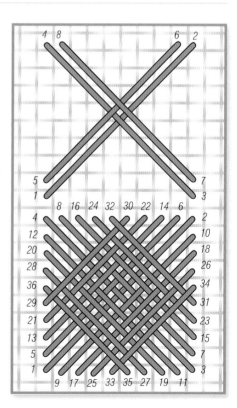

Oatmeal

This stitch combines two different sizes of diagonal square stitches, which are worked at opposite angles to each other.

Begin by working a diagonal row of interlocking square stitches. Make a tent stitch across one intersection of the canvas, then below it make stitches across two, three, four, three, two then one intersection again. Repeat this pattern across the diagonal of the area being worked.

Once this row is complete make the smaller square stitches in the spaces. These begin with a reversed tent stitch, then a stitch across two, three, two then one intersection of the canvas. Repeat these along the row. The longest of the stitches should touch at the corners.

The next row is a repeat of the first. The longest stitches of these squares should touch the longest stitches of the previous row of large diagonal squares.

USES

The two different directions of the stitches in this pattern give it an interesting texture. Oatmeal stitch has a fairly large pattern repeat, but it is good for backgrounds.

VARIATIONS

This stitch carefully interlocks two different stitches together. There are many stitches that follow this diagonal design and could be put together. For example, the smaller square could be replaced with a fan stitch (see page 106).

Oblong double-tied cross

This stitch is worked in bands of oblong crosses. First, make an oblong cross stitch across two by five canvas threads. Always make the top stitch bottom left to top right. Next, tie it twice in the centre with two horizontal stitches across two threads of canvas. Make the next cross and again tie it in the centre. Repeat across the row. Work the next row directly beneath the first.

USES

Oblong double-tied cross is a fairly large raised stitch with a definite horizontal striped effect.

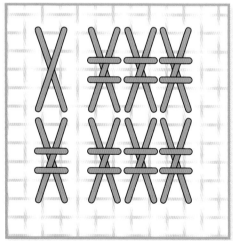

VARIATIONS

The rows could be worked vertically. After working the first cross, the second could begin two canvas threads down, giving a diagonal stepped effect.

RELATED STITCHES

Without the tying stitches this is just oblong cross stitch. Worked across three vertical threads and tied just once in the middle the stitch becomes oblong tied cross stitch.

117

Parisian

This simple stitch is worked in horizontal bands. Make a vertical stitch over two threads of canvas. Next to it, make a vertical stitch over four threads of canvas. Repeat these two stitches alternating between two and four threads of canvas.

  For the second row, place the small stitch directly below the longer stitch and vice versa. Repeat on each following row.

USES

Parisian is a medium-sized flat stitch that fills in areas quickly. It is good for slightly textured backgrounds.

VARIATIONS

To work a smaller version of the stitch, stitch across one and three threads of the canvas. Parisian stitch can also be worked in vertical bands.

RELATED STITCHES

If worked diagonally, by alternating the stitches across one and two intersections of the canvas, the stitch becomes condensed mosaic stitch.

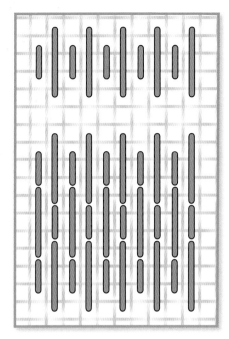 

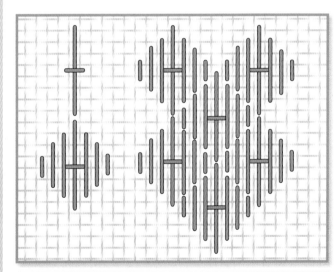

Pavilion, tied

This is a large diamond-shaped pattern made up of vertical stitches. Make the tied central stitch of the diamond first. This is a long vertical stitch over eight canvas threads, tied in the centre with a horizontal stitch across two canvas threads. With this in place, start to fill in the diamond shape with two vertical stitches, each over six canvas threads, to either side of the tied central stitch. Next, add vertical stitches over four canvas threads on both sides and finally add vertical stitches over two canvas threads at the edges.

  Work the pattern in horizontal rows, beginning at the top of the next diamond eight threads across from the top of the previous diamond.

USES

This is a large flat stitch that covers the canvas quickly.

VARIATIONS

The stitch can be worked without the tie.

  A smaller diamond pattern can be worked with five stitches rather than seven, the first over six canvas threads.

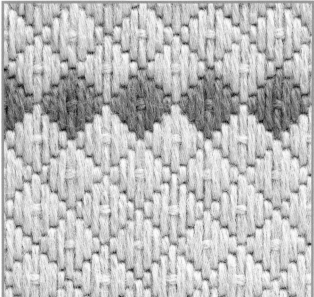

Berlin wool work
This small piece of canvaswork includes plush work in the central flowers, and also bead work. Late 19th or early 20th century. (RSN Collection)

Dragon
A design influenced by a dragon on a William De Morgan ceramic vase. Large patterns are used individually in 'spots' on the background. 21st century. (Personal collection of Jacqui McDonald)

119

Perspective, variation

This is an overlapping stitch, worked in horizontal bands. The rows of this stitch must always be worked from top to bottom.

Make a diagonal stitch across two intersections of canvas, from top left to bottom right. Make two more in the same way directly underneath the first. To the right of these, make three diagonal stitches that angle from bottom left to top right to meet the first three. Repeat this six-stitch chevron pattern horizontally across the area to be worked, leaving no gaps between.

For the row below, the chevrons are repeated, but rather than point down, they now point up. Where the six chevron stitches above meet in a downward point, the same canvas holes are used for the upward point of the chevron stitch below. Complete the row in the same way.

The third row will be the same as the first. Continue the rows, alternating the direction of the chevron.

USES

A medium-sized decorative stitch with good texture.

RELATED STITCHES

For perspective stitch, work twelve stitches in each chevron (i.e. six stitches and six stitches) and overlap only the bottom three stitches of each row.

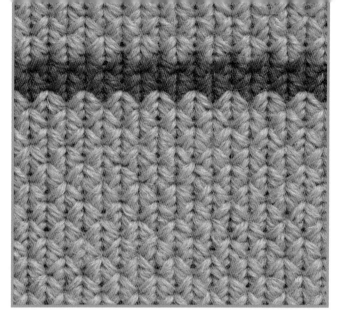

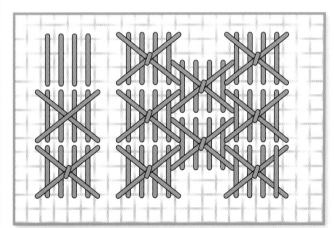

Pineapple half drop

This stitch is worked in vertical columns of crossed blocks of pineapple stitch, with a half drop to each column.

Make four vertical stitches over four threads of canvas to make a block. Next, bring the needle up one thread across from the top left-hand corner and take it down one thread across from the bottom right-hand corner. Make a second diagonal stitch across the block from the bottom left-hand corner to the top right-hand corner. Always make the top stitch of the cross in the same direction. Tie down the cross with a vertical stitch across the centre of the cross and over one vertical canvas thread. Make the next block in the same way directly beneath the first, and continue in a vertical line.

For the next column to the right, begin the block two threads above the lower right-hand corner of the last block. The cross of the next row should tuck under the vertical edge of the previous row.

USES

This is a medium to large stitch with a lot of texture and a fairly raised appearance. It can be used individually as a single motif.

RELATED STITCHES

This stitch can be worked in vertical or horizontal rows to make a grid. The stitch then becomes pineapple stitch.

Note that the corners of the crosses should meet for pineapple stitch, and this leaves a small gap between the blocks.

Plait

This is a heavy horizontal stitch that looks like a row of plaited braid. All the stitches on the reverse of the canvas should be vertical. Make a diagonal stitch from bottom left to top right across four intersections of canvas. Bring the needle out four canvas threads below the top corner of this stitch, then make a diagonal stitch up four and across two threads of canvas to the left. Bring the needle out vertically below the end of this stitch.

Repeat these two stitches across the band of the plait. The following rows should be worked in the same direction as the first (i.e. left to right).

USES

This stitch gives a firm raised band of pattern and fills in quickly.

VARIATIONS

For a smaller plait, work the band across two horizontal threads of canvas, making the first stitch across two intersections of canvas.

RELATED STITCHES

This stitch is also called Spanish plait stitch.

Algerian plait stitch is identical in appearance to plait stitch on the front of the canvas, but on the reverse has horizontal stitches. It is worked like a herringbone stitch: after the first stitch is made, take the needle back across two vertical threads of the canvas to the left.

Make a second stitch that crosses the first and again take the needle back across two vertical threads of the canvas to the left. Continue across the band of the plait.

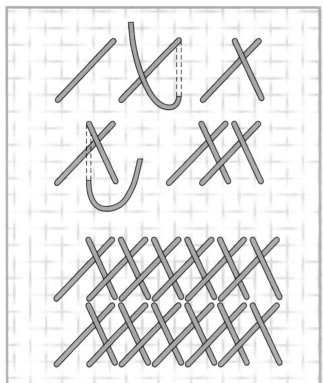

Raised spot

This is a very dense stitch, best worked with several threads in the needle at once. Make a vertical stitch across three threads of the canvas, then repeat the stitch through the same holes several times, until you cannot get any more thread through. Make a note of how many times you are wrapping around each stitch and keep this consistent throughout.

Move two canvas threads to the right and repeat to make the next stitch, making sure to match the number of times you wrap around each stitch. The second row fits into the gaps of the first, encroaching by one canvas thread.

USES

This is a raised small stitch that gives great texture. It is very slow to work.

VARIATIONS

The stitch can be made smaller or larger and can vary within the area being worked to create a more random texture.

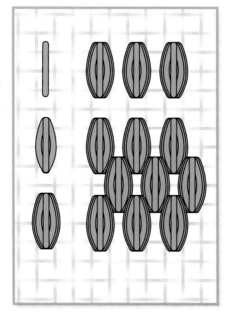

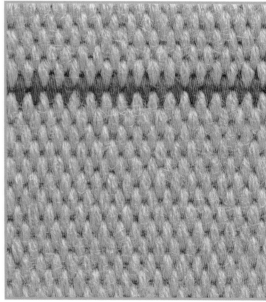

Rhodes

This stitch is made up of raised squares worked in a grid pattern. Each completed square measures six threads by six threads of canvas.

Begin one canvas thread in from the bottom left-hand corner and take this over to one thread in from the top right-hand corner of the complete square (i.e. across four threads and up six threads of the canvas).

Return to the bottom edge and make a stitch one thread to the right of the first and one thread to the left of the top edge of the first stitch. Continue in an anti-clockwise direction around the square, fanning the stitches. The sixth stitch should be from the bottom right-hand corner to the top left-hand corner.

Continue around the square until twelve stitches have been made. The last of these should be from the top right-hand corner to the bottom left-hand corner. Move to the next square, either below or across. Always work the stitches in the same order and direction, so that the last stitch is always the same.

USES

This is a very raised large stitch, and it creates a strong textured grid.

VARIATIONS

The same stitch can be worked at any size, smaller or larger. A combination of sizes can work well together.

If the stitch is made much larger, a single tent stitch can be placed in the centre to hold the long final stitch in place.

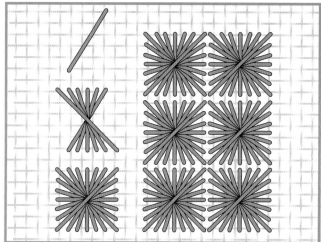

Rice

This is a large cross stitch with a cross over each of its corners. Begin by making a cross stitch across four by four threads of the canvas. Make sure that the top stitch is always bottom left to top right. Now, beginning at the top left-hand corner, make a diagonal stitch across two intersections of canvas, crossing the corner of the first cross. Repeat at each corner, so that these stitches meet at the centre points of the sides of the cross. Repeat the rice-stitch block in horizontal rows.

USES

This is a good basic medium-sized stitch. It is a little raised and has an even-textured appearance. It can be used as a single motif or as part of a pattern.

VARIATIONS

Rice stitch can be worked larger or smaller, as long as it is across a square of any number of even threads.

RELATED STITCHES

This stitch is also known as crossed corners.

When worked with horizontal and vertical stitches, it produces a diamond-shaped pattern called straight rice stitch. To produce this, make an upright cross over four threads of canvas, then cross the stitch ends across two threads of canvas.

Romanian couching

This stitch uses small diagonal stitches to hold down one long stitch. Make a long horizontal stitch across the area to be couched from left to right. Bring the needle up two canvas threads to the left of the end of the first stitch. Make a diagonal stitch from the bottom right to the top left, across the long stitch and holding it to one horizontal canvas thread. Next, miss two vertical canvas threads then make the second diagonal stitch. Continue across the width of the first stitch holding it down at these intervals.

For the next row, make a second long stitch under the first and work back across it, placing diagonal stitches directly beneath those of the first row. Always work this stitch from top to bottom.

USES

This is a quick stitch that covers smoothly and gives a lightly textured surface.

VARIATIONS

Try keeping the length of the holding stitch consistent (two threads by one, in this example) but varying its position. You could brick the holding stitches on successive rows, or make some closer together or further apart.

RELATED STITCHES

When the laid thread is held down with a single reversed tent stitch this becomes Bokhara couching. Place the holding stitches three threads apart and brick the pattern on the second row.

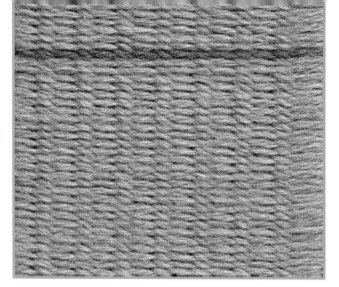

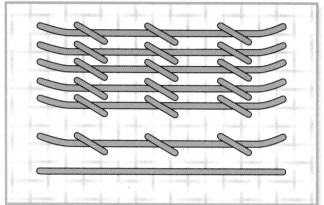

Scotch

This is a diagonal stitch made of interlocking squares. Make a tent stitch across one canvas intersection. Below it make a stitch across two canvas intersections, then further stitches across three, two and one canvas intersections. This makes the first square.

Repeat the sequence diagonally: across one, two, three, two, one, two, three, two etc. Continue in diagonal rows. The shortest stitch of the next row will sit next to the longest stitch of the previous row and vice versa, so the second row should interlock with the spaces of the first.

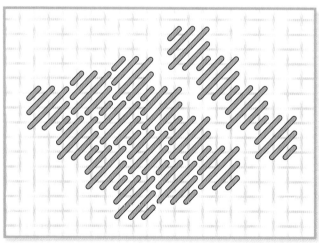

USES

This is a flat medium-sized stitch that fills in quite quickly.

VARIATIONS

The size of the square in this stitch can be increased or reduced.

RELATED STITCHES

This stitch is also known as condensed cushion stitch.

Shell

This decorative stitch is worked in several stages. First the vertical bars are put in over six horizontal threads of canvas. Each stitch has five of these bars. The last in each group and the first of the next group share the holes of the canvas. Work these across the row.

Next, each group is tied together with a horizontal stitch over the two central threads of canvas. You will need to angle the needle out from the stitches and tuck it back round each group.

Now the groups are linked together with one continuous surface thread. Starting somewhere to the left of the groups, thread the needle under the first holding stitch from top to bottom. Take the needle across to the second group and thread it through this group from bottom to top. Again take it through the first and second holding stitches in the same directions. Do not pull the yarn too tight.

Take the needle across to the third holding stitch and through from top to bottom, then back to the second holding stitch and through from bottom to top and finally to the third holding stitch and through from top to bottom. Continue across the row, linking the groups, then work as many rows of the stitch as required.

To cover up any bare canvas that might show when finished, work a back stitch across two threads of canvas between each row where they meet.

USES

This is a large, very decorative stitch with surface decoration.

VARIATIONS

The stitch can be worked without the looped thread, although this will leave canvas showing that will need to be covered with something else.

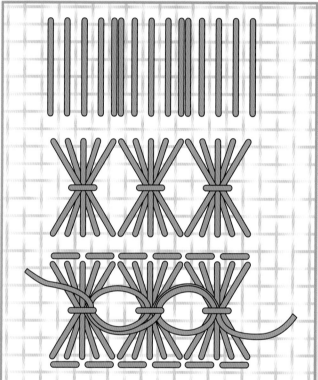

Tent

This is the simplest and most common stitch in canvaswork and the foundation for many other stitches. Tent stitch is usually worked across a single intersection of canvas from bottom left to top right. How you travel between tent stitches can be worked in several different ways, each with its own name: continental, basketweave and half cross.

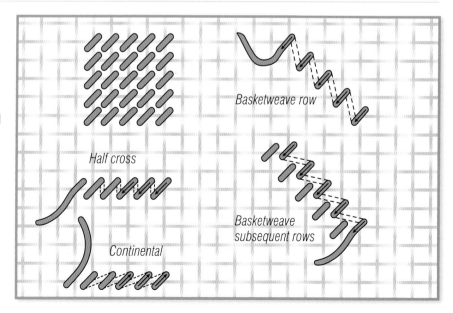

Half cross

Continental

Basketweave row

Basketweave subsequent rows

CONTINENTAL

This variant is worked in horizontal or vertical rows and makes a diagonal stitch on the back, larger than that on the front. This is a fairly hardwearing stitch.

Working from right to left, make a tent stitch from bottom left to top right. On the reverse of the canvas make a diagonal stitch across two threads of the canvas and bring the needle up one thread to the left of the bottom corner of the first canvas stitch. Continue across the row in the same way, making the stitches from bottom left to top right.

To work a row from left to right, the order of the stitch is reversed: i.e. top right to bottom left.

BASKETWEAVE

This is the most hardwearing of the three variants and the least likely to warp the canvas. It should always be used in large areas of tent stitch. It is worked in diagonal rows, either from the top right-hand corner down, or from the bottom left-hand corner up.

Working the tent stitch area from the bottom left-hand corner, make a diagonal row of tent stitches, each from top right to bottom left, and with a vertical stitch over two threads on the reverse. On the return row, fit the tent stitches between those of the first row, this time making a horizontal stitch across two canvas threads on the reverse. When working down a basketweave row, there will be a horizontal stitch on the reverse, and when working up a row there will be a vertical stitch on the reverse. When worked carefully the back of the work should have a neat woven appearance.

HALF CROSS

This variant is worked in horizontal or vertical rows and uses the least amount of thread. It is also the least hardwearing variant and can warp the canvas if worked over a large area.

Working from right to left, make a tent stitch from top right to bottom left. On the reverse of the canvas make a vertical stitch over one thread of canvas. Begin the next tent stitch, again working from top right to bottom left. The back of an area worked in half cross will be quite open and will all be vertical stitches.

To work a row from left to right, the order of the stitch is reversed: i.e. bottom left to top right.

USES

Tent stitch is versatile and can be fitted into any shape. It is very useful for fitting into gaps left at the edges of other stitches.

VARIATIONS

The angle of this stitch can be reversed to lean from bottom right to top left. Rows of reversed tent stitch can be alternated with rows of tent stitch.

RELATED STITCHES

When worked on a single thread of double canvas this stitch is called petit point. It is often used for the small detailed areas of a design and combined with other stitches on double canvas.

Landscape

This landscape uses larger textural stitches in the foreground, which reduce in scale and texture to the horizon. Stranded cotton was used for the smoothly blended sky. 21st century. (Personal collection of Yukari Suai)

Canvas chair seat

A canvas design by Nikki Jarvis, worked by the RSN Studio staff and apprentices. 20th century. (RSN Collection)

Turkey rug knot

This can be a looped or cut stitch depending on the desired effect. In both cases, it must be worked from the bottom upwards. With no knot and a loose tail end on the top of your canvas, take the needle down through the canvas where you wish to start. Bring the needle up one thread to the left of this. Holding the working loop of the thread to the top of the work, take the needle down two threads across from where it came up but do not pull it tight yet. Bring the needle back up where you initially started and pull the loop tight. This will form a horizontal holding stitch to the tail ends of the thread.

Take the needle to the right of the horizontal holding stitch and, again, without pulling the thread tight, loop it around to one canvas thread across from the last stitch. Take the needle down and bring it up one thread to the left of this, through the same hole as the previous stitch. Holding the working loop of the thread to the top of the work, take the needle down two threads across from where it came up but do not pull it tight yet. Bring the needle back up where it first began and pull the loop tight.

Continue looping stitches across the row. Cut the thread at the end of the row and return to the left-hand side of the work. Make a second row above the first, beginning one thread to the left, so that the stitches are bricked. When the area is complete the loops can either be left as they are (see the left-hand side of the photograph) or cut short for a more fluffy appearance (right-hand side of the photograph).

USES

This stitch gives a very fluffy texture to an area and can give real height to the work. However, it is also very slow to work.

Turkey rug stitch should always be the last stitch to be put in your design as it is very difficult to fit other stitches around it due to its dense nature.

RELATED STITCHES

This stitch is also known as Ghiordes knot.

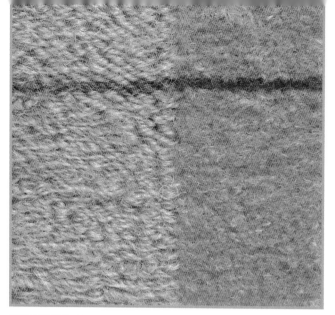

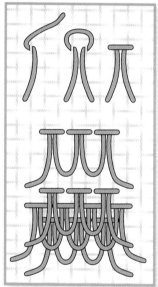

Upright cross

This is a small cross stitch worked upright. First make a vertical stitch over two canvas threads then cross it with a horizontal stitch across two canvas threads. Make sure the top stitch is always horizontal. Work the crosses in horizontal rows. The second row should fit into the spaces of the first.

USES

This is a very small stitch with a raised texture. It is particularly good for small areas.

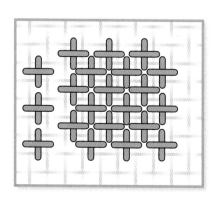

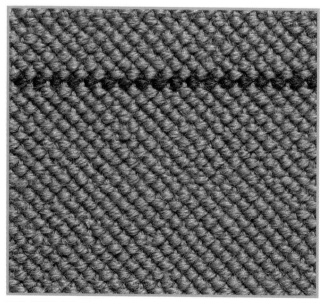

RELATED STITCHES

This stitch is also known as straight cross stitch. This stitch can be alternated with a regular cross stitch across two by two canvas threads and it becomes reversed cross.

Victorian step

This is a diagonal stepped stitch worked in vertical stitches. Begin with a vertical stitch over four canvas threads. To the bottom right of this stitch make three vertical stitches over two canvas threads. In line with the top of these stitches, begin another long stitch over four canvas threads which should end two canvas threads below the last stitches.

Continue stepping the stitches, making three smaller stitches then one long one.

The second row should be fitted into the gaps of the first, with the first long stitch of the next row sitting to the left of the leftmost long stitch of the previous row. The top of the long stitch should be at the same level as the short stitches in the previous row.

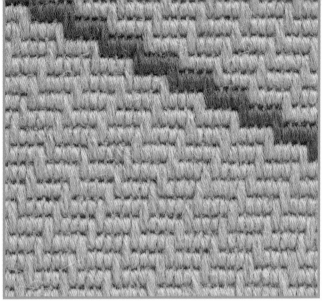

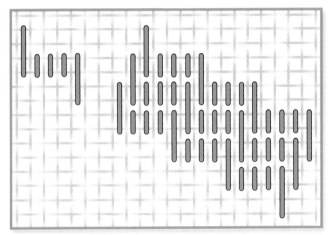

USES
This stitch has a medium-sized pattern repeat and gives a smooth appearance of diagonal lines running through the area.

VARIATIONS
The steps can be made longer or shorter by increasing or decreasing the number of smaller stitches in each step.

Web

This stitch of couched diagonal lines gives a woven appearance. Begin at the top left-hand corner of the area with a cross stitch over two by two canvas threads. Make sure the top stitch goes from top left to bottom right. Start the next (long) stitch two threads down from the bottom left-hand corner of the cross stitch, and take it across to two threads to the right of the top of the cross stitch. Work back across this thread with diagonal stitches, always taking them from bottom right to top left and tucking them under the previous couched thread. Lay the next long thread and again couch back across it. Continue the pattern by laying threads and then immediately couching them down.

USES
This stitch gives an even woven appearance without having to weave the threads.

RELATED STITCHES
If this stitch is worked horizontally, it becomes Bokhara couching.

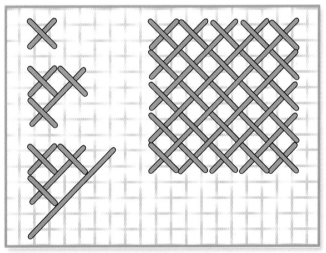

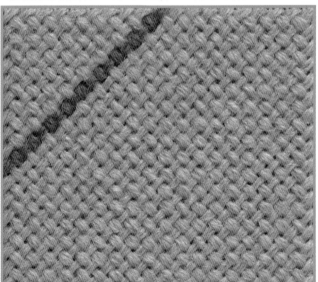

128

MOVING ON

Stitch blending

Within an area of a design, several different stitches can be blended organically from one to the next, in order to create depth or texture or simply to create interest. Stitch blending needs to be gradual and with room to take place. One stitch stopping dead and another immediately starting will look too sudden. The second stitch needs to be introduced slowly into the pattern of the first.

The most successful blending of stitches occurs between stitches that are of a similar scale or direction: two diagonal stitches of similar sizes would be easy to blend, for example, while a large diagonal stitch would be difficult to blend into a small horizontal stitch.

Magpies
21st century. (Rachel Doyle's personal collection)

Here, from the bottom left corner upwards, the rice stitch is reduced in scale, and gradually becomes upright cross stitch. This is reduced again and becomes a simple cross stitch.

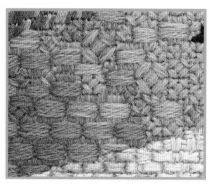

Broad cross stitch is blended into a rice stitch by gradually introducing individual rice stitches into the broad cross pattern.

Colour blending

Colour blending is an important part of any design. It will give shape to objects and depth to the design. Use your original image as a guide and refer to it constantly while stitching.

It is important to remember that you are stitching an interpretation of the original design. Due to the restrictions of the stitches and materials you are working with, you will not be able to get every detail into your piece. But that is part of the process. Choose what is important and leave out what is not.

Smooth shading

This is a controlled method of shading. The sky is worked in stranded cotton with a range of three shades to create the shaded effect. To blend smoothly from one shade to the next, the darkest shade was gradually faded out and the next shade gradually introduced across each diagonal line of the pattern. Work with several needles at once, each threaded up with a different shade. Do not try to change colour too quickly and try to be as free as possible with your shade placement.

Windmill
21st century. (Rachel Doyle's personal collection)

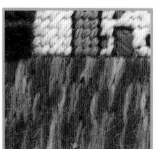

Random shading

The field in the foreground is shaded in a more random way. This method uses blending in the needle. Three shades of crewel wool were used to create the effect. The shades were paired up into three different combinations, i.e. light with dark, light with medium and dark with medium. These were then all used at once in a completely random order to create a mottled effect.

BLACKWORK

Blackbird

Worked by Becky Hogg. In this design I have used the octagonal square pattern (page 151) as a silhouette border around the bird. The pattern also forms the edge of the leaves, giving them a delicate finish. On the bird itself, rather that realistically representing the feathers, I went for a more stylised approach with bold patterns, including triangular darning (page 153) and scattered triangle (page 149).

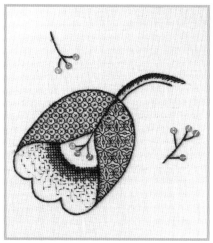

La Marinera Peruana

Worked by Bella Lane. In this piece the embroiderer has carefully chosen suitable patterns and used effective shading to achieve the ruffles and folds in the dancers' costumes.

See also page 159.

See also page 142.

FROM THE AUTHOR

I first encountered blackwork as an Apprentice at the Royal School of Needlework, where I was introduced to the amazing variety and vast number of intricate stitches that it encompasses. There was a particular book in the library that had been well thumbed and seemed to hold more stitches than I could comprehend. Between the tutor, the library and the school's amazing historical collection of embroidery, I was quickly hooked on the subject. Visits to the Victoria & Albert Museum in London only intrigued me more as I studied the exquisite embroidery of 16th century blackwork pieces in the British Gallery.

What I love most about blackwork is the intricate nature of the patterns, which have a graphic quality quite unique in embroidery. I am also drawn to the monochrome nature of this technique, which gives it such a striking and defined appearance where stunning shading effects can be achieved.

The geometric patterns in blackwork are called 'diaper' patterns, of which there are hundreds. However, blackwork appeals not only because of its diversity of pattern, but also because of the shading possibilities. Shading can be carried out in two ways: by varying the thickness of the threads, or by fragmenting the diaper patterns to achieve really delicate, subtle edgings on a design as the stitches fade away to nothing.

Because of the sophisticated degrees of shading it offers, blackwork has been popular for portraiture as well as for designs that pick out the light and dark qualities of a picture, such as reproductions of etchings, pen-and-ink drawings and photographic subjects.

Today, blackwork still has much appeal, due to the diversity in the patterns and materials available. By using traditional blackwork methods as a foundation, it is possible to create unique embroidery for both practical and decorative purposes.

In this section I will be introducing you to the methods of blackwork, showing you how to begin a project, inspiring you with stitches and explaining the methods of shading. This will be followed by ways in which you can develop your style and expand on the traditions of the technique in a more creative way. There are a vast number of diaper patterns to discover and once you have mastered a few, you will be able to make up your own. I hope you are inspired to enjoy blackwork and to develop your skill and knowledge so that you can create good and exciting embroideries.

Becky Hogg

THE HISTORY OF BLACKWORK

Blackwork was popularised in England during the reign of Henry VIII (1509–1547). This technique was generally thought to have been introduced by Catherine of Aragon (Queen of England from 1509-1533), who brought it from its Moorish roots in Spain.

This fine technique was a counted embroidery worked in black silk thread on a fine linen cambric or Holland fabric, and was famed for its textural patterns and illustrative qualities throughout the Tudor period and into the early 17th century.

There are several different methods that come under the heading of blackwork through its history, including the double running stitch method, the diaper pattern style and later the speckling style. The characteristics of the technique changed as developments in materials and styles progressed.

Blackwork diaper patterns shared their use of geometric pattern tessellation and repartition with Moorish design; many patterns used in blackwork can also be found in Moorish architecture such as at the Alhambra in Granada, Spain. These designs developed into complex and intricate patterns as a response to the Muslim faith, which forbids figurative representation. Diaper patterns were very intricate and almost

lacy in appearance, creating incredibly complex arrangements through adjoining back stitches. They would often be used to fill an area, for example a leaf or flower, which was then outlined with stem or chain stitch, and this is the method of blackwork which is most popular today.

During the rule of Henry VIII, blackwork became fashionable on linen garments including women's jackets and smocks, and on the collars, sleeves and cuffs of men's shirts. These shirt edgings were decorated with geometric patterns worked in a black double running stitch, which embroidered the reverse of the fabric as neatly as the front.

Examples can be seen in portraiture of the time by the artist Hans Holbein, who had been Henry VIII's court painter. As so many of Holbein's paintings depicted the technique, the famed double running stitch was named Holbein stitch after him.

Paintings remain a valuable historical source of research into blackwork, as original examples are rare, partly due to the iron mordant used to set the black dye, which would cause the silk thread to decay over time. Some fascinating examples can be seen where the needle holes of the embroidery are still visible but the thread has disappeared, revealing the inked out pattern beneath. The care of garments and the

Detail of a blackwork cushion cover. (RSN Collection 1305)

Detail of a blackwork pattern sampler. English 20th century. (RSN Collection 573)

132

variation in the recipes for the black dye also played a significant part in the longevity of the embroidery.

The English style of blackwork developed in the 1590s as printed pattern books (inspired by herbals, nature books and engravings). These became more available and were widely used as a source of inspiration for embroidery design. The geometric, counted diaper patterns were now replaced by a technique called 'speckling'. It is thought that the development of speckling stitches used in the embroidery reflected the quality of the woodcut printing in these books. Speckling was a technique made up of a series of small seed-like running stitches or back stitches, which would become slightly longer and denser towards the edge of a motif to give subtle shading effects. As well as using monochrome black thread, white linen and black silk were spun together to achieve the desired woodblock effect. This was then outlined with stitches including chain, stem or buttonhole. Designs included scrolling patterns of leaves, fruit, flowers, insects, fish, figures and even mythical beasts, which appeared in popular pattern books like Richard Shorleyker's 'A Schole-House for the Needle', published in London in 1624.

There was definitely a visual affinity between black on white embroidery and printed illustration. As well as the popular black silk embroidery, the technique was also worked in red, blue and green and would often be embellished with precious silver-gilt threads and spangles.

Quene Elizabeth's Blackwork Sleeve Unpick'd

Worked by Nicola Jarvis. This artwork was inspired by the paintings of the Tudor period, showing blackwork embroidery as seen on the clothing of the time. The design brings together drawing and stitch.

Elizabeth I painted in 1590 by an unknown artist. The original painting is at Jesus College, Oxford.

TOOLS AND MATERIALS

Threads and needles

Though silk was the traditional choice of thread for blackwork, embroiderers today also use cotton. The most widely used is stranded cotton, of which you can apply between one and six strands. You can also use coton à broder no.16, which is a thick, soft, twisted cotton for denser stitching, or a very fine no.50 machine thread, which is ideal for lighter tonal values. Varying thicknesses of very fine silk gossamer are also available and are used to create even finer more delicate patterns.

It is good to have a range of threads, as this will give you more variety when shading, and as long as the thread passes smoothly though the holes in the fabric, there are no limitations.

By tradition, metal threads and spangles were also used to highlight and enrich areas of a blackwork design. Today these can include stranded metallic threads, or metallic machine threads, which can be used in the needle to stitch the patterns or to define outlines. Spangles are like sequins but are finely cut pieces of metal from a tightly coiled wire. These can be used to create pattern in the background or to form a little speck of highlight.

Tapestry needles are used when working any counted embroidery technique, including blackwork. The needle should pass with ease through the holes in the evenweave linen without forcing the grain to separate too much. Having a blunt end ensures that none of the fibres of the fabric are caught. The size of needle largely depends on the gauge of fabric, so the thickness of the needle should be approximately the thickness of one of the threads of linen, for example, a 35-count linen would need a no.24 or no.26 tapestry needle.

There are occasions in blackwork when a sharp embroidery needle is required. At any point where you are piercing the grain of the fabric to create an outline or stitching down a spangle, a sharp needle is key. A good all-round size is a no.9 or no.10 embroidery needle, however, if you are using a thicker coton à broder thread, then a no.7 is better. The lower the number, the thicker the needle.

It is good to keep your needles in an organised needle case, so it is easy to find the correct size for different projects.

Stranded cotton, coton à broder and machine black threads, metallic threads, strong threads for framing up, cotton machine threads for tacking, blunt tapestry needles, sharp embroidery needles (no.s 9 and 7), a needle cleaning strawberry and a needle case.

Fabric

Blackwork is always worked on an evenweave fabric – this means that the warp and weft have the same number of threads per inch (TPI) and although natural slubs may appear, the fabric is even and easy to count.

The TPI will determine the scale of each stitch you make within a blackwork diaper pattern, so it is very important to choose the scale that suits your design.

For a very detailed embroidery or small design, a 35TPI Edinburgh linen works well, or for a large-scale design, something like 20TPI Cork linen.

Other counts of linen include 25, 28, 32 and 40TPI. The higher the number, the finer the fabric, and so the smaller the stitches will be.

Linen
Three different gauges of evenweave linen, fine through to coarse.

Blackwork Tudor rose and leaves cushion cover worked in brown thread. English, 20th century. (RSN Collection 109)

135

DESIGN

In its most basic form, blackwork is a counted embroidery technique; therefore it is possible to plan your design on a grid, stitch by stitch, as you could for cross stitch or canvaswork. Designing blackwork like this tends towards patterns that are small and geometric, with no variation in tone.

At the Royal School of Needlework, we teach a method of blackwork combining counted and non-counted techniques that takes full advantage of blackwork's scope in terms of shading and richness of tone. Undoubtedly blackwork's biggest strength and appeal is the ability to shade from dark to light within continuous patterns, so we practise a method of blackwork that encourages this approach.

The design is tacked on to the fabric, outlining the edges of shapes, as well as the key shading changes within the design. This tacking is temporary. We then fill in the spaces that have been tacked, using the different diaper patterns, thinking of each pattern as a different colour that we are painting into the tacked-on shapes. The patterns are continuous and counted out within each area, creating a freer style of embroidery.

A good design for blackwork will have a lot of tonal contrasts, which will enable you to really explore the shading possibilities within the diaper patterns. Really light, or even white areas can be left totally devoid of any stitching, and design lines can be created by the surrounding embroidery (see the clouds on the *White Horse at Cherhill* design shown below).

As well as bold contrasts in tone, really subtle shading can also be achieved to create delicate edges without the need for an outline. This is suitable when you want a very gradual change. All of these things help in deciding on a design.

A design can be produced from something as simple as a photocopy, or for a more individual design, a black-and-white sketch could be drawn from life or from an existing image. The most important thing that will help in producing the embroidery is to have a clear image of the tonal values in the design. This will also help to suggest the weight of stitch and density of patterns you choose when you start stitching.

It is also advisable to do a stitch guide on a paper copy of your design. Try sketching out the rough shape of the patterns you are thinking of using to see if they suit the shape and scale of your design.

The White Horse at Cherhill embroidery part worked. Here the shapes in the design are being filled with different patterns up to the tack lines, using varying thicknesses of thread to change the tone.

The design for the White Horse at Cherhill embroidery, which I created using computer software.

The finished embroidery. The strong tonal contrasts are interpreted in blackwork stitches, with the use of clever shading and pattern.

STITCHES

The following pages display the fundamental stitches you will need to know for blackwork. Back stitch is the most important stitch, and is used to make up all the diaper patterns for which blackwork is so famous. A very simple stitch to learn, it is made up of a series of small stitches joined together to make a solid shape or outline. Once you have mastered this, you will be able to work any of the diaper patterns from pages 140–154. The patterns in the embroidery shown right will all have been worked using back stitch. Double running stitch is very similar to back stitch and is used if the piece needs to be reversible, as the stitch looks the same front and back.

Stem stitch, chain stitch and sketched satin stitch are not compulsory to use in blackwork, but are useful to know if your design requires an outline or definition to a shape. None of these stitches requires counting out, and they are all stitched with a sharp embroidery needle, which gives you a smoother line, particularly on a curved or complex outline.

Blackwork pattern sampler with over 100 different designs worked in squares. English 20th century. (RSN Collection 573)

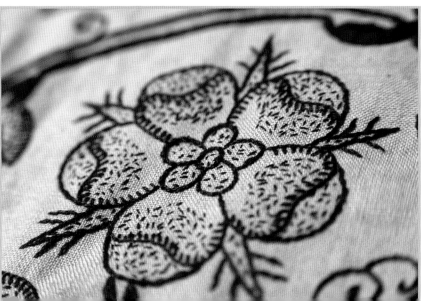

Detail of blackwork cushion cover. (RSN Collection 1305)

BLACKWORK STITCH FINDER

Stitch	Page
BACK STITCH	SEE PAGE 57
DOUBLE RUNNING STITCH	SEE BELOW
CHAIN STITCH	SEE PAGE 62
SKETCHED SATIN STITCH	SEE OPPOSITE
STEM STITCH	SEE PAGE 56

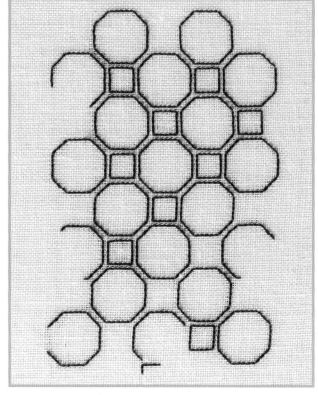

This sample illustrates how a row of back stitches can form a solid smooth line, worked either straight with the grain or diagonally across.

Double running stitch

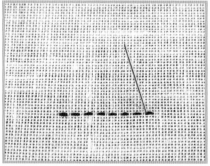

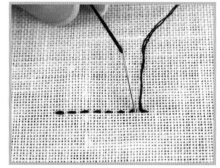

1 Having secured your thread, stitch over two threads, leave two, then continue to the end of your stitch line.

2 Come up in the end hole of your last stitch.

3 Make a stitch over the gap, and continue filling in all the gaps.

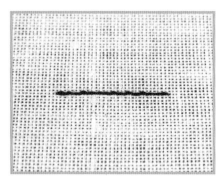

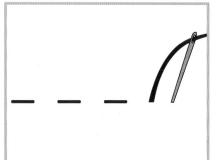

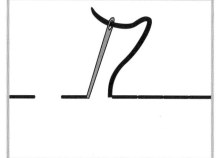

The end result looks the same as back stitch.

Diagram, stage 1.

Diagram, stage 2.

Sketched satin stitch

Sketched satin stitch can be used in blackwork to create a delicate, broken border on a design. It is made up of a row of straight stitches that lie at a 90° angle to the design line, and can either be solid or have space in between the stitches.

Each stitch is a slightly different length to the last, to create a feathered and broken edge. It is good for making a dark border on a design. This example uses two strands of stranded cotton on a 35TPI evenweave linen.

1 Come up and go down to make a long stitch.

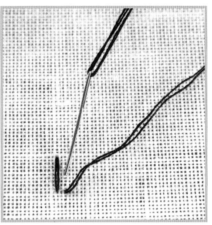

2 Make a shorter stitch beside the first one. I have left two strands of fabric between the two for clarity, but you can work them closer together if you wish.

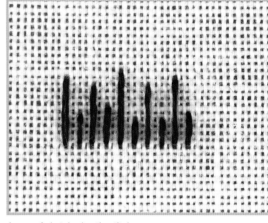

A row of sketched satin stitch.

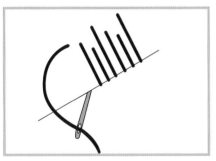

Sketched satin stitch.

This sample illustrates how sketched satin stitch can create a thick but delicate edge which enhances and gives form to a border.

PATTERNS

Once the design has been finalised, the next stage is to look at the patterns that will give your piece the desired texture and feel.

Look at the shapes in the design and see how the patterns fit into them, and if the texture, scale and direction is suitable. The size of the pattern will obviously depend on the 'threads per inch' (TPI) of the evenweave fabric. In some cases the stitch can be scaled down from the original, or altered slightly to suit. Using tiny patterns will give you intense, dark effects, in contrast to the more open patterns that would be more suitable for lighter tones. In some cases in blackwork, less is definitely more, as you can achieve really effective embroidery by using very few patterns and just concentrating on the shading methods.

It is always advisable to do a test of the pattern on the edge of the fabric to determine the density and scale on the gauge of linen chosen for the embroidery, as unpicking can be time-consuming and leave marks on the fabric.

A good method is to look at rounded patterns for organic shapes, and longer, more architectural patterns for pointed or elongated shapes, but it really depends on the outcome you want to achieve. Choose a pattern that gives you the appropriate texture for the subject. The angle of some patterns can also be rotated or flipped to suit; for example, an elongated pattern may work better horizontally than vertically to fit the direction of the shape that it is filling. It is really useful to see how a pattern will work when you leave stitches out, as this will totally change the appearance and give a different texture. The other thing to take into consideration is that some patterns will allow you to add extra stitches. For example, if it is a large pattern that incorporates a square, a simple cross could be added inside it, making the tone of the stitch much darker.

When you start a pattern, it is easy to become confused at the complex make up of it, but if you look at the different shapes within it, you can easily break it down. For example, a pattern with crosses and squares, when complete, looks like a hexagon (see octagonal square, page 151). Once you have started playing around with the patterns and have become familiar with their make up, then it is easy to invent your own. It can sometimes be useful to work out a new pattern on graph paper beforehand.

On the following pages I have illustrated a selection of diaper patterns you can use in your designs. The names are used for reference and are not historical. There are a variety of different shapes and scales of pattern, with some sample embroideries to show how you could apply them to your own designs. I have suggested suitable areas and the rough scale for each pattern, but if your design suits the texture and decoration of a pattern, then don't be afraid to try it! All patterns are worked on a 35TPI linen using one or two strands of stranded cotton.

When working any of the following patterns, it does not matter which part you choose to stitch first, as long as you work methodically through it using the back-stitch method. Avoid jumping across large distances, as this will give you long stitches on the reverse which may show through. All the diagrams are shown on a grid and each square represents one thread of the fabric.

Hexagonal lozenge

This pattern is made up of adjoining polygons with a long stitch through the centre. It is a fairly open pattern and works well horizontally or vertically.

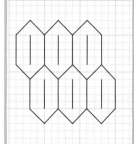

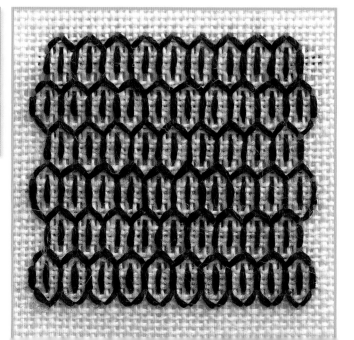

Fan

This pattern is made up of adjoining fan shapes and is a very open in nature. It is ideal for grassy textures as well as fur or feathers.

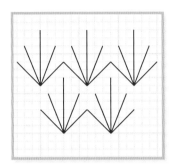

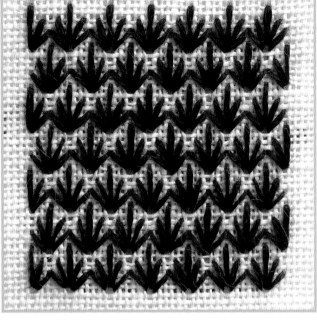

Small diamond

This pattern is made up of diagonal squares with a vertical straight stitch inside. It is a small-scale pattern suitable for darker tones.

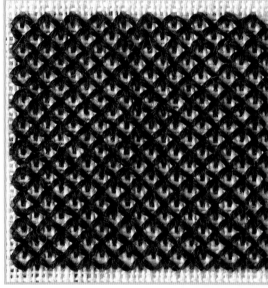

Octagon star

This is made up of small squares and larger octagons with a star inside. It is a mid-scale pattern and is suitable for more rounded, organic shapes.

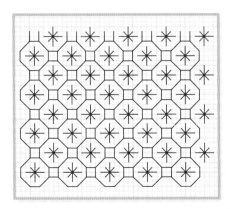

141

Lace

This is a complex decorative pattern made up of an open cross shape and a lozenge. It is a larger scale of pattern and is suitable for rounded shapes and for depicting the natural world.

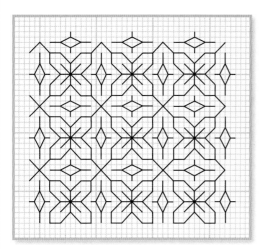

Elizabethan Flower

Worked by Becky Hogg. This stylised flower has three different patterns to create the decorative textures. These patterns were chosen for their ornamental qualities, but also for their scale and shape. This embroidery also benefits from the use of a stem-stitched outline and sketched satin stitch stem to give it definition.

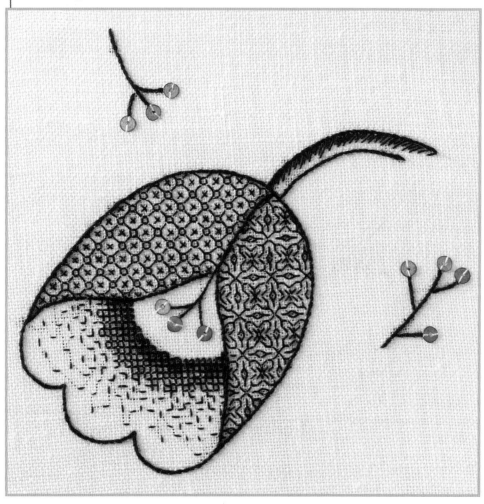

Waffle

Here is a detailed pattern made up of a diagonal square surrounded by a small parallelogram. It is fairly small in scale, making for a denser pattern, and is suitable for rounded, natural shapes.

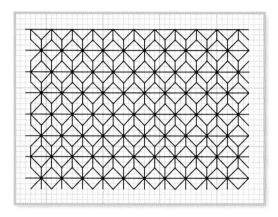
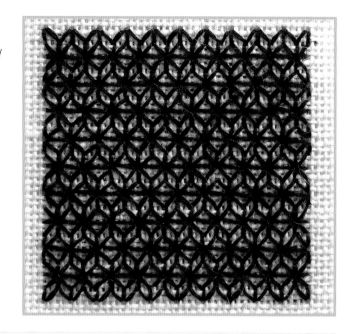

Interlocking 'I's

This pattern is made up of rows of long straight stitches with a bar at either end. It is fairly large in scale and is good for creating a linear texture, worked either horizontally or vertically.

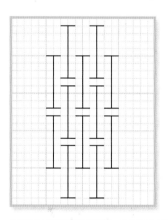
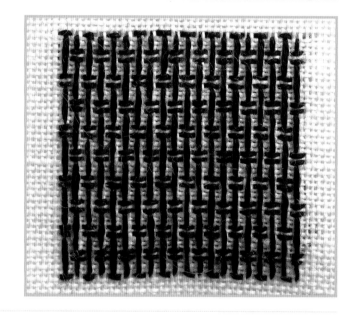

Interlocking 'Z's

Here is a pattern made up of diagonal stitches, one long and two short. It is good for filling more architectural shapes and can be effective both horizontally and vertically. It is a slightly more open pattern where the individual lines overlap but are not linked.

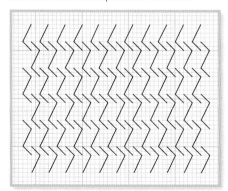
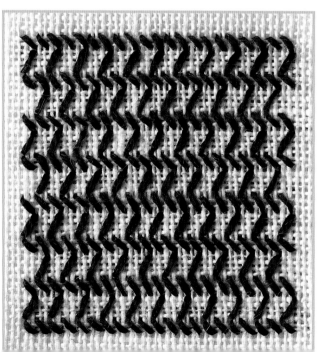

Interlocking 'Y's

This pattern is made up of straight and diagonal stitches, giving a slightly more open structure where the individual shapes overlap. It is suitable for more architectural shapes.

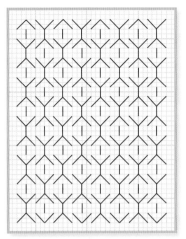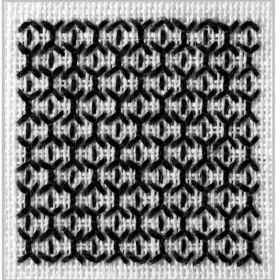

Chevron

A pattern made up of diagonal 'V' stitches with vertical stitches in between. It is a small, dense pattern and good for linear designs.

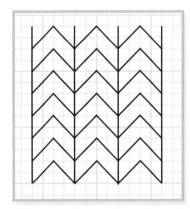

Open lace

A decorative pattern made up of adjoining grouped diagonal squares and grouped straight squares. It is quite an open, large-scale pattern good for more organic areas of designs.

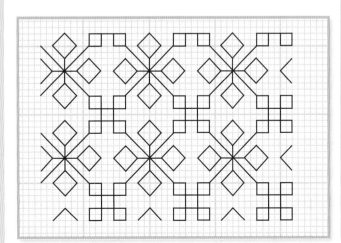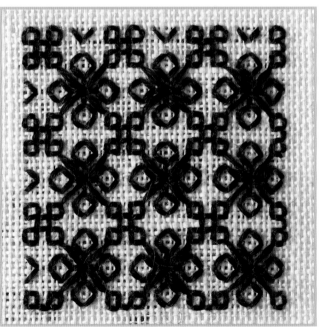

De La Warr Pavilion

Worked by Margaret Dier. This embroidery has four patterns, which have been chosen to suit the more architectural nature of this design. The chevron pattern gives texture to the seat, whereas the interlocking 'Z's pattern gives the table a smoother surface. The outlines are embroidered with back and stem stitch.

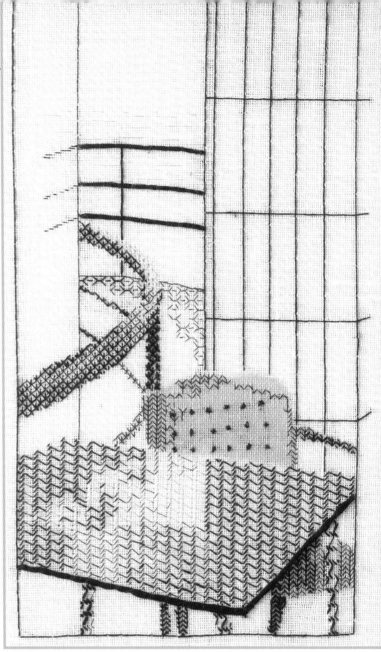

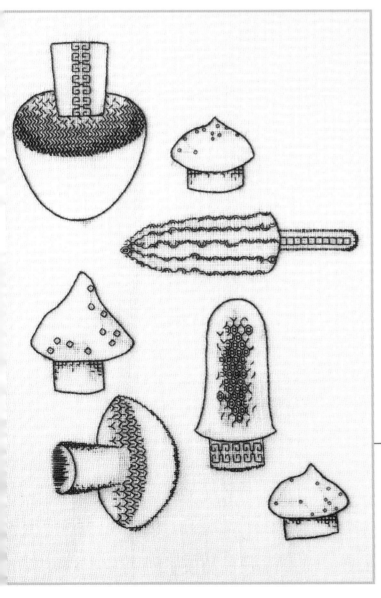

Mushroom Pattern

Worked by Becky Hogg. The linear formation of the zigzag pattern in the top mushroom gives the appearance of the underside of the cap, and the small diamond pattern is used to form the spotted patterning of the toadstool. The outlines are embroidered in stem stitch and the Grecian curl pattern in the stalks adds a more stylised, graphic touch.

Grecian curls

This pattern is made up of adjoining groups of 'G' shapes. It is a very open, larger scale pattern and is suitable for creating a graphic effect.

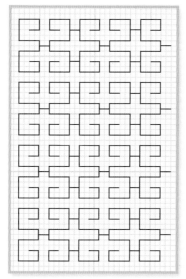

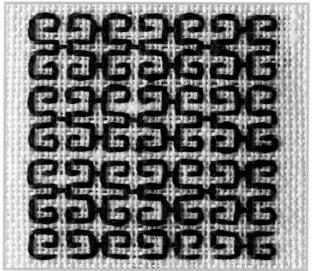

Leaves

This pattern is made up of a series of small diagonal squares and angled shapes and is quite complex in its make up. It is a larger scale pattern and well suited for more rounded shapes.

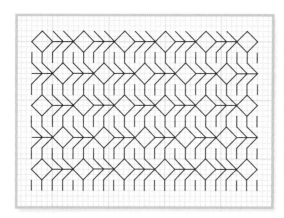

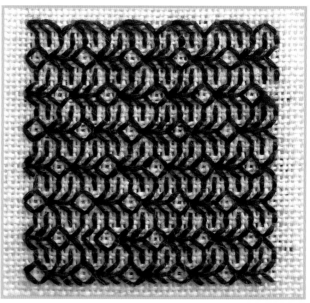

Diagonal weave

This complex pattern is made up of large and small rectangles with a diagonal stitch in the middle of each. It is a fairly dense pattern and works well in architectural shapes.

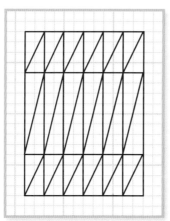

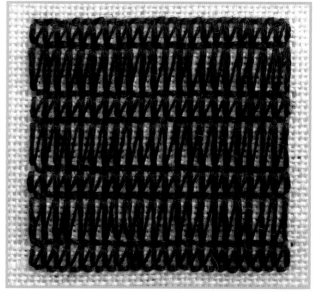

Zigzag

In this pattern lines are formed by rows of zigzags, with each stitch worked diagonally over the linen. It is quite a dense pattern, good for creating a linear effect.

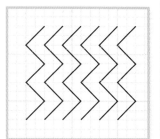

Open zigzag

This pattern is made up of rows of zigzag lines stitched diagonally over the linen, with an added horizontal stitch at each point. It is a mid-scale pattern and is suitable for creating a geometric effect within more linear shapes.

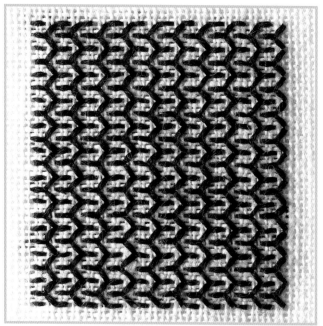

Honeycomb

This pattern is made up of a series of hexagons with a box inside and is a mid-scale pattern. Its honeycomb effect makes it good for more natural designs.

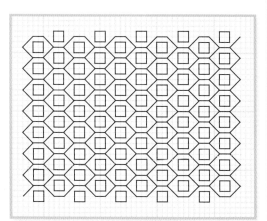

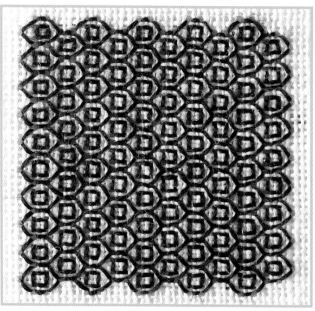

Diamond eyelet

This decorative pattern is made up of little squares in diagonal rows that make up a larger square, with a star shape inside.

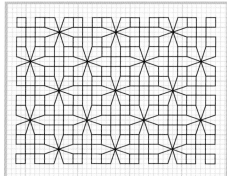

It is quite a complex pattern, which is very detailed, but you could try leaving out the central stitch in places to simplify it.

Diagonal trellis

This pattern is similar to diamond eyelet, above, but adding a cross stitch in alternating squares totally changes the effect. It is quite an open pattern.

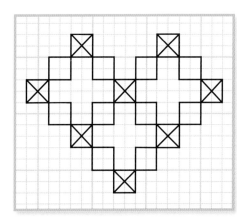

'T' blocks

This pattern has the appearance of a capital 'T' or a bricked pattern with a diagonal line running through the centre. It is a very detailed pattern and works well in more linear formats.

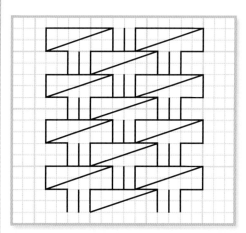

Open honeycomb

This pattern is made up of slightly flattened octagon shapes with a vertical stitch inside. As a fairly rounded pattern, this works well within more organic designs.

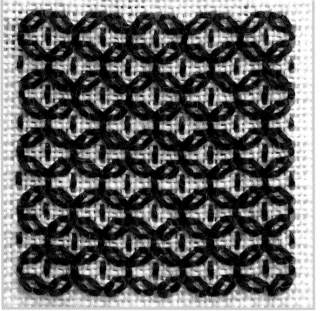

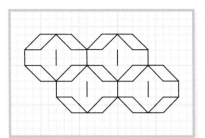

Floral lace

Here is a pattern made up of straight squares with adjoining cross stitches, which work to make little hexagons. A larger cross stitch is also placed inside. This is a larger scale pattern, good to use in more organic shapes.

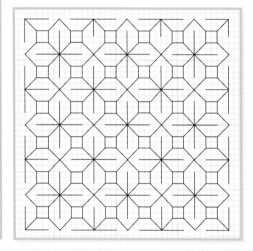

Scattered triangle

A pattern made up of a series of small triangles that is very free in its nature. Try grouping them closer together for darker areas and further apart for a more open pattern.

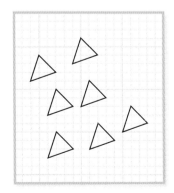

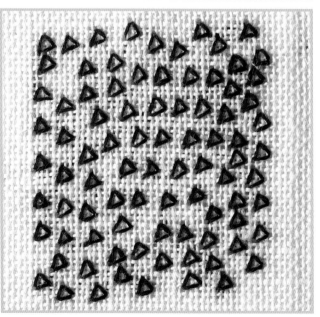

Diagonal tile

Here is a pattern made up of rows of diagonal boxes with slanted adjoining lines. It is a fine-scale pattern good for either architectural or organic shapes.

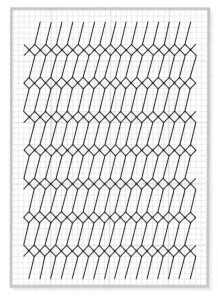 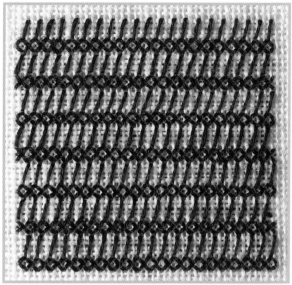

Diamond tile

This pattern is very similar to diagonal tile, above, except that the adjoining lines are straight, and larger in scale. These two patterns work well together to create curvature in a shape, as seen in the centre of the geranium leaf on the opposite page.

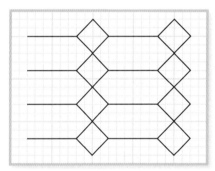 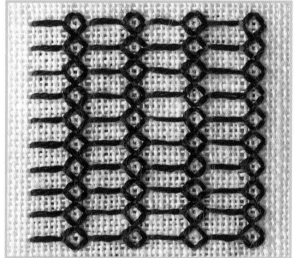

Compressed lace

This pattern is made up of a series of lozenge shapes with a central diamond, and is a larger scale pattern. This would work well in natural shapes.

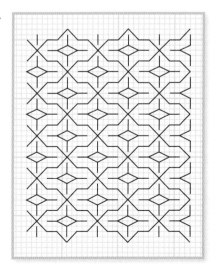 

Geranium Leaf

Worked by Becky Hogg. The patterns used in this design are a good example of how the angle of a pattern can be changed to suit the curvature in a shape. The middle of the leaf has the diagonal and diamond tile patterns, which change angle as the shape curves. The closed diagonal darning (see page 153) is a really dense pattern and here it is used to create the shadow of the leaf's turnover edge. The sketched satin stitch around the edge of the leaf is stitched at a 90° angle to the design line and adds definition and shading to the outline.

Rounded eyelet

This is a fairly complex pattern made up of larger octagons joined together by squares. The octagon has a star-like stitch in the middle. Though this is quite a large pattern, it works well in darker areas.

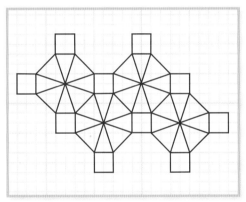

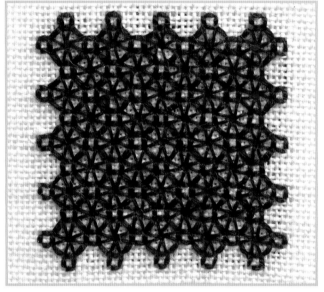

Octagonal square

This pattern is made up of crosses and squares and is a fairly small-scale pattern good for natural shapes.

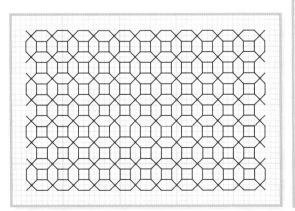

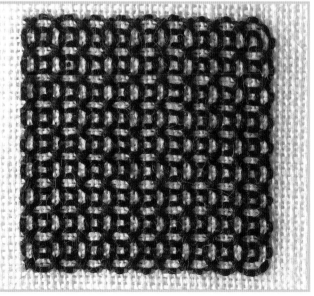

151

Block trellis

This pattern is made up of spaced squares which, when joined, form a cross shape. It is a fairly open pattern and is good for natural designs.

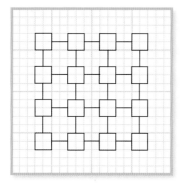

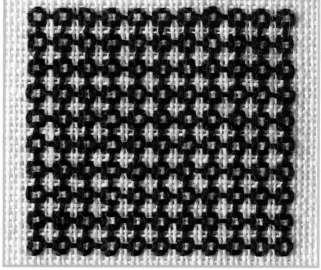

Tulip

This pattern is made up of a series of interlocking hexagons, joined in columns by a straight stitch. It is a mid-scale pattern and works well in more organic designs.

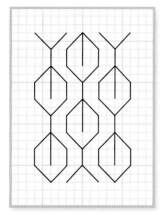

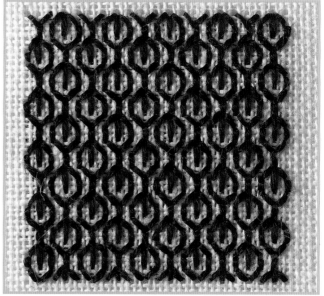

Bricked wave

This pattern is made up of horizontal and vertical straight stitches which develop into a zigzag structure.

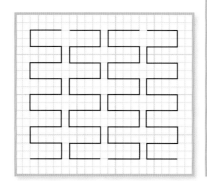

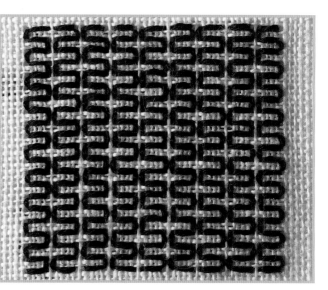

Darning patterns

The following three patterns are known as darning patterns and are used in blackwork to give a denser coverage in a design. They are made up of parallel stitches, which can be varied in length to suit.

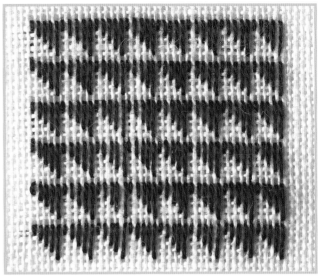

TRIANGULAR DARNING

This pattern is made up of a diagonal block of stitches that increases in size within each block and has quite a dense coverage. It is an effective pattern, which can create texture in a design, as seen in the bird on page 130.

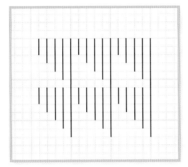

CLOSED DIAGONAL DARNING

A pattern made up of densely worked horizontal stitches in diagonal rows that are worked over each grain of fabric. This stitch is good for silhouettes or dark shadows.

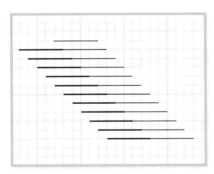

CLOSED HERRINGBONE DARNING

This pattern is made up of closely worked zigzag rows, which completely cover the linen. It is good for silhouettes or dark shadows and is also effective as a background.

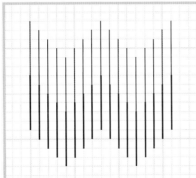

153

Diamond trellis

This pattern is made up of diagonal squares joined up with straight crosses and has the effect of a trellis pattern. This is a mid-scale pattern and works well in more architectural shapes.

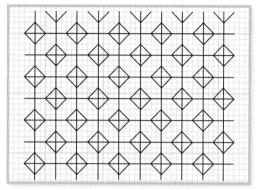

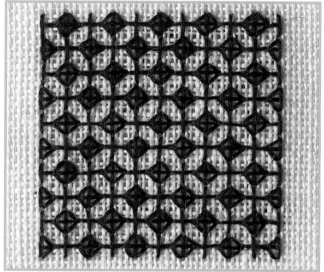

Diagonal wave

Here is a pattern made up of very large and very small diagonal stitches in a zigzag formation. It is a large-scale pattern and works well in more linear designs.

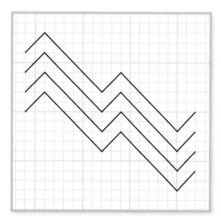

Harlequin

This pattern is made up of diagonal stitches forming an elongated diamond shape. It is quite a small pattern, so is good for creating detail in a design.

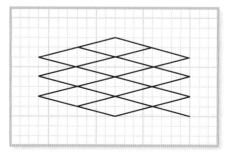

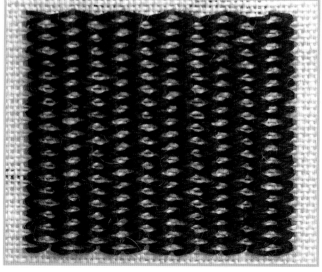

SHADING

Shading is one of the fundamental methods to master in blackwork and is what makes it so appealing. Though the diaper patterns are beautiful when worked in one flat tone, they are also effective as a tool to shade with. They can be utilised in different ways to give the various tonal values, be it subtle or dramatic, to suit the design. The two main methods of shading patterns are changing the thickness of the thread and breaking up the pattern. These two methods can also be combined to get the most dramatic effects.

By missing out the stitches in a pattern and using a fine machine thread or gossamer silk, you are creating really light areas of stitch, and in some cases you can leave out the pattern completely. In contrast, by using the full pattern with the thickest thread, you are creating the darkest effect.

Light and dark contrasts can be worked to create very intricate shapes or textures, like the shapes in a bird's feathers, as seen in the owl, right.

Owl

Worked by Lizzy Lansberry. The owl is a fine example of the effects of shading in blackwork. The main body of the bird is worked in one pattern, interlocking 'Y's (page 144), but fully explores the thickness of thread and pattern disintegration to create the desired texture. A smaller square pattern is used in the head, which is suitable for the size and shading required, and a very thick thread is used in the branch to give a strong shadow.

CHANGING THREAD THICKNESS

Working with different thicknesses of thread within the same pattern gives the effect of shading. The thickest area in the example below was worked in coton à broder no.16, which is a twisted cotton thread roughly the thickness of one strand of the 35TPI linen. The thickest thread should still pass with ease through the fabric, so that it does not distort it. When you want the pattern to get lighter, a finer thread can be used, for example one strand of stranded cotton (it depends on how dramatic a change you want). The idea is to integrate the two threads gradually, as in step 1, where the hexagons are stitched with the finer thread but the little inside stitch is in the coton à broder. At this stage it is advisable to have one needle threaded up with the coton à broder, and another threaded up with the stranded cotton. This means you can easily pick up the thread you need as you gradually merge the thicknesses within the pattern. This method is continued until you reach the finest thread.

There is no rule about what part of the pattern you use to merge the thicknesses; it is purely a matter of judgment and how the design dictates your decision.

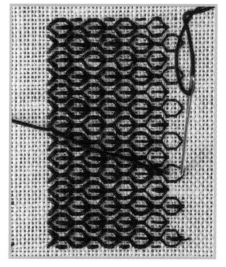

1 Begin this pattern with the thickest thread, which is coton à broder. Some way along, begin to stitch the hexagons with one strand of stranded embroidery thread, which is thinner. Continue placing the stitches inside the hexagons with coton à broder. This makes the shading more gradual.

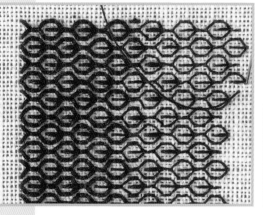

2 As you continue with the pattern, begin to fill the hexagons with one strand of stranded embroidery thread, which will give the pattern a lighter, less dense look.

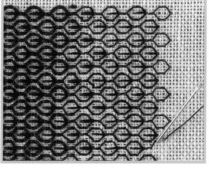

3 Begin to stitch the hexagons with a machine thread, which is the finest of the three.

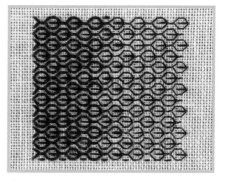

4 Continue to place the straight stitches inside the hexagons with the previous thickness – one strand of the stranded embroidery thread.

5 Finish the pattern by filling in the hexagons with straight stitches in the finest machine thread. This completes the gradation from a dense, dark pattern to a lighter look.

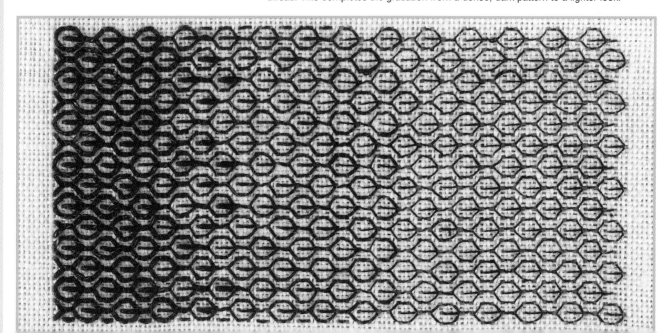

BREAKING UP THE PATTERN

The diaper pattern itself can be used as a tool for shading, as the complex make-up of each pattern can be fragmented into little pieces to create lighter effects. The pattern can be worked in any thickness of thread, and purely by removing elements within it, shading can be achieved. For the darkest part of the area, the pattern is worked in full, then as you progress to a lighter part, the stitches can be gradually removed, or in some cases made smaller. The process can be dramatic or gradual, and sometimes creates a whole new look to the pattern.

As you work the pattern, you still count the stitches that you have chosen to omit, so they are in the correct place. Doing this creates the pleasing effect of a complex geometric pattern dissolving and fragmenting, and if it were to reform, everything would be in the correct place.

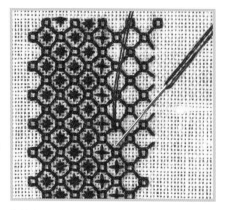

1 To begin breaking up the pattern, replace the stars in the centres of the hexagons with a simpler cross shape.

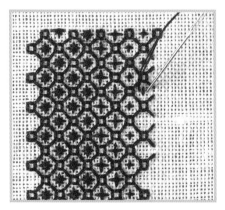

2 After a couple of rows of crosses, reduce the size of the crosses as shown.

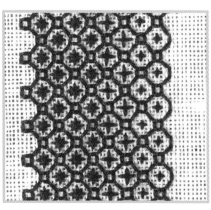

3 Continue in this way for two rows.

4 Next, begin to place crosses in alternate hexagons only. Then leave a row empty, and in the next row place crosses in every third hexagon. After this, do not stitch any more crosses.

5 Begin to leave off one side of the squares between the hexagons, opening up the shapes as shown.

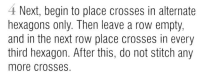

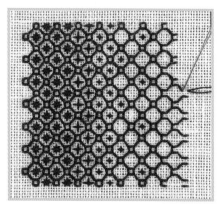

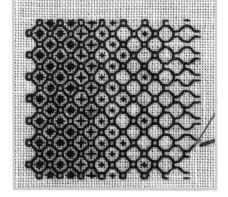

6 Continue in the same way, breaking up the pattern gradually so that the shapes end up with only four sides instead of six, and then gradually become diagonal lines only.

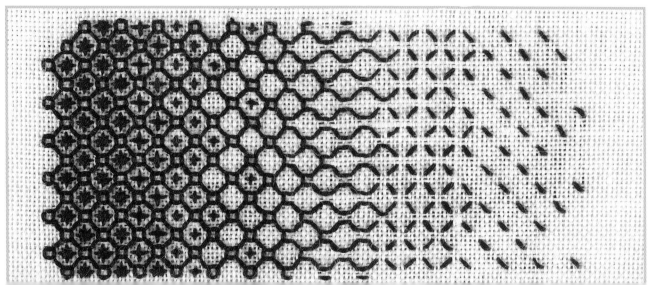

COMBINING THE TECHNIQUES

Changing the thickness of thread and breaking up the pattern can be combined to create really
dramatic effects. In a small design area there may be a sudden contrast between the shades,
so by combining changing the thickness of thread with breaking up the pattern, the tone can be
changed very quickly.

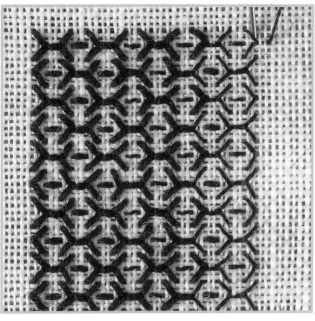

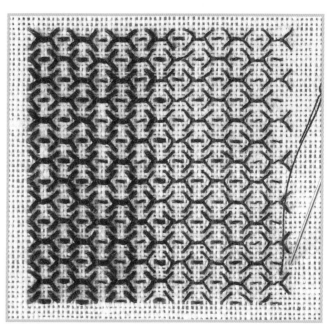

1 The beginning of this pattern is stitched in thick coton à broder, then
the Ys change to one strand of stranded cotton thread, which is finer.
For one row, the straight stitches are still in the thicker coton à broder,
then in the next row the straight stitches, too, are stitched with the finer
embroidery thread.

2 As the pattern continues, the even finer machine thread is introduced.

3 The pattern continues in the finest machine thread,
and then the pattern begins to break up.

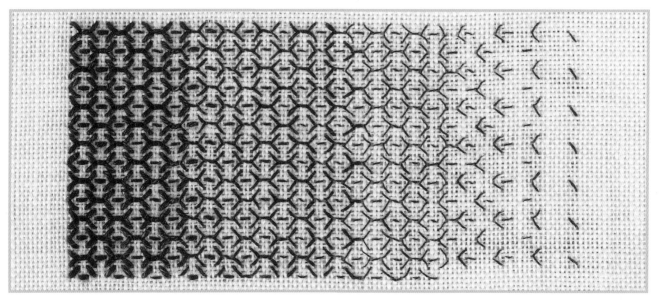

Penguins

Worked by Rachel Doyle. This image of emperor penguins makes great use of the very dark, densely embroidered patterning on the heads and back, contrasting starkly with the white on the belly of the birds. Note how the birds are not outlined but use the structure of the pattern (either as a full or fragmented pattern) to create the edges. By breaking up the pattern, the embroiderer has delicately changed the tone from grey to white.

Tiger

Worked by Sarah Homfray. This dramatic image of a tiger illustrates that within the patterns you can create very defined changes in tone by varying the thickness of thread. This is evident in the striking patterning on the fur where thicker threads are used for the dark patches against fine thread and the white of the fabric.

159

Richi

Worked by Kate Cross. The shading in this portrait shows off the expressions of the couple to full effect. To create the mid-tones, the embroiderer has kept the main structure of the pattern and missed out the central stitch. This is a great way to shade your pattern to a lighter tone.

Cheetah

Worked by Heather Harrison. In this design it is interesting to note how quickly you can fragment a pattern to nothing, as seen above the eyes of the cheetah. This is effective when a sudden change in tone is needed. Again, you can see how in just one pattern you can create interest through the use of tone.

MOVING ON

Once you have mastered the patterns and shading of blackwork, you need not be restricted to black thread! Historically blackwork was not only stitched in black but in red (see right) and also blue and green, and would often be embellished with metal threads or spangles. Though black is still the predominant colour for this technique, because of its striking, graphic appearance, colour can also work beautifully.

When using colour in this technique, the methods of pattern and shade are the same, but shading can be achieved not only through breaking up the pattern and changing the thickness of thread, but also by using different tones of colour. It may be that you only need one colour for the design, as the shading in the stitches will give it form, as it would with black thread.

Colour can also be applied with fabric paints prior to the embroidery being worked. The open nature of the diaper patterns means that the dyes can work together with the stitching, showing through the tiny gaps between the patterns. Another alternative is to stitch on a coloured fabric, or try reversing the traditional black stitching on white, by having white stitching on a black fabric.

Fine metallic threads can be added to act as a highlight or add a contrast of texture, or just form part of the pattern itself. Some metallic thread is fine enough to stitch with and can also be used in the same needle as a stranded cotton thread, in effect mixing the colours within the needle. Another effective way to incorporate the metallic thread is to use it as an outline, stitched in chain or stem stitch. Gold and silver work well with black, but other metallic colours are available too.

Metal spangles or sequins can be used in blackwork for patterning in the background or again as a highlight.

It is also interesting to try different scales of fabric and thread, for example, using 2-ply wool on 20TPI linen, to create a much coarser, chunkier quality of stitch. Working on a coarser fabric will automatically enlarge the patterns, and in contrast working on a very fine fabric will turn them into minute lace-like stitches. As long as the fabric is evenweave, the patterns will always work. Happy stitching!

Blackwork sampler of forty-nine stitches, worked in red silk on linen incorporating counted and needle lace stitches. English 18th century. (RSN Collection 248)

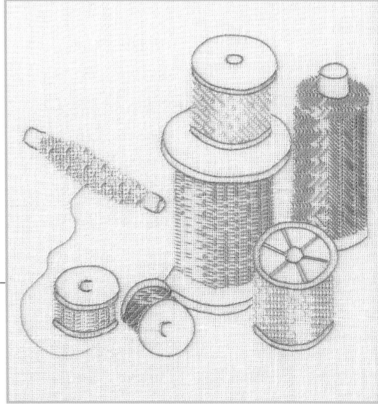

Cotton Reels

Worked by Becky Hogg. When I was thinking about using colour with the diaper patterns, I was in my studio, where I have a shoebox full of reels of threads bursting with different colours, and I thought it would be fun to translate some of them into stitch. The reels each use only one tone of colour but they are given shape and form by the shading of the pattern. I also tried to pick stitches that represented the texture of a spun cotton reel.

161

SILK SHADING

Endless Ocean

This piece brings together all of the techniques and stitches explained on pages 178–179. See also page 180.

See also page 173.

See also page 165.

See also page 164.

FROM THE AUTHOR

Silk shading, painting with a needle, long-and-short stitch embroidery, thread painting: this technique goes by many names but the basis is one stitch, known as long-and-short stitch. One stitch, I might add, that consists only of putting straight stitches together in a row! For the purposes of this book I will stick to the term silk shading, but feel free to substitute any of the alternative names instead.

This technique never fails to impress. Its photographic quality makes the subject matter instantly jump out at you. The colours are sumptuous, the finish is luxurious and the design often portrays the beauty of the world that surrounds us. All of this can make the technique feel out of reach. So many times I have heard the phrase, 'That's lovely, but I could never do it!' I put it to anyone who follows the steps that they certainly can do it, and not only do it, but do it well.

Embroidery should be accessible to all, so I have given options on different methods and approaches wherever possible, so that you can choose the one that best suits you. All you need to start is a few basic materials and, most of all, a little patience. If you want to learn something well it cannot be done in an hour, so be prepared to dedicate a little time to practise and your efforts will be well rewarded.

Here I will attempt to guide you through the stages of this beautiful technique, teaching you not just how to work long-and-short stitch but also about colour, composition and where to find inspiration along the way. So grab a bit of cotton fabric, a needle with a point, some cotton thread and have a go!

Sarah Homfray

THE HISTORY OF SILK SHADING

The history of silk shading is a complex subject, intertwined with the history of embroidery itself. Silk shading can be split into two halves: the stitch and the technique.

Let us first look at silk shading as a stitch. The long-and-short stitch is the basis of all silk shading. However, the stitch appears in several other techniques, including crewelwork, for example. Because of this, while all silk shading is long-and-short stitch, not all long-and-short stitch is silk shading.

There are many examples of long-and-short stitch embroideries found throughout history from all over the world. Some of the oldest pieces, such as those found in Coptic cemeteries in Egypt, date back as far as the 5th century BC.

It is hard to define the point in history at which silk shading became the technique we know it as today, but it was most likely first practised in China, where it is more commonly known as needle painting. China is well known for its silk production throughout history, which is thought to have existed as far back as 5,000–6,000 years ago. Archaeological excavations have found embroideries that date back to at least the 2nd century BC.

In England, silk shading was first used in *Opus Anglicanum* embroidery (also known as English work), a technique used in the Mediaeval period. It is thought that *Opus Anglicanum* was first worked by nuns, and the technique was later taken up by professional men and women who had completed a seven-year apprenticeship in the technique. This level of professionalism and skill meant that silk shading embroideries were restricted to the very wealthy. Most surviving examples of *Opus Anglicanum* silk shading are seen on church work and comprise silk-shaded faces, angels and animals.

The Black Death of 1348 is estimated to have killed half of the population of England, including many of the embroiderers of *Opus Anglicanum* work. However, the need for fine embroideries was still great and a new faster shading technique was developed to meet the demand. This meant that embroidery was no longer something only royalty could afford and the nobility began to adorn their clothing with it.

By the 17th century, an increase in trading by the East India Company made silks more readily available and silk shading started to appear in other types of embroidery. For example, it was used for faces on the stumpwork boxes of the 17th century, and long-and-short stitch was used heavily in Jacobean crewelwork designs.

The art of silk shading is still alive and well today. It is worked extensively in China to very high standards, although now the clientele are tourists, not emperors! The Royal School of Needlework continues to teach this beautiful technique in new and innovative ways, introducing a technique steeped in history to the embroiderers of this and future generations.

Floral panel with exotic birds

This silkwork panel demonstrates how effective silk shading can be at representing floral and bird motifs. English 20th century.
(RSN Collection)

Magnolias

This is a piece stitched by Miss Bartlett, worked in natural shading using unspun silk. The shading on the petals is very subtle, but the contrast between the light tones of the petals and the dark tones of the branches makes this a very striking piece. English 20th century. (RSN Collection)

TOOLS AND MATERIALS

Fabrics

While you are learning silk shading I recommend that you use the fabrics described below, at least initially. Once you have learned to master the essentials of this technique you can be more creative with the types of fabrics you use.

BACKING FABRICS

Silk shading produces quite dense stitching, so you will need a good strong base on which to stitch. Back your chosen embroidery fabric with either **calico** or plain white **cotton** sheeting to give extra stability. They are both readily available and inexpensive to buy.

EMBROIDERY FABRIC – SILK

Silk is one of the strongest natural fibres available and it is this quality that makes it suitable for silk shading. Silk is produced by farmed silkworms. The worms are fed mulberry leaves until their weight has increased 10,000 times. The silk worms spin a cocoon around themselves and it is this that can be unravelled when soaked in hot water, producing filaments that can be up to a mile in length. The silk is then processed to remove the sericin: a natural gum that protects the fibres and causes them to stick to each other as the cocoon is spun.

Silk is a protein fibre, similar to wool or to human hair. This means that silks will have some irregularities, known as slubs. This is the nature of silk fabric, so do not worry about finding the perfect piece.

A good quality silk is an excellent surface for silk shading. It has a very tight weave allowing for great accuracy. It gives a good sheen, comes in a wide variety of luxurious colours and can be kept very tight during stitching. Silk comes in different forms and weights. A silk dupion is suitable for silk shading as it is stronger than other silks, and I have also used a lighter-weight silk, a sheer, plain-weave fabric known as pongee or China silk (see Marbles on page 193).

EMBROIDERY FABRIC – LINEN

Linen is made from the fibres of the flax plant. It has a long individual fibre length in comparison to cotton and other natural fibres, but it is coarser than silk due to the shape of its cross section.

To get the longest fibres, the plant is pulled up whole or very close to the root. The fibres are then loosened from the stalk by using bacteria to break down the pectin that binds the fibres together. The fibres go through more refining processes until just the soft flax fibres remain. This is then spun and woven into a fabric. Like silk, linen is labour-intensive to manufacture, making it a more expensive fabric. It is thought to be one of the oldest known fabrics in existence and the Egyptians used it to wrap their mummies as a display of wealth.

Linen is a durable and strong fabric. The fibres themselves do not stretch, and this low elasticity means that they cannot be continually folded in the same place without becoming damaged. Slubs in linen, unlike silk, can be a sign of low quality, as the poorer fibres of the plant have been used. A good-quality linen uses threads with a consistent diameter, so keep your eye out for this when choosing. Linen is natural in colour; white linen will have been bleached.

EMBROIDERY FABRIC – COTTON

Like linen, cotton also comes from a plant, the aptly named cotton plant! It is a fibre that grows around the seeds and aids in seed dispersal. The cotton fibres can simply be lifted off the plant and spun into threads. This makes it an inexpensive fabric and any good-quality cotton is great for silk shading. It can easily be printed, painted and drawn on to, making it a versatile fabric to use.

Threads

As with fabric, there is a wide variety of suitable threads available. Use stranded cotton initially to gain an understanding of the basic technique, then you can start to experiment later.

Note that threads are dyed in batches. While every attempt is made to ensure the same colour each time, colours can vary between batches. Every project in this book has used one skein or less of the same colour, but if you are working a lot of silk shading, and need more than one skein, choose skeins from the same dye lot if you can.

Whichever thread you decide to use, the following pages will give you some basic knowledge on how to handle and store your threads for the best results.

SILK

This thread is the most traditional – hence the name silk shading! This thread was used in embroidery before the advent of more modern synthetic threads. It gives a lustrous finish and is nice to work with.

FLOSS SILKS

These are silk fibres that have not been twisted together to make one strand. This is the thread traditionally used in most silk shading embroideries from the Far East. It can be split down into extremely thin fibres, but this makes it harder to use.

RAYON

Rayon is a synthetic fibre that imitates the feel and texture of silk. It can easily be dyed and is an affordable silk substitute.

COTTON

Cotton threads are readily available in a huge variety of colours. They are inexpensive, making them great threads with which to learn. Cotton threads do not have the sheen that silk has, but they are durable and easy to use.

Cotton threads within a range are numbered, to help identify unique colours. Each range has its own set of numbers, and there are a number of ranges, most commonly DMC and Anchor.

HANDLING A SKEIN

A skein is a length of thread wrapped in a figure-of-eight shape, so that when you pull one end, the thread should pull out of the skein easily. Leave the labels in place and pull out only what you need, then strand the individual threads (see below). Wrap any remaining strands around the skein so that you will know from which colour they come – colours can look similar when you can only see one strand.

STRANDING COTTON THREADS

Most makes of cotton threads come in four to six strands. Separate these strands and use an individual one for silk shading. To do this, part the ends and pull one of the strands vertically upwards out of the group. This will avoid knotting the rest.

HANDLING A HANK

A hank is a longer length of thread, used when you have something larger to work. This is not wrapped in a figure-of-eight but round in a continuous loop. To stop a hank becoming tangled, open out the threads into a circle. Cut straight though all of the threads in one place. Fold the threads in half and, getting someone to hold the folded part, divide the threads into three and loosely plait them together. When you want to use a thread, pull one length out from the top and strand as before. Some makes of cotton also come in this configuration.

CARE OF YOUR THREADS

Keep your threads away from sunlight and damp to preserve their properties. Try not to let them get tangled, as untangling them will result in damage to the individual fibres. Use them in a clean environment (wash your hands regularly) as dirt can harm the fibres – especially with silk threads.

Needles

Needles are a vital part of all embroidery and it is important that you use the correct one for the type of embroidery that you are working. There is a baffling array of needles available, but here are some guidelines that you can follow to help you choose the right one:

• The higher the number, the finer the needle. Silk shading uses the finest, so look for sizes 9–12.

• Throughout this silk-shading section, size 12 and 10 embroidery needles are used for the silk-shading technique itself, while a size 9 is used for surface stitches.

• The crewel needle is used for framing up, and the curved needle is used when mounting your work.

• Use a needle with a point to pierce the fabric. Blunt needles (tapestry and ballpoint) are for counted fabrics (canvas and cross-stitch fabrics). Do not use these needles for silk shading.

• If you can hear the thread passing through the fabric, then your needle is too small. The needle, not the thread, should make the hole for the thread to pass through the fabric, so if you choose a thicker thread, you will need a bigger needle. Note that if your needle is too big, it will make a hole in the fabric.

WHAT TYPE OF NEEDLE FOR SILK SHADING?

Use embroidery needles for silk shading. These have a point and a long slender eye, making it easy to thread embroidery cottons. Do not get them confused with sharps, which have short round eyes and are used for general-purpose sewing. Use sizes 9, 10 and 12 embroidery needles for silk shading. Refer to the table below to help you choose when to use which needle:

From the top: embroidery needles sizes 12, 10, 9; crewel needle size 5; curved needle.

NEEDLE SIZE	9	10	12
THREAD TYPE	Larger weave, thicker thread		Tighter weave, fine thread
FABRIC TYPE	Linen	Cotton	Silk

HOW TO THREAD A NEEDLE

Silk shading generally uses the smallest needles available, so it is important to know how to thread them correctly. This will save you a lot of time and much frustration. Needle threaders are usually too big to use on very fine needles. There are different ways of threading a needle and the method used will depend on the technique you are stitching and the size of the needle, but the following technique will work well for both cotton and silk threads.

1 Silk-shading needles are too small to fold the thread in half around the needle so, using a sharp pair of embroidery scissors, cut the end of the thread cleanly and at an angle of about 45° for a sharp end to thread through the eye.

2 Hold the thread in the hand you normally use for writing, between the pads of your thumb and your index finger. Hold it right at the end so you can only just see the end of the thread between your index finger and thumb.

3 Take the eye of the needle right up to the end of the thread and move the thread towards the eye by straightening your finger and thumb.

4 This pushes the thread towards the eye. Because you are only exposing a very small portion of the thread, it has nowhere to go other than through the eye of the needle.

DESIGN AND USING COLOUR

In the case of silk shading, the term 'design' encompasses the image you want to embroider and also colour and composition. Designing is not a 'black art' and can be taught, just as embroidery can be. While you can copy an existing piece, it can be tremendously rewarding to design your own piece of work.

I suggest reading through the following pages on design and when you are ready to design your own piece, come back to them and try to apply the principles. Once you have finished your piece, you will truly be able to say it is all your own work.

Colour

It is essential to have a broad understanding of colour where silk shading is concerned. Colour can be a powerful and very personal tool, so it is worth taking the time to understand the basics: learning them will make the next stages so much easier.

HUE

Hue is a name for a specific colour: ultramarine and duck egg blue are both specific hues of the colour blue.

TONE

A measure of how dark or light something is. White is a light tone, grey a mid tone and black a dark tone. Light tones are tints of a particular colour, while dark tones are shades.

PRIMARY COLOURS

Red, yellow and blue. In painting, these cannot be mixed from other colours, but all other colours can be made from a mixture of these three.

SECONDARY COLOURS

Green, violet and orange. These colours are created when you mix together two primary colours. On the colour wheel (see below), they are the colours halfway between the primary colours used to make them.

COMPLEMENTARY COLOURS

Red/green; yellow/violet; blue/orange. These pairings of primary and secondary colours are opposite each other on the colour wheel (see below). These pairings will always go well together in a colour scheme.

OTHER COLOUR GROUPINGS

Contrasting colours are those that are opposite each other on the colour wheel, such as red and green, or blue and orange. These can be used to create striking effects: try picking a contrasting colour for your background to make your embroidery really stand out.
Analogous colours are colours that are next to each other on the colour wheel, such as red and orange, or blue and violet.

COLOUR TEMPERATURE

Broadly speaking, reds, oranges and yellows are warm, and blues and greens are cool. These overlap each other and you can get warm blues and cool reds, but all you need to worry about for embroidery is the basic warm and cool colours above, and that warm colours come forward while cool colours recede. If you are working a warm red flower, for example, you might want to consider a cool blue background to bring the flowers to the forefront of the design.

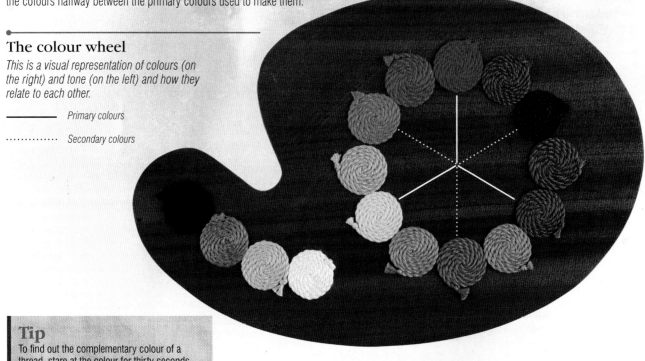

The colour wheel

This is a visual representation of colours (on the right) and tone (on the left) and how they relate to each other.

———— *Primary colours*

·············· *Secondary colours*

> **Tip**
> To find out the complementary colour of a thread, stare at the colour for thirty seconds then move your eyes to a white surface and the complementary colour will appear before your eyes!

COLOUR NUMBERING SYSTEM

Most commercial threads have a number to identify their unique hue. These colour ranges have often been altered over time, as some colours have been removed and new colours have taken their place, so what was once a logical numbering system is now rather disjointed. However, you can still use the numbers to help you choose your colours.

Colours come in family groups. You will find the numbers on the larger of the two labels. Take the Anchor stranded cottons 264–269, shown right, as an example. This range of six colours are all the same colour of green dyed in different tones from light to dark. The lightest tone is 264 and the darkest is 269, indicated by the last of the three numbers. (In other manufacturers this can be the other way around).

If you want to achieve a harmonious shading effect, make sure that the colours you use are from the same family group. This ensures that they all go together and that each skein has a different tonal value. Always try to use the lightest and darkest tones available in your piece to produce a really three-dimensional effect, even if it is just a little of each. For a dramatic shading effect put colours together with drastically different tonal numbers (e.g. a 1 with a 9). For a subtle, muted effect, use colours with tones in the middle of the range.

Anchor stranded cottons 264–269: different tones of the same colour.

Tip
If you put different colours that are the same tone together, then they will blend well together even though they are different colours. To test if colours are the same tone, photocopy them in black and white. If they come out the same grey colour they are the same tone. There are anomalies in all colour ranges so do not ignore your instincts.

DOS AND DON'TS WHEN CHOOSING COLOURS

- Do look at whole family groups of thread to see the range that is available to you.
- Do choose all of your colours together so you know that they all work well with each other.
- Do pick a good range of different tones, and include the lightest and darkest.
- Do look at and choose the colours in daylight, as artificial light will change how the colours appear.

- Don't pick too many colours, as this can get very confusing. Silk shading is about using colours together well, so let your eyes do some of the colour mixing for you. Remember, less can often be more.
- Don't rush this part. Take time to make sure you are happy with your selections.

Understanding colour will take a while to get the hang of, but once you do you will be applying it to all your embroidery from then on!

Tip
Investing in a shade card is worthwhile if you are going to do a lot of silk shading. You can see all the colours in front of you before you commit to buying individual ones.

Planning

A little bit of planning before you start your silk shading will make the embroidery stage so much easier. You may not use these stages so much as you become more experienced, but just the process of going through them on paper will help to clarify the stages in your head. Complete the following information for every piece you do, use it, and you cannot go wrong.

OUTLINE REFERENCE

This is a line drawing of your final design. Make sure that your lines are neat and that nothing is ambiguous. Rub out any lines that are mistakes so it is clear which lines are the final ones. Make copies of the outline reference drawing, both to use for the next planning stages and so you can make notes. You can also use this reference to make a pricking if you are pricking and pouncing on your design (see page 20 for more information on this technique).

Make this outline drawing clear and accurate. You could draw it in pencil first, and when you are happy with it, go over it in pen.

COLOUR AND TONAL REFERENCE

Your colour reference picture will usually be the photograph or painting that originally inspired you. Use it to select your thread colours. In addition, make a tonal reference (a black and white one!) of this picture. The easiest way to do this is to copy the colour picture on a black and white photocopier or scanner. This will help you to see the different tones without the confusion of the colours.

STITCH DIRECTION REFERENCE

This will help you to place your stitches so that they point in the right direction for the effect you are trying to achieve.

STITCH ORDER REFERENCE

This will tell you in which order to stitch the different parts of the design. In silk shading we start with the elements at the back so that the ones on the top can sit neatly on top of the back elements.

Note

Do not forget that every stage you do in a piece of embroidery affects the accuracy of the next stage, so be as accurate as you can from the beginning. Anything worth doing is worth doing properly.

Tip

You can also stitch the same design in a completely different colour range just by using the tonal reference picture.

This design board is for an iris image. It includes the original photograph that inspired the piece, thread ideas and an initial sketch in coloured pencils.

Tip

If you cannot remember to start with the elements at the back, just think 'silk shading is back to front'!

Note

A stitch direction reference is only needed if you are working your embroidery in natural shading (see page 174), not tapestry shading.

SILK-SHADING STITCH FINDER

Stitch	Page
ADDING BEADS	SEE PAGE 176
ADDING SEQUINS	SEE PAGE 176
BULLION KNOTS	SEE PAGE 67
EYELET STITCH	SEE PAGE 175
FRENCH KNOTS	SEE PAGE 66
LONG-AND-SHORT STITCH	SEE PAGE 174
RUNNING STITCH	SEE PAGE 57
SPLIT STITCH	SEE PAGE 58
STEM STITCH	SEE PAGE 56

Snow Scene
A delightful snow scene, that shows how light and texture can be suggested with silk shading. The origin of this piece is not known. (Personal collection of Shelley Cox)

Japanese panel
Japanese 19th century. (RSN Collection 1235)

STITCHES

Long-and-short stitch

This one stitch is what silk shading is all about. It is not a complicated stitch, but you should take the time to practise and understand it to help you with the later stages of creating embroideries. All silk shading is worked in long-and-short stitch. The angle of the stitch, however, defines the type of silk shading. The technique is split into two categories: natural silk shading and tapestry silk shading.

NATURAL SILK SHADING

The long-and-short stitch varies in direction depending on the shape of the design. For example, if a shape curves, then the stitches will curve with it (see Marbles on page 193). There is more information on natural silk shading on pages 184–185.

TAPESTRY SILK SHADING

In tapestry silk shading, the stitches are always worked in one direction (vertical or horizontal), regardless of the design shape (see *Houses* on page 197 for an example). As a result, for this type of shading you will not need to complete the stitch-direction reference stage of the planning.

In the example shown here, I have used a different colour for each row so you can clearly see what is happening. Use a size 10 or 12 embroidery needle; cut the length of embroidery cotton no longer than 30cm (12in) and pull out one strand from the cut length. Use a holding stitch (see page 39) to start and finish your threads.

- Note how much of each colour is visible when finished. Remember to allow for this later on, as you may need to work several rows in the same colour to achieve the effect that you want.
- To blend smoothly and avoid ridges across your stitching where each row starts, vary how far back you bring the needle from the previous row of stitches.
- Do not crowd your stitches together and, equally importantly, do not space them too far apart. They should lie comfortably next to each other.
- Finally: practise, practise, practise!

> ## Note
> *The horizontal lines are a guide to show you where to start and stop the rows. It is good practice to draw these on when you first work the stitch, but you will find you do not need these guides as you grow in experience.*

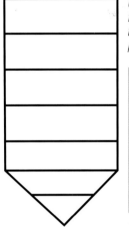

Copy this template on to a piece of cotton or silk. Back the fabric with cotton or calico and frame it up following any of the techniques on pages 16–19. Use a single strand of cotton to practise this stitch.

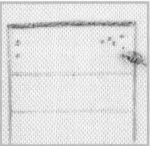

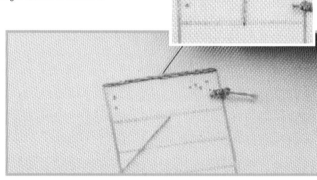

1 Work a row of split stitch (see page 58) along the top of the shape in one strand of the first colour you are going to use.

2 Start a new thread in the same colour near to the top of the shape. As the name suggests, the stitch consists of alternate long and short stitches. Make your first stitch a short one. Bring it up on the first line below the split stitch in the centre and take it down over the split stitch edge, tucking the needle as close as possible to the split stitch; pull through (see inset).

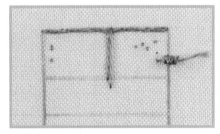

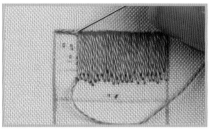

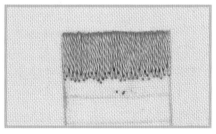

3 Work a longer stitch next to the first short stitch. Ensure the stitches lie next to each other and tuck in closely over the split-stitch edge.

4 Work to the right, stitching alternate long and short stitches until you reach the edge of the shape, then go back to the middle and work to the left.

5 Finish the thread inside the shape with two stab stitches near to where your last stitch finishes. Bring the needle to the top and cut off the thread close to the surface.

Note

In the first row, because you are working from the edge of the shape, the stitches are all of different lengths. From the second row onwards, all of the stitches will be of a similar length.

The stitches from this point on are brought up at different heights in the previous row of stitches, then down a uniform distance into the fabric. These two points ensure that the stitches blend well together.

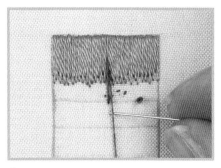

6 Start off the next colour in the same way as before, bringing the first stitch up in the centre through the previous row, splitting the stitches, then going down into the fabric near the second line and pull through. Work the row from the centre to one side edge, then from the centre to the other side, as before.

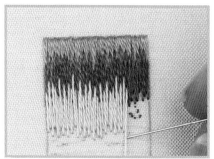

7 Repeat for the next rows, changing the thread colour for each row. Stagger where you bring up the needle for each stitch on these rows of stitches so that the colours blend smoothly.

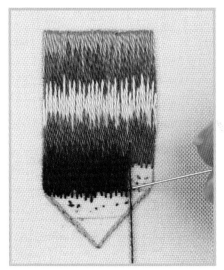

8 When you get near to the bottom of the shape, work a row of split stitch along the bottom in the colour of the final row. For the last two rows, take your needle down over the split-stitch edge as you reach it.

Note

Do not worry about changing direction at the moment, as this is covered later on. Simply practise threading needles, starting and finishing your threads and blending rows together.

9 Tuck the needle in closely to get a neat finish.

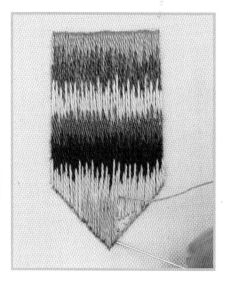

Eyelet stitch

This stitch is good for flowerheads and background decoration. It does not matter which part of the eyelet you start with, but always work your way round in a circle, finishing back at the point where you started.

• The centre is shared by all of the threads, so do not make a new hole for each one: always take your thread down in the centre of the stitch.

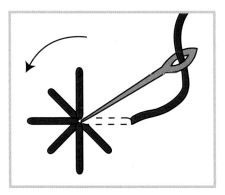

1 Bring your needle up at the edge of the eyelet shape, then down at the centre. Bring it up a little further along the edge of the eyelet shape, then down again in the centre. Repeat until you have completed the circle.

This is how the stitch will appear as you work. Make as many eyelets as you need.

You can vary the lengths of each spoke and the size of each eyelet for a different effect.

ADDING BEADS AND SEQUINS

The availability of such a huge variety of beads and sequins makes creating exciting designs easy. Use them sparingly but carefully to enhance your work and give it texture and reflections. For more ways to add beads, see pages 377–385.

Note

Make sure you use a needle small enough to go through the hole in the bead.

BEADS

1 Bring the thread up where you want the bead to sit, and thread the bead on to the needle.

2 Push the bead to the bottom of the thread. Take the needle into the fabric at the end of the bead.

Beads secured in place with stitches.

SEQUINS

1 Bring the needle up in the fabric where you want the centre of the sequin to lie. Thread the sequin on to your needle.

2 Push it down the thread until it lies flat on the surface of the fabric. Take the needle back down at the edge of the sequin.

SEQUINS AND BEADS

1 Bring the needle up where you want the bead and sequin to sit. Thread on the sequin and then the bead.

2 Push the sequin only to the bottom of the thread then take the needle back through the hole in the sequin.

 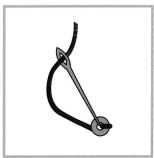

3 Draw the needle through, then bring it up on the opposite side of the sequin.

4 Take the needle back down through the centre of the sequin to secure it.

3 Pull the thread tight to secure both the sequin and bead in place.

A row of sequins secured in this way.

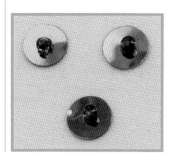

Sequins held in place with small beads. This method is good for showing as little thread as possible.

PADDING

You should use the technique of silk shading to make your piece look three-dimensional, but sometimes, when you are working silk shading with another technique, it helps to bring the silk shading forward. You can do this in two ways, depending on the shape and how much you want to pad something.

PADDING WITH FELT

This gives the embroidery a cushion to sit on and is a good method to use for padding a large area (see Endless Ocean on page 180).

> **Tip**
> When you draw around something it always comes out bigger. Cut to the inside of the line when you cut your shape out of the felt.

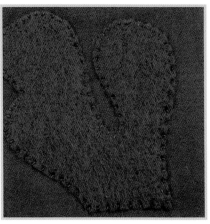

1 Choose a felt in a colour appropriate to the embroidery threads you will be using. Carefully cut out the required shape and use this as a template.

2 Pin the felt in place on your embroidery, then use stab stitch to work around the felt shape in a thread matching the colour of the felt.

3 Work your silk shading on top of this felt as you would on a single piece of fabric.

PADDING WITH STITCHES

You can also simply use stitches to pad smaller areas.

> **Tip**
> You can work more than one layer for deeper padding, but ensure that each subsequent layer is worked at a right angle to the previous layer and that the long-and-short stitch is worked at a right angle to the final layer of padding.

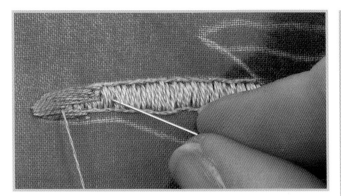

1 Use a similar colour for the padding as you want the area to end up. Work straight stitches inside the shape to fill the area you wish to be padded. Next, work long-and-short stitch (exactly as you would on an unpadded piece of fabric) at 90˚ to the direction of the layer of padding stitches.

Padding in this way gives you a lot of control over the depth of your piece, and is a good way to add texture and interest.

USING THE SURFACE STITCHES

The following pages show details of a completed piece of silk shading (see page 180). Every stitch explained has been used in this piece, but this is fairly unusual. You should aim to use the stitches where appropriate and to add to your work, not overpower it.

Stab stitch
Small stitches, half hidden at the bottom of the piece, have been used here in order to hold down the felt that makes up the coral.

Long-and-short stitch
As the focal point of the image, long-and-short stitch has been used to produce the fish's body, effectively re-creating the stunning colours and striking blend of textures.

Split stitch
The fish's fin has been worked in split stitch (see page 58) to give a lighter texture that is reminiscent of a real fish.

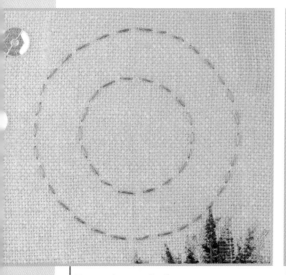

Running stitch
This stitch has been used to produce a subtle effect on the painted background.

Stem stitch
This is a great stitch for producing stem and plant effects, and so it has been used here to represent the seaweed on the rocks.

Eyelet stitch
This stitch helps to create an effective texture on the rocks.

178

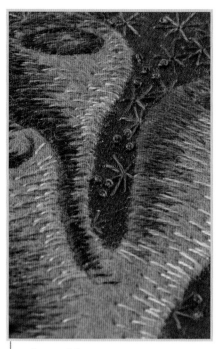

Felt padding
The coral was brought forward from the rocks with felt padding (see page 177).

French knots
Used alongside the eyelet stitches on the rocks, French knots help to create texture.

Bullion knots
Good for creating texture and interest, bullion knots were used here to create plants.

Beads
Applied to the bottom of this piece, beads add an extra layer of depth and give a sparkle to the sea floor.

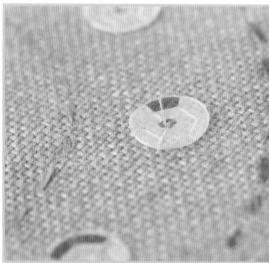

Sequins
Sequins have been used sparingly across the piece to add a sparkle to the water.

179

Endless Ocean

Worked on a painted background fabric and utilising a range of techniques, this piece is a playful example of what is possible with silk-shading embroidery.

Detail from Egyptian Panel

The background is linen that has been hand-painted with watercolour paint to look like papyrus. The falcon is completely worked in natural silk shading, while the hieroglyphs are hand stitched in a fine sewing thread. English 20th century.
(Sarah Homfray's personal collection)

GETTING STARTED

Simple shapes

Now you know all of the basics, you can begin silk shading. Frame up a small piece of fabric (I have used a piece of painted cotton for the sample) with a backing piece of calico or plain cotton in a ring frame. Make the fabric big enough to go on your chosen frame. Transfer the vase design on to your fabric using the outline drawing below. If you are using a lightbox or window, do this before you frame up the fabric.

TAPESTRY SHADING – VASE

Use just three colours to start with: a light tone, a medium tone and a dark tone. The colours I have used are Anchor stranded cotton 109, 110 and 112. Pull out a strand no longer than 30cm (12in) in the medium tone and thread a size 10 embroidery needle.

Tip
You can use the tonal reference picture if you want to use different colours: blue instead of purple, for example. Just pick a light, medium and dark thread in the colour of your choice.

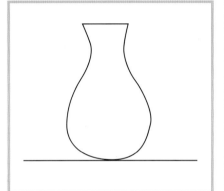

The outline reference picture for the vase worked in tapestry shading (actual size).

The colour reference picture for the vase worked in tapestry shading.

The tonal reference picture for the vase worked in tapestry shading.

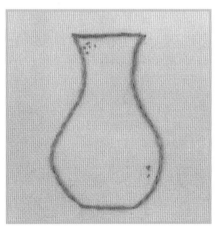

1 Starting at one of the corners, work split stitch (see page 58) around the whole of the shape in the medium tone. Start and finish your thread within the shape using holding stitches (see page 39).

2 Using the darkest tone, start your thread in the shape near to the top. Start your long-and-short stitch in the middle with a long stitch. Come up inside the shape and go down over the split-stitch edge. Using the same colour for the whole of the first row, work first to the right-hand side, then go back to the middle and work across to the left-hand side, keeping all of the stitches vertical.

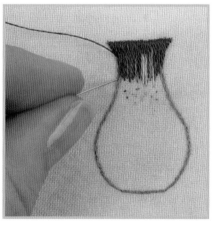

3 For the second row, thread strands of the other two tones and start both needles off inside the shape. Work the second row in long-and-short stitch using the two lighter tones, swapping between the needles to get the correct colour as you work, using the colour or tonal reference picture as a guide.

182

4 Continuing to refer to the colour or tonal reference picture, work the remaining rows in the same way. Do not jump about with your stitches; try to keep to the system of working in rows, changing your colours regularly.

You can turn your shape into a simple finished design by adding some of the stitches previously covered. Here, I have added stem-stitch stems (see page 56) and French knots for the flowers (see page 66) and a row of long-and-short stitch for the vase to stand on.

NATURAL SHADING – VASE

Here we work the same shape but with natural silk shading, where the stitches flow with the shapes of the design.

Start as before, framing up your fabric, transferring your design and split stitching around the edge in the mid-tone colour. You could work both versions on the same piece of fabric.

The outline reference picture for the vase worked in natural shading (actual size).

The colour reference picture for the vase worked in natural shading.

The tonal reference picture for the vase worked in natural shading.

The stitch-direction reference picture for the vase worked in natural shading.

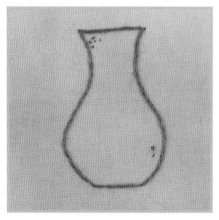

1 Starting at one of the corners, thread a size 10 embroidery needle and work split stitch around the whole of the shape in the medium tone. Start and finish your thread within the shape using holding stitches.

Tip

You may find it helps to draw stitch-direction lines straight on to your fabric as I have done. Use a colouring pencil that is a similar colour to your threads and put on the minimum number of lines you need to guide you.

2 Start your first row in exactly the same way as you do for tapestry shading (see step 2 on page 182). Start from the middle and work to the right. Refer to the stitch-direction plan to see which direction each stitch should go. In this first row, the stitch direction changes only very slightly; as you come to the end of the row, the bottom of the stitches start to lean towards the centre of the shape. Note that there are two colours in this first row, the medium tone and the dark tone. Bring your second colour in as you work to the left, working just a few stitches in this colour.

3 The second row contains all three colours so make sure these are threaded in separate needles and ready to use. Again, start from the centre and work to one side first and then the other, carefully placing your stitches next to each other. Use the directional lines to make sure they point in the right direction.

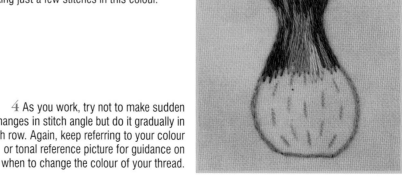

4 As you work, try not to make sudden changes in stitch angle but do it gradually in each row. Again, keep referring to your colour or tonal reference picture for guidance on when to change the colour of your thread.

5 Continue to work the remaining rows in the same way. Do not jump about with your stitches; try to keep to the system of working in rows, changing your colours regularly.

Adding some of the other stitches helps turn this exercise into a finished design. Here I have added stems using stem stitch, bullion knots for the flowers and rows of stem stitch for the vase to stand on.

COMPLEX SHAPES

TAPESTRY SHADING – CARROT

When you have got the hang of long-and-short stitch in the vase shape, why not try something a little more complex? This carrot is worked in tapestry shading and is made up of several sections so now there is more to think about. Do not panic; apply each stage of the process, as previously discussed, and you will be fine.

Preparation

Start by choosing your fabric. This example is worked on silk dupion. Trace the outline design on to your fabric (I would suggest the lightbox or window transferring method, shown on page 20), then place it on top of the backing fabric and frame up.

Next, use the colour reference picture below to choose your colours. You can use the colours that I used or choose your own if you feel more confident. Note that all the orange tones are from the same family group and the green tones are another family group.

Stitching

Work split stitch around the whole of the carrot (I shaded my split stitch dark on one side and light on the other in line with the colours that the carrot will be shaded in) then choose the colours for the first row.

The leaves are behind the carrot, so work them before you start the carrot or before you finish the last section. I coloured the leaves in with coloured pencils (these work nicely on silk) and worked the outline and inner detail with split stitch.

Starting at the tip of the carrot, work your first row of long-and-short stitch, placing your first stitch right into the point of the tip. Next, work up to the first line on the outline reference picture. When you reach this line, work split stitch along the line then stitch the next row of long-and-short stitch over the split stitch to get the ridges.

As you work, refer to the colour-reference picture for changes in colour. Break the carrot down into individual shapes and work each one separately, as if it was a single shape on its own. Work up to each line before you split stitch it. This makes it much easier to work and you do not get carried away with an area you are not yet ready to start.

The tonal reference picture for the carrot.

The colour reference picture for the carrot. All threads are Anchor stranded cotton. The colours used: oranges: 300, 301, 302, 303 and 304; greens: 255, 256 and 258.

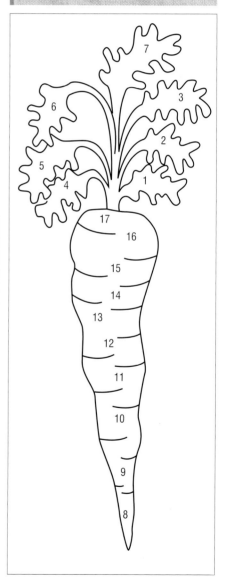

The outline reference and stitch-order diagram for the carrot.

186

Carrot

This carrot was worked on silk dupion and is a good example of how tapestry shading can give a full, rounded appearance. The leaves were worked in coloured pencil and split stitch.

NATURAL SHADING – BANANA

This project shows how to work a more complex shape in natural shading. Again, follow all the design stages carefully and remember to use this information as you stitch. Bananas have a lovely natural gentle curve to them so this is a good project in which to practise changing stitch direction.

The colours of a banana are very subtle, so look carefully. You will probably be surprised at which ones you choose! Bananas are readily available, so get an actual one and work from that.

Frame up your desired fabric and transfer your design as before, then split stitch around the top of the banana in a colour similar to one you will be stitching with. Choose a neutral colour for the split stitches if you are unsure.

Look at the colour reference picture and stitch-order diagram and choose the colours that are going to be in the first row. Thread them ready to use. Use the stitch-direction diagram and colour reference picture to work the banana.

Tip
Cover the area of the reference picture you are not working on with a blank piece of white paper. This helps you to focus on just the area you are working.

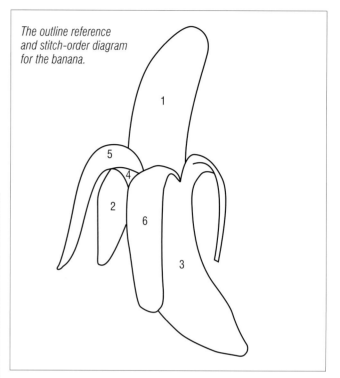

The outline reference and stitch-order diagram for the banana.

The colour reference picture for the banana. All threads are DMC stranded cotton. The colours used are: 732, 733, 734, 372, 307, 445, 3819, ecru and black.

The tonal reference picture for the banana.

The stitch-direction reference picture for the banana.

Tip
If you are choosing colours from an image, turn the image upside down. This helps the brain to detach itself from what the item actually is and you can look at the colours more objectively.

Banana

Like the carrot on the previous pages, this project was worked on silk dupion. Note how the natural shading allows the curve of the shape to be realistically represented.

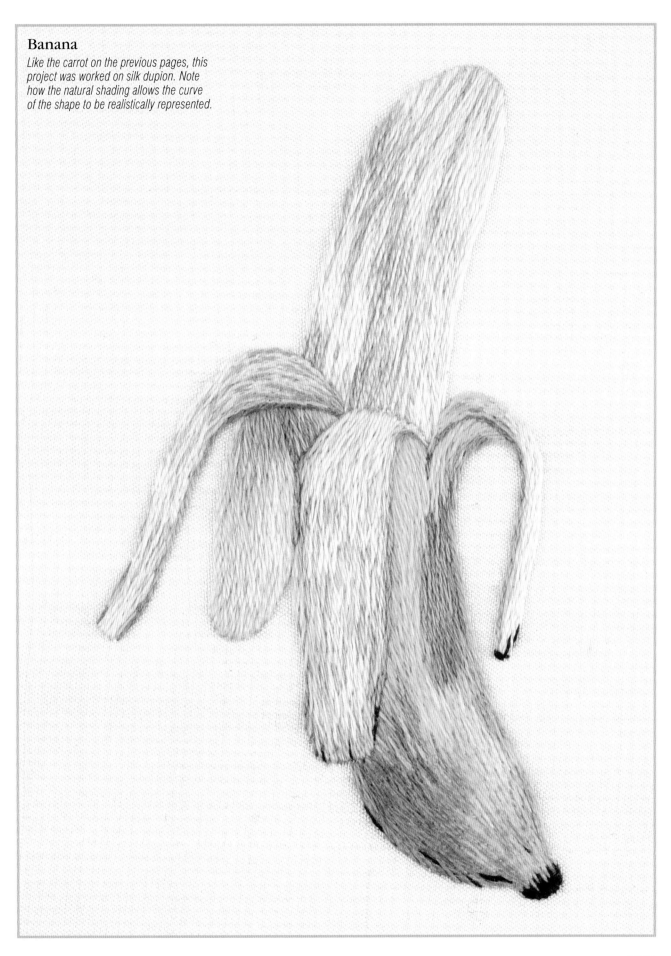

PROJECTS TO STITCH

The following pages look at some examples of silk shading in more detail, with each finished piece shown alongside notes to help you stitch it. Each project helps to develop a specific skill, building up to the more complex and rewarding Autumn Leaves on pages 198–199.

Blue Curves

This exercise aims to give you practice at getting around tighter curves by working separate parts of a piece. Once you have mastered this, you will find it easy to tackle any shape.

Select an area of the design to practise on and choose just three tones to work with. You can, of course, work the whole design if you like!

The curves are tight on this design, so shorten your stitches to get round them. Do not panic and turn them too soon. Turn each row slightly more than the last one and you will get comfortably around the shapes.

Split stitch around the shape and work from the outside edges towards the point with your long-and-short stitches. Until you get the hang of working tighter curves, it is a good idea to mark your stitch direction lines faintly on the fabric.

The tonal reference picture for the curves.

The outline reference picture for the curves.

The stitch-direction reference picture for the curves.

The colour reference picture for the curves. All threads are Anchor stranded cotton. The colours used are: 133, 131 and 130.

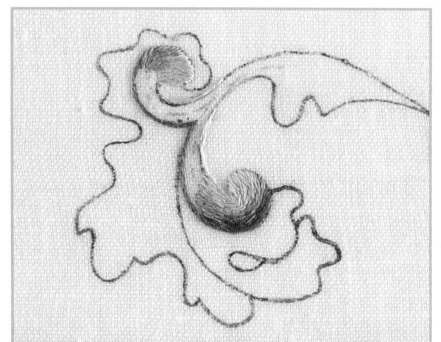

All of the elements involved are shown here: the split-stitch edge, direction lines and the first few rows of long-and-short stitch.

Sections from the Blue Curves

Look carefully at the angles of the stitches around the curves. Use this picture to help you with your practice.

Marbles

This is a good exercise in blending different tones together. Marbles are smooth and shiny, so you want to try to blend your colours together as smoothly as possible. This means picking tones that are similar and from the same colour family if possible.

I used the tissue-paper method (see page 20) to transfer this design on to my chosen silk. I was not confident of creating perfect circles so the stitching allowed me to make any corrections I needed to.

I started with the red area on the right-hand marble. The only part of the design to have a split-stitch outline is the outer edge of each marble.

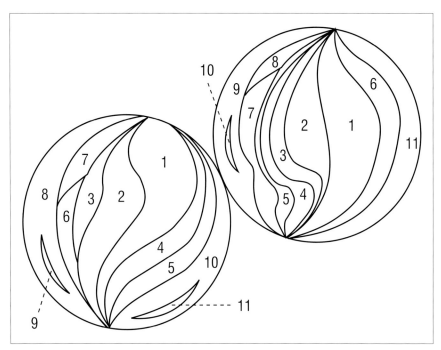

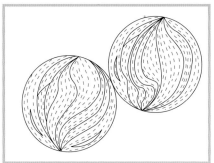

The stitch-direction reference picture for the marbles.

The outline and stitch-order reference picture for the marbles. Note that since each marble is completely separate, each has a stitch order starting from 1. Pick whichever you like to begin.

The tonal reference picture for the marbles.

The colour reference picture for the marbles. All threads are Anchor stranded cotton. The colours used are:
reds: 36, 42 and 43;
blues: 132 and 134;
turquoises: 185, 187, 189, 1068 and 1092;
greens: 254, 255 and 258;
browns: 906, 907 and 277;
white: 2.

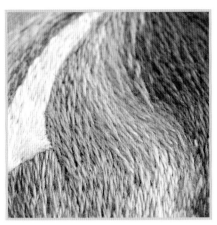

Concentrate on blending the colours together within the bands of colour to get a smooth-looking effect on the finished piece.

Note how the stitches change direction around the bottom of the blue area as the shape curves more dramatically.

Marbles

The finished marbles, worked on a China silk background.

Poppy

Flower subjects lend themselves beautifully to the technique of silk shading. They have subtle curves, rich colours and come in an endless variety of shapes and sizes. They are, however, often very complex. This poppy will introduce you to stitching a simple flower. There are only three petals to stitch and some gently curving stems.

Red can be a difficult colour for the embroiderer. If you want to use red, I advise checking the colours available first. Different tones of blue, for example, become light blue or dark blue, whereas red actually changes colour when it is lightened or darkened and can become pink, salmon, brown or orange.

Note

This stylised poppy shows that your designs do not always have to be true to life to be effective.

The outline and stitch-order reference picture for the poppy.

The tonal reference picture for the poppy.

The stitch-direction reference picture for the poppy.

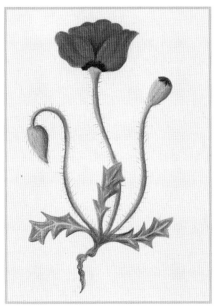

The colour reference picture for the poppy.
All threads are Anchor stranded cotton.
The colours used are:
reds: 11, 13, 45 and 799;
greens: 243, 244 and 246;
black: 403.

Hairs on the stem have been suggested with
the use of single stitches.

Black is a very strong colour, so use it sparingly
to enhance your silk shading.

Poppy

I wanted this design to look like an old
botanical painting where the paper has aged.
To achieve this I took a piece of white linen
and dyed it with a tea bag (see page 205 for
more information on this technique). It is a
simple process, but one that puts the design
into context.

Houses

This design aims to show you the type of subject that suits tapestry shading. The stitch goes straight up and down so I have picked a fairly simple design of buildings, which is good for practising the technique.

Up until now I have used fairly plain backgrounds. Now I have brought in a patterned background to show you what effect this can have on the overall design. Choose carefully, as the background should complement the design, not overwhelm it.

The stitch order may look complicated, but essentially I have worked the windows and doors first then just worked left to right with the houses.

As your design gets more complicated, the planning stages become more important, so do not neglect these.

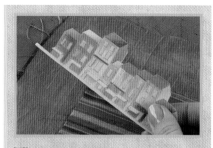

Tip

If you are not sure about the background, photocopy the image you want to shade, cut it out and place it on top of different fabrics to see what effect they will give.

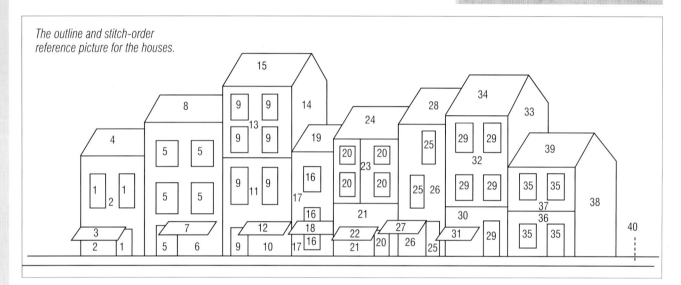

The outline and stitch-order reference picture for the houses.

The colour reference picture for the houses. All threads are Anchor stranded cotton. The colours used are:
pinks: 1029, 85 and 89;
browns: 905, 341 and 359;
reds: 20 and 47;
greens: 255 and 268;
yellows: 290 and 293;
oranges: 314, 319 and 326;
windows: 1090;
shades: 254.

The tonal reference picture for the houses.

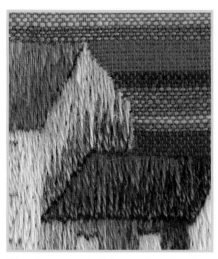

Where two areas of stitches meet, such as in this detail, make sure that there are no gaps between the stitches.

I have used two rows of stem stitches to ground the houses (see page 14 for more information on grounding).

Houses

This design was inspired by the coloured village buildings of the Cinque Terre coast on the Italian Riviera. It is stitched on cotton fabric.

Autumn Leaves

This subject is one that I love: nature when it is past its best and nearing the end of its life. Unexpected shapes develop and the colours change dramatically as the leaf enters its final moments. Often studying natural forms like this can inspire more interesting designs than a perfect green leaf.

I found these leaves on the ground outside my house and photographed them. I then did a watercolour study of them, changing the composition slightly to improve the leaves' positions relative to each other. It is from this study that I took my direction when working the embroidery.

In order that the stitches flowed with the shapes of the design, I decided to work the embroidery in natural shading (see pages 184–185 and 188–189). This meant I needed a stitch-direction reference picture.

The watercolour painting of the leaves (top) provided me with my colour reference picture; the original leaves are shown below. All threads are Anchor stranded cotton. The colours used are:
reds: 336, 338, 339 and 341;
browns: 1086 and 1088;
orange: 1004;
beiges: 361, 362, 363, 4146 and 914.

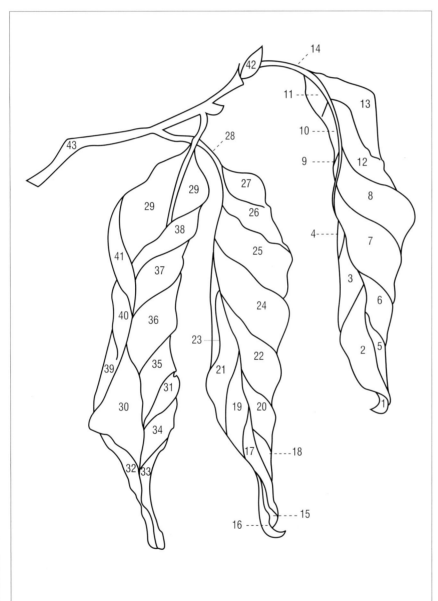

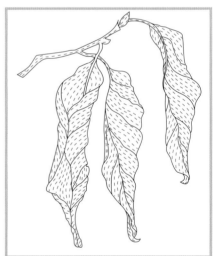

The stitch-direction reference picture for the leaves.

The stitch order for this piece looks complex, but if you follow the numbers from 1–43 you will see a logical system emerge. If you work this out beforehand, you can concentrate on the embroidery. Again, apply all the same processes and rules as before and work one section at a time.

This piece is quite an involved one, so just concentrate on one leaf at a time, one area at a time. There are a lot of colours, so you might have about six or seven different colours threaded up and in use at once. If you need to change the thread for one or two stitches then do so, it is this detail that will give the piece realism.

Autumn Leaves

This piece has been composed to give the impression that the leaves are at the end of their life and about to drop from the branch. While they are not really going to drop, the space below the leaves helps to place this idea in the viewer's mind, which gives a dramatic effect.

Single stitches have been used carefully to add texture.

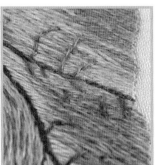

Stem stitch has been used in order to represent veins on the leaves.

When areas of silk shading cross over each other, such as the twigs in this detail, the area at the back must be worked first.

Here you can see the effect of natural shading, with three areas of stitching worked in three distinct directions.

TAKING YOUR WORK FURTHER

Other designs

Once you have got the actual method of silk shading perfected, you can start to think about design a little more. Flowers are a popular subject, but there are many others for which silk shading is appropriate – just think outside the box a little! Why not use an abstract painting as your inspiration? You could add other stitches and other embroidery methods into your piece.

ABSTRACT DESIGNS

All abstract pieces of art come from somewhere and often start life as something quite figurative (i.e. something that is clearly derived from a real object). The following piece was inspired by an artist called Kandinsky. Kandinsky started off painting figurative works, but as time went on his pieces became more abstract as he reacted to what was happening politically at the time.

This design is inspired by his later work and uses geometric forms and simple lines. I have used subtle muted colours and added felt and sequins for extra texture. I tried many design variations and colour combinations on paper first before settling on the final design. If you are going to spend a long time stitching something, it is worth taking the time to get it right.

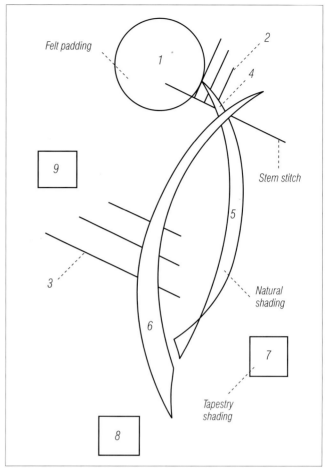

The outline and stitch-order reference picture for the abstract design.

The colour reference picture for the abstract design. All threads are Anchor stranded cotton. The colours used are:
greens: 264 and 265;
pinks: 48 and 49;
turquoise: 1092.

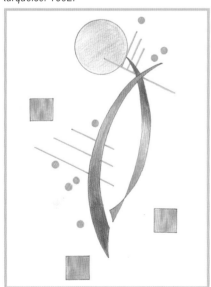

The tonal reference picture for the abstract design.

200

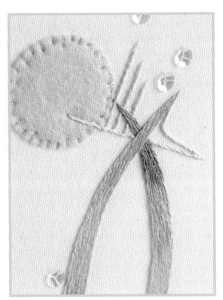

When using different techniques together, think carefully about the order in which you work them. Here, I stitched the felt first, then the stem stitch and finally worked the silk shading.

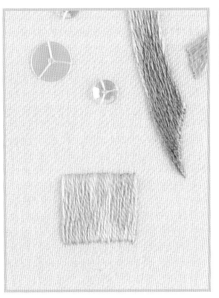

A combination of tapestry and natural shading has been used in this piece, and the contrast between the two is important. It is therefore essential that the straight stitches in the squares are perfectly straight. Ensure you stitch them on the grain of the fabric.

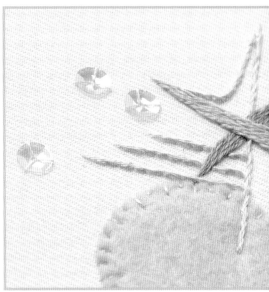

The sequins have been stitched down individually. Each has three stitches worked into the centre to hold them securely in place.

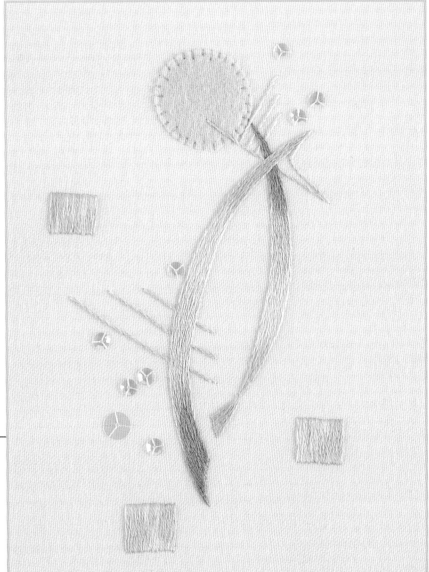

After Kandinsky

The finished design is stitched on soft cotton using felt, cotton threads, stem stitch and long-and-short stitch and is embellished with sequins.

Working with different threads

All of the projects on the previous pages have been worked mainly in cotton, but the name of this technique is silk shading, so it is only appropriate that we have a look at silk more closely. Silk can come in different forms and twisted silk can be used just as stranded cottons are used. This section concentrates on unspun floss silk, as this is the material in which pieces from the Far East are traditionally worked.

FLOSS SILK

Because floss silk is unspun, it does not have anything to hold the fibres together when you stitch with it. You need to temporarily stick the fibres together while you stitch with them. One way of doing this is to wet them. Dampen a piece of kitchen paper and slide the thread through this just before you stitch with it. It will dry very quickly and the fibres will lie smooth and flat.

Use short lengths so the thread does not dry before you finish stitching with it. Depending on the thickness of your silk thread, which can vary from supplier to supplier, you should use either a size 10 or 12 needle. For very fine work you can strand the fibres down further.

Note

You do not have to work long-and-short stitch in different colours. Stitch blocks of colour as I have done here for a flatter effect. This works well in silks as the light catches the fibres giving an impression of more tones.

Stylised Flower

I worked this simple stylised flower with floss silk. It is harder to use than stranded cottons, so start with something simple until you get used to working with this thread.

Tip

If you cannot find the colour of silk fabric you want, why not paint your own as I have done? Silk paints are widely available in different colours and are easy to use. I practise on a spare piece of silk (see above) to try out different colour combinations and effects.

Silk flower placemat

Lots of everyday items benefit from some decorative embroidery work, such as this beautiful placemat worked in silk. Chinese 21st century. (Sarah Homfray's personal collection)

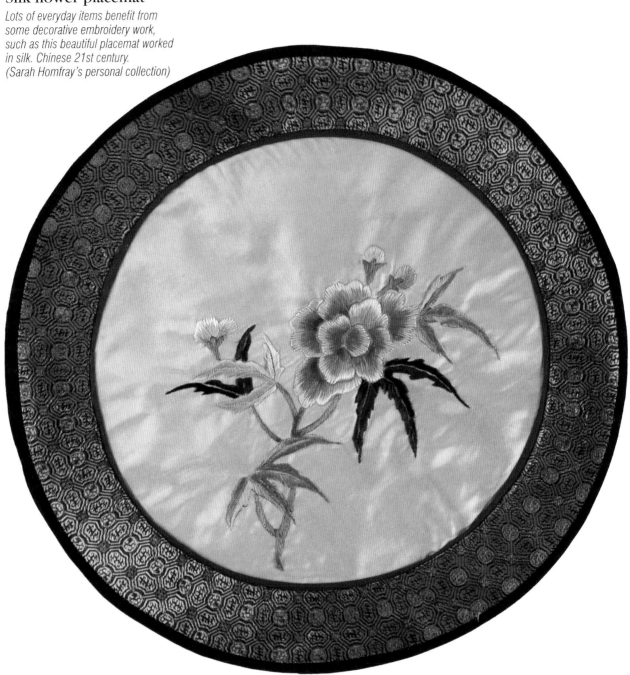

The leaves are stitched in a single colour, but note how the shine of the silk gives the impression of different tones.

This detail of a flower is a good example of a stylised design that still looks realistic.

Working with different fabrics

Although silk is a fabulous surface on which to work the technique of silk shading, do not be afraid to have a go on something completely different.

Denim is a great modern fabric, known for its hard-wearing qualities and tough structure. It is not something you would immediately associate with the delicate art of silk shading! They may seem like incompatible materials and techniques at first, but as this example demonstrates, they can offer a great contrast.

DENIM

I used this stylised peacock feather design to embellish a pocket on a denim jacket that I had. Think about what threads might best suit the design you are working. I have used rayon threads here; they have a shimmer to them that seemed to mimic the iridescence of a peacock feather.

An actual peacock feather provided the inspiration for the final design.

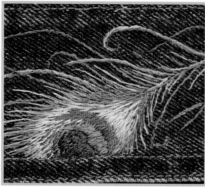

Stem stitch was used to represent the stem and individual parts of the feather. The feather has been stitched to fit the shape of the pocket. Think carefully about the placement of motifs like this before you start your silk shading.

If you wish to try this yourself, you can use this coloured-pencil drawing as your outline and colour reference drawings.

Peacock jacket

The fabric is heavy, so I was not too concerned about getting it drum tight in the frame, as it would not be at this tension when finished. I did not back the denim as the stitching was not going to be that dense and denim is already a heavyweight fabric.

Painted backgrounds

One way to put your design into context is to place it on an appropriate background. You may need more than just a different coloured fabric or a patterned fabric, so why not have a go at painting your own? You do not have to be an artist to do this; a simply painted background can be just as effective.

There are many paints suitable for fabric, and for the silk shading projects in this book. I have used fabric paints (see Endless Ocean on page 180 for an example), silk paints (see **Stylised Flower** on page 202) and watercolour paints. These are all water based, which means you can mix them with water to thin them down. Clean your brushes in water afterwards.

Use a plain white cotton fabric for trying out the following samples. This is an excellent material for painting on and is inexpensive so you do not have to worry if it does not come out as you wish the first few times. Frame up a piece of fabric – interlocking frames or silk-painting frames are good for this. Get yourself two pots of clean water, some kitchen paper and several soft brushes of different shapes and sizes, and then begin.

Note

Fabric paints and silk paints are already watered down to a consistency with which you can paint. If you use watercolour paint, you will need to dilute it with water to get it to a workable consistency.

MARK MAKING

Use different parts of the brush to make marks on the fabric in paint. Roll it, dab with the point, make long lines and try some circles. Just experiment as much as you can to see what effects you can get, as in the example below.

COLOUR MIXING

For a spontaneous effect drop the paint on and let it spread. Dip the brush in the paint and hold it over the fabric until the paint drips. Change colours to see what happens when the colours mix. Try just dropping clean water on to the fabric. This will affect the way the colour mixes. Do not fiddle with the paint, just drop it and let the paint mix itself (this works best with very watery paints). If you do not like the effect, wait for the piece to dry, then drip more paint on. You can also sprinkle on rock salt while the paint is wet, as shown below. It will soak up the paint and leave interesting marks.

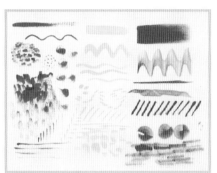

Tip
Painting can produce unexpected results. Sometimes you might like the result and other times you will not, so allow yourself some extra material and practise first. Do not be afraid to experiment and have a go. After all, the worst that can happen is that you will need to get a new piece of fabric.

TONAL PAINTING

Paint over the top of previous layers to add depth. Paint one layer and wait for it to dry before adding another layer. To make an area lighter, dab the fabric with a damp piece of tissue to soak up some of the paint.

OTHER BACKGROUNDS

Another way of getting a different background is to dye it. There are commercial dyes available that are easy to use, and many different methods of dyeing. One method that you can do at home without buying any equipment is tea-bag dyeing.

Make up a container of tea using tea bags. Use less water and more tea bags for a stronger dye, and vice versa for a more subtle dye. Place the fabric on a piece of plastic (you could use plastic carrier bags) and dab the tea bags on to the fabric. Press them down harder to get a stronger effect. If you wet your fabric first (as previously) the colour will soak into the fabric more evenly. Leave it to dry for a more marbled effect.

The tea will dry lighter so remember to allow for this. Again experiment with different strengths and application methods. If the effect is too strong you can rinse it under the tap to wash out some of the tea.

BLENDING

Blend different colours together. Paint two separate colours next to each other, then use a clean brush dampened with water to blend the two colours together.

Safety note

You will need to pick up the tea bags so it is important to let the water cool down to body temperature.

I used this technique on Poppy (page 195) to create an aged look. The tea dye was made up in a cereal bowl and used two tea bags, which gave quite a strong result. This technique is also good for toning down a bright white fabric.

Putting it all together

We have had a look at the two types of silk shading, different materials to stitch on, different threads to stitch with, composition, colour and context. The project that follows uses all of these aspects of silk shading together.

The design was inspired by a model of a Jicarilla Apache. The skin colours and textures were what drew me to this particular piece. However, I did not want simply to place the figure in the middle of a piece of fabric.

I researched the Jicarilla Apache and found images of the types of terrain in which they live. Because of the difference in scale between the head and the landscape, I chose to place my Apache in the foreground of the design. The background (painted in watercolour paints on cotton) suggests he is in his home environment, perhaps away from his settlement hunting.

The outline and stitch-direction references diagram for the Apache.

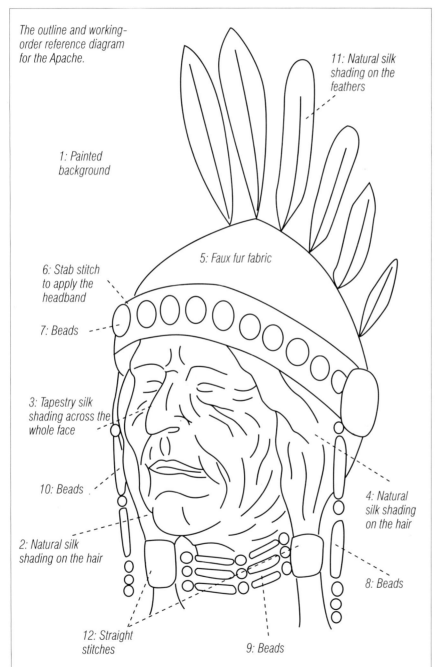

The outline and working-order reference diagram for the Apache.

11: Natural silk shading on the feathers

1: Painted background

5: Faux fur fabric

6: Stab stitch to apply the headband

7: Beads

3: Tapestry silk shading across the whole face

10: Beads

2: Natural silk shading on the hair

4: Natural silk shading on the hair

8: Beads

12: Straight stitches

9: Beads

The tonal reference diagram for the Apache's face and hair.

206

The background is painted on white cotton using watercolour tube paints. Details were added once the paint was dry.

This detail of the stitching on the face demonstrates how you can get lots of shading into a tapestry-stitch design, even though all of the stitches are straight.

The Apache is heavily adorned with animal furs and beads. I thought these would look flat in stitching so I applied faux fur fabric for the headwear and used real beads for his adornments.

Jicarilla Apache

The face and the mountains are placed according to the divisions of the rule of thirds. The Apache faces inwards but is actually looking at the viewer. This keeps the viewer looking within the picture. To finish I added some surface stitching to the bushes on the left to bring them to the front of the landscape and to tie the background and Apache together.

FURTHER IDEAS FOR YOUR OWN DESIGNS

Highland Cow

The white space is important in the design, as it indicates that the cow is standing in deep snow, so only small areas of the linen background were painted with watercolour paints. English 20th century. (Personal collection of Derek Watson)

Rose Canina

Note the variety of colours used in the leaf and stem of this dog rose, and how natural shading conveys the soft curves and delicacy of the petals. English 21st century. (Personal collection of Anja von Kalinowski)

Biggles

This wirehaired dachshund is worked in natural silk shading, a versatile technique that is perfect for capturing the texture of fur. English 21st century. (Personal collection of Derek Watson)

TROUBLESHOOTING

Whenever you are learning how to do silk shading, you may come across problems that you are not sure how to solve. The following pointers should help you to get past any problems you might come across on your stitching journey.

THE THREADS LOOK FLAT AND FLUFFY

When you are nearing the end of a piece, the threads you have stitched can start to look fluffy and flat. This is where you have leaned on the work or covered it with tissue or cotton to keep it clean. Run a needle point lightly along the length of the threads. This will separate them and they will look fresh and newly stitched.

AT WHAT ANGLE SHOULD THE STITCHES BE WORKED?

If you are working tapestry shading, all of your stitches are always vertical or horizontal. If you are working natural shading, the stitches flow with the direction of the object. This is illustrated well on the Banana (see pages 188–189). You may find drawing faint guide lines on to your design in a coloured pencil (similar to the thread colour you are using) helps you.

THE THREADS ARE GETTING TANGLED

Use shorter lengths of thread. Bring any thread that you are not currently using to the top of the fabric to help prevent it from becoming knotted. If your threads keep breaking, again, use shorter lengths or loosen the tension.

WHICH COLOURS SHOULD I CHOOSE?

Look at your source material and choose what you can actually see and not what you think you can see. Do not choose too many colours – keep it to a maximum of about fifteen for a bigger project. Look at family groups and try to pick light tones and dark tones. Look at the section on colour on pages 170–171.

THE STITCHING IS LUMPY

You have too many stitches in your work. Go back to the long-and-short stitch example on pages 174–175 for more practice on placing your stitches slightly further apart.

I CAN SEE THE FABRIC THROUGH THE STITCHING

You do not have enough stitches in your work. Again, go back to pages 174–175 and practise placing your stitches closer to each other.

I DO NOT KNOW WHICH PART TO STITCH FIRST

Silk shading is always worked from the back to front: i.e. the elements that are behind other elements are worked first, and those on top last. Number your design, starting with number 1 for the part of the design that is the furthest away. See page 172 for more information.

ON WHICH OF THE EDGES SHOULD SPLIT STITCH BE WORKED?

Final edges need a split stitch under them. Split stitch gives a neat edge to the work and is used to raise one design edge over another. If two areas of stitching meet, then the area on top should have a split-stitch outline where the two parts meet. If you can remember this, you should be able to work out which edges need split stitch.

THE EDGES ARE NOT VERY NEAT

Make sure your split stitch is neat (make smaller stitches if you need to) and tuck your stitch closely into the split-stitch edge.

I AM FINDING IT HARD TO GET ROUND A CURVE

Shorten your stitches and check against the drawing that you are working the same angle. Draw directional lines straight on to your embroidery if you find it necessary. See pages 190–191 for more information.

THE COLOURS DO NOT LOOK BLENDED

Use more colours, and change between them more regularly. Thread up lots of needles in different colours before you start, as if they are ready you are more likely to use them.

THE ROWS OF STITCHES APPEAR RIDGED

To avoid unsightly ridges, make sure you stagger where you bring the needle out of the thread itself when splitting it with the needle. Make sure each stitch is started further forward or further back than the one it sits next to. See pages 174–175.

Apples

Still-life studies are a very popular subject for natural silk shading.
English 21st century. (Personal collection of Helen Wharam)

Sam

This rendering of a Siamese cat in natural silk shading shows wonderful tonal balance. Note the subtly patterned background in a cool blue colour. This has the effect of bringing the cat forward. English 21st century. (Personal collection of Rebecca Ray)

GOLDWORK

Fearless Freedom
*Worked by Helen McCook. Japanese thread, copper, gilt and silver bright check thread,
and assorted stranded cotton threads on a linen ground. See also page 220.*

See also page 255.   See also page 215.   See also page 256.

FROM THE AUTHOR

Long before I ever held an embroidery needle and became immersed in the fine tradition that is the world of bespoke embroidery, I recognised that the beauty of metal thread work held a strong appeal for me – with its sculptural, tactile qualities, its deeply rooted symbolism and simply for the look of it and the way it catches the light.

Metal thread work is such an intriguing part of embroidery for many reasons, but perhaps part of its allure is the glamour that it evokes with all its embedded associations in our psyche and across so many differing cultural, political and religious backgrounds.

Let us not forget the qualities of the metal itself, which has an innate warmth and universal appeal. It is no surprise that almost every civilisation has revered this metal and used it to celebrate the most important landmarks in their lives. Some might say that this is the chosen material of the elite, used to emphasise their elevated status.

It is tactile before even being worked, becomes more so through the craftsmanship and diligence of our splendid gold and silver wyre drawers, and is enhanced by the artisan hand embroiderers who strive to use this most popular of techniques to better what has gone before and bring beauty to others through their efforts.

The subtle manipulation of the padding, type and size of metal thread chosen, the direction in which the thread is stitched, and the colour chosen to hold the metal thread down, create a delicate shift in the way the textile reflects the light and can alter it from simply being a flat embroidery to a piece that interacts with the light. The light – and therefore the viewer's eye – should dance across its surface.

A particularly intriguing facet to the art of metal-thread embroidery is the fact that it is an ever-changing art form, not only in style of design but also in its basest form; the very thread with which you work is made to change. The tarnishing process is a natural part of this technique to the extent that some might call goldwork the study of elegant decay. It is this response to time, damp, heat and the air – all of the elements, in truth, that we ourselves respond to – which ultimately makes metal thread work fascinating to me. It emphasises the limits to my control. I may be able to spend hours fashioning the thread into a beautiful embroidery but ultimately it will be fashioned by greater forces than myself. And everybody reacts to that fact differently: some try to control this alteration, with airtight frames, carefully controlled room temperature and storage conditions, or simply by their choice of threads. Others embrace the unpredictability of the alterations. It is truly a technique that encourages you to embrace the differences not only in it but also in yourself!

I hope I can introduce you to a subject that offers so much variety and encourages you to try a new technique, and also that it will offer a sound reminder of the traditional methods of metal-thread hand embroidery for those of you who have used this technique before but need a helping hand to iron out any general problems. There is, of course, a limit to what can be achieved when handling a subject that is so varied, but when used in combination, the given techniques will keep you endlessly occupied in hours of happy, sometimes challenging but hopefully always productive stitching.

Helen McCook

THE HISTORY OF METAL THREAD WORK

As suggested earlier, goldwork has become synonymous with splendour and as such was utilised in many countries by various cultures and faiths. What can be seen as a common thread between all of them is that the ability to have finely rendered and embellished goods, particularly those made in gold, has always been used as an indicator of wealth, power and status. As such, the history of goldwork really deserves an in-depth study, however, if we look at some of the important development features in relation to the Royal School of Needlework, it may be easier to tackle this subject.

Some of the earliest surviving examples of metal thread work in Great Britain are the textiles associated with Saint Cuthbert that can be seen in the Treasury at Durham Cathedral. These are vestments in the form of a stole and maniple and date to the tenth century. It is interesting to note that on these early pieces of church textiles, golden threads acted as a decorative surround or background to throw the fine embroidered detail into the fore. This use of gold as a dazzling background became honed during the medieval period in England, a period in which this work became known as Opus Anglicanum (English work). It was the skilful rendering of goldwork in a technique called underside couching at this time that helped to make this work so famous and highly sought after. It was, in fact, so highly prized that it was used as political gifts across Europe.

One of the reasons that the Church used gold was to celebrate the majesty of God. May Morris, who taught at the RSN during the Victorian period, noted: 'The old workers knew what they were about when they lavished mysterious splendour of gold and broken colour on their altar apparel and priests' vestments; such a method lost little through distance of its power of impressing the spectator with a vague sense of beauty and richness entirely appropriate to the spirit of the building'.

Later, gold was used in secular embroidery, which was seen as a reflection of the divine right of kings, although there is far less of this early secular embroidery still in existence. This may be due to the huge costs involved in the materials alone. These valuable metal threads were often recycled or even melted down, a technique known as drizzling and parfilage.

It is important to remember that during this early period there was a strict hierarchy in place, but equally this meant that a churchman and a king had appearances to uphold – after all, they had been favoured by God for high placement. During a time of widespread illiteracy, the impact of the written word was restricted but this gave images and the visual realm more power over the senses and the mind. These images would be used to inform and mould your audience. The pomp and circumstance created by the awe-inspiring use of metal threads in church work was observed keenly by kings and emulated where possible. We still see evidence of this today in the use of golden braids and embroidery in military uniforms, court dress and ceremonial items such as the imposing Lord Chancellor's purse, the most recent of which was worked by the RSN with mixed techniques (including many that can be seen in this stitch guide) over high-relief padding, lending a sculptural effect to the impressive finished piece.

Silk crane on goldwork ground. Japanese, twentieth-century, Jean Panter bequest. (RSN Collection 1474)

Nineteenth-century envelope case from India, which contained greetings to Queen Victoria. Metal-thread embroidery on red velvet. (RSN Collection)

Close-up of a sampler featuring counted patterns in silk and metal threads. English, late eighteenth century. (RSN Collection 215)

There are also, of course, the Robes of Estate of our monarchs. The RSN has been honoured to design and produce the embroidery for both Queen Elizabeth the Queen Mother and for our current Queen Elizabeth. This is a wonderful opportunity for us to honour our patrons and play a small, if vital, part in the spectacle of the Coronation Day. The embroidery is used only on the female robes, the male robes having only golden braid. The chosen symbols for the Coronation robe are extremely significant as they are meant to represent what that monarch hopes for in her reign to come. The Queen Mother, for example, chose flora and fauna from some of the Commonwealth countries to show that her interests lay in the Commonwealth as a whole, whereas the Queen chose wheat sheaves and barley ears to represent peace and prosperity, which is what the Queen and in fact the whole country hoped for in the post-World War Two period.

The embroidery on the robes is a mixture of standard and complex metal-thread techniques worked to the highest traditional technical level. Multiple embroiderers worked on the robes at the same time and each had to stitch in a uniform way to give the impression that only one hand had embroidered them. This, in itself, can be a complex process, but add to that the time constraints and you can appreciate that the Robes of Estate are a unique chance to showcase the extraordinary craftsmanship, attention to detail and loyal discretion with which the RSN is synonymous.

This technique requires discipline, understanding, patience and careful handling alongside creativity, attention to detail and the desire to mix tactile sculpting with striving to achieve the elusive beautiful light play across the surface that has been created. It is a combination of all of these factors that has led to the longevity of our love affair with metal thread work, a love affair that continues today and thankfully shows no signs of abating. It seems that we are still enthralled by the splendour of gold both on a primitive instinctual level and from a purely aesthetic perspective.

Antependium (altar hanging), designed by Matthew Webb and worked by the RSN in silk and metal threads. English, twentieth century. (RSN Collection 101)

Peacocks in heavy metal thread work with silk. Indian, nineteenth or twentieth century. (RSN Collection T33)

TOOLS AND MATERIALS

Metal threads

I always liked the look of metal thread embroidery, but before it was explained to me, the subject seemed unfeasibly complicated! The thing to note, however, is that it is very much like any other form of embroidery in so far as it has a variety of different threads, all of which have their own names and most of which are available in a variety of sizes. They also have specific purposes. Once you become familiar with the differences between these threads and learn how to handle them, there is an almost infinite variety of ways in which they can be used.

There are numerous types of metal threads that can be purchased, but as a guide they can be divided into the following categories:

Gold-plated metal tends never to have more than 2 per cent gold content.

Gilt-plated metal tends to have approximately 0.5 per cent gold content.

Silver metal contains a maximum of ninety nine per cent fine silver.

Silver-plated metal has a silver content of no more than 1.5 per cent.

Copper metal tends to be either hard drawn or to consist of copper alloys.

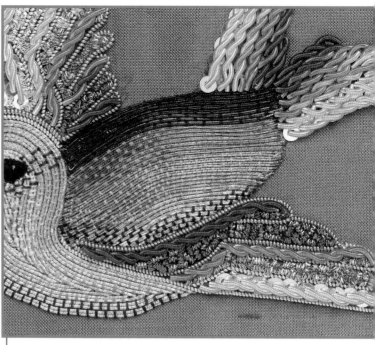

Spring Flight (detail)
Worked by Helen McCook in assorted silver, golden, copper and bronze metal threads; spangles; and a variety of colours of stranded cotton threads on a silk dupion ground. See also page 255.

COUCHING THREADS

These are threads that are applied to the surface of the fabric, generally in pairs, and are held down with a small holding stitch (see couching on pages 227–231). They tend to have ends that can unravel or fray and therefore the ends of the threads are later plunged through the surface of the fabric to the back of the embroidery and fastened with additional overstitches. Any excess thread is then neatly snipped off. Threads that come into this category include the following:

Japanese gold is essentially composed of a thread core with flat, paper-backed gold wrapped around it.

Passing has a thread core which is twisted in one direction, and the fine metal thread is then wrapped neatly over the core in the opposite direction, resulting in a reasonably strong and stable thread. Wavy passing has a rougher finish and is far rarer than the more commonly used smooth passing.

Twist is generally composed of three metal-wrapped cores which are then twisted around each other to produce something very similar to a cord.

Elizabethan twist is a much finer version of the twist mentioned above and, instead of being three-ply, is generally two-ply. It is slightly different from the other threads in this category in so far as it can be used in a needle to sew through the fabric as well as being couched with.

Rococo is composed of a central, twisted-thread core which is then wrapped with another thread to create a wavy effect. The whole core is then neatly wrapped with a fine metal thread in the opposite direction to the twist. Rococo threads have a gentle open-wave effect.

Check is made in much the same way as rococo thread, but has a tighter effect with its waved pattern.

A variety of metal couching threads on reels (check, passing, twist and Japanese).

Pearl purl is made with wires that are considerably thicker than the wires used to make the other purl threads (see opposite). It is therefore far more robust, in many senses, than the others. The wire is beaded into a horseshoe or stirrup shape and then wrapped around itself into a coil.

CUTWORK THREADS (PURLS)

There are a number of different purl threads, but they all have certain characteristics in common: they are made of a wire that is tightly coiled like a spring; they do not fray and therefore do not need to have their ends taken through to the back of the fabric to be fastened off; and they should be stitched invisibly so that you do not see the stitch attaching them to the face of the fabric. These threads should be handled carefully so that they are not damaged or overstretched and therefore rendered useless for traditional goldwork embroidery effects. If this happens, you should store them separately for possible use on creative metal-thread projects at a later date. Threads that come into this category include the following:

Smooth purl is essentially a round, spring-like thread but the surface of its metal has been burnished or flattened slightly so that it is very shiny.

Rough purl is made the same way as smooth purl but the surface of the metal is left rounded and therefore has a more matt appearance than the smooth purl.

Bright check is made in a similar way to smooth purl and is also shiny, but instead of being spring-like and circular in appearance, the coils have angles added at regular intervals that catch the light.

Wire or **dull check** is made in the same way as bright check but is matt in appearance in a similar way to rough purl.

Spangles, seed beads, whipped plate, kid, pearl purl, and smooth and bright check threads in copper, gold and silver metals.

Miscellaneous materials

There are, of course, any number of materials that can be combined with metal thread embroidery to create interesting effects, for example washers, screws, safety pins and jewellery findings, but for a traditional approach we are left with items such as kid leather, spangles and plate. There are sections dedicated to the basic application of each of these techniques further on in this chapter of the book.

Kid leather is a supple leather that has been treated to have a metallic finish on one side. Alternatives to animal hide can be purchased according to the financial or ethical leanings of the individual. It should be noted that some metalised faux kid can lose its flexibility and develop the appearance of cracks as it dries out over time.

Spangles are essentially metal sequins, however they all have a small slit to one side due to the manufacturing process. Spangles are made of tightly coiled, heavy wire that is cut and flattened. Each cut coil produces one spangle, the cut being evident in the spangles still as the aforementioned slit.

Plate or **broad plate**, to give it its traditional name, consists of a piece of wire that has been flattened by rollers enough times to achieve the sufficiently smooth width. Other members of the plate family are whipped plate, which has a fine thread wrapped around the plate to create an alternative effect, and crinkle plate, which sees an even ribble or crinkle put into the metal with shaped rollers.

There are, of course, many other threads and braids but these are the ones used most often and therefore the most useful to mention.

Embroidery threads

There are no hard-and-fast rules regarding which embroidery threads you should use in combination with metal threads. It is very much a case of personal preference and choice of colour palette to complement your design. For most goldwork designs you will require self-coloured thread (a thread to match the colour of the metal) and contrasting shades to create impact.

Needles

The needles most commonly used are sizes 9, 10 and 12 embroidery needles as they pass comfortably through the gold for cutwork. You need to remember that the smaller the size of the gold, the finer the needle will need to be to pass through the purl. A larger needle may be utilised for use with a lasso to plunge ends (generally a size 18 chenille needle or a size 18 tapestry needle). Curved needles can be very useful when tying threads off on the back of the embroidery (though some people prefer a straight embroidery needle).

Pins and needles should be stored in a pincushion or needlecase for ease of use.

An assortment of fabrics including velvet, silk dupion, satin and organza.

Fabrics

Metal thread work is traditionally worked on rich fabrics to complement the richness of the thread, the most commonly used fabrics being jewel-coloured silks and velvets. However, this technique can essentially be worked on any fabric. On the whole, the fabric is applied to a calico base to help strengthen and support the fabric and metal thread work. To see how to do this, refer to the section in the book on 'framing up' (pages 16–19) and attach your silk to a calico base at step 13. Sew it on with long-and-short stitch before tightening the frame (see below).

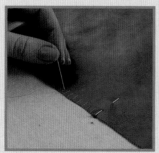

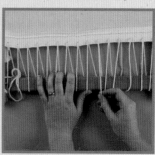

1 Cut a piece of fabric to the size you wish to work and secure it in place in the centre of the backing fabric, with a pin in each side and in each corner.

2 Thread a size 9 or 10 embroidery needle with strong thread. Starting from the centre of one of the sides, work long-and-short stitches up to the corner.

3 Start again from the centre and work to the other corner; repeat on the other sides and remove the pins.

4 Tighten the frame following steps 14–15 on page 18.

OTHER SEWING TOOLS

Other tools that are especially useful to the embroiderer wishing to work with metal threads are as follows:

Wax: there are many types of wax and wax-related products available, however the one which consistently yields the best results is pure beeswax. This is used to coat the working thread (usually a Gutermann sewing thread) to smooth and strengthen it, which will ease the use of the metal threads and help to prevent any sharp ends from catching and stretching.

A mellor is a metal tool with one wide rounded end and one tapered pointed end. The rounded end is used to help mould the shape of couched or cut metal threads and the pointed end can be used to help manipulate the threads with more precision. The tapered blade is used to manipulate cut threads over so that they bend easier, thus reducing the likelihood of any cracks and blemishes occurring.

Tweezers can be used for manipulating the metal threads and helping to withdraw threads if any problems have occurred while stitching. They can also be very helpful when using pearl purl to aid in the working of sharp points or when trying to merge two ends together to close a shape, for example a circle.

Gold scissors look like normal embroidery scissors but have a very sharp point and the blades are serrated to help cut the gold without crushing it and without it rolling out of the blades.

Gold board: this is board that has velvet on both sides. The velvet on the lower side ensures that the board may rest on areas that have already been embroidered and the velvet on the upper surface is used to nestle the gold against that will be cut (for cutwork, see pages 235–239). The pile of the velvet helps to keep the gold still while you are measuring it and also stops any cut pieces from rolling around and escaping before they can be stitched down.

FELT AND STRING

There are various methods of padding associated with goldwork, for which felt and string are required. Traditionally, yellow craft felt and carpet felt are used, and soft and hard string, depending on the method used (see pages 224-227).

An assortment of useful tools: a gold board, mellor, thimbles, pins, needles, curved needles, a bracing needle, a mechanical pencil, a fine paintbrush, a pricker, tweezers, a waterproof fine-line marker pen, watercolour and gouache paint, beeswax, a tape measure and a paint palette.

Webbing for use during framing up; calico to use as a backing fabric; craft felt for craft-felt padding; soft string and hard string for soft- and hard-string padding respectively.

DESIGN

Virtually any design can be adapted for use and interpretation with metal thread work, as the range of threads and varied ways of working and applying the threads offer huge versatility and endless possibilities.

One of the most important aspects of metal thread work design is texture. Our talented gold and silver wyre drawers go to great lengths to cunningly create a sparkling array of threads made in a variety of ways to enable us, as embroiderers, to have as many options as possible when it comes to stitching using this technique. Arguably the major reason for the importance of texture is that light bounces off different textures in various ways, and it is the play of light across a piece of metal thread work, in conjunction with its combinations of textures, that can really make it interesting, or otherwise. Therefore it is important to look at combining different textures to get different effects. You should also look at ways of enhancing the qualities of different gold threads. For example, certain types of threads may suit different areas of your design. You can also sometimes be limited to what type of thread goes where.

Just as we appreciate light by understanding the depth of darkness, so too we should appreciate that no piece of embroidery should be a solid mass of stitch. There should be a harmonious blend of boldly and heavily worked areas foiled against a backdrop of delicately and lightly worked open spaces. It takes both to make us truly appreciate the differences they offer.

Think carefully about the flow of the lines within the piece. This can be altered drastically depending on the direction in which you lay your metal couching threads or the angle in which you stitch down your cutwork, for example. I find drawing the different options for the flow of gold on to a photocopy of the outline design particularly helpful when pondering this issue.

Once you have thought about and learnt the rules above, you can apply them to any design. Having done so, you should think about the height of your padding across the piece. Metal thread embroidery works in the realm of three dimensions and you should utilise all of the padding techniques appropriate to your chosen design to enhance your work further.

You could additionally consider introducing coloured threads into your metal thread work and experiment with shade play across the piece. This could be abstract, pattern based or simply something to aid the three-dimensional effect. Again, I find it helpful to draw on to a copy of the outline design to aid me with this. There is, however, no right or wrong way of approaching this and as you become more experienced in working with metal threads, you will be able to trust more to instinct and less to rigid planning.

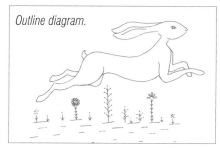

Outline diagram.

Shading plan.

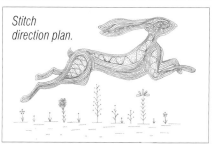

Stitch direction plan.

Colour plan.

The stages in the development of my design for Fearless Freedom. I may also draw up a stitch plan, in which I write my initial stitch choices on to the stitch direction plan.

Fearless Freedom

The finished piece worked by Helen McCook. Japanese thread, copper, gilt and silver bright check thread, and assorted stranded cotton threads on a linen ground.

STITCHING TIPS

Working thread

Always use a double thread to go through the centre of a thread (chips and cutwork) and a single thread to go over threads. This is because if your stitches are visible, you generally wish to see the gold rather than the holding stitch, unless you wish your holding stitches to be decorative, for example in the case of Or Nué (see page 249).

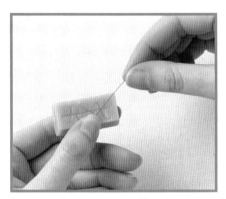

For gold embroidery, your working thread should always be run through beeswax to strengthen it and smooth off any loose fibres.

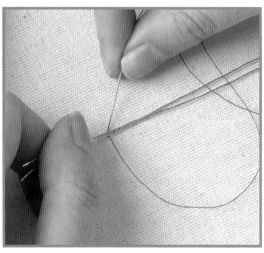

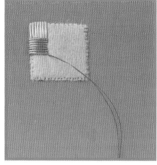

Use a double thread to go through the centre of a metal thread (chips and cutwork), as shown above, and a single thread to go over metal threads, shown on the left.

A section of an altar frontal featuring high-relief goldwork over card padding with chain stitch or tambour work in silk on a cream silk satin ground. (RSN Collection)

GOLDWORK STITCH FINDER

Stitch	Type	Page
ATTACHING PLATE OVER FELT	PLATE	SEE PAGE 244
ATTACHING PLATE OVER SOFT STRING	PLATE	SEE PAGE 244
BASKETWEAVE	STITCHES	SEE PAGE 234
BRICKING	COUCHING	SEE PAGE 230
CARPET-FELT PADDING	PADDING	SEE PAGE 226
CHAIN STITCH	STITCHES	SEE PAGE 245
COMBINING THREADS	COUCHING	SEE PAGE 227
COUCHING IN A CIRCLE	COUCHING	SEE PAGE 231
CUTWORK CHIPS OVER FELT	CUTWORK	SEE PAGE 236
CUTWORK PURLS OVER FELT	CUTWORK	SEE PAGE 237
CUTWORK PURLS OVER SOFT STRING	CUTWORK	SEE PAGE 237
DIAPER COUCHING	USING COLOUR	SEE PAGE 248
FEATHER STITCH	STITCHES	SEE PAGE 246
FELT PADDING	PADDING	SEE PAGE 226
FLAT CUTWORK	CUTWORK	SEE PAGE 239
HARD-STRING PADDING	PADDING	SEE PAGE 225
JAPANESE GOLD	COUCHING	SEE PAGE 228
OR NUÉ	USING COLOUR	SEE PAGE 249
OR NUÉ WITH PAINT	USING COLOUR	SEE PAGE 250
PEARL PURL	COUCHING	SEE PAGE 232
PEKINESE STITCH	STITCHES	SEE PAGE 246

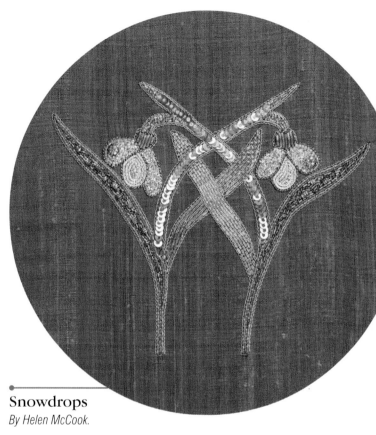

Snowdrops
By Helen McCook.

S-ING	CUTWORK	SEE PAGE 240
SOFT-STRING PADDING	PADDING	SEE PAGE 224
SPANGLES HELD ON WITH PURLS	SPANGLES	SEE PAGE 242
TRELLIS STITCH	STITCHES	SEE PAGE 247
TURNING AND PLUNGING	COUCHING	SEE PAGE 228
TWISTS	COUCHING	SEE PAGE 233
USING KID	APPLIQUÉ	SEE PAGE 239

ORDER OF WORK

There are often specified ways to plan your order of work depending on the techniques chosen. The order of work for metal thread embroidery is very important. The reason for this is that you need to build up your work, beginning with the padding and then stitching the most stable metal threads, and ending with the most delicate embroidery. This is the order in which you would generally work a piece of metal thread embroidery:

1 Padding

The first stage is to attach any padding required for the raised areas of your embroidery. This could be felt or carpet-felt padding, soft or hard string or indeed a combination of any or all of the above depending on the desired effect. If your design is large, you may wish to stab stitch your paint lines prior to padding to ensure the fabrics do not pucker.

2 Kid and surface stitching

Any appliqué should be worked next, including kid, and it is also appropriate to add any decorative surface stitching at this stage as it tends to be closer to the face of the fabric than the metal thread. Working the surface stitching now also stops the embroidery threads catching on the metal and stretching it out of shape.

3 Couching

Couching is done next, using Japanese thread, rococo, check, twist, Elizabethan twist or passing. You would also apply any pearl purl threads at this stage. This stage in the order of work is essentially to fill areas or to create outlines.

4 Cutwork

Cutwork can be worked using bright check, dull or wire check, smooth purl or rough purl. Techniques include chips (generally using bright, dull or wire check), cutwork, s-ing and s-ing with spangles.

5 Finishing touches

This is when you would complete the piece by adding embellishments in the form of beads or crystals, for example, or any additional surface stitching that needs to be placed after the goldwork has been executed.

Marguerite Daisy
By Helen McCook.

Spring Flight (detail)
Gilt metal threads, spangles and seed beads on a silk ground. See page 255 for the complete embroidery.

1 Soft-string and craft-felt padding are applied.

2 Couching is used to outline the petals.

3 Overstretched pearl purl with a coloured core is applied for the stem and leaf outlines. Spangles held down with beads embellish the flower centre.

4 Chips and cutwork provide the finishing touches.

PADDING

People often seem inclined to hurry through the padding phase of goldwork, generally because they are so keen to move on to working with the metal threads themselves, but it is important to remember how key the padding stage is to achieving a good piece of metal thread work. A good analogy is this: if a house does not have good foundations, it will not stand well, and it is exactly the same with metal threads. If the padding is not strong, smooth and even enough then the metal threads will not lie evenly or be supported sufficiently, and this could lead to some of the metal threads cracking, which in turn will speed up the tarnishing process. It is therefore worth taking your time over this important process to ensure that your gold will be sufficiently cushioned.

Another reason to add a single layer of felt padding is to create a complementary coloured background on which to work chips or couching. This will blend the background into the colour of the stitching and make it less obvious if there are any tiny gaps.

Note

Don't rush your preparation.

Sample showing the padding stages of the Palais Pansy by Helen McCook, working in soft string and craft felt.

Soft-string padding

This type of padding is created to raise up and support cut goldwork and sometimes plate embroidery. Soft string, sometimes known as cotton bump (or bumph), is run through some beeswax and then cut to lengths that are longer than the designated shape to be filled by about 4cm (1½in) at each end. Ideally you want the length of the shape to be filled, and you also want to have sufficient numbers of threads to fill out the width at its widest point and to be a pleasing height. To ensure that you achieve this, cut your lengths and then twist them together and hold them in position over the shape to be worked. This will help you get an idea of the height and width that will be left after the soft string has been stitched in place. Add more string until you are happy with the appearance.

Note

The beeswax which the soft string is gently run through is to help smooth off any fibres, but also to make the string more malleable and easier to mould if need be.

  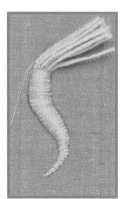 

Soft-string padding, worked within a curved shape. If you are filling an irregular shape like this, always start stitching at the widest point. Use a waxed double thread to stitch the soft string down. To help you to determine how much soft string is needed to fill the widest parts of your chosen shape, and also to see how high the string padding will be, start by twisting the threads together gently. You will need to remember to untwist them when you start the stitching.

If you wish to taper the string towards a point then you will need to first lift the bulk of the soft string upwards from the face of the fabric. You will then need to separate out a few of the string lengths from the central underside and snip them away by placing the point of your scissors towards the point of the shape that you are working towards, and ensuring that the blades of the scissors are at approximately 45° to the base fabric. Smooth the remaining threads back over and keep stitching your way towards the end of the piece. By snipping a few lengths at a time from the underside you will find it easier to achieve a gently tapering, smooth-surfaced piece of soft-string padding, and by the time you come to the end of the shape you need only snip off the excess soft string at the appropriate angle and stitch it down.

Note

See also the section on cutwork over soft-string padding, on pages 237–238.

Hard-string padding

Hard string is used as the base over which to stitch couched metal threads to form patterns. These patterns can take the form of chevrons, diamonds, stripes and so on, or can be more complex, in which case they are known as basketweave (see page 234).

When using gold, it is advisable to soften the harsh white appearance of the string by dyeing it, generally using tea. Once it is dry, run it gently through some beeswax to help make it a little more malleable. If you are using silver, thc string can be left undyed.

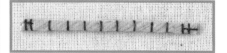

1 To start this technique, begin your thread using the waste-knot or holding stitch technique (see page 39) in an area that will be covered.

2 When executing the couching, place your stitches at a distance of approximately 3mm (⅛in) apart.

3 Ensure that you finish the ends of the string by putting a stitch from the fabric at the very end of the string and going down into the string itself.

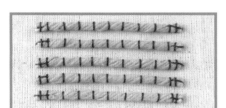

4 Couch lengths of hard string down securely and carefully, ensuring that they lie in straight, parallel lines (for basketweave) or in whatever configuration suits your design. Make sure that the distances between the pieces of string are even. Generally this should be between one and a half and two times the width of the string, depending on the desired effect and design.

Tudor Rose

First-year apprenticeship goldwork embroidery by Helen McCook, executed in a variety of golden metal threads and silk floss on linen ground, showing felt and hard-string padding.

Felt padding

Felt padding can consist of one layer or multiple layers of felt in a colour that complements the chosen metal: yellow for gold, white or light grey for silver and brown for copper or bronze. If there are multiple layers of felt to build up a slightly higher shape, then the smallest piece of felt is stitched down first and the largest is stitched down last. This is so that the external finish is smooth rather than stepped, which would be the resulting appearance if the largest were stitched down first and the smallest last.

To ensure that you have achieved the correct size of felt for your shape, you could place your design on a lightbox, trace it through the felt and then trim it off. Alternatively, you could use a copy of the design to create a template that can then be pinned on to the felt and cut round, or you could use prick and pounce to transfer the design (see page 20).

APPLYING MULTIPLE LAYERS OF FELT

1 To start stitching, thread a needle with multipurpose thread in a complementary colour to your felt and metal threads. Use the waste-knot or holding stitch technique to start your thread (see page 39). Bring your needle up in the fabric and take it down into the edge of your first piece of felt at a slight angle (about 45° to your base fabric). This will make a small stitch on the top surface of the felt that will pick up more of the felt as you move through it. Stitch all the way around the piece leaving gaps of about 1.5–2cm (⅝–¾in) depending on the size of the piece of felt. This will secure your felt in place.

 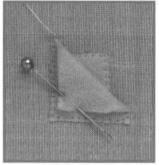

2 You then need to go back around your shape, filling in more stitches with a gap of no more than 2 to 3mm (about ⅛in) between them.

3 Once the whole shape is held down like this, you then either add the next (larger) layer of felt or you can finish off the thread by executing two more tiny stab stitches on or next to each other, either in a nearby area that you know will be covered or angled out slightly from underneath the newly applied felt.

4 Add a third layer, following the same method, if required.

Carpet-felt padding

Whilst a fair amount of height can be achieved by using layers of felt, in order to create a higher, more sculptural effect it is worth considering the use of carpet felt. In this instance it is best to utilise a copy of your original design to use as a template, which you can pin to the carpet felt and cut around. The largest piece of carpet felt should be fractionally smaller all round in size than the painted or drawn outline for the shape. Before stitching the carpet felt you should chamfer the edge. Do this by holding your scissor blades so they lie against the side of the felt at an angle of approximately 45° and effectively cut off the top corner of the felt.

1 The largest piece of carpet felt is stitched down first using a waxed double thread. Begin by laying herringbone or cross stitching over the piece in order to secure it in place (carpet felt is very easily broken down by stitching directly into it). If you are working with a substantial piece of carpet felt or are working an unusual shape that will need definition, then you should now gently work long and short stitches along the edge of the carpet-felt padding.

2 If there are any additional smaller layers you should stitch these in order from the largest to the smallest, having first chamfered (shaped) the edges by angling your scissors to cut or round off the top corner on the edge of the felt. The reason for chamfering is to help create a smooth overall shape by easing the edges of the separate pieces of carpet felt together. You may also need to work long and short stitches around the edge on these additional layers.

3 Having stitched all of the required layers of carpet felt, apply a single layer of craft felt over the top using exactly the same technique as that used to attach felt padding (described opposite). This layer of felt will help to trap in all the fibrous matter from the carpet felt and provide a smooth surface to settle the gold against. It should be a complementary colour to your chosen metal.

METAL THREAD METHODS

There are many options that may be used in combination with each other to create a seemingly endless array of appearances in metal thread work. This section explores the most commonly used of these.

COUCHING

Couching is the most commonly used way of filling areas of your chosen design with metal thread. There are a number of different ways of doing this, depending on how you decide to lay your threads and where you decide to plunge your ends. The type, colour and size of threads also drastically alter the appearance and light play with this technique. In the following sections, the couching methods used for various metal threads are discussed. A single waxed machine thread or strand of stranded cotton is the most common choice of sewing thread with which to make the couching stitches, however any thread that is relatively stable and even in width can be used.

Combining threads

Using combinations of threads, for example rococo, Japanese gold, passing, check and twist, when couching will help you to achieve different effects. Each of these may be stitched at a variety of angles. These threads, in a range of sizes, colours and directions, can be used to create different textures and to alter the play of light across the surface of the work.

Different sizes of gold rococo and silver check couched down in pairs in parallel rows.

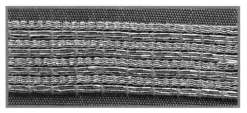

Japanese gold threads couched down in pairs alternating with pairs of silver check strands.

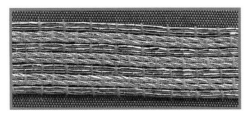

Japanese gold threads alternating with silver twist, both worked in pairs.

Silver twist couched down in pairs alternating with pairs of gold rococo.

Japanese gold

Japanese gold is stitched down in pairs. Either use two reels and leave the threads on the reel, or cut off an appropriate length of thread and fold it in half. Start your stitching 4–5cm (1½–2in) from one end of the gold threads.

1 Take the first stitch over the gold threads, ensuring it is at 90° to the threads. Avoid pulling the stitch too tight – it should be tight enough to hold the gold securely but not so tight that it dents the threads.

2 Pull the needle through and position it ready for the next stitch. Stitches should usually be approximately 3–4mm (¼in) apart, but this depends on the pattern.

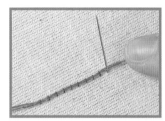

3 Continue to stitch along the gold thread, ensuring the stitches are evenly spaced and all lie at 90° to the threads. Make sure the gold threads don't twist over as you work, and do not over-tighten the stitches.

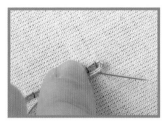

4 To turn the gold thread back through 180°, first bend the thread back on itself. Hold the gold threads firmly in place, and bring the needle up on the outer side of the threads in the second row, just below the last stitch.

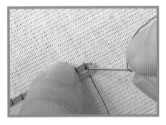

5 Take the needle down through the hole at the end of the last stitch.

6 Tighten the stitch, making sure the two pairs of gold threads are still lying parallel, and make the next stitch halfway between the last two stitches of the previous row.

7 Continue working along the gold threads, placing the stitches in between those of the previous row, in a brickwork pattern (see page 230). When you have finished couching, take the thread through to the back of the work ready for fastening off (see below).

Note

When couching adjacent rows of gold, always work from the outer to the inner edge, and angle the needle underneath the previous row to help pull the two rows of gold threads together neatly.

Turning and plunging

Just as there are a variety of ways to fill shapes with couching, so too there are a few ways of turning. The one shown above is probably the most commonly used, but two methods for turning around corners and angles are given on pages 229 and 230.

This is also a good time to mention plunging. The threads that we use for couching can tend to fray so they need to be secured. The most aesthetically pleasing way of doing this is to plunge the ends individually through to the back of the fabric, oversew them and snip off the excess thread to create a neat finish.

PLUNGING AND FASTENING OFF

1 When you have finished couching, cut off the gold threads so that the tails are the same length as those at the start.

2 Take a bigger needle and pass the two ends of a length of buttonhole thread through it to form a loop.

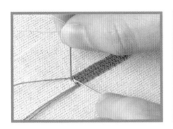

3 Lift the gold threads out of the way and insert the needle where you wish to plunge them.

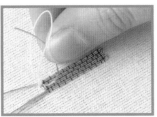

4 Pull the thread through, leaving a loop on the surface. Pass the end of one of the gold threads through the loop.

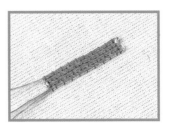

5 Pull the loop through. Ensure the end of the gold thread is not too close to the loop, otherwise it could be damaged. As you tighten the loop, the gold thread will be pulled through to the back.

6 Repeat for the remaining gold threads.

7 To fasten off the gold threads on the back of the work, pull a pair of threads back over the work and work a couching stitch over them, picking up a little of the previous stitching and the calico.

8 Work three or four more stitches over the top of the first and cut off the tails.

9 Finish the remaining gold threads in the same way.

10 Take the sewing thread through to the front and make a tiny stitch at the edge of the work, angling the needle underneath the gold.

11 Make two further stitches in the same place, bring the needle through to the front and cut off the thread close to the fabric.

Note

Some people prefer to use a curved needle to fasten the ends off at the back of their work. You should try both a straight and a curved needle and decide which one works best for you.

COUCHING AROUND A RIGHT-ANGLED CORNER

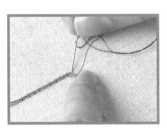

1 Having couched the gold threads to the corner, turn the gold threads through 90°. Bring the needle up on the corner and work a diagonal stitch across it.

2 Continue couching, positioning the stitches so they match those on the first side of the right angle.

3 Turn the gold through 180° to encourage it to bend (see opposite) and work back towards the corner. At the corner, make a diagonal stitch. Bring the needle up on the outside edge and take it down through the same hole as the first diagonal stitch, angling the needle underneath the first pair of gold threads as you do so to help keep the row together.

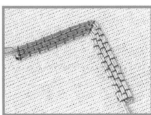

4 Continue couching in the same way, turning the gold at the end of each row and making sure the diagonal stitches at the corner are aligned, as shown.

FISHTAILING AROUND AN ACUTE ANGLE

It is difficult to make a sharp corner by the usual plunging method, so acute angles are worked by plunging the ends of the threads in a fishtail arrangement.

  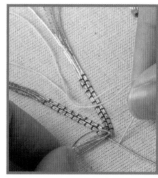 

1 Couch down a pair of gold threads. When you reach the corner, cut off the ends, leaving long tails for plunging later. Lay a second line of gold threads across the first, creating a 'V' shape. Couch it down, starting just above the crossing point and aligning the stitches with those in the first row.

2 Cut off the gold threads, leaving long tails as before, and lay another pair alongside the first, inside the 'V'. Couch the threads down, taking the stitches over from the outer to the inner edge and angling the needle underneath the first row to draw the two rows together. Lay the couching stitches in a brickwork pattern (see page 228 and below).

3 Continue to lay pairs of gold threads in this way. When you have finished, lift all the gold threads out of the way apart from the first pair. Plunge these through to the back (see page 228).

4 Plunge the second pair of gold threads just above the first pair.

5 Continue in this way, plunging the pairs of threads in the order in which they were worked, and each time taking them through at a point just above the previous threads, as shown.

An interesting effect can be achieved by couching down different coloured metal threads in a 'V' shape. Here, pairs of gold, copper and silver threads have been couched down using bricking (see below).

Crozier Border
Worked by Helen McCook. Inspired by the Luttrell Psalter and worked in couching, flat and raised cutwork, pearl purl, chips, spangles and beads.

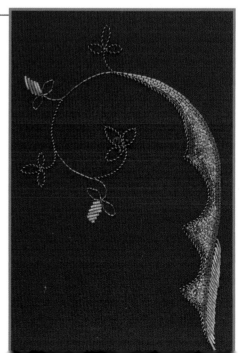

Bricking

Bricking is the most common method for holding down the couched threads. If it has been executed correctly, it creates a firm, stable embroidery with a beautifully even finish. The stitches should be evenly spaced, sit at 90° to the metal thread they are holding down, and all be pulled to the same tension so that none of them lie higher or lower on the gold's surface than the others. However, even where a pattern has been worked well, the odd rogue stitch can often be overlooked. Bearing in mind that the human eye is trained to pick up patterns, it is important to point out that the single rogue stitch will always be the one that the eye is drawn to even when all the others are perfect.

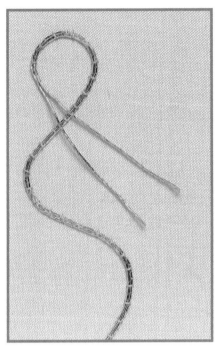

First row of bricking pairs of gold thread in a curve.

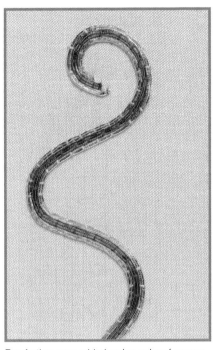

Two further rows added, using pairs of copper and silver threads.

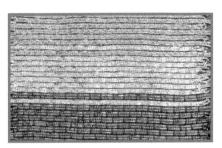

Here, bricking has been used with different coloured metal threads couched to create a strong design.

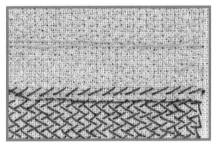

The back of the design reveals the nature of the stitching.

Couching in a circle

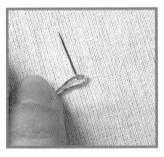

1 Create a fold in the gold and lay a stitch over it to form the centre of the circle. Bring the needle back through at the edge of the gold, approximately 3–4mm (¼in) away from the first stitch

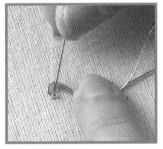

2 Make the second stitch over both threads, then bend the gold back on itself to form a tight curve. Stitch over the top of the curve, bringing the needle through on the outer edge of the gold and angling it back down under the gold you attached in step 1.

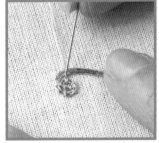

3 Continue stitching the gold in a tight circle, working the stitches from the outside of the circle in towards the centre and angling the needle underneath the previously worked gold threads. Ensure that all the stitches are evenly spaced and placed at 90° to the gold.

4 As the circle grows, make sure it maintains a good shape and does not distort, and that the gold threads lie flat and parallel without twisting.

5 When the circle is the desired size, plunge the gold threads through to the back of the work (see page 228).

6 Bend the gold threads back on themselves and oversew them firmly in place on the back of the work using either a curved or a straight needle, whichever you are more comfortable with. Trim off the excess gold to finish.

231

Pearl purl

Pearl purl can be used in lines of couching or overstretched and wrapped with a coloured thread as its core, but it is generally used to create lines or to outline areas. When overstretching, you want to achieve an even pull across the entire length so that the individual twists in the metal appear at regular intervals. The central core can be anything you wish it to be – stranded cottons, silks, chenille threads or even other metals – as long as they sit comfortably in the twist of the pearl purl.

Note

Although pearl purl does not fray and can be snipped off when you have finished with it, the central core will probably be a thread that will fray. You will therefore need to plunge it and fasten off at the back as you would with some of the other couching threads (see page 228).

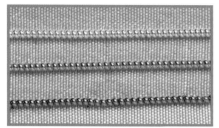

Pearl purl.

Overstretched pearl purl.

Overstretched pearl purl with a coloured core.

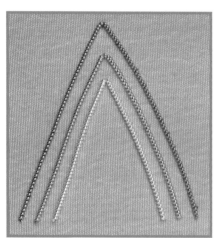

Pearl purl worked in an inverted 'V' shape.

STRETCHING PEARL PURL

Before using pearl purl, you need to stretch it slightly to loosen the coils. This allows the thread with which you attach the pearl purl to sit comfortably between the coils. Do not confuse this with overstretched pearl purl (see above), which is used to produce very different effects.

A comparison of unstretched pearl purl (top) with stretched pearl purl (bottom).

ATTACHING PEARL PURL

1 Bring the thread to the front and take it over the pearl purl, about 1cm (½in) from the end.

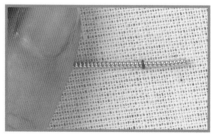

2 Pull the thread tight to form the stitch. Here, the stitch is lying on top on the pearl purl and is clearly visible.

3 Keep pulling until the thread 'pops' between the coils and becomes invisible – this is the correct way to attach pearl purl.

Note

For clarity, I have used a thread of contrasting colour with which to attach the pearl purl in this demonstration. In reality it is best to use a self-coloured (matching) thread to work pearl purl.

TURNING PEARL PURL INTO A CIRCLE

1 If necessary, twist the pearl purl to position the first stitch approximately 1cm (½in) from the end. Continue stitching, bringing the needle up underneath the pearl purl and taking it down as close as possible to (but not through) the same hole.

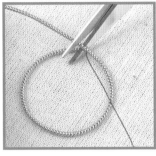

2 When the circle is complete, snip off the pearl purl so that the two ends meet but do not overlap.

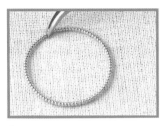

3 Place the final stitch over the end of the pearl purl and pinch the ends together using a pair of tweezers so that you cannot see the join.

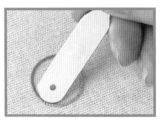

4 Refine the shape of the circle using the round end of a mellor to eliminate any kinks in the pearl purl.

Twists

Twists can be stitched down in pairs using the couching technique or they may be stitched down in individual strands that require an invisible stitch. The latter technique is demonstrated below. To show the technique clearly I have used a thread of contrasting colour, but you would normally use a self-coloured (matching) thread to couch down twist so that you do not see any of the holding stitches.

ELIZABETHAN TWIST

Elizabethan twist is a small-scale twist thread, generally used in conjunction with a coloured thread to fill small areas with gold and a decorative pattern at the same time. An example of Elizabethan twist used in this way is provided by the small leaves on the Tudor Rose, shown on page 225.

3-ply twist consists of three strands – the top thread is normal 3-ply twist and the bottom thread is 3-ply twist unravelled.

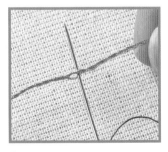

1 To start off the sewing thread, bring it up through the fabric and pass it through the twist – over the bottom strand and under the top two strands.

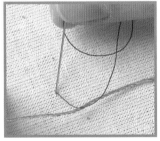

2 Take the needle back down through the same hole.

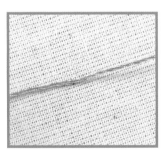

3 Pull the thread through to create an invisible stitch.

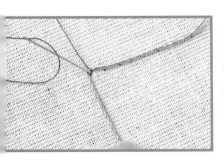

4 Continue stitching, passing the thread through the twist as described above and spacing the stitches approximately 3–4mm (¼in) apart. To turn a corner, bend the twist round at the last stitch made and place a second stitch over the top of it. Lay this stitch over all the strands to create a sharp corner. As you make the corner stitch, twist the end of the gold thread tightly in the direction of the plies to hold the strands together.

5 Continue stitching along the twist as before.

Basketweave

Basketweave involves couching over hard string. This is a very versatile technique as you can lay the threads down in many different patterns. Begin by dyeing the hard string (generally using tea) to soften the colour (see page 225). When dry, run it gently through some beeswax to help make it a little more malleable, then cut it into several pieces, all the same length. The following method requires an odd number of strings.

A fleur de lys, which, along with the pomegranate on page 241 and the crown on page 236, forms part of an early twentieth-century student-diploma piece using gold and cotton threads. The fleur de lys features a basketweave pattern. (RSN Collection)

APPLYING THE GOLD THREADS OVER THE PADDING

There is a huge variety of basketweave patterns that can be achieved by stitching over different numbers of strings in various combinations. Smooth metal threads, for example Japanese gold or smooth passing (which is the thread used in the demonstration below), generally work better than textured threads, which can create a confusing finish.

Begin by cutting two pairs of gold threads, approximately 4cm (1½in) longer than the padding at each end. Attach the first pair, then use the second pair to measure the third pair against and so on. That way, you will avoid cutting any threads the wrong length.

Note

For clarity, I have used a contrasting sewing thread in the demonstration, but it is best to use a self-coloured (matching) thread to work over the hard-string padding.

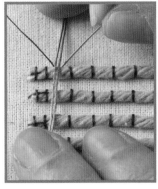

1 Lay a pair of gold threads across the padding and take a stitch over the gold using a suitable sewing thread, next to the top of the first string. Start a little way in from one side, as shown.

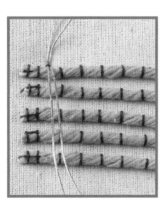

2 Pull the thread tightly so that it holds the gold firmly against the string.

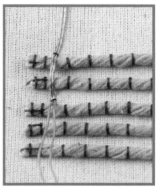

3 Take the gold threads over two strings and lay another stitch halfway between the second and third strings. Pull the stitch tight.

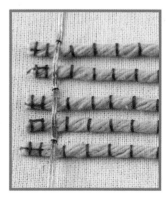

4 Lay the gold threads over each subsequent pair of strings, holding them in place with a stitch, as above. Keep the line of gold threads as straight as possible, and make sure it doesn't twist.

Note

Placing the first row of gold may initially displace the strings. After you have worked several more rows, the strings should look even again.

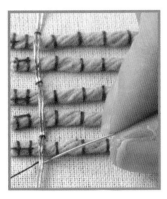

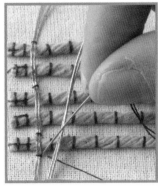

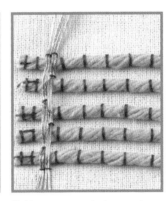

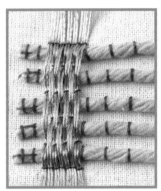

5 Finish the row with a small holding stitch over the gold threads, just below the last piece of string. Leave the thread in the needle and use it to work the next stitch.

6 Lay the next pair of gold threads adjacent to the first. Work the first stitch over the threads next to the bottom of the last string.

7 Work up towards the top of the padding, laying the gold over pairs of strings and finally over a single string. Work all the stitches from the outer edge inwards to help keep the lines of metal thread together.

8 Continue in this way and gradually build up the basketweave pattern. Work up and down the rows of string, and across a little way to the right then out to the left.

CUTWORK

Cutwork involves the cutting of soft-spiral or spring-like threads which have a hole in the middle. These need to be snipped down to the required size and then stitched down like a bead with a double thread through the central hole. These metals will need careful handling so that there are no sharp ends on the metal to catch on fibres and pull out. They also crush and crack easily. You can tell if a thread is cracked when a dark line appears across the surface of the metal. If this happens, you need to dispose of that thread or save it for creative metal thread embroidery, where it may come in useful. The threads often tarnish quicker from the cracks and this is a good reason to dispose of cracked threads for traditional metal thread work.

CUTTING THE METAL THREAD

We tend to use a gold board on which to cut the metal thread so that the threads are cushioned a little by the velvet's pile and are therefore protected from crushing. Also, the metal threads don't bounce around and get lost during the cutting process or once they are cut.

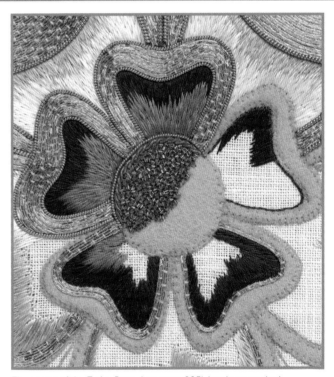

The centre of the Tudor Rose (see page 225) has been worked traditionally using small, flat chips, which give a dense, glittering finish.

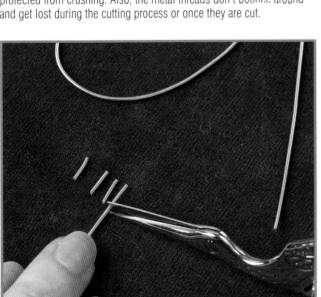

> ### Note
> *Always keep a separate pair of scissors for cutting metal threads, as this can damage the blades.*

Cutting smooth purl into a number of small pieces, all the same length, on a gold board.

235

Cutwork chips over felt

There are clearly many different colours of metal thread that can be used to execute cutwork, but generally bright or dull check are used to fill areas with chips. These can be purchased in differing scales, which creates a variety of different effects.

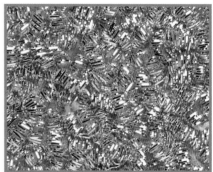

Copper and gold bright check, randomly placed at different angles to create a glittering, metallic surface. The chips have been cut relatively long in order to provide a looped, rough textural finish.

Traditionally, the chips are cut slightly shorter than those shown here, which results in them overlapping slightly and creating a textural finish.

ATTACHING THE CUTWORK CHIPS

Chips are most commonly cut into very small pieces and stitched down flat, at random angles, to create a glittering surface of metal, as in the Tudor Rose on page 225. They can also be cut longer and stitched down into loops or so that they overlap each other to create entirely different textures and effects. The following demonstration shows how to attach cutwork chips.

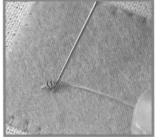

1 Cut tiny pieces from a length of gold thread and retain them on a gold board.

2 Bring a waxed, doubled thread through to the front and pick up a chip with the needle. Push the chip down to the end of the thread and secure it with a tiny stitch.

3 Position a second chip next to the first, varying the angle, and secure it in the same way.

4 Continue to add chips until the desired effect is achieved. The chips should be worked to fill the whole shape densely, as desired, so that none of the felt is visible. Smaller chips can be added at the end to fill any little gaps.

The crown which, along with the pomegranate on page 241 and the fleur de lys on page 234, forms part of an early twentieth-century student-diploma piece using gold and cotton threads. Cutwork is shown in the form of chips applied to the top, decorative section of the crown; cutwork over soft string has been utilised in the two narrow horizontal bands bordering the lower section; and s-ing has been worked around the jewels.
(RSN Collection)

Cutwork purls over felt

Cutwork is mostly seen over high padding to give a sculptural feel to a piece, but it can be worked flat to the ground fabric or over craft-felt padding as well as over soft-string padding. The finished result looks very different depending on the pattern, angle and types of threads used, as well as the level of padding.

1 Thread a needle with a double thread and wax it. Start the thread (see page 39) a purl's length from the edge of the shape and pick up a single purl on the end of the needle. Avoid touching the gold.

2 Take the purl down to the end of the thread and nudge it right to the end using the needle.

3 Take the thread down at the edge of the felt. Use the point of a mellor to make sure the thread runs smoothly and prevent it from knotting.

4 Pull the thread tight to secure the purl and bring the needle back through adjacent to the end of the first stitch. Pick up another purl and position it next to the first. Make sure the two purls lie parallel, with no gap in between.

5 Continue to lay the purls in parallel lines.

6 To create a chequerboard pattern, attach enough purls to make a square, then change to a different coloured smooth purl and lay the cut purls at 90° to those in the first row.

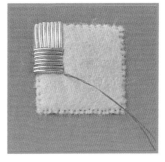

7 Complete the second row of purls.

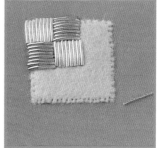

8 Build up the chequerboard pattern, using alternately gold and copper-coloured purls.

Cutwork purls over soft string

As previously illustrated, cutwork may be worked flat to the fabric or over craft felt, but it is most commonly used over soft-string padding to create a dramatic, sculptural effect.

High-relief padding emphasises the textural qualities of the metal threads and also acts as a stable support.

Still Waters Flow (detail)

By Helen McCook. This enlarged section of a finished piece includes an example of cutwork over soft string, spangles, beads, pearl purl, overstretched pearl purl with a coloured core, twist, silver passing thread with coloured bricking, s-ing, kid and patterned couching. The entire piece is shown on page 247.

ATTACHING CUTWORK PURLS OVER SOFT STRING

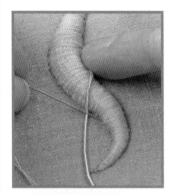

1 Using a waxed double thread, bring the needle up from underneath the padding approximately halfway along the right-hand side. The thread should be just touching the padding. Take a length of stretched pearl purl. Starting where the sewing thread comes through the fabric, take the gold across the padding at 45° so that it hugs the padding. Hold it firmly in place and use the needle to dent the gold at the point where it meets the fabric. This dent marks the length to which you need to cut the purls.

The dented smooth purl, marking the length of the cut purls.

2 Working on a gold board, cut off the first purl at the dent using a pair of very sharp scissors and use it as a guide for cutting off several more.

3 Working with the cut purls nearby, pick up a purl with the needle and take it gently down to the base of the thread. Lay it across the padding at a 45° angle. Take the needle down through the fabric, close to the side of the padding and tucked underneath so that the gold hugs the padding.

4 Place the tip of a mellor under the gold to ease it into shape and prevent it from cracking.

5 Bring the needle up a little below the first purl on the left-hand side, allowing enough room for the second purl to just touch the first. Pick up a second purl and attach it as before.

6 Attach the rest of the purls, working first towards the bottom of the padding and then towards the top. Here I have alternated smooth and bright check to enhance the pattern.

The partly worked cutwork over padding.

Note

Allow slightly more room for the gold where the needle comes up than where it goes down, as the second purl will naturally roll towards the first as the thread is tightened.

238

Flat cutwork

Cutwork can also be worked flat on to the face of the base fabric or over a single layer of felt. The following demonstration illustrates this.

Note

Cut purls can be attached at either 90° or 45° to the felt, depending on the effect you wish to achieve. When working at 90°, you can start to attach the purls at one end and work along to the other. When working at 45°, it is better to start in the middle of the shape and work first to one end and then to the other.

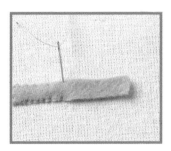

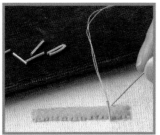

1 Cut a single strip of felt and attach it to the background fabric using tiny stab stitches worked 2–3mm (about ⅛in) apart (see the section on felt padding, page 226).

2 Begin with a waxed double thread and bring the needle through to the front of the fabric from underneath the felt, close to the bottom edge of the shape. Hold the length of smooth purl across the shape and dent it using the needle at the point where it touches the fabric on the other side. Snip off the purl at this point and use it as a guide to measure and cut several more. Pick up a purl with the needle and push it gently to the end of the thread. Stitch the purl in place, working at right angles to the felt.

3 Work the subsequent purls in the same way. Working over a single layer of felt produces a pleasing curve that complements the gold well.

USING KID

The application of kid is a good way to cover an area swiftly or to create a smooth effect. It is available in various colours and textures and faux kid leather is also available. Kid can be attached directly to the background fabric, or worked over felt or soft-string padding. The method is the same in each case. If you are applying a large piece of kid, you may wish to baste it to the fabric prior to stitching to hold it in place.

Note

If you are working an edging, always attach the kid before applying the edging. The demonstration shown here uses a coloured thread that is clearly visible against the kid, however if a self-coloured thread is used, the stitches will be virtually invisible.

Note

Kid is a tough material to stitch through. Once you have inserted the needle into the kid, 'wiggle' it slightly to help ease it through. Wear a thimble to protect your fingers. You may wish to consider using a leather needle when applying kid as it will cut through the kid easier than a normal embroidery needle. Do be aware that they are very sharp, however.

TRANSFERRING A SHAPE TO KID

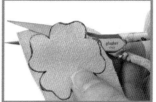

1 Lay the template face down on the back of the kid and draw round it using a fine-liner pen.

2 Snip around the shape.

The cut-out shape.

ATTACHING KID

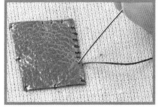

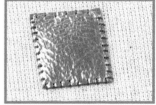

1 Using a single thread, bring the needle up through the fabric at the edge of the kid and take it down through the kid to form a tiny stitch.

2 Begin by securing the kid using widely spaced stitches placed close to the corners and in the centre of each edge.

3 Work the stitches in between the initial holding stitches, spacing them approximately 2–3mm (about ⅛in) apart.

The kid stitched in place.

S-ING

S-ing is essentially stem stitch worked in metal threads. It can be used to create a fine, sinuous line of metal with a rope-like appearance or it can be executed using longer pieces of metal, which may be stitched to create interlinking loops when viewed from the side. S-ing may also be used with spangles.

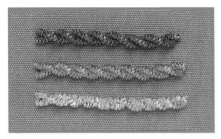
S-ing with copper, gold and silver bright check purl.

S-ing with copper, gold and silver smooth purl.

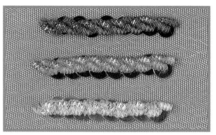
S-ing with copper, gold and silver bright check purl with spangles.

S-ing with copper, gold and silver smooth purl and spangles.

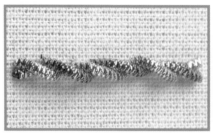
Looped s-ing with gold and copper bright check. See below for instructions.

Looped s-ing with spangles and smooth purl. See page 242 for instructions.

1 Cut several equal short lengths of gold and copper purl on a gold board. Take a waxed double thread and bring the needle through to the front of the fabric. Pick up a gold purl with the needle and push it down to the end of the thread. Lay it flat, and take the needle back down just underneath the end of the purl.

2 Pull the thread through so that the purl lies flat against the surface of the fabric.

3 Bring the needle and thread back through about half-a-purl's length in front of the purl.

4 Pick up a copper purl and push it to the end of the thread. Take the needle down under the first purl and approximately halfway along.

Note
Take care when s-ing not to damage your previous purl with your needle or by pulling the thread too tight.

6 Continue to create loops using alternating gold and copper purls. To finish, bring the needle through to the front at the end of the last loop, thread on a small chip and take the needle back down approximately one-third of the way along the last loop. Secure the sewing thread.

5 Secure the purl, then bring the needle through about half-a-pearl's length in front of it, as in step 3, and thread on a gold purl.

The first three purls.

This pomegranate forms part of an early twentieth-century student-diploma piece using gold and cotton threads. Twist has been used to finish the edges of the fruit and leaves, and Elizabethan twist to embroider the leaves. (RSN Collection)

SPANGLES

Spangles may be stitched down in a variety of decorative ways, either individually or in lines. You may decide that you want fancy stitching with coloured silk threads. Alternatively, they could be held down with chips, looped chips, beads or, invisibly, in fish-scale-style stitching which results in the overlapping spangles concealing the stitch that holds down the previous spangle.

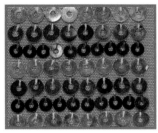

3mm copper sequins and 4mm gold and silver spangles worked in rows. Each spangle is held down with a single stitch.

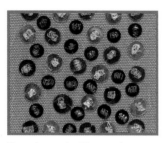

Spangles worked in a random pattern, each held down with a chip.

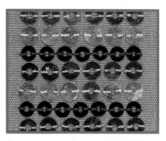

Rows of spangles, each held down with two stitches.

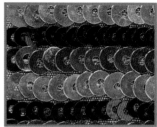

Spangles worked in a fish-scale design. The spangles are overlapped to hide the stitching.

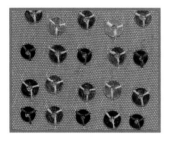

Spangles held down with three stitches.

Spangles held down with beads.

Spangles held on with purls

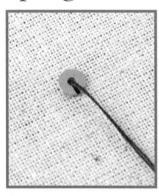

1 Take a waxed double thread and bring the needle through to the front of the fabric. Thread on a spangle and push it down to the end of the thread.

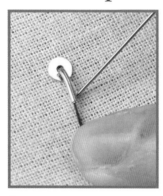

2 Pick up a purl with the needle and push it to the end of the thread. Lay the purl flat and take the needle down underneath it about one-third of the way back along its length.

3 Pull the thread through and bring the needle out on the other side of the spangle. Make sure the ridge on the spangle is concealed underneath the purl. Thread on another spangle and push it down to the end of the thread.

4 Pick up another purl and push it to the end of the thread. Take the needle through to the back on the opposite edge of the first spangle. Use the pointed end of a mellor to guide and shape the purl carefully.

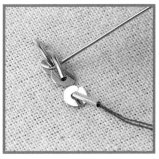

Note

Always position the spangles so that the ridge is concealed under a purl.

5 Pull the thread through to tighten the stitch.

6 Bring the needle back through just above the second spangle and thread on a third spangle. Pick up a purl and this time take the needle down through the hole in the centre of the first spangle.

7 Continue in this pattern, taking the needle down through the second spangle back from the one you are securing. To finish, work a final purl without the addition of a spangle. Fasten off the thread on the back.

PLATE

Plate is a thin, flat metal that can have a smooth or textured surface. It can be used flat or over hard or soft string, and may be stitched so that it is folded back on itself. Either no gaps can be left; gaps left unfilled; or gaps left and filled with decorative stitches, beads or chips of metal.

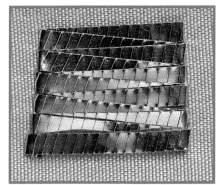

Whipped plate folded backwards and forwards across a shape with no gaps.

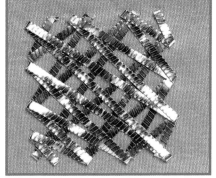

Whipped plate worked in an open pattern to create texture.

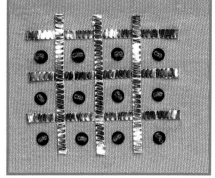

Whipped plate worked in an open grid pattern with spangles and chips in the gaps.

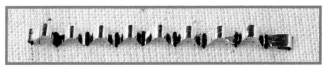

Crinkle plate attached with a coloured thread.

Crinkle plate attached with beads.

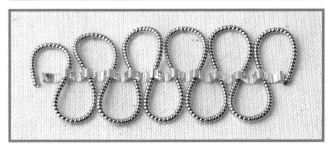

Crinkle plate with pearl purl.

243

Attaching plate over soft string

1 Begin by creating a hook at one end of the plate using a pair of curved tweezers.

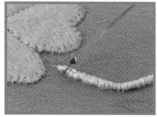

2 Make a loose stitch on the fabric, positioned where you wish to attach the end of the plate, and hook the end of the metal through the loop.

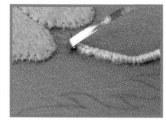

3 Pull the thread tight so that the plate lies securely against the fabric. Lay the metal across the padding, as shown.

4 Place a second holding stitch over the plate, abutting the other side of the padding.

Note
Use tweezers and a mellor to fold and position the plate rather than your fingers – handling the metal too much can cause it to tarnish.

5 Pull the thread firmly to form a tight stitch.

6 Fold the metal back across the padding at a slight angle, ensuring it covers more of the padding while at the same time overlapping the previously placed plate. Secure it with a holding stitch worked close to the padding, as in step 4.

7 Continue working back and forth across the padding.

Attaching plate over felt

1 Begin by creating a hook at one end of the plate, as above. Make a loose stitch on the felt where you wish to attach the end of the plate, and hook the end of the metal through the loop.

2 Pull the stitch tight to secure the metal to the felt. Lay the plate across the padding and secure it on the other side with another tight stitch.

3 Fold the plate across to the other side of the padding, angling it so as to cover more of the padding and overlap the previous row of plate.

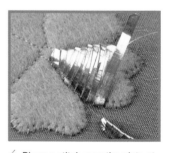

4 Place a stitch over the plate at the next fold, then bend the plate back in the opposite direction against the stitch, again at a slight angle. Continue in this way until the padded shape is covered.

5 Snip off the plate, leaving a sufficient length to bend under into a hook (as in step 1).

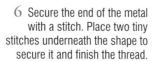

6 Secure the end of the metal with a stitch. Place two tiny stitches underneath the shape to secure it and finish the thread.

The completed plate over felt.

STITCHING WITH GOLD THREADS

There are a number of surface stitches that can be executed in metal threads. A few examples of these are shown below and include feather stitch, trellis, chain and Pekinese stitch.

Pomegranate and Gillyflower (detail)
By Helen McCook. Couched trellis with looped chips, overstretched pearl purl with coloured thread core, flat cutwork with beads and rough purl, feather stitch in rough purl, couching and surface stitching. See page 257 for the complete embroidery.

Chain stitch

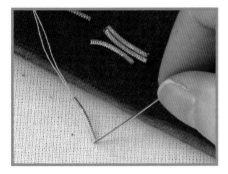

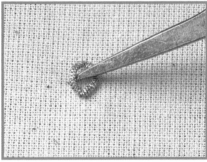

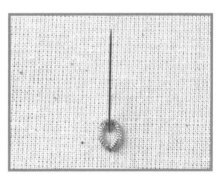

1 Cut a number of short lengths of copper and gold bright check, all the same length. Take a waxed double thread and bring it through to the front of the fabric then pick up a gold purl on the needle. Push the purl to the end of the thread and take the needle back down through the same hole.

2 Pull the thread through and use the pointed end of a mellor to ease the metal into shape. This will help prevent twisting and cracking.

3 Bring the needle back through inside the loop.

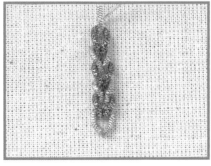

4 Pick up a copper purl and work a second stitch in the same way as before.

5 Continue to work stitches in alternate gold and copper purls, ensuring all the stitches are the same size. To finish, put a tiny purl in place at the end to hold the final stitch in place.

The completed chain stitch.

Feather stitch

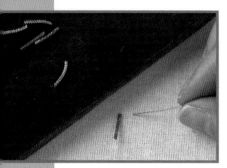  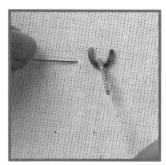 

1 Cut a number of short lengths of copper and gold bright check, all the same length. Take a waxed double thread and bring it through to the front of the fabric then pick up a copper purl on the needle. Push the purl to the end of the thread and take the needle back down a stitch length to the right.

2 Guide the stitch around the pointed end of a mellor to ease it into a 'U' shape and to prevent the metal from twisting and cracking.

3 Bring the needle through to the front inside the loop, towards the base of the 'U', and pick up a gold purl on the needle. Push it down to the end of the thread and take the needle back down a little way to the left to create a second stitch. Make sure this stitch is the same size as the previous stitch.

4 Shape the stitch as before, using a mellor. Now bring the needle back through inside the loop. Pick up a copper purl and create the third stitch.

5 Continue to work stitches in alternate gold and copper purls, ensuring all the stitches are the same size. To finish, put a tiny purl in place at the end to hold the final stitch in place.

The completed feather stitch.

Pekinese stitch

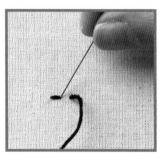 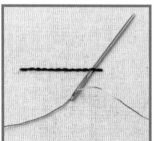 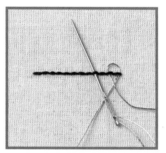 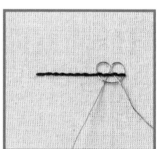

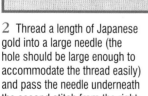

1 Begin by working back stitch using six strands of six-stranded cotton. Keep the stitches as even as possible.

2 Thread a length of Japanese gold into a large needle (the hole should be large enough to accommodate the thread easily) and pass the needle underneath the second stitch from the right.

3 Take the thread underneath the first stitch in the opposite direction and pull it through to form a loop. Pass the needle underneath the fourth stitch in the same direction as it went through the second stitch.

4 Pull the thread through to make a loop, then take the needle underneath the third stitch to form a second loop on the top of the line of back stitching. Try to make the loops as even as possible.

Note
Be aware of the amount of tension on the gold thread while you are stitching – avoid pulling the thread too tight.

5 Continue in this pattern to form the Pekinese stitch. Finish by plunging and finishing the ends (see page 228).

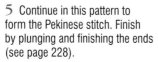

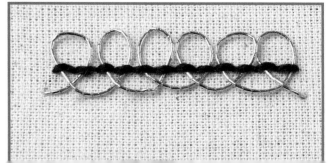

Trellis stitch

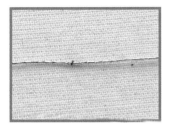

1 Take a single strand of Japanese gold, lay it on the fabric and stitch over the gold near one end.

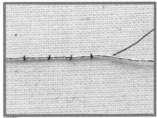

2 Continue stitching along the gold using small, evenly spaced stitches worked at right angles to the gold.

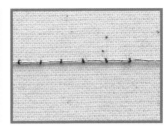

3 Continue stitching in this way until the desired length has been achieved. Finish off the sewing thread at the end.

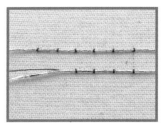

4 Lay a second strand of gold thread alongside the first and stitch it down in the same way, placing the stitches parallel with the first set.

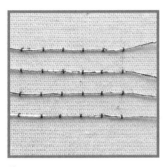

5 Stitch on more lines of gold until you have the required number, spacing them evenly.

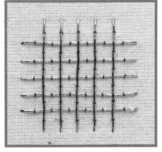

6 Lay more strands at 90° to the first, placing them in between the stitches on the horizontal lines. Stitch these down in the same way, placing the stitches in between the lines of gold.

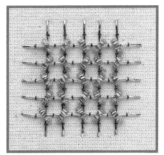

7 Decorate the trellis, for example by stitching purls across the intersections, as shown here.

USING COLOUR

Metal threads are, of course, beautiful, but when you add colour the lustre of the metal is given another dimension and depth. There are a number of ways in which to do this, including overstretched pearl purl (page 232) and using a coloured thread to create a pattern as shown with the Elizabethan twist threads (page 233). This section shows you how to create diaper or trellis couching, how to draw a pattern on to your base fabric and then go over it in thread, and Or Nué, which is a technique in which you can fill a whole area with gold held down with coloured threads or break it up by interspersing it with painted areas. Colour and gold is a very versatile combination and can be experimented with extensively.

Still Waters Flow

This piece, by Helen McCook, includes an example of cutwork over soft string, spangles, beads, pearl purl, overstretched pearl purl with a coloured core, twist, silver passing thread with coloured bricking, s-ing, kid and patterned couching. A close-up of the central section is shown on page 237.

Diaper couching

Begin by drawing your design on to the background fabric. The lines represent where the couching stitches are to be placed and at what angle. In the pattern, stitches that fall on the diagonals are worked at 45° to the metal thread, and those on the verticals are worked at 90° to the metal thread. Stitches that fall in between the lines are worked in a self-coloured thread and are therefore invisible; those on the lines are worked in a coloured thread.

1 Take two strands of metal thread (here I have used silver) and lay them down one side of the shape. Thread two needles – one with a single strand of self-coloured thread and the other with two strands of pink six-stranded cotton. Work a single holding stitch using the self-coloured thread at the top of the shape, then work a diagonal couching stitch on the first diagonal line using the pink thread.

2 Continue to couch down the silver threads, placing a regular number of horizontal holding stitches in between the diagonal pink couching stitches.

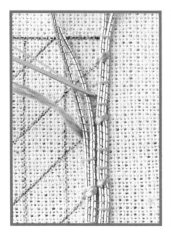

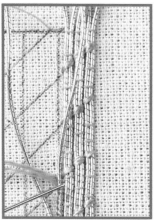

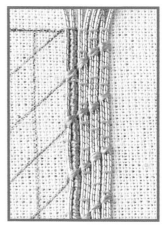

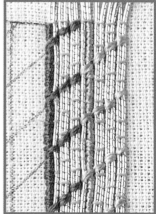

3 When you reach the bottom of the shape, lay another pair of silver threads alongside the first and couch back up to the top of the shape in the same way. Work the holding stitches in between those in the previous row to create a brick pattern.

4 Continue across the shape to the first vertical line. Here, place a holding stitch over two silver threads, as before. Couch down only the right-hand thread on the line using the pink thread and closely worked, horizontal couching stitches.

5 When you reach a diagonal, work a single, diagonal couching stitch over both silver threads. Work to the top of the shape. Secure both silver threads with self-coloured holding stitches.

6 Work the next vertical block in the same way as the first, using a different coloured thread. To finish, take all the sewing threads through to the back, plunge the metal and fasten off.

Or Nué

Begin by drawing your design on to fabric and choose your thread colours, then thread two needles – one with a self-coloured thread and one with a contrasting thread. If you are using more than one contrasting colour, start with the first one that you will be using in the design. You will start from the top of the design and work downwards.

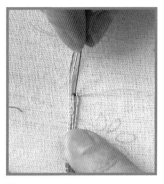

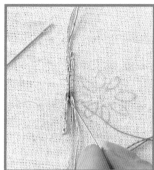

Note

If you are working individual strands of Japanese thread or do not mind a slightly bulkier turn, then you could turn the ends and work the whole piece with the same metal thread and only plunge at the start and finish of the piece. This is something to consider at the design stage.

1 Cut a length of Japanese gold that is about twice the width of your design plus 8cm (3in), fold it in half and lay it across the top of the design with the loop level with the left-hand side. Secure the loop with a stitch in the self-coloured thread. Continue to couch down the two threads, changing to the coloured thread where required.

2 Start the next piece of metal thread at the opposite end to where you started on the first row. Start the thread in the same way, ensuring that the gold will sit close to the previous row with no visible gaps.

3 Work your way along the gold as before, placing couching stitches in self-coloured thread where you wish the stitches to be invisible, and changing to the coloured thread and working close stitches where colour is required.

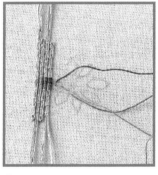

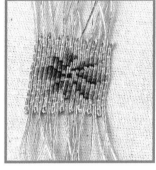

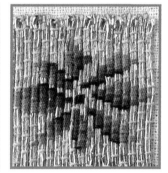

Note

Ensure that you come up on the outer edge of each new piece of gold and take the needle down into the fabric on the edge which is against the previous row of gold (in the same way that you would for normal couching).

4 As you progress back and forth across the design, introduce more contrasting colours as demanded by the design. Work the coloured stitches close together for solid areas of colour; space them out for a more subtle effect.

The completed design.

The completed design with the ends plunged.

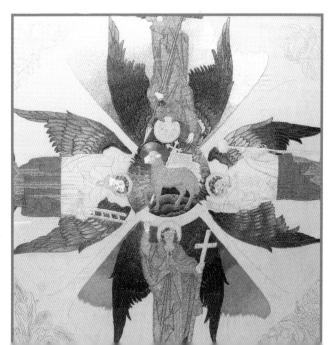

Early twentieth-century Or Nué training piece depicting angels, worked by RSN students and left unfinished for training purposes. Silk shading and Or Nué on linen. (RSN Collection 96)

Or Nué with paint

There are two approaches to working Or Nué over a painted background: either fill the entire background with colour and use it as guidance only for the colour of the stitching; or leave some areas of the background unpainted and stitch only in these areas, leaving the coloured areas unstitched. Watercolour, fabric or silk paints are suitable mediums for colouring the fabric.

CREATING BLOCKS OF STRONG COLOUR

In this example, a strong surface pattern is created by couching down pairs of gold threads using a contrasting thread. The pattern is painted on to the background fabric and provides a guide for the placement of the coloured couching stitches.

1 Take two strands of Japanese gold and lay them down one side of the coloured shape (see page 249). With two strands of six-stranded cotton/mouline thread in your chosen colour, couch down the gold using closely worked stitches with no gaps in between. Stitch with the coloured thread only where the background is painted; where the background is unpainted, secure the gold by couching in a brickwork pattern using a self-coloured thread.

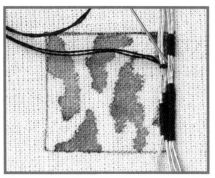

2 Couch down the second pair of gold threads in the same way, working from the bottom of the shape to the top.

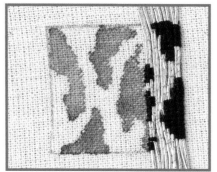

3 Continue working in this way across the shape.

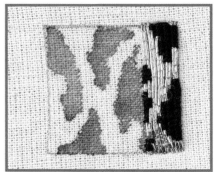

4 To finish, take all the sewing threads through to the back, plunge the gold and fasten off (see page 228).

CREATING A RANDOM EFFECT WITH TWO COLOURS

Here, a more irregular pattern has been created using randomly spaced stitches and two different coloured threads.

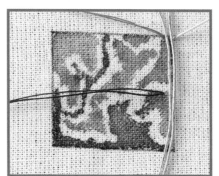

1 Begin by laying a pair of Japanese gold threads down one side of the coloured shape. Thread two strands of six-stranded cotton in two different colours into separate needles. Bring each thread through to the front where you intend to start stitching in that colour. Place the first couching stitch at the top of the shape.

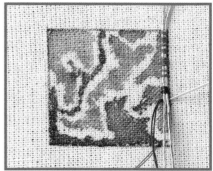

2 Work from the top to the bottom of the shape, stitching only within the coloured areas. Use randomly spaced stitches so that the gold shows through. Take the gold across the uncoloured shapes, securing it using one or two stitches worked in a self-coloured thread only where the gap is large.

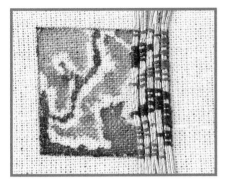

3 Continue working in this way across the shape.

4 To finish, take all the sewing threads through to the back, plunge the gold and fasten off (see page 228).

Note

If crossing a large unpainted area, hold the gold in place with one or more stitches worked in a self-coloured thread.

CREATING SUBTLE SHADING EFFECTS

In the example below, the thread colour is varied to reflect changes in the colour of the background. Gaps are left between the lines of gold so that the background is still visible, creating a subtle play of colour and light.

1 Take a single strand of Japanese gold and lay it across one side of a coloured shape. Choose a six-stranded cotton thread that matches the colour of the background at the start of the gold thread. Using two strands of your chosen cotton, couch down the gold using small, evenly spaced stitches.

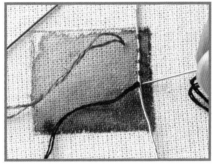

2 Change to a different thread to reflect the change in the background colour. Leave the first thread on the needle and use a new needle for the new thread. Bring the first colour through to the front of the fabric ready to resume stitching – to the left of the first row, halfway between the first two stitches.

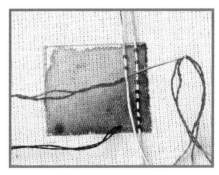

3 Stitch to the end of the gold in the second colour, then lay a second gold strand down alongside the first, leaving a small gap in between. Position the second colour to the left of the new strand, halfway between the last two stitches, and resume stitching in the first colour at the top of the new strand. Place the stitches in between those in the first row.

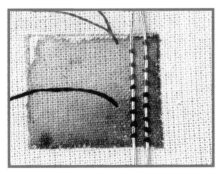

4 Continue stitching in this pattern, changing from one colour to the other to reflect the changes in the background.

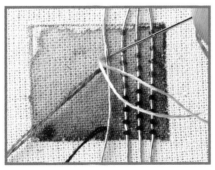

5 Introduce further colours for a more subtle effect or even greater tonal variation. Use a different needle for each thread.

6 To finish, take all the sewing threads through to the back, plunge the gold and fasten off.

In the example below, the technique from page 251 has been applied on a larger scale to achieve a highly contemporary design that uses traditional goldwork techniques to achieve a more painterly effect.

1 Draw on the design with Indian ink permanent marker and paint it with watercolour.

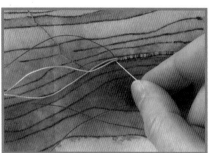

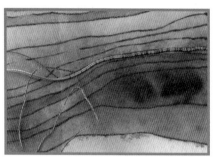

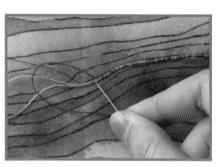

2 Lay a pair of silver threads along one of the contours and couch it down using a coloured cotton thread. Use randomly spaced stitches, varying the spacing depending on the intensity of colour you wish to achieve.

3 Vary the thread colour to match the background, using a different needle for each colour. Mark the points along the line at which the colour changes by bringing through threads in the appropriate colour.

4 When you change colour, work stitches in the second colour between the stitches worked in the first colour to achieve a blending effect.

COMBINING TECHNIQUES

This section is an opportunity to show you a few finished embroideries, with close-up images, in order to illustrate how the different techniques described in previous sections of the book may be worked together, and hopefully to help inspire you to develop your own ideas. Remember that these are just a few options and the techniques can be mixed and matched to suit your design.

Ageing Acanthus (detail)
Spangles, surface stitching and couching.

Ageing Acanthus (detail)
Spangles, cutwork and couching.

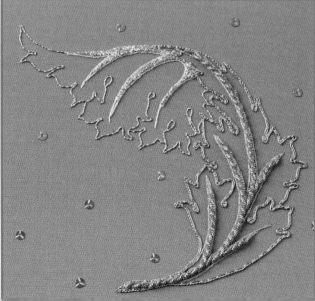

Three Wishes

Finished size: 48 x 25cm (19 x 9¾in).

If you ever play the three wishes game with friends, you will notice that the first dream wish is often very simple, the second dream wish is a little bigger and more complex and the third wish often expands into a grandiose and intricate story. It was this expansion and growth from small and simple to large and complex and the hidden depths that these dreams reveal in your friends and loved ones that inspired this embroidered panel, which shows three differently sized stars with intertwining shooting tails and flashes.

MATERIALS

Silver, gold and copper metal threads, including rococo, Japanese, pearl purl, bright check, organza appliqué, spangles and crystals, worked on a mole-grey velvet ground fabric.

TECHNIQUES

Overstretched pearl purl, spangles with single stitches and chips, crystals with chips, couching, cutwork, bright check chips and appliqué.

Having designed the composition, I framed up and transferred the design to the fabric. I then worked the appliqué, followed by couching, pearl purl, chips, crystals and spangles.

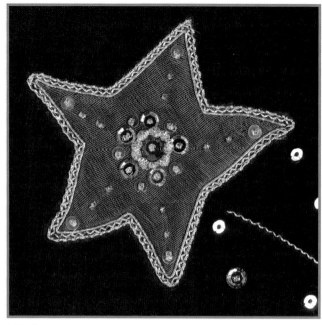

Wish One.

Wish Two.

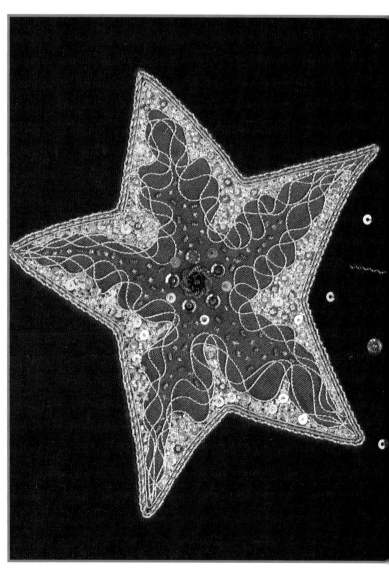

Wish Three.

Indian Summer

Finished size: 10 x 15cm (4 x 6in).

Having been born and raised in Birmingham, I've learnt to appreciate the vibrancy of colour and culture all around me. As such, I wanted to pay a small homage to that by looking at hot, spicy Indian silk fabrics and creating a design that was a little reminiscent of the traditional *mehndi* patterns with their delicacy and happy associations.

Hot, spicy orange and azure blue silks are balanced with a mixture of golden threads and orange metallic thread in a scrolling floral design.

MATERIALS

Gilt smooth purl and bright check, pearl purl, Japanese, rococo, coloured metallic twist, spangles, sequins and seed beads applied to a silk ground.

TECHNIQUES

Pearl purl, spangles with chips, sequins with beads, couching, cutwork over soft string, bright check chips, beadwork and appliqué.

The finished piece (shown left) and the initial colour drawing (above).

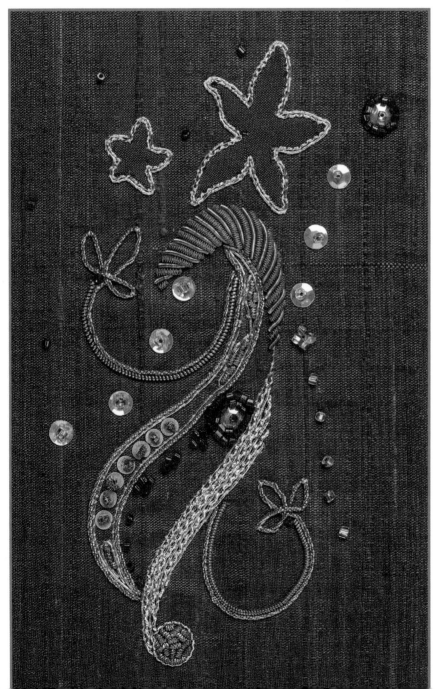

I carefully transferred the design on to the silk using a lightbox and then put the fabric into a ring frame, ensuring that the tension was nice and tight all round. I worked the soft-string padding and executed the appliqué areas. I then embroidered down all of the couched threads, plunged their ends and fastened them neatly and securely at the back of the piece. Next came the pearl purl and chips, followed by sequins, spangles and beadwork. Last to be worked was the area of cutwork over soft string.

Spring Flight

Finished size: 30 x 35cm (11¾ x 13¾in).

This piece is a celebration of new beginnings and renewal. Every year, the blossom bursts forth and the birds return from their winter retreats, and with them come fresh colour, warmer weather and hopeful, happier attitudes. Every spring offers a turning point; longer, lighter days and new life. This piece embodies that celebration for me.

This piece combines a delicate balance of heavily worked areas with finely wrought, open areas utilising a mixture of cherry blossom reds and pinks with the bronze, copper, gold, silver and blue contrast of the bird in flight.

MATERIALS

Silver, gilt, copper and bronze fine passing threads, copper, gilt, silver, pink and red rough purl, silver, gilt and copper bright check, silver and gilt spangles, gilt pearl purl, gilt and coloured metallic twist, seed beads and sequins on an eau de Nil silk ground.

TECHNIQUES

Couching, cutwork, s-ing with spangles, chips, and overstretched pearl purl.

I stretched my fabric into a slate frame and then carefully transferred the design on to the silk using the prick-and-pounce method. I then worked the carpet-felt padding and craft-felt padding, followed by the couching threads and pearl purl. The next stage to be worked was the chipping, sequins, spangles and beadwork, followed by the cutwork to the wings, tail, beak and flowers.

The complete embroidery.

   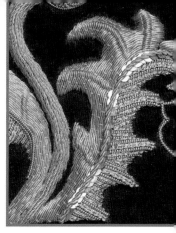

More a Scottish Thistle than an English Rose

Finished size: 71 x 68.5cm (28 x 27in).

This piece was worked while I was in my second year as an apprentice at the RSN in 2002. The requirement was to take inspiration from Coronation robes from the past and create a new design. Mine was quite a personal response based upon my Scottish heritage (represented by the thistle) but also showing reference to the fact that I was born and raised in England, which is represented by the acorn and rose leaves. The five laurel leaves on the right-hand stem symbolise the five members of my family and the stems intertwine and curl towards each other to show that we are all a product of our environment and culture. The leaves face outwards to represent the space that is essential for every individual in a family so that there is room for them to grow and follow their own path.

MATERIALS

Assorted gilt and gold metal threads including plate, rococo, twist, Japanese thread, passing, gimp, bullion, spangles, pearl purl, smooth purl, rough purl, bright check threads and dull/wire check threads, worked on a dark blue velvet ground.

TECHNIQUES

The techniques employed across the piece are very traditional and include couching, couching over hard string, pearl purl, chips, cutwork over soft string, cutwork over carpet felt, s-ing, s-ing with spangles, plate over felt, chips and looped chips.

Having framed up the calico and velvet in a slate frame I pricked, pounced and carefully painted the design on to the fabric to ensure I had a fine, even line. I then applied the carpet-felt padding, craft-felt padding, soft-string padding and hard-string padding. All areas of couching were then embroidered, and had their ends plunged and neatly secured at the back of the fabric. I then worked all areas of pearl purl, followed by the chips. The gimp was then applied and the plate was stitched down. All areas of cutwork were then completed.

Above, from left to right: rough, smooth, dull check and bright check purls over soft-string padding with s-ing detailing; rough and smooth purls over soft string, looped chips and plate over felt, and combination couching over craft-felt and carpet-felt padding; rough and smooth purls over soft-string padding, couching over hard string, combination couching over carpet-felt and craft-felt padding, rough, smooth, dull check and bright check purls, and chips over carpet felt and craft felt with a pearl purl edge; combination couching and couching over hard string, carpet felt and craft felt with pearl purl and s-ing with spangles, cutwork with spangles, pearl purl and cutwork over soft string and carpet and craft felt.

Left: the complete embroidery.

Pomegranate and Gillyflower

Finished size: 15 x 16cm (6 x 6¼in).

This piece derives its inspiration from the Elizabethan and Stuart floral designs that were so often translated on to items of clothing and accessories in embroidery, and also from the texture and pattern of Jacobean embroidery.

I hoped to create a robust but feminine floral design with areas of varying texture and colour, and with bursts of rich colour to delight the eye in the same way that the original embroideries did, and still do today.

MATERIALS

Seed beads, sequins, fine copper mesh, copper bright check, coloured rough purl, stranded cotton, rococo, coloured metallic twist, gilt Japanese thread and fine silver passing thread.

TECHNIQUES

Chain stitch, straight stitch, stem stitch, metal mesh appliqué, trellis with looped chip decoration, couching, overstretched pearl purl with coloured core, feather stitch in coloured rough purl, sequins with bead centres and beads.

I carefully transferred the design on to the fabric using a lightbox and then placed the fabric into a ring frame, ensuring that the fabric was taut and stretched evenly. As the first stage for the embroidery, I worked all of the areas of surface stitching using stranded cottons, followed by the couching and pearl purl. All sequins, copper mesh, beads and chips were then applied, followed by the cutwork. In the case of the pomegranate stem, the beads were worked at the same time as the cutwork, as they need to be worked in order.

The finished piece (shown right) was based on my initial colour drawing above. An enlarged section of this piece is shown on page 245.

STUMPWORK

See also page 299.

See also page 269.

See also pages 274 and 279.

See also page 284.

FROM THE AUTHOR

I have grown to love the subject of stumpwork not for its designs, which are imperfect in form, or for its less-than-brilliant use of colour, but for its uninhibited playfulness, its eclecticism, humour, innocence and often naïvety. As an embroiderer, stumpwork encourages me to explore and experiment within design and stitching, but most importantly to remain creative. Apart from the need to capture the essential 'spirit' of stumpwork, there are very few rules within this technique, enabling modern embroiderers still to create contemporary and relevant work.

In every 17th-century stumpwork piece there is always something new to learn, not just in the stitching, but also about the embroiderer herself. Were they professional or amateur, royalists or lovers of mythology? What was their favourite plant, and did they have a weakness for high fashion? Through this medium embroiderers reflected the age that they lived in, and on the fabric lie intriguing tales of social and political history.

Within my own work I have never concentrated on just one technique, preferring to use stitches and materials, however varied, that best convey a required effect. Stumpwork as a subject uniquely reflects this same idea of working. It uses an array of different materials and ingeniously blends multiple embroidery techniques such as silk work, goldwork, counted work, flat stitching, raised stitching, beadwork, padding and needlelace. Design themes are also very broad in their nature. Sometimes themes are political or relate purely to the social history of the day, but very often they act as a sort of artistic and emotional 'pin-board'. These embroideries reveal favourite

designs and motifs and harbour treasured objects, such as precious shells, possibly gathered from trips to the coast, nestled within the layers of embroidery. For this reason, stumpwork can be very well suited to a modern approach.

Within a subject such as this, vast in technique and possibilities, this section of the book has been written as a way of clearly demonstrating the essential practices of stumpwork. It strives to help readers uncover or take a fresh look at this incredible subject, and by doing so help to create work which is vibrant and contemporary, without losing any of its intrigue.

The way in which this section is ordered helpfully reflects the stages in which stumpwork can be best executed. Due to the nature of the work and its sculptural effect, various layers of embroidery and padding will be built up in several stages. Do not be daunted by this; once you have read through the different sections and come to grips with the system of work, you will very quickly realise that it is self-explanatory. For instance, I first work all of the flat stitches because they lie underneath layers of padding. Wired shapes will be inserted last in order for them not to be damaged when working other raised stitches. Different design processes will be discussed and demonstrated, as well as methods shown to prepare the fabric ready for stitching. All the most useful stitches will be illustrated and at the end of the chapter we will take a thorough look at constructing a figure.

Kate Sinton

THE HISTORY OF STUMPWORK

Stumpwork, a term coined in the 19th century, known as raised or embosted work in the 17th century, reached its height of popularity between 1650 and 1690. With the influence of the European 'broderie en relief', a highly padded and naturalistic form of ecclesiastical embroidery and a technique that can be traced back to the 15th century, raised work gradually became popular for domestic and decorative embroidery. Although it was not until the mid-17th century that stumpwork reached its peak, during the Elizabethan period many of the popular plants of the day were worked in detached buttonhole, an essential stumpwork stitch, and padding and metal work could often be found on gauntlets and expensive gloves. Alongside these similarities in technique, many of the same motifs used in the Elizabethan and early Stuart periods can be identified on stumpwork pieces.

Privileged young girls practised a diverse and broad range of stitches on spot motif and band samplers. The decorating of caskets, mirrors and pictures provided a great opportunity to explore the potential of these stitches and patterns, and many girls spent years working on such projects. Professional embroiderers who travelled the country visiting large country houses largely sustained the fashion for stumpwork. Ready-drawn designs on linen or satin could be bought or drawn up 'in house' along with carved hands and fruit that would later be placed on the work. These pedlars knew exactly which scenes would attract most customers, and by drawing figures dressed in the latest fashions of the day, young girls found them irresistible. These early forms of embroidery kits could go a long way to explaining the similarity of design and choice of motif in many historical pieces.

Stumpwork objects displayed a high level of imagination in design, and were predominantly adorned with pictorial images drawn from biblical stories and classical mythology. Other popular images were large formal portraits, often framed in oval cartouches. Whatever the main subject, the background was enlivened with animals, birds, insects, trees and buildings. These were joyously placed around figures to fill spaces, sometimes in a more ordered way, sometimes playfully haphazard. The embroiderer copied many motifs without changing the scale, which had the effect of merely adding to the fantastical nature of the scenes. A favourite image of mine is worked on a mid-17th-century piece and shows a bird standing on a roof with a worm in its mouth. The bird is nearly as large as the roof itself and the worm bigger than the windows or chimneys. Most motifs were taken from printed sources, of which there were many to choose from. New pattern books, herbals and bestiaries were circulated, many thorough in their chosen subject; one published in 1630 by Thomas Johnson was called *A book of Beaste, Birds, Flowers, Fruits, Flies and Wormes, exactly drawne with their Lively Colours truly Described*.

Random spot sampler

English School, 1630. This sampler exhibits a wide repertoire of stitches and patterns. Stitches include eyelet, bullion knot and tent worked in silk and metal thread. These samplers provided young girls with inspiration as they moved on to working a stumpwork piece. (Dorset County Museum, 1917.8.2)

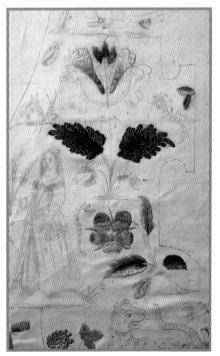

Looking Glass Border, 1690s

This partially worked panel (above) shows a beautifully balanced design with some of the separate images set on hillocks. The drawing in black ink is probably the work of a highly skilled professional embroiderer. On the left is shown a detail taken from the lower right-hand corner. (RSN Collection 1420)

Raised-work casket

English School, after 1685, worked on satin-weave silk in silk thread, metal braid, wax, mica, parchment, pearls, metal purl and bullion, straw, glass beads, silk cord, linen ribbon, wood and padding. One of the five panels on this box depicts the Jewish biblical heroine Judith, symbolising humility, holding the severed head of her people's enemy, Holofernes. See also page 264. (Dorset County Museum, 1955.2.9)

Stumpwork, although always used to adorn luxury objects, never maintained the formal repetitions you see in many of the decorative arts. Through its pictorial nature it developed a rich symbolism of its own, which was largely informed by the turbulent years from the execution of Charles I through to the Restoration. Many of the male biblical characters in these scenes, as well as the regal lions, bear some resemblance to Charles I or Charles II. Portraits of both monarchs were occasionally stitched, and are instantly recognisable.

Embroiderers sometimes expressed their loyalty to the royalist cause through emblems or hidden images. The caterpillar, it has been suggested, is a badge of Charles I and a butterfly, oak and acorns badges of Charles II. The symbolism was extended further still. One could choose from a splendid range of subjects, including sheets of flowers, fruit, birds and animals. Carnations suggested love and bees diligence and orderliness. Many embroiderers would know full well the meaning of each motif, but many were chosen just because they liked the curved line of a petal or the potential for stitchery within a snail's shell or lion's head.

The restoration of Charles II brought a more literal approach to this symbolism. The figure of his father, Charles I, became synonymous with that of King Solomon. The marriage of King Solomon to the Queen of Sheba is one of the more common themes and represents the marriage of Charles I to Henrietta Maria. Charles II and Catherine of Braganza were also represented. Other scenes from the Old Testament such as Esther and Ahasuerus were also popular and recurred again and again, however always varying through the different applications of embroidery.

Work by the amateur embroiderer ranged from comparatively crude and simple pieces to works that showed great skill. At its peak both amateur and professional embroideries could be highly intricate and inside many caskets lay three-dimensional gardens in sunken trays, trees and plants standing proudly upright surrounded by fantastic topiary worked in encrusted embroidery.

The popularity of stumpwork only continued, however, until the end of the 17th century when the Western imagination became entranced by anything oriental. This style dramatically influenced the designs and techniques used on both furniture and furnishings, but interestingly these designs too often had a novel and appealing way of using scale and perspective.

17th-century picture

Randomly placed images worked on silk satin. Techniques include silk work, metal thread work, tent stitch slips and plush work in silk chenille. (Private collection)

TOOLS AND MATERIALS

FABRICS

Traditionally, stumpwork was embroidered on ivory-coloured silk, satin-weave silk or plain-weave linen. If worked on silk, areas of the background cloth would be left visible or very often spotted with metal spangles or feathers. It is fairly common, however, to see large areas of the silk covered in silk-work stitches such as laid work, silk shading or burden stitch (see page 48). Stumpwork on a linen background was almost always filled in with counted work such as fine tent stitch or gobelin filling stitch.

Obviously, there are no rules concerning what the contemporary embroiderer should use and any fabric can be used as long as the fabric is strong enough to support some of the heavier padded and raised elements.

In addition to the background fabrics described, various other fabrics are also used in stumpwork. Calico, for example, is used to act as a support fabric when constructing detached needlelace pieces in a ring frame. Silk organza is used as a base fabric for wired pieces filled with embroidery and fine linen or canvas is used for counted tent-stitch slips. Silk, silk tissue, silk organza or any other fine fabric can be used to create wired fabric shapes. If you have a fabric that you particularly like, the only way to see if it is suitable is to sample and experiment.

THREADS

Traditionally, stumpwork was worked in floss, twisted silks and metal threads. Sometimes linen threads were used to string beads. Today, stranded cottons, perlé cottons, crewel wool and many other threads are easily obtained and can be used in stumpwork embroidery to great effect. The trick is to experiment with threads through sampling and find out if they achieve a good result.

SILK RIBBONS

Silk ribbon is a fantastic material to work with and extremely adaptable. It can be stitched down in straight stitches to create leaves or petals, left looped on the surface of the fabric or wrapped around a large bead, which shows off its lustrous quality beautifully (see page 296).

In the 17th century metallic bobbin-lace ribbons were frequently sewn down to frame a picture or cameo portrait, or to line the outside edges of a casket or mirror. Unfortunately these intricate ribbons are expensive and difficult to find today, but I find silk ribbon to be a fair exchange and a much more versatile product.

SILK CORDS

Fine silk cord was one of the most popular materials used in 17th-century stumpwork, and you will see it on almost all period pieces. These shiny, smooth cords were couched down with a single thread and embroiderers found it extremely useful for outlining motifs or filling large areas, such as tree trunks and even whole animals. The cords were very often shaded in colour as they were laid down. Such fine silk cords, plentiful in the 17th century, are near impossible to find today. However, slightly larger cords can be bought and will add authenticity to any contemporary stumpwork design.

Any thread can be used for stumpwork, but above are the threads that I find extremely useful. Stranded cottons, rayon machine threads, polyester machine threads, fine semi-transparent threads, perlé cotton, pure silk embroidery threads, flower thread, silk cord and silk ribbon.

METAL THREADS AND WIRES

Traditionally, most of the metal threads used in stumpwork would have been silver gilt or metal wrapped with coloured silk. The type of metal threads used were Japanese thread, smooth purls, bright check purls, plate or lizerine wire. Most of these metal threads and wires can still be purchased from specialist suppliers, as well as an array of new coloured threads. Embroiderers were, and still are, extremely inventive with the use of metal threads and if you study traditional stumpwork pieces you will see that there are no set rules on how and where these threads can be used.

Shown right are some of the metal threads that can be used in stumpwork embroidery. Japanese thread, plate, smooth purl, bright check and pearl purl along with some spangles.

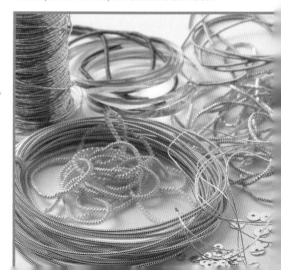

NEEDLES

The choice of needle depends largely on the embroidery technique and thread that are being used. A large variety of techniques and threads can be used in stumpwork, reflecting the broad array of needles that is required. Needles are numbered according to their size; the higher the number, the finer the needle.

EMBROIDERY/CREWEL NEEDLES

Embroidery/crewel needles are slender, sharp-pointed needles. Their small eyes help to hold the thread well in the needle. Numbers 10 and 12 are used for fine work and are best used with fine silk or cottons. If you find these needles too small to thread, a no.9 will work just as well. Use the finest needle you can to stitch any form of slip on to the base fabric, for example when making detached needlelace and faces. When using a slightly thicker thread such as a perlé cotton or several strands of stranded cotton, use a no.9 or no.7.

CHENILLE NEEDLES

Chenille needles are longer and thicker than embroidery/crewel needles and have larger eyes to accommodate heavier or larger numbers of threads. Numbers 24 and 22 are very useful when using thicker perlé cotton threads or more than one strand of crewel wool. I find a no.20 chenille needle a very useful size for plunging Japanese metal threads, silk cords or bundles of couched threads to the back of the fabric.

TAPESTRY NEEDLES

Tapestry needles have large eyes and are blunt at the end. This blunt point makes them perfect for weaving threads and therefore executing stitches such as woven wheels (see page 68) or tent-stitch slips. Some embroiderers enjoy using a fine tapestry needle when needlelacing, as they do not catch on other threads as easily.

BEADING NEEDLES

Beading needles are fine and long – perfect for threading up long lines of beads or pearls. Many people prefer sewing beads down with these needles, but personally I would always use very fine embroidery/crewel needles such as no.12 or no.10, which are shorter and easier to handle.

OTHER MATERIALS

Fabric paint: any fabric or watercolour paint can be used to colour backgrounds or give definition to embroidered faces.

Padding materials: cotton felt, soft sheep's wool, pelmet Vilene, cotton string and wood are all used for padding.

Wires: fine, paper-covered cake wires are extremely useful when creating stumpwork embroidery. As well as wrapping them with threads to produce hands or antennae for insects, wires can be used as an edge to fabric or buttonhole shapes.

Fine card: this can be wrapped with thread before being folded into a loop and stitched down (see page 296). Fine card or parchment is also a traditional material to paste on to the back of fabrics to add support.

Leather: fine, soft leather can be cut and stitched down with small stab stitches. Leather is a useful material for figure work and can be used for boots and shoes, cuffs or belts.

Seed pearls: traditionally, seed pearls were used to embellish figures and were stitched down to create necklaces, bracelets or buttons. In contemporary stumpwork seed pearls can be used in many different ways.

Wooden beads: these can be found in various sizes and are easily wrapped with threads or ribbon.

Glass beads: these can be stitched on to padded slips or used to embellish various areas of your stumpwork.

Mica or shisha mirror: mica is a natural mineral that was often used in traditional stumpwork. Small pieces would be stitched on to embroideries to form the windows for castles. It is difficult to find today and a good substitute is small pieces of Indian shisha mirror.

Found objects: to provide areas of intrigue, small objects can be stitched or glued on to your stumpwork embroidery: bells, beads, shells or anything of personal interest.

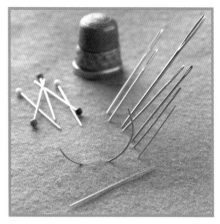

Stumpwork can use a vast array of different needles for all the many different techniques.

Some of the padding materials used in stumpwork, as well as paints and wires.

A collection of beads, feathers, leather and all sorts of other favourite found objects, for example shells and old buttons.

STUMPWORK DESIGN

The design of stumpwork is almost more essential to its character than the techniques used. It is this character that should be captured by the contemporary embroiderer. In the 17th century, the use of chosen images, varying and unrelated in scale, meant that a flower could be as big as a dog and a butterfly could match a lion or a castle in size. This idiosyncratic use of scale alludes to a world of imagination and playfulness rather than one of constrained realism, whether intentionally or not. The application of this approach in modern design should be a very useful tool, but as important as it was for the young girls of the Stuart period to produce work that reflected the age they lived in, with the use of new and relevant images it is vital for us to create work with a contemporary style.

Stumpwork designs usually fall into one of three distinct groupings, and these too can usefully be applied to modern design.

SCATTERED OR MIRRORED IMAGES

The design is treated like a sampler with single images or small scenes scattered on the fabric either haphazardly or in a more orderly fashion. A good example of this is shown on page 261. Often images with similar qualities or proportions were mirrored on either side of the design. Sometimes these images 'floated' on the fabric but at other times they were set on small mounds or hillocks. These acted as a useful device for isolating one incident or character from another. The embroidery design shown at the bottom of page 260 is an excellent historical example of this type of design, and the image on page 274 shows a more contemporary take on it.

As spoken about in the introduction on page 259, this embroidery illustrates beautifully the 'pin-board' effect you can create with a few favourite motifs, images or ideas. This contemporary piece successfully follows the 17th-century tradition of scattered images, yet retains a very modern feel.

SMALL IMAGES SURROUNDING A CENTRAL FIGURE OR FIGURES

This type of design features single images or small scenes surrounding a main group of figures or a large central portrait. The image on the lid of the casket shown below is a good example of this.

IMAGES FORMING A NARRATIVE

A narrative-style design is one in which a story or a single scene from a story is illustrated. Designs of this type were very often found on the side panels of caskets. Whilst they use a much more realistic perspective they still retain that naïve quality that makes stumpwork so unique.

Raised-work casket

English School, after 1685. The lid of this casket shows clearly small images surrounding the main central figures, and the side panels demonstrate the more narrative style of design. See also page 261. (Dorset County Museum, 1955.2.9)

264

APPLIQUÉ

All sorts of different appliqué methods can be used in stumpwork and it is one of the most well-used techniques. All slips and needlelace shapes are applied to the fabric using small stab stitches. Other fabric shapes can be cut slightly larger and have their edges turned under before being appliquéd to the work. Both of these methods will be described later in the book.

Iron-on adhesives such as Bondawcb can be fused to the back of fabrics before ironing them into place. A line of stitching can be placed over the edge to secure the fused fabric more firmly. This method is shown in the demonstration below.

Areas of flat appliqué should be placed on the base fabric before any stitching is worked. Other applications, such as slips or needlelace cordonnets, are applied when all the layers of the embroidery that lie underneath them have been worked. Always consider the grain of the fabric before applying it to the background fabric. Usually, fabric is applied on the straight grain, but if you need flexibility when applying a fabric (such as the neck or face fabric on a figure, cut the fabric on the cross.

Begin by cutting out a square of fabric approximately 2.5cm (1in) larger all round than the appliqué shape. Press if necessary.

This piece shows layers of fabric fused to the background using Bondaweb. The bird has been applied to the background using stab stitches before being padded (see pages 284–285). A couched line of thread has then been applied on top.

 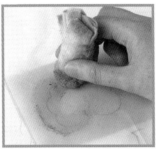  

1 Cut a piece of adhesive web (for example, Bondaweb) approximately 1cm (½in) smaller all round than the fabric. Place the fabric over a piece of tissue paper and iron the adhesive web on to the fabric using a fairly hot iron.

2 Make a pricking of the appliqué shape and transfer the image on to the fabric using pounce (see page 20).

3 Remove the pricking and draw in the outline using a fine, blue soluble pen.

4 Cut out the shape on the line.

TRANSFERRING THE SURFACE STITCHING LINES

Once all the layers of flat appliqué have been worked and any painting done on the base fabric, all the areas of flat stitching that will lie underneath more raised areas can be worked.

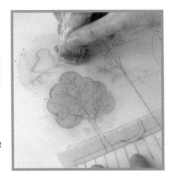  

5 Position the template on the background fabric and secure it with one or two pins. Peel the protective backing off the adhesive web and place the appliqué shape on the fabric, underneath the template, aligning it with the corresponding part of the design. Lift the template away and iron the appliqué shape in place under a sheet of tissue paper.

1 Make a pricking of the elements that will be stitched flat to the fabric. Transfer them to the background fabric as described above.

2 Remove the pricking and mark in the outlines with a fine, blue soluble pen.

3 Brush away any excess pounce with a soft brush.

265

STUMPWORK STITCH FINDER

See also page 265.

See also page 284.

Stitch	Type	Page
BACK STITCH	FLAT SURFACE STITCH	SEE PAGE 57
BUTTONHOLE BARS	FLAT SURFACE STITCH	SEE PAGE 274
BUTTONHOLE COURONNES	FLAT SURFACE STITCH	SEE PAGE 272
BUTTONHOLE SCALLOPS	FLAT SURFACE STITCH	SEE PAGE 275
CEYLON STITCH	NEEDLELACE STITCH	SEE PAGE 278
CHIP WORK IN BRIGHT CHECK	METAL THREAD WORK	SEE PAGE 281
CHIP WORK IN COLOURED PURLS	METAL THREAD WORK	SEE PAGE 281
CORDED BUTTONHOLE STITCH	NEEDLELACE STITCH	SEE PAGE 278
COUCHING A GOLD THREAD	METAL THREAD WORK	SEE PAGE 280
COUCHING A SILK CORD	FLAT SURFACE STITCH	SEE PAGE 268
COUCHING THREADS	FLAT SURFACE STITCH	SEE PAGE 59
COUNTED CANVAS SLIPS	SLIPS	SEE PAGE 290
DOUBLE BRUSSELS STITCH	NEEDLELACE STITCH	SEE PAGE 277
FABRIC SLIPS	SLIPS	SEE PAGE 288
FELT PADDING	PADDING	SEE PAGE 284
FINISHING STITCH	FLAT SURFACE STITCH	SEE PAGE 39
FOUND OBJECTS	EMBELLISHMENT	SEE PAGE 298
NEEDLELACE SLIPS	SLIPS	SEE PAGE 292
PEARL PURL	METAL THREAD WORK	SEE PAGE 280
PLATE	METAL THREAD WORK	SEE PAGE 282
RAISED LEAF STITCH	FLAT SURFACE STITCH	SEE PAGE 272

RAISED STEM BAND STITCH	FLAT SURFACE STITCH	SEE PAGE 271
RUNNING STITCH	FLAT SURFACE STITCH	SEE PAGE 57
SATIN STITCH	FLAT SURFACE STITCH	SEE PAGE 46
SINGLE BRUSSELS STITCH	NEEDLELACE STITCH	SEE PAGE 276
SPANGLES	METAL THREAD WORK	SEE PAGE 280
STEM STITCH	FLAT SURFACE STITCH	SEE PAGE 56
STARTING STITCH	FLAT SURFACE STITCH	SEE PAGE 39
STITCHED PADDING	PADDING	SEE PAGE 284
STRAIGHT STITCH	FLAT SURFACE STITCH	SEE PAGE 269
STRING PADDING	PADDING	SEE PAGE 286
TREBLE BRUSSELS STITCH	NEEDLELACE STITCH	SEE PAGE 277
TURKEY RUG STITCH	FLAT SURFACE STITCH	SEE PAGE 70
VILENE PADDING	PADDING	SEE PAGE 285
WIRED FABRIC SLIPS	SLIPS	SEE PAGE 289
WIRED NEEDLELACE SLIPS	SLIPS	SEE PAGE 295
WIRED SLIP FILLED WITH STITCHING	SLIPS	SEE PAGE 291
WOOD	PADDING	SEE PAGE 286
WOVEN PICOTS	FLAT SURFACE STITCH	SEE PAGE 270
WOVEN WHEELS	METAL THREAD WORK	SEE PAGE 279
WRAPPED BEADS	WRAPPING	SEE PAGE 296
WRAPPED PAPER	WRAPPING	SEE PAGE 296
WRAPPED WIRES	WRAPPING	SEE PAGE 297

See also page 283.

See also page 274.

FLAT SURFACE STITCHES

Couching a silk cord

In 17th-century stumpwork, silk cords were couched down using a fine silk thread. I prefer to attach the cord with small stitches that catch the edge of the silk using a semi-transparent thread, as I feel this disturbs the lustre of the silk less. This method also hides the couching stitches better and therefore gives a neater finish to your work. Use silk-wrapped cord and the finest thread you can find in a colour that matches the cord. The needle should be either a no.12 sharps or a no.10 embroidery needle. In this demonstration, I am outlining a piece of appliqué (see page 265).

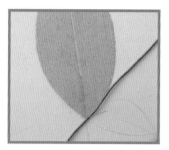   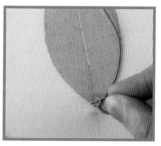

1 Begin by making the starting stitches, and lay the cord along the first part of the line, with an extra 4–5cm (1½–2in) tail that will be plunged behind. Work the first stitch 1–2mm (⅛in) from where the cord will be plunged. Bring the thread up on the outside of the shape, then take the needle back down, splitting the cord through the middle as you do so.

2 Pull the thread through and make the next stitch 3–4mm (¼in) along the cord. Continue to catch one side of the cord in the same way along its length, all the time guiding the cord with your left hand so that it lies neatly around the shape. The sewing thread should be hidden within the silk cord.

3 To plunge the cord once you have finished couching, first make a hole where you wish the cord to go through using a stiletto, a mellor or a large tapestry needle.

4 Cut a length of sewing thread, fold it in half and thread the two ends through a needle (any ordinary sewing needle will do). Pass the needle through the hole and pull the thread through, leaving a loop on the top. Catch the cord in the loop and pull the rest of the thread through, pulling the cord through with it.

5 Cast off on the back of the fabric using the same method as that used for finishing a couched thread (see pages 228–229).

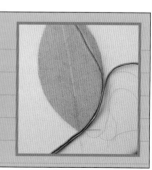

Note
If you are laying two or more cords next to each other, always lay the first cord on the outline and the subsequent cords on either side of it. To lay these cords, bring the thread up on the outer edge and take it down in the middle of the cord, towards the cord that has already been secured.

A line of silk cord edges the appliqué of this tree. A further line of cord is stitched down the centre to create the trunk before lines of outline stitch are worked up against the cord as a shadow. The leaves have been made using wired slips filled with stitching (see page 291) and the background is dotted with spangles.

Straight stitch

Straight stitch is an extremely useful stitch and one that is often overlooked. It can be worked in any thread and can add areas of interest and texture through small and delicate stitches or larger and heavier ones. Straight stitch is a particularly useful stitch when working with fine silk ribbons. Groups of single straight stitches, worked using thread, ribbon or a combination of both, can be used to create clumps of grasses, legs of insects, leaf veins, and so on.

Avoid working with lengths of ribbon greater than 20cm (8in), because ribbon can start to look worn very quickly. Start off and finish as you would a couched thread or cord, but if there is no suitable space for casting off invisibly, thread through the existing stitches on the back.

- Always hold the needle on top with your left hand and keep your right hand underneath the fabric all the time (reverse this if you are left-handed). This will speed up your sewing.

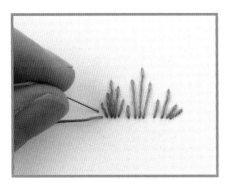

1 Work groups of single straight stitches with a thread to create a clump of grass. Always pull the thread through completely at the start and end of each stitch.

2 To make a straight stitch with ribbon, pass the ribbon through to the front of the fabric, hold it taut in your left hand and take the needle down through the centre of the ribbon.

3 Pull the ribbon through to the back of the fabric.

4 Use the ribbon to make some more stitches of varying length.

This embroidery includes straight stitches worked in ribbon. Woven wheels in metal thread (see page 279) are used for the flowers, and the rest of the design is painted.

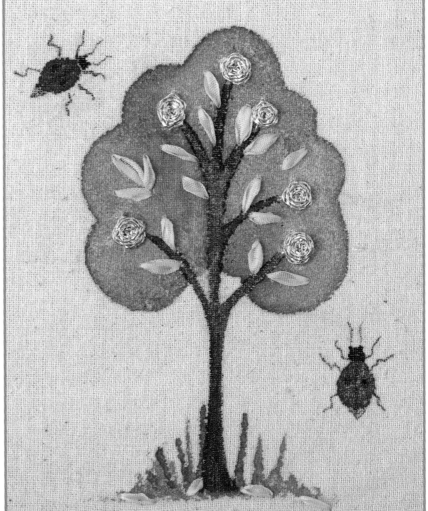

Woven picots

Woven picots can be worked large or small, thin or wide. Picots that are attached to the fabric at both the base and the point can be worked with two, three, four or five prongs. Detached picots attached to the supporting material only at the base can only be worked with three or five prongs. Try using fine beading wire for the outside prongs of a detached picot to create shapes that you can bend and manipulate.

TWO-PRONGED PICOT

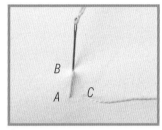 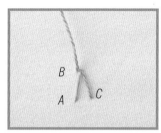  

1 Make a stitch from A to B, then a second stitch from C to B to form a point. This will be the size of the finished woven picot.

2 Bring the needle through to the front of the fabric just to the left of B.

3 Weave backwards and forwards across the shape, from top to bottom, using either the eye of the needle or a tapestry needle. Push the thread up with the needle as you work to ensure the rows are tightly packed.

4 Continue to the bottom of the shape, finishing the stitch in the centre of the base, tucking the thread up underneath the weave.

THREE-PRONGED PICOT

1 Make the initial shape with two stitches (see step 1 above), then work a third stitch halfway between them. Weave backwards and forwards across the shape as before.

2 Work down to the end of the shape and end on whichever side you finish weaving.

Note
Start a three-pronged picot by going under the first thread, over the middle one and under the third thread.

This stumpwork pin uses detached woven picots worked over felt to create the petals (see opposite). The tips of alternate picots have a bead placed at the point. The centre of the flower is a slip of French knots and beads edged with a metal wire called lizerine (see page 280).

DETACHED WOVEN PICOTS
- Detached woven picots can only be worked on three- or five-pronged picots.
- The maximum length of a detached woven picot is approximately 1.5cm (½in) – any longer than this and they become a little unstable.

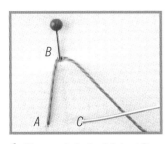

1 Place a pin in the fabric at B to mark the top of the picot. Bring the thread up at point A (as in step 1 opposite), wrap it round the pin and take it down at C.

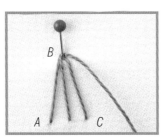

2 Bring the needle back through halfway between A and C and wrap the thread around the pin again.

3 Do not take the thread through to the back of the fabric, but instead weave the thread backwards and forwards across the shape, as you did before. Take the thread through to the back of the fabric on the side on which you finish weaving.

4 Remove the pin and bend the picot upwards, away from the fabric, with the end of the pin.

Raised stem band

This stitch makes a solid, slightly raised shape with a wonderful texture of regimented horizontal bands. It is the perfect stitch to portray insect bodies or perhaps the bark of a tree. Any thread and sharp-ended needle (embroidery needle) can be used. The bars can be anything between 5mm and 1cm (¼–½in) apart, depending on the size of the shape.

Note

If the 'twists' in the second row look like mirror images of those in the first row, the needle has been pointed towards the wrong side of the outer edge.

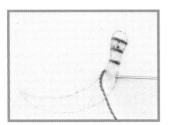

1 Lay bars across the shape, evenly spaced at approximately 6mm (¼in) intervals and at right angles to the length of the shape. Take the needle through the fabric on the outer edge of the outline.

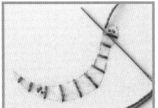

2 Start a new thread. Make a starting stitch and bring the needle through to the front of the fabric on the outline at the top right-hand corner of the shape. Change to a tapestry needle. Pass the thread over and under the first bar, pointing the needle towards the top outer edge of the shape.

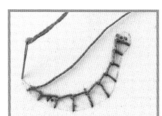

3 Continue working over and under each bar. Avoid over-tightening the stitches – they should lie flat without distorting the bars. Take the needle through to the back of the fabric when you reach the end of the shape.

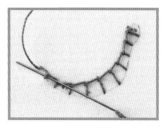

4 Come up as close as possible to the end of the last stitch, and work back towards the top of the shape, passing the thread over and under the bars, as before, this time pointing the needle towards the bottom outer edge of the shape.

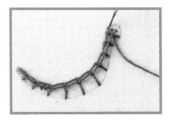

5 At the end of the row, take the needle down at the edge of the shape as before.

6 Continue to fill the shape. Notice that the more rows you put in, the denser the stitching becomes. As you approach the lower edge, you will need to bring the needle up further towards the middle of the shape to fill the small gaps that are left.

7 To completely fill the shape and obtain a neat, compact finish, you may sometimes need to force the needle under the stitches.

Buttonhole couronnes

These small circles of buttonhole stitch can sometimes be difficult to master, but keep practising as they can prove to be extremely useful. Use variously sized knitting needles or wooden dowelling to produce different-sized circles. Any type of thread can be used for this stitch.

- Couronnes can be attached to the fabric at either one point or two to four points using a fine thread in a matching colour. Bring the needle up on the outside of the circle and take it back down through the centre of a stitch.

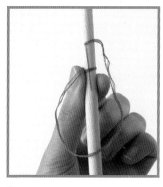

1 To make a large couronne, thread two strands of perlé cotton through a needle and double it to form four strands. Hold the threads firmly in place on the dowelling (form), leaving a long tail.

2 Wrap the thread around the back of the form and cross it over at the front.

3 Take the needle down behind the wrapped thread and bring it up through the loop.

4 Tighten the buttonhole stitch firmly around the form.

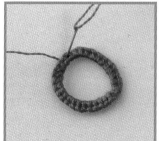

5 Make the second stitch just to the right of the first.

6 Continue around the form, placing each buttonhole stitch firmly against the previous one to form a tight circle of stitches. Complete the couronne by taking the thread up through the first stitch. Leave the thread threaded through the needle.

7 Remove the couronne and use the needle and thread to attach it to the fabric. Take the tail thread through to the back of the fabric and use a separate single thread to stitch the couronne in place. Cast off all threads on the back.

Raised leaf stitch

Raised leaf stitch is one of my favourite stitches and it is most effective when worked small. Experiment with the width of card used, but if the stitch becomes too large the loops of thread will become difficult to control and the finished effect can look untidy. Begin by cutting a small rectangle out of card – no wider than about 1cm (½in) and significantly longer than the leaf. Any thread can be used for this stitch, and any sharp-pointed needle. For this demonstration I have used a piece of card 8mm (³⁄₈in) wide, and three strands of stranded cotton.

- Practise this stitch using different widths of card and different numbers of stitches to see how it changes the shape and size of the leaf.

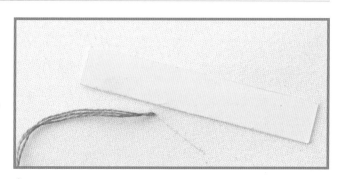

1 Mark the position of the leaf with a single line drawn on to the fabric. Bring the thread through to the front of the fabric at the tip of the leaf.

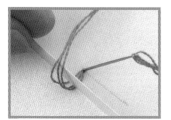

Note

Only the first stitch needs to go up and down through the same hole.

2 Hold the card at right angles to the fabric and stitch over it, making sure that the thread of the first stitch is taken down through the same hole as it came up (this will ensure a sharp point to the leaf).

3 Pull the thread through to form the stitch, then bring the needle back up on the opposite side of the card just in front of the last stitch.

4 Continue to form stitches along the card. When you have worked approximately six to eight stitches, bring the needle up on one side of the card and pass the eye-end of the needle under all the stitches back to the tip.

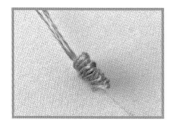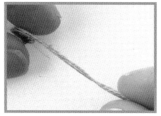

5 Pull the thread through, then hold on to the stitches with your left hand and remove the strip of card with the other.

6 Hold the stitches upright and gently pull the thread over towards the base of the leaf.

7 Shape the leaf gently and take the thread down through the fabric at the base of the leaf.

The completed leaf.

Note

Try using a thread in another colour to work a single stitch from the centre to the end of the leaf. This will add variation to the central vein and stem.

The leaves of this tree are made using raised leaf stitch in five different colours of stranded cotton. A separate straight stitch in brown thread has been placed down the middle of each leaf to define the central veins.

273

Buttonhole bars

Buttonhole bars can be attached to the fabric securely at both ends or detached at one end to produce a stitch with movement and flexibility.

- The distance A–B determines the length of the buttonhole bar or scallop.
- Hold the thread taut in your left hand as you form each stitch to maintain the shape of the preceding one.

ATTACHED BUTTONHOLE BARS

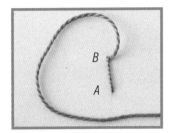 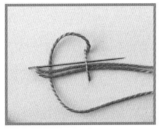 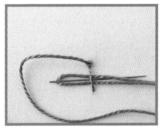 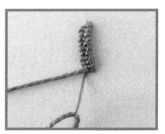

1 Make a stitch from A to B, which will be the length of the finished buttonhole bar. Bring the needle back through to the front of the fabric just to the right of B.

2 Form a loop to the left of the bar and push the eye-end of the needle under the bar from right to left, taking the needle through the loop.

3 Tighten the buttonhole stitch and form the next stitch in the same way.

4 Continue down the bar, making the buttonhole stitches as even as possible. At the end of the bar, take the needle through to the back of the fabric and cast off.

This embroidery was created using only those stitches demonstrated in this section. By carefully following the step-by-step instructions provided, similar effects can be achieved.

DETACHED BUTTONHOLE BARS

In the following demonstration, a detached buttonhole bar is used to make a tiny carrot.
They can, of course, be made using a single colour, and the buttonhole stitches worked
along the entire length of the wrapped thread.

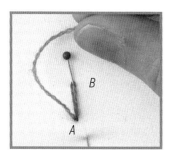 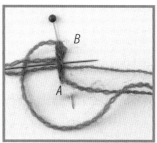 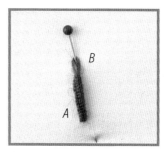 

1 Insert a pin into the fabric and
bring the green thread up just
to one side of it, at A. Wrap the
thread around the top of the pin
(B) once and take it back through
the same hole at A. Repeat two or
three times.

2 Cast off and change to an
orange-coloured thread. Bring
the thread up at A and work a
buttonhole stitch just down from B.

3 Continue to form buttonhole
stitches to the end of the wrapped
green thread. At A, take the thread
through to the back of the fabric
and secure it.

4 Remove the pin and cut
through the green loops to form
the top of the carrot.

Buttonhole scallops

Buttonhole scallops are very adaptable. They can be stitched singly or in lines, large or small.
The outline of a scallop can be stitched or it can be a densely filled-in shape.

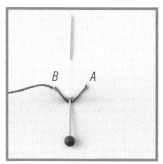 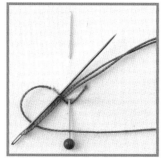  

1 Insert a pin vertically into the
fabric and make a stitch from A
to B, taking the thread around
the head of the pin. This will be
the size of the scallop. Bring the
needle back up just to the left of B.

2 Form the first buttonhole stitch
by taking the eye-end of the needle
under the stitch and through the
loop that has been formed.

3 Continue along towards A,
removing the pin as you approach
the centre of the scallop.

4 At A, take the needle through
to the back of the work.

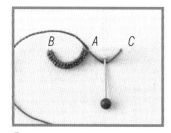 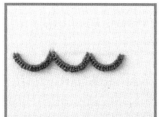

5 To make a row of scallops,
bring the needle up at C and down
at A, taking the thread around a
pin as before. Bring the needle
back up just above A, to start the
buttonhole stitches.

6 Work buttonhole stitches
along the second scallop and
repeat for as many buttonhole
scallops as you wish. Subsequent
rows of scallops can be made to
good effect.

*Four rows of buttonhole scallops were placed on the breast of this owl
after the padded tent-stitch slip had been worked (see page 290).*

NEEDLELACE STITCHES

Needlelace is probably the most identifiable stitch within stumpwork and one that was passed down to the Stuart embroiderers from the Elizabethan period. In many 17th-century pieces extraordinarily fine buttonhole stitch was worked and often contrasted with a slightly heavier buttonhole stitch to great effect.

There are a great many different buttonhole stitches and most can be worked directly on to the base fabric, over padding or as a slip on a separate frame. These slips are called cordonnets and refer to the support threads couched around the outside edge of the shape. Cordonnets can be filled with many different stitches, the most effective being corded buttonhole, and single, double or treble Brussels stitch.

When working directly on to the fabric the most effective stitches used are corded buttonhole and Ceylon stitch. To ensure that you do not pick up any of the background fabric or padding you can use a tapestry needle.

The demonstrations on the following pages show four of the more common versions of needlelace, but their appearance can be varied, for example by working the first row fairly loosely and working three buttonhole stitches into each loop of the previous row, or by working it tightly and making a buttonhole stitch in every second or third loop of the previous row.

Jenny Adin-Christie has used wired buttonhole slips to create the centre of this orchid. Corded buttonhole stitch has been used, and metal threads and changes of colour and direction incorporated to wonderful effect.

Single Brussels stitch

This stitch can be worked densely, as below, by working the first row of buttonhole stitches close together or as a more open stitch by spacing them further apart.

- When working an organic shape in needlelace, for example a leaf or a petal, work from the base to the tip.
- Needlelace is attached to the background fabric only at the edges.

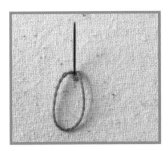 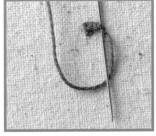  

1 In the top left-hand corner of the shape, take the needle through to the front of the fabric and bring it back down just to the right of the thread, forming a small loop. Bring the needle back through the loop just under the top outline.

2 Form the stitch, then repeat along the row to the right-hand edge of the shape. Take the needle down on the right-hand edge, then bring it back through on the line, just below the first row. Work another row of buttonhole stitches from right to left, passing the needle through the loops of the previous row.

3 Continue to the left-hand edge of the shape, take the needle down, and bring it back through on the line just below the last row.

4 Continue to work rows of buttonhole stitch backwards and forwards across the shape, forming each stitch by passing the needle through the loop just above it. On the final row, pass the thread through the fabric as you form each stitch.

The filled shape. A more open version of this filling stitch can be achieved by making the loops of the buttonholes slightly bigger.

Double Brussels stitch

This is a more open filling stitch than single Brussels stitch, so make the buttonhole stitches a little wider.

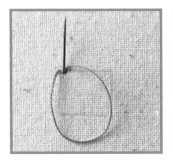

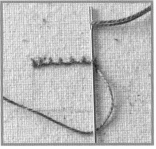

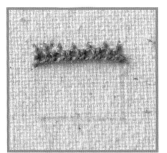

1 Work a buttonhole stitch in the top left-hand corner of the shape, as for single Brussels stitch.

2 Make a row of fairly wide buttonhole stitches across the top of the shape. Take the needle down on the line at the end of the row and bring it back through just below it, then form a buttonhole stitch through the last loop of the first row.

3 Work a second buttonhole stitch into the same loop, then continue along the row working two stitches into each loop of the previous row.

4 Continue working backwards and forwards across the shape in the same way until the shape is filled. On the final row, pass the thread through the fabric as you form each stitch.

Treble Brussels stitch

For this Brussels stitch, where three buttonhole stitches are inserted into one, it is best to use a finer thread, for example a twisted silk.

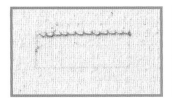

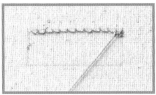

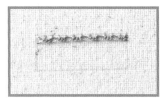

1 Following the instructions for double Brussels stitch, work a row of fairly loose buttonhole stitches across the top of the shape.

2 Start the second row, and work three buttonhole stitches into the last loop of the first row.

3 Miss out the next loop of the previous row, and continue to work three buttonhole stitches into alternate loops of the first row.

4 For the next row, work three buttonhole stitches in each of the large loops of the previous row and miss out the triple buttonholes.

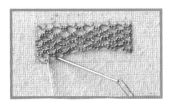

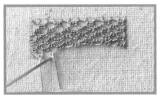

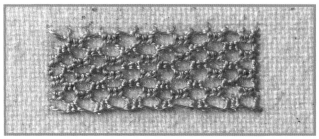

5 Continue working backwards and forwards across the shape. On the final row, take the needle down through the fabric as you pass the thread through the loop of the previous row ...

6 ... and bring it back through on the lower edge of the shape as you form the stitch.

The completed treble Brussels stitch.

Note
There will be a tendency for the current row to 'flip up'; this will lie flat when the final row has been stitched down.

Corded buttonhole stitch

This is an extremely useful stitch and probably the most common of the buttonhole stitches.
It creates a dense finish and is the easiest stitch to use to create a regular stitch surface.

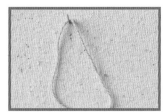

1 At the top of the shape, take the needle through to the front of the fabric and back down on the line just to the right to form a small loop. Bring the needle back through the loop just under the top outline.

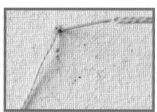

2 Pull the thread through and tighten the loop, then take the needle back down on the right-hand edge of the shape, next to the loop, to form the buttonhole stitch.

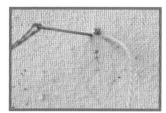

3 Bring the needle back through on the right-hand edge of the shape, just below the first row, and take it down on the line on the left-hand side.

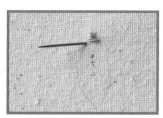

4 Pull the thread through to form a cord going across the shape, then bring the needle back through on the left-hand edge just below it.

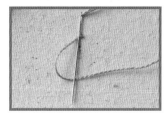

5 Work a buttonhole stitch, taking the needle through the loop of the first row, as well as under the cord. Take the needle through the loop that has formed.

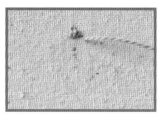

6 Pull the thread through to form the buttonhole stitch, then work further buttonhole stitches into the previous row of loops and along the cord to the right-hand side. Take the needle down through the fabric at the end of the row and bring it back up just below it.

7 Lay another cord across the shape as before and work another row of buttonhole stitches along the cord from left to right. Continue to fill the shape.

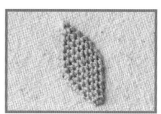

The shape, completely filled.

> **Note**
> If the shape gets wider, you may only have the cord to work the next buttonhole stitch into.

Ceylon stitch

This stitch takes on the look of a knitted sweater. It is therefore a good stitch to sample in wool, but can be just as effective in any thread. The sample below was worked using perlé cotton.

- When filling small shapes, it may not be necessary to couch down the foundation line.

1 Begin by laying a foundation line across the top of the shape. Make a starting stitch on the left-hand side, then lay a stitch across from left to right. Couch it down using a fine cotton thread in a similar colour to the embroidery thread. Cast off the sewing thread.

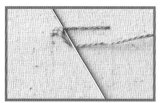

2 Bring the embroidery thread back through on the left-hand side of the shape, just below the foundation line, and work a row of loops across the shape. Pass the needle under the foundation line as you work each loop.

3 At the end of the first row, take the thread through to the back of the fabric and bring it back up to the front on the left-hand side, just beneath the previous row. Pass the needle through the second loop of row 1 and back out through the first (without piercing the fabric).

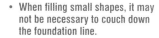

4 Pull the thread through to form the first stitch of row 2.

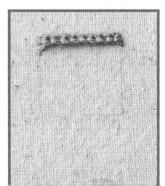

5 Work the next stitch by passing the thread through the third loop and out through the second loop of row 1. Continue in this way to the end of the row, then take the thread through to the back of the fabric.

6 Continue working in this way until the shape is filled. On the last row, take the needle down through the fabric as you work each stitch and bring it up through the next loop along.

METAL THREAD WORK

The use of metal threads in stumpwork is essential to its look and goldwork makes up a large portion of its stitch repertoire. Most traditional pieces use at least some metal threads, and others use it in large quantities. In the past, threads were usually silver gilt and a huge variety of different types of threads and techniques were used. The most common threads selected were twist, Japanese threads, cut purls, lizerine (a flat, square pearl purl wire), spangles and plate.

Today, we can buy many coloured metal threads but in the 17th century thin wires were covered in silk thread and coiled around a long darning needle to make 'purlings'. Metal thread can be worked on to any fabric, from silk organza to velvet.

Chip work in bright check (see page 281) is used here to create some of the blooms in this vase, and metal spangles (see page 280) dot the background silk. Yellow woven wheels (see below) in silk ribbon have been worked to complement the chip work.

Woven wheels

Also known as spider's webs, these raised circular shapes were commonly worked in metal threads during the Elizabethan period, but can be worked in any thread to great effect. First, a foundation is worked consisting of an odd number of evenly spaced straight stitches radiating from a central point. Five or seven is the usual number of these 'spokes'. The needle is then brought up in the centre of the circle, between two stitches, and the thread woven over and under the spokes in a spiral towards the outer edge of the wheel, without picking up the base fabric. See page 68.

Note
Keep a separate pair of embroidery scissors for working with metal, as it will blunt them.

Couching a gold thread

For couching, use a no.10 crewel embroidery needle threaded with either white sewing thread (if working with silver) or yellow sewing thread (when working with gold). Pass the thread through a beeswax block before starting to stitch.

Begin by making a starting stitch a little way in from the start of the stitching line. Lay two metal threads on the line, extending beyond the start of the line by approximately 2.5cm (1in).

- Couched metal threads look more effective when couched down in pairs.
- As a general rule, use one sewing thread to stitch over something (for example Japanese gold) and two sewing threads to stitch through something (such as a bead of cut purl).

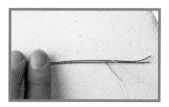
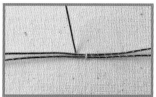
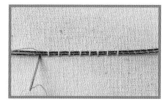
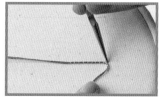

1 Bring the sewing thread up on one side of the line and make a vertical stitch over the metal threads. Hold the metal threads taut in your left hand as you do so.

2 Form the stitch, then bring the needle up approximately 3mm (⅛in) along the line ready to form the next stitch.

3 Continue along the gold threads, keeping the couching stitches neat and evenly spaced.

4 First cast off the sewing thread, then make a hole at the end of the stitched line using a stiletto, a mellor or a large chenille needle.

Note

Do not make the couching stitches so tight that the metal threads bunch up and overlap each other; they should be loose enough to hold the metal threads in place alongside each other comfortably.

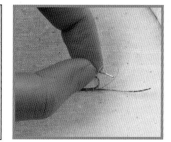

5 Make a 'lasso' with a double sewing thread and use it to pull first one then the other gold thread through the hole to the back of the fabric (see page 228). Stitch the threads down on the back of the fabric.

Spangles

Spangles are flat pieces of metal shaped like a sickle and used frequently in stumpwork to fill spaces on the silk between separate motifs. To begin, wax a single thread and form a starting stitch where the spangle is to be placed.

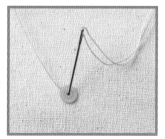

1 Come up on one side of the spangle and take the needle back down through the centre.

2 Secure the spangle using three evenly spaced stitches; smaller spangles can be held with just two stitches.

Pearl purl

Pearl purl is a thicker metal thread than either purl or check. It can be used as an edging thread. The version used in this demonstration has a round cross-section, though a square-cut version is also available, known as lizerine. This would have been the type used in traditional stumpwork.

Begin by cutting a length of pearl purl and stretch it slightly to tease out the coils. Do this by holding it at the very ends and then snipping them off when stretched.

- When forming the couching stitches, make sure the thread 'clicks' down between the pearls and does not sit on top of the wire.

1 Lay the pearl purl in position, make a starting stitch and lay the first couching stitch over it between the first and second pearls.

2 As you pull the thread taut, it should make a distinctive 'pop'. Make the next stitch between the second and third pearls to ensure the end is well secured, then continue to stitch along the wire at intervals of two or three pearls.

3 Approximately 1cm (½in) before the end, cut off the pearl purl to the required length and continue to couch it down, ensuring the last two pearls are secured. Cast off the sewing thread.

280

Chip work in bright check

Bright check is a metal thread with a hole down the centre, similar to a bead. The thread has been formed by wrapping it around a long, thin, triangular form. Small chips of gold are stitched down individually, either filling a space completely (as below) or with spaces in between. A filled shape can be worked either as a slip (see page 288) or directly on to the base fabric.

- If you are outlining a shape, work the outline first before filling.
- Use two strands of sewing thread to stitch the chips down.

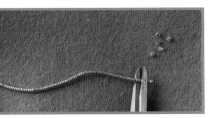 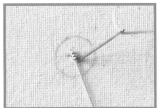 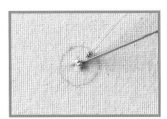 

1 Cut short sections of bright check over felt or velvet (this prevents them from jumping or rolling away).

2 Make a starting stitch in the middle of the shape to be filled, pick up a chip and push it down the thread to the fabric surface, then take the needle back through at the edge of the chip.

3 Come up a short distance away from the first chip that is equal to the size of a chip, pick up another chip and push the needle towards the last stitch to ensure the chips lie close together. Work all the chips at different angles to each other.

4 Continue in this way until the shape is filled. Working the stitches in different directions results in a more 'sparkly' finish.

Chip work in coloured purls

Smooth or rough purl can be purchased in a huge array of colours and is a metal thread with a hole through the centre. It has been formed by wrapping it around a long, thin, cylindrical form and can be cut to any length required.

 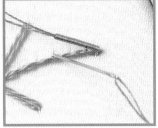  

1 Cut the chips of purl as described above. Make them a little longer this time. Measure each chip against the previous one so that they are all the same length.

2 Using two strands of cotton thread in a colour similar to that of the purls, make a starting stitch and thread on a purl. Push the purl down to the fabric and make a stitch that is slightly smaller than the purl so that the purl curves slightly to form the side of a leaf.

3 Attach a second purl on the other side of the stem to complete the leaf.

4 Take the thread across the back of the work and create an adjacent leaf following the same method. Repeat for all the remaining leaves.

USING METAL PURLS TO MAKE RAISED LOOPS

1 Using two strands of thread, make a starting stitch and thread on a chip of purl. Take the needle back down near the same hole and allow the purl to create an upright loop.

A collection of loops formed on the fabric.

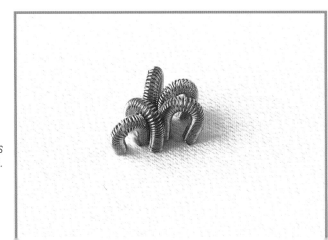

Plate

Here, a broad silver plate is used to work a crescent moon over a string padding. Narrower plate is available, but is more difficult to work with. Gold gilt is also available. Instructions for the string padding are provided on pages 286–287.

- Only tension the metal as you are pulling on the thread underneath, and be careful not to over-tension it.

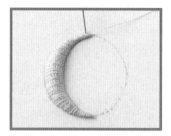

1 Thread a needle with a piece of well-waxed white cotton thread and bring the thread through to the front of the fabric at the tip of the shape. Make a single stitch down the outer edge of the padded shape that is the same width as the plate.

2 Bend over the end of the plate using tweezers and place the hook under the stitch.

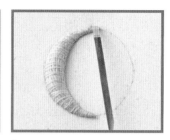

3 Pull on the stitch so that the fold in the plate sits on the edge of the shape, and lay the plate across the shape.

4 Bring the thread through at the tip again and make a stitch over the plate on the inner edge of the shape.

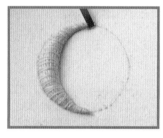

5 Pull the thread tight to form a crease in the plate and fold the plate over to the outer edge while maintaining tension on the sewing thread below.

6 Being careful not to pull on the metal, bring the needle up on the outer edge halfway along the first stitch.

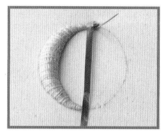

7 Make another stitch over the metal, taking the needle down on the line, pull the thread tight and at the same time fold the plate over to the other side. Bring the needle back through on the inner edge halfway along the stitch, as before.

8 Continue taking the plate from one side to the other, stitching it in place each time, until the whole shape is covered.

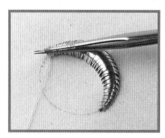

9 To finish, cut off the plate and fold over the tip using tweezers to form a hook as you did at the start.

10 Pass the thread through the hook, take it down through the fabric and cast off in the normal way.

Broad plate has been used for the upper part of the bird's leg and stitched down as demonstrated. Silver plate has also been laid flat and stitched over with a coloured thread to create the tail feathers. This piece was worked by Becky Hogg.

282

TECHNIQUES

Stumpwork is characterised by the use of techniques such as padding, slips, the wrapping of various materials and the addition of found or treasured objects to the embroidery itself. All these techniques are described here.

As discussed previously, flat and raised stitches play a huge part in the vocabulary of a stumpwork piece, but it is only when these are used in combination with padding or slip work that an embroidery truly becomes a piece of stumpwork or raised embroidery.

Five different forms of padding will be discussed and demonstrated, as well as six different types of slip (a slip being any piece of embroidery worked off the base fabric and applied later). The final section explores different types of wrapped materials and the application of found objects. These two techniques are what give stumpwork its more intriguing quality; the playfulness and eclecticism spoken about in the introduction on page 259.

The centre of this poppy, shown in close-up on page 267, is worked in two different rows of turkey rug stitch and a third row of looped silk ribbon. A large wrapped bead has been placed on top. The petals are painted felt with a wired and silk cord edging. The piece is finished, in a somewhat flamboyant fashion, with the addition of individual feathers purchased from a craft shop.

A large wooden bead has been wrapped with silk ribbon, forming an apple hanging from a branch of couched silk cord. The stalk of the apple is made using wrapped wire inserted into the top of the bead, and the leaves are made using wired buttonhole slips. Straight and stem stitch have been worked in stranded cotton on the leaves and branch to add detail.

Bullion knots make up the bodies of these ants, and beads and straight stitches form their heads and legs. The ants at the front of the line carry a leaf constructed using a corded buttonhole slip edged on the darker side only with a further buttonhole stitch.

PADDING

In the 17th century, materials such as horsehair, sheeps' wool, fine card or vellum, and bundles of linen thread were regularly used for padding. Today, animal wool is still the best material for padding felt shapes or slips, but carpet felt is a comparable modern material to use instead of horsehair, and bundles of cotton string are used instead of linen thread, which today is much more expensive. For more on padding, see pages 224–227.

The body of the bee has been constructed using felt padding stuffed with wool. The yellow and black stripes have then been stitched on top using satin stitch worked in stranded cotton and silk ribbon. The head of the bee is a wrapped wooden bead.

Stitched padding

Stitched padding is used when padding needs to be inserted into a small area. It is normally worked in stranded cotton, but any thread relative to the space being filled can be used. Three strands are usually sufficient, though any number between two and five can be used depending on the size of the shape and how well it needs to be padded.

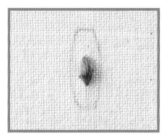

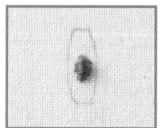

1 Knot the thread and take it down through the centre of the shape. Work two or three vertical stitches over the knot.

2 Work three or four stitches horizontally across the vertical ones.

3 Continue to build up the padding in this way until the shape is filled, ensuring that the final layer of stitching lies just within the outline and is at right angles to the first layer.

Note

Start each stitch by bringing the needle back through the fabric as close as possible to where it went down. This will ensure all the stitching is on the front of the fabric and the back (shown above) is as flat as possible.

Felt padding

Cotton felt is an extremely useful padding material that produces a smooth area ready for stuffing and covering. Small shapes can be stitched down and stuffed with wool in preparation for a layer of detached buttonhole stitch or appliqué. When creating figures, larger shapes are cut, stitched and stuffed before clothing is placed on top (see page 302). Begin by transferring the shape you wish to pad on to felt using pricking and pouncing (see page 20), and cut it out a little larger than actual size (approximately 1–2mm or 1/8in all round).

• When securing felt padding, always start at a point on the outline that it is essential to position accurately, for example a point, corner or tip, rather than part of the way along an edge.

• Secure the felt to the background fabric and stuff it in sections working from the top downwards.

1 Using a very fine needle (no.12 or no.10) and a single sewing thread, work a starting stitch on the fabric. Position the felt padding on the fabric and secure it with a small stab stitch, here at the base of the neck, taking the needle up on the line and down through the felt.

2 Place another stab stitch on the opposite side of the shape and one at the top to anchor the felt in position, then fill in the gaps in between with stitches placed 1–2mm (1/8in) apart. Secure a section, in this case the head.

Note

Notice that, because the felt is cut slightly larger than the shape, it will dome slightly when attached to the background fabric. This allows room for stuffing.

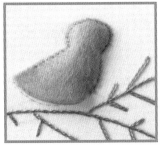

3 Take a small wad of fleece or cotton wool and push it into the stitched end of the shape with a pair of tweezers. Continue stuffing until the head is stuffed firmly.

4 Continue stitching down the sides of the shape until two-thirds of the shape is secured and stuff as before.

5 Complete the remaining third of the felt padding. To see how this bird is finished, see page 290.

Vilene padding

Pelmet Vilene is used as padding when a crisp, firm edge is required. It can be stitched over, wrapped with fabric or stuffed with a little padding to increase its height.

SATIN-STITCHED VILENE

1 Transfer the design on to Vilene and cut it out on the line. Using a single strand of white sewing thread, make a starting stitch (see page 39) within the shape on the fabric and position the Vilene over the top. Bring the thread through just inside the edge of the Vilene and make a small running stitch (see page 57).

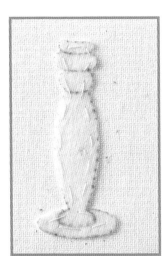

2 Continue stitching around the edge of the Vilene using running stitches.

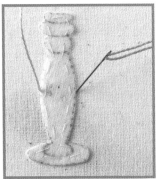

3 Using a single strand of coloured thread, work a starting stitch in the middle of the Vilene. Bring your needle up through the base fabric near the centre of the shape at the very edge of the Vilene.

4 Take your needle back down through the base fabric on the other side of the Vilene and continue to cover the top part of the Vilene shape with satin stitch.

5 Change the thread colour where necessary and bring your needle back to the middle of the shape to then fill the bottom half. For this table leg, the feet were added with French knots (see page 66).

Each petal of this rose is a separate piece of pelmet Vilene, which has been stitched to the base fabric before being worked over with satin stitches. The centre of the flower is a wooden bead covered with buttonhole stitches.

1 Transfer the shape to the Vilene using pricking and pouncing and draw in the line with a blue soluble pen. Mark the top with a 'T'. Cut out the shape on the line.

2 Completely cover the back of the shape with double-sided sticky tape. Trim off the excess and peel off the protective layer.

3 Lay the non-sticky side of the Vilene on the back of a piece of fabric and cut around it neatly leaving a 5mm (¼in) border. Fold the edges of the fabric over and secure them on the back of the Vilene.

4 Where the fabric may need to be smoothed in areas, use a matching thread and lace backwards and forwards across the back of the Vilene.

5 Thread up one strand of machine thread and attach the covered Vilene shape to the background fabric using stab stitch. Work the stitches by bringing the needle up through the fabric at the very edge of the shape and taking it back down through the background fabric.

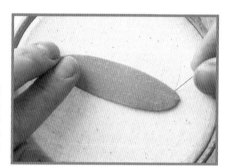

Wood

Small pieces of wood can be carefully carved to form noses that are then placed under fine cotton slips. In the 17th century, one could buy hands, pears or oranges carved in wood or wax. Often the fruit mouldings would be covered in needlelace and today you can buy various-sized wooden beads that can be used in a similar way (see the rose on page 285, and wrapping a wooden bead on page 296).

See page 306 for a demonstration of how wood can be used to pad a nose in figure work.

String padding

String makes a fairly dense, firm padding and is used for cutwork and metal plate work. Always use white cotton string when working with silver and yellow cotton string when working with gold. Begin by waxing the string heavily.

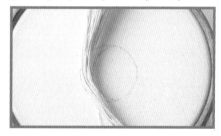  

1 Fold the string up and make sure it fills the shape you wish to pad sufficiently (in this case, a crescent moon). The bundle should be at least 4cm (1½in) longer than the shape at both the top and the bottom.

2 Cut through the loops at the top and bottom of the bundle of string.

3 Using a double strand of waxed white thread, make a starting stitch in the middle of the shape. Lay the bundle of string on the shape and work two stitches over the middle of it, 2–3mm (⅛in) apart. For each stitch, bring the needle up on the line on one side and take it down on the line on the other.

4 Hold the strings to one side and make a holding stitch underneath the padding in the centre of the shape to secure the first two stitches.

5 Find the bottom layer of strings and, holding the top ones back with the needle (be careful not to include any from the sides), cut them off at the base.

6 Lay the strings back in position and make two more stitches over the bundle, just above the previous two, followed by a holding stitch.

Note

By cutting away strings from the underneath layers, the padding retains a smooth surface while it is being tapered.

7 Repeat step 5, this time taking out a few more strings than before, or however many are required for the shape you are filling.

8 Make two more stitches followed by a holding stitch, and repeat steps 5 and 6 until you reach the top of the shape. Try to gauge how many strings to remove at each stage in order to be left with just two or three at the end.

Note

Make a note of how many strings you remove at each stage so that you can repeat the sequence on the other side. This ensures the padding is evenly shaped at the top and bottom.

9 Taper the last strings into the corner of the shape using a sharp pair of embroidery scissors.

10 Bring the needle up at the end of the shape and take it down into the padding. Pull the thread through, then form two stitches over the point.

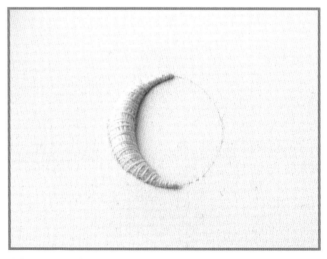

11 Complete the padding on the other side of the shape following the same method, removing the same number of strings at each stage as you did on the first side. See page 282 to cover this shape with metal plate.

SLIPS

A slip is any separate piece of embroidery worked off the frame and then applied to the main embroidery, for example a piece of needlelace or a wired fabric shape. Slips can be any shape (though highly complicated shapes should be avoided) and can be unpadded, stuffed or laid over padding.

Fabric slips

Various fabrics can be used to make fabric slips; silk organza will support any stitch, including goldwork, and folds under well, and is therefore a popular choice. Fabric slips can be left uncovered or filled with stitches such as French knots, bullion knots, turkey rug stitch, loops or chips of metal thread and bead work. For these slips use a fine fabric such as silk organza or a lightweight calico. Remember to keep the shape of the fabric slip fairly simple as it can be hard to achieve more difficult shapes.

In the following demonstration, a silk organza slip is filled with French knots, though the same method will apply whichever stitch you use.

This embroidery was made using silk work, metal threads and beads. The blackberries are French knot slips inserted with a little wool padding before being completely stitched down (see below).

FRENCH KNOT SLIP

   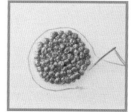 

1 Begin by securing a piece of silk organza in a small embroidery hoop and draw on the shape, slightly larger all round than the final shape to allow for shrinkage when turning and padding (if required). Use a blue soluble pen.

2 Fill the shape with a filling stitch, starting at the centre and working outwards. Here the shape is being filled with French knots (see page 66).

3 Continue to fill the shape up to the blue outline, ensuring there are no gaps. Cast off the thread.

4 Thread a needle with a length of sewing thread, put a knot in one end and work small running stitches around the slip, approximately 5mm (¼in) from the edge (more intricate shapes may require smaller stitches). Leave a long tail thread; do not cast off.

5 Remove the fabric from the frame and trim neatly around the slip using a sharp pair of embroidery scissors, approximately 5mm (¼in) outside the running stitches. Be careful not to cut the sewing thread.

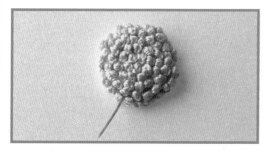  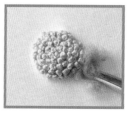 

6 Pull the thread to gather up the fabric under the slip and secure it by lacing across the back three or four times. Leave a long tail thread and use this to attach the slip to the background fabric, beginning with a single stitch placed on the edge of the slip. Bring the needle up just inside the slip and take it down through the fabric, angling it in towards the slip as you do so.

7 Work the stitches all the way round the slip, leaving a small gap for stuffing if desired.

8 Take a small wad of fleece and push it into the slip using a pair of tweezers.

9 Continue to stitch around the gap and cast off.

Wired fabric slip

A wired fabric slip is fairly time-consuming to make, but well worth the effort. Wired fabric slips can be used to make beautiful flower petals or, with fine silk organzas, the wings of an insect.

The petals of both these flowers were created using wired fabric slips. The yellow flower has had internal detail added using lines of double running stitch (see page 138). The central points, where the wires have been inserted, have been covered with large beads.

Note

Cut a length of paper-covered wire that is long enough to go all the way round the shape leaving a long tail at each end of approximately 4cm (1½in).

1 Secure the fabric in a small hoop and mark on the shape. Knot a thread and take it through to the back of the fabric on the line, approximately 1cm (½in) away from the base of the shape. Bring it up at the point on the line where it will be attached to the embroidery. Work a stitch over the wire.

2 Continue to couch over the wire, working back towards the knot. Leave no gaps between the stitches – a technique known as trailing.

3 When you reach the knot, cut it off and continue around the rest of the outline. Tuck the finishing stitches inside the shape at the base of the shape.

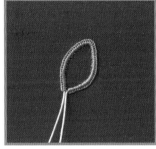

4 Using a new thread, work close buttonhole stitches over the couched edge. With each stitch, take the needle down inside the shape and bring it up, through the loop, outside the shape.

5 When you have completed the buttonhole edging, again tuck the finishing stitches inside the shape at the base of the shape.

6 Work any internal detailing within the shape and cast off.

7 Remove the fabric from the hoop and cut out the shape. Cut as close as possible to the shape, pushing the scissors just under the lip of the buttonhole edging.

8 Make a hole in the background fabric where you wish to attach the slip and pass the wires through the hole.

9 Bend the wires over on the back of the embroidery and stitch them down using a curved needle and white sewing thread (to match the background fabric).

10 Cut off the wires and trim the thread.

The attached slip.

Counted canvas slips

Counted canvas slips are finished off and applied to the fabric in a slightly different way from a fabric slip. Use a fine, evenweave linen, such as a 28 threads per inch (TPI) linen, or fine canvas and fill the shape with a counted stitch such as tent stitch, gobelin or cross stitch.

TENT STITCH ON A LINEN SLIP

First, trace the shape from the template on to silk organza, adding 2mm (¹⁄₈in) all round if it is to be worked over padding. Make sure it is the right size by laying it over the padding and trim or add to the shape where necessary.

- Before you begin the tent stitch, work out how many threads of stranded cotton or other thread you need to use in order to fill the holes in the linen comfortably. Here, three threads have been used.
- When working tent stitch, always work the long stitches at the back of the work.

1 Put the linen in a small embroidery hoop and draw around the silk organza shape on to the linen using a blue soluble pen.

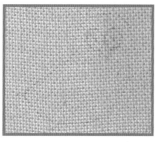

2 Use pricking and pouncing to transfer the elements inside the shape, in this case the eyes.

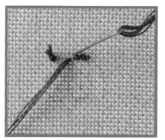

3 Knot your thread and take it down in the top left corner of the shape. Bring it back through on the right-hand side of the shape. Working from right to left, make a row of small diagonal stitches, each worked from bottom left to top right across the intersection of the first horizontal (weft) thread that lies within the shape and the vertical (warp) threads of the linen.

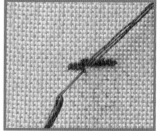

4 Cut off the knot and work the second row from left to right over the next weft thread down. Lay the stitches in the same direction as before, but this time work them from top right to bottom left of the stitch.

5 Continue backwards and forwards across the shape until the shape is filled. Change colour where necessary. Add the surface detailing when you have finished, here using stem stitch, French knots and straight stitch.

6 Paint diluted fabric glue around the edges of the embroidery on the back of the fabric to secure it before cutting out the slip. Make sure the glue covers the edges of the stitching and the linen.

7 Remove the linen from the hoop and cut around the shape, close to the edge.

8 Using a fine needle and either cotton thread in the same colour as the embroidery or invisible thread, make a starting stitch on the padding.

9 Cut off the knot and bring the needle up through the fabric as close as possible to the edge of the padding, on a corner or bend. Here, the first stitch is placed on the right, where the head joins the body. Find the corresponding point on the slip and make a tiny stitch.

10 Place two further holding stitches on the left-hand side of the neck and the top of the head, then fill in with the remainder of the stab stitches around the head, placed 2–3mm (¹⁄₈in) apart.

Note
If you need to tuck the slip underneath, work the stab stitches by coming up through the slip and down through the fabric.

11 Attach the body in the same way, working three or four holding stitches first, and then the remaining stitches in between.

12 Couch a silk cord or a bundle of threads around the shape. Bring the couching thread up through the fabric and go down through the edge of the slip. Follow the method described on page 268.

The completed embroidery.

Wired slip filled with stitching

A wired slip filled with stitching (in this case a leaf) is best worked on a strong, fine fabric. Silk organza is a very useful fabric for this technique and a huge variety of stitches can be applied on top, including satin stitch, silk shading, chain stitch, stem stitch and straight stitch. Begin by cutting a length of paper-covered wire to the correct length (see page 289).

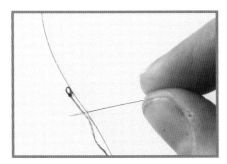

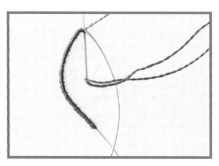

1 Secure the silk organza in a small hoop and mark on the shape. Knot a single thread and take it through to the back of the fabric on the line, approximately 1cm (½in) away from the base of the leaf. Bring it up at the point on the line where it will be attached to the embroidery. Work a stitch over the wire.

2 Continue to couch over the wire, working back towards the knot. Place the stitches very close together, with no gaps in between (this technique is known as trailing). When you reach the knot, cut it off.

3 Continue to couch over the remainder of the wire.

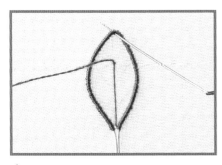

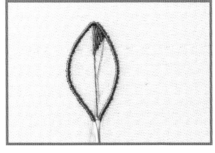

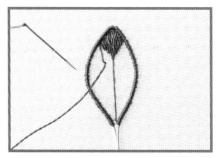

4 When you have couched around the entire outline, bring the needle through to the front of the fabric on the central vein, at the base of the first segment, and work a stitch to the top of the leaf.

5 Fill the top right-hand segment of the leaf with satin stitch (see page 46).

6 Bring the needle back through just to the left of the start of the first stitch and fill the top left-hand segment in the same way. Place a holding stitch further down within the shape.

continued overleaf

291

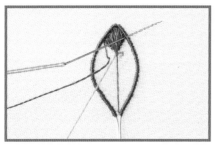

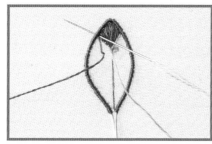

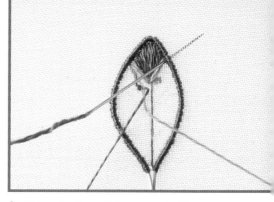

7 Start a new thread in another colour for the veins and make a starting stitch. Bring the thread up on the central vein at the base of the top segments of the leaf and work a stitch across the lower edge of the right-hand segment.

8 Work the left-hand vein in the same way.

9 Add another two stitches on each side to strengthen the veins, then bring the needle through on the central vein at the base of the next segment down. Secure the thread, still threaded through the needle, at the side of the work.

10 Take up the main colour thread again and continue down the leaf following the method described above.

11 When the shape is filled, cast off. Start a new double thread in the second colour and work the central vein in stem stitch, from the bottom of the leaf to the top.

12 Cast off by running the thread through the stitches on the back of the work.

13 Starting at the base of the shape, work a tight buttonhole edging around the shape, ensuring that the ridge is on the outer edge of the shape by taking the needle down inside the shape and up on the outside.

14 Complete the buttonhole edging and cast off. Remove the fabric from the hoop and cut away the fabric as close as possible to the shape.

15 The completed shape can be attached to the background fabric following the method described on page 289.

Needlelace slips

Needlelace cordonnets are pieces of needlelace worked on top of a support fabric. An outline thread, the cordonnet, is stitched down first in order to act as a support for the stitched area. A piece of tracing paper is used to draw the design on to, as well as creating a barrier between the support fabric and the needlelace. The following demonstration is the sleeve of the figure on page 294.

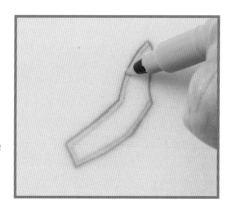

1 Begin by tracing the shape from the template. Make another tracing, this time drawing the outline approximately 1–2mm (⅛in) outside the first one on the edges that will increase due to padding; in this case, every edge apart from the top seam.

2 Cut out a rectangle around the shape, leaving a generous border. Use herringbone stitch or running stitch to attach the tracing to a piece of cotton fabric that is stretched in a hoop.

3 Thread a needle with a contrasting thread and make a starting stitch in the fabric just off the tracing paper. Bring the needle through on the edge of the shape, on a corner or bend.

4 The cordonnet and the needlelace are worked in the same thread. Take a long length of this thread and double it. The doubled thread should be long enough to go right round the shape, plus 5cm (2in) for finishing off. Take the needle down through the loop close to where it came up.

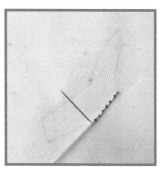

5 Pull the contrasting (red) thread through and couch down the cordonnet threads around the shape. Work the stitches fairly close together (approximately 2mm or ⅛in apart).

6 When you reach the start of the cordonnet, thread a needle with the cordonnet threads and pass them through the loop.

7 Pull the threads through the loop then unthread the needle and lay one thread in one direction on the outline and one in the other direction. Use the couching thread to secure the base of each thread with two or three stitches.

8 Cut off the ends of the cordonnet threads and cast off the couching thread away from the tracing paper.

9 Using the same thread as that used for the cordonnet, make a starting stitch away from the tracing paper, as far as possible from where you intend to start the needlelace. Bring the needle through just outside the shape, on a corner or bend.

10 Work a row of buttonhole stitches across the top of the shape from left to right, taking the needle under the cordonnet with each stitch (not through the fabric).

11 When you reach the right-hand edge of the shape, slide the needle under the cordonnet, take the thread back over to the other side (as in corded buttonhole stitch, page 278) and take it under the cordonnet on the left. Work the first buttonhole stitch, taking the needle through the first loop of the previous row and under the cord.

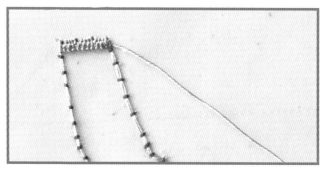

12 Work buttonhole stitches in the same way across the row, passing the needle under the cordonnet when you reach the right-hand side and starting the next row as before.

13 When you are ready to change colour, take the thread under the cordonnet at the end of the row and wrap it around the cordonnet two or three times. Secure the needle at the side of the embroidery and wrap the thread around it neatly to hold it in place.

14 Thread a needle with the second colour and take the knot down through the base cloth away from the tracing paper, some distance from the end of the last row. Bring the needle through just outside the shape on the right-hand side and wrap it once or twice around the cordonnet, ready to start the next row of needlelace.

15 Work the required number of rows in the second colour and secure the thread at the side of the work as before.

16 Pick up the first colour, work the cord across the shape and continue as before.

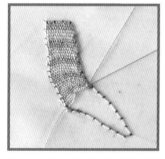

17 Continue in this way until you reach the first corner. To turn, lay the cord from right to left as before, but then work only part of the way along the row. Lay a cord back to the left again and continue in this manner to create a wedge shape.

18 Once the corner is turned, work all the way across to the right and continue filling the shape as before.

19 When you have filled the shape, leave the threads intact – do not cast off.

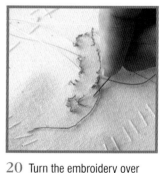

20 Turn the embroidery over and cut off all the long threads as close to the ends as possible. Remove the red threads.

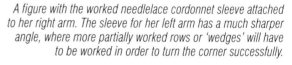

A figure with the worked needlelace cordonnet sleeve attached to her right arm. The sleeve for her left arm has a much sharper angle, where more partially worked rows or 'wedges' will have to be worked in order to turn the corner successfully.

21 Turn the embroidery back over to the front and lift off the needlelace slip. Remove any remaining red threads with tweezers.

22 The detached needlelace slip can be attached to the embroidery using the long tail threads.

Wired needlelace slips

Wired needlelace slips are attached to their base support at one point or along one edge, and left to form a raised three-dimensional area of embroidery. Use paper-covered wire, which can be painted to match the needlelace. Begin by tracing the shape from the template on to tracing paper and attaching it to the fabric, as described in steps 1 and 2 on pages 292–293. Make sure you start with enough wire to go round the shape and leave a 4cm (1½in) tail at each end.

Note

As an alternative to working in rows, you can work the first row of buttonhole stitches around the entire shape, and gradually work your way into the middle, as shown on page 283.

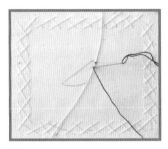

1 Thread a needle with a contrasting thread and secure it just outside the edge of the tracing paper. Bring it up at a corner or bend on the outline. Lay the wire in position and, leaving a long tail, start to couch it down.

2 Finish couching around the shape and cast off the thread outside the tracing paper. Cut off the ends of the wire leaving tails of approximately 4cm (1½in). Stick these down with sticky tape, if you wish, before starting the needlelace.

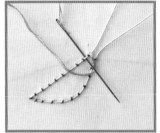

3 Start the needlelace where you intend to attach it to the embroidery. Make a knot at the end of the thread and take it down through the support fabric, away from the tracing paper. Bring the needle up through the fabric, piercing the tracing paper, at the edge of the wired shape. Form the first buttonhole stitch over the wire.

4 Work the remainder of the first row, forming each buttonhole stitch over the wire. Stop at the next corner.

5 Wrap the thread around the wire at the end of the row and work the second row back in the opposite direction, passing the thread through the corresponding loop of the previous row as you work each stitch. This shape has been filled with double Brussels stitch (see page 277).

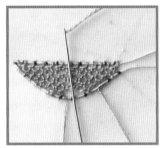

6 At the bottom of the shape, take the thread under the wire as you work each stitch.

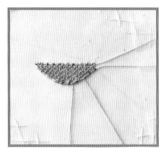

7 When the shape is completely filled, wrap the thread around the length of wire two or three times and cast off away from the tracing paper.

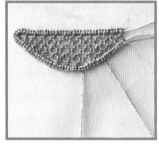

8 Start a new thread and work a tight buttonhole-stitch border over the wire. Make the starting stitch away from the tracing paper and begin from the point that will be attached to the embroidery. Catch in the outer stitches of the needlelace as you work.

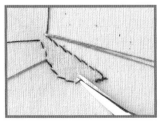

9 Turn the work over and cut away all the couching threads.

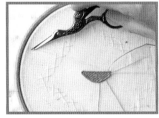

10 Next, trim the knots from the needlelace threads in order to detach the slip.

11 Detach the slip and remove any thread remnants from the needlelace using a pair of tweezers. The long tail threads can be used to attach the slip to the embroidery, or cut off the long threads that are not in the correct position for plunging (they have been woven securely into the buttonhole edging and will not unravel).

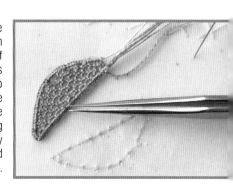

WRAPPING

Wrapping various materials with threads was an extremely popular technique in the 17th century and beautiful effects were achieved. Materials such as fine parchment, straw or raffia were commonly used.

Beads

Use wooden beads, available in many different sizes, with a large hole through the centre. Silk ribbon is ideal for wrapping as it covers well and is easy to handle. Different widths of silk ribbon are available – here 4mm (¼in) wide ribbon has been used. For wrapping larger beads, use ribbon that is 7mm (³/₈in) wide.

1 Thread the ribbon through a chenille needle and take it up through the centre of the bead.

2 Clasp the tail end in your left hand and wrap the ribbon around the bead by taking the needle back up through the hole and pulling it through.

3 Wrap the ribbon evenly around the bead. With each wrap, overlap the previous wrapping slightly to ensure the bead is completely covered.

4 Pass the tail back through the hole, using the needle to catch a few threads of the ribbon within the hole along the way. Use the two tails to attach the wrapped bead to the embroidery.

Papers and cards

Originally vellum would have been used to wrap threads around, but any thick paper, card or Vilene can be used. You can cover each side of the paper with double-sided tape to secure the threads if you find it easier. You can also colour the paper with watercolour paint to match the wrapping thread.

 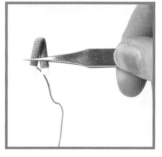 

1 Take a single strand of cotton thread, hold it on the paper and start to wrap, from right to left, covering the tail. Continue to wrap for as long as you wish.

2 To finish, knot the thread and cut it off leaving a long tail with which to attach the wrapped paper to the embroidery. Fold the paper into the required shape, if necessary.

This detail taken from a larger piece shows grasses worked using various techniques. From left to right, they are straight stitch in silk ribbon; stem stitch in stranded cotton and perlé cotton; and wrapped card in stranded cotton.

Wires

Wires are a useful and adaptable material in stumpwork, and represent a simple way of creating a sculpted look. Single covered wires can be wrapped individually and arranged into various shapes or inserted into the edges of fabric, needlelace or stitched slips. Wired hands are also a common feature of stumpwork figures (see pages 304–305). Here is how to wrap a wire.

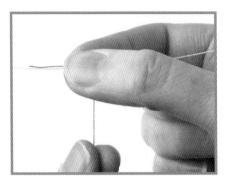

1 Hold a strand of cotton thread on the wire, leaving a short tail extending beyond the end of the wire, and clasp the other end of the thread in your other hand.

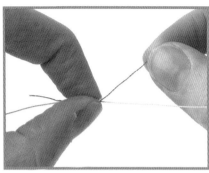

2 Start to wrap the thread tightly around the wire from right to left, wrapping over the tail thread.

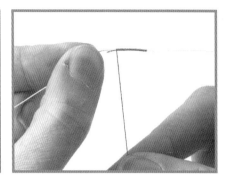

3 Continue wrapping the thread tightly and evenly around the wire.

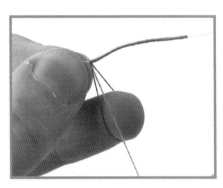

4 To finish, keep the thread taut and tie it in a simple knot around the wire to secure it. Trim the wire but leave a long tail thread with which to secure the wrapped wire to the embroidery.

5 If necessary, bend the wire into the required shape.

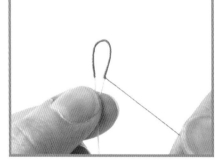

Note

Use a water-based glue to support the knot if you wish to make it even more secure.

Sarah Stevens has used fine wrapped wires to create this beautiful flower, worked as part of a larger piece.

FOUND OBJECTS

Placing found objects such as shells and pieces of coral on to embroideries is an intriguing aspect of stumpwork and one that enhances its fascinating and curious character. The 17th-century embroiderer was following the trend for collecting and admiring quite unconnected objects, a well-used technique in the arts today.

The idea is to put anything that is special or of interest to you or the person for whom the embroidery is intended on to the embroidery. I love indulging in this practice, placing such things as bells, buttons and even snail shells on to my work. When attaching objects to the fabric, use stitching as much as possible, but if an object is difficult to work with in this way, use a small amount of fabric glue to secure it down instead.

A twig from my garden was used to create this tree of beads and found objects, designed to illustrate the range of items you can use to embellish your embroidery. The flowers and leaves are formed using shisha mirrors, feathers, leather, buttons, bells, small clothes pegs, bugle beads, pearls and crystals. A snail's shell has been glued to the base of the tree.

Attaching embellishments

Beads and other items should be attached using a doubled thread to match the background fabric. The thread can be waxed. Use either a beading needle or a no.10 or no.12 embroidery needle.

Note
As a general rule, always use doubled thread when passing the thread through something such as a bead, and a single thread when stitching over something.

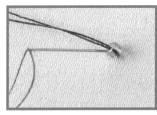

Bring the thread through to the front and thread on a bead. Push the bead down to the bottom and take the needle down close to the bead on one side.

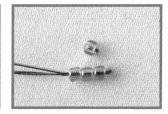

Attach short rows of beads by threading on two or three beads at a time and securing as described for one bead, left.

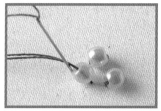

Individual beads, such as these seed pearls, can be attached individually or in clusters.

Bugle beads are attached in the same way.

Buttons can be attached using two or three stitches placed through opposite holes.

Crystals, like spangles, are attached using three evenly spaced stitches.

Rocks and chippings can be stitched on following the same method used for beads.

To attach a small bell, pass the thread through the hook at the base three or four times.

298

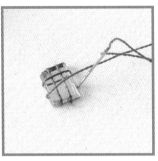

To attach a shell, paint a water-based fabric glue on to the base of the shell then press the shell firmly in position on the fabric.

Mica and shisha mirrors may need to be cut into the required shape using glass cutters. Glue them on to the fabric first and then stitch over them first in one direction and then in the other.

Feathers can be attached by placing a single stitch over the spine. Use a single thread and a no.10 or no.12 embroidery needle.

Cut out tiny leather shapes and stab stitch them in place. Always bring the needle up through the fabric and take it down through the leather.

A detail from an embroidery worked by Sarah Stevens. She used silk floss and wrapped wires as well as fine leathers to create this delicate dandelion.

FIGURES

Historically, figures in stumpwork never stood alone on the fabric but were surrounded by small motifs and scenes. Sometimes figures were placed within a medallion shape and surrounded by decorative details, or placed on the sides of caskets in a more narrative style. Very often, solitary figures or small figurative scenes made up part of a sampler-style design with other motifs like trees, flowers, insects and animals, all of a similar scale, scattered amongst them.

Designs for figurative work were copied from printed sources. For example, in 1553 a small Bible picture book was published in Lyons and the vignettes, one to each page, were used in needlework for more than a century. Other printed pattern books, normally traced back to Continental sources, displayed mythological scenes, often from Ovid's *Metamorphoses*. Scenes from the pages of these books were copied fairly exactly, mostly by professional draughtsmen, and then rendered with some freedom by the domestic embroiderer.

This unselfconscious way of designing can inform the contemporary embroiderer. Unlike the 17th-century embroiderer, we have a wealth of visual imagery around us, and in magazines, books and on the Internet we can find an infinite supply of pictures of the human form. A good starting point might be to take an image from a favoured artist or to simplify a naturalistic figure to render it more appropriate to textiles, accentuating the essential features, for example the eyes or hair.

A detail from a larger embroidery by Rachel Doyle (see page 264). The focal point of this contemporary figure is the stunning embroidered skirt, which has been wired at the base. The fabric for the legs, arms and face have all been cut on the cross of the fabric for flexibility, and the delicate buttonholed shoes and vest have been applied on top. The clever use of colour set against a printed cloth makes for an extremely striking image.

Traditionally, figures were worked in one of two ways. Silk was worked directly on to the fabric with often small amounts of low-relief detail added, or alternatively different methods of padding were used to create a more realistic sense of form. The latter method is popular with embroiderers today. As well as felt padding being used to create the body of the figure underneath the clothes, slips of fine cotton or silk can be stuffed and moulded to create characterful faces; hands can be made by wrapping paper-covered wire; and skin can be created by covering felt or Vilene with flesh-coloured cloth. All these techniques will be shown over the next few pages.

Common ways of making clothes and fabric included the use of buttonhole cordonnets; the application of embroidered or intricately woven cloth; or metal threads couched closely together with silk in a technique known as *or nué*. Usually more than one of these techniques would be used and worked in suitable textures and weights depending on the scale of the figure.

There are no hard-and-fast rules for assembling a figure. Different layers of padding and clothing will be built up depending on the specific stance or dress of each design. The 'order of work', in other words, is specific to the design and to your own preferred way of working. Within this chapter, however, a figure has been worked in a particular order to help you better understand the process.

The various types of buttonhole stitch on this embroidery by Jenny Adin-Christie have been expertly worked and are fascinating to study. However, it is the wonderful character achieved in the fisherman's face and the found objects that go to make up his glasses, fishing rod and hat that make this figure so enchanting.

Some of the same motifs and images that went to make up the embroidery on page 274, like the vase of flowers on the table, the rug and the ladybird, have been used to place this figure in a narrative setting. The images differ in scale but are still slightly distorted, maintaining the sense of playfulness and lack of naturalistic perspective that are essential to creating the spirit of a stumpwork piece. The fine cotton skirt has been embroidered with silk and gold, and a silk ribbon has been placed on the waist to act as a belt. Fine twisted silk has been used to make up the buttonhole shirt, which contrasts with the heavier embroidery used to create the flowers and leaves in the vase.

TECHNIQUES FOR STUMPWORK FIGURES

Begin your embroidery by making a line drawing of the design, and a drawing showing the essential lines of stitching ready for pricking.

The final line drawing of the design.

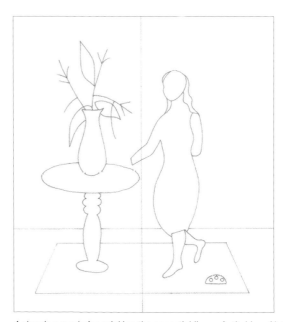

A drawing ready for pricking the essential lines of stitching. Note that the areas of raised embroidery or slip work have not been added; these will later be added by eye or by the use of a template.

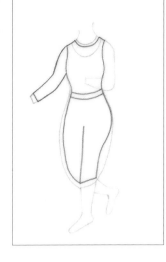

Padding

This drawing shows the first layer of felt padding. This will be stuffed during the process of stitching it down. Note that the felt is cut slightly lower than the neckline of the outfit and slightly shorter than the edge of the sleeve. The felt follows the contours of the body rather than the outline of the skirt. Any internal lines are marked on to the felt and a double back stitch used to mark lines where necessary.

The first layer of felt padding.

ATTACHING THE PADDING TO THE FABRIC

Note

When attaching padding to a background fabric, bring the needle up through the fabric and down through the felt padding. This will ensure a precise line.

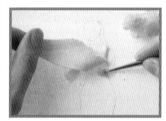

1 Pounce the outline for the body on to the background fabric – only transfer those lines that will be needed as stitch guide lines. Elements that will be made separately, for example the hands, do not need to be transferred. Draw over the outline with a blue soluble pen and brush away any excess pounce.

2 Pounce the outline for the padding on to felt. It should be slightly smaller all round than the outline for the body marked on the background fabric. Mark on the waist. Lay the padding in position and stab stitch the top part, down to the bust, in place. Back stitch along the line joining the body and the arm.

3 Stuff the top part of the body using small wads of fleece manipulated into place using a stiletto, a pair of tweezers or a mellor. Shape the bust carefully, and be careful not to over-stuff the neck and chest.

4 Continue down the body, stitching and then stuffing one section at a time. Use back stitch to mould the figure's shape where necessary, for example around the bust and along the waist. Pack the stuffing firmly and carefully to ensure you achieve a good shape.

5 When the padding is complete, cast off.

Legs

The legs are cut out of pelmet Vilene, then fabric shapes cut on the cross and wrapped over the Vilene. The technique for covering Vilene is described on page 286. The legs are then stitched down on to the background fabric, butting up against the bottom edge of the felt padding.

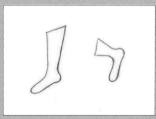

The legs are cut out of pelmet Vilene.

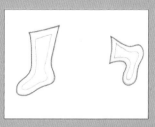

Fabric shapes are cut on the cross and wrapped over the Vilene.

Neck

Work out the area of neck fabric required. The top and bottom edges will be covered by the head and clothing, so it can be stab stitched into place. The left and right edges will be visible and so will need excess fabric cut for turning under.

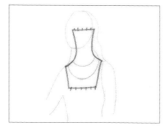

The area of neck fabric is worked out.

Final pattern for the neck fabric.

1 Secure a piece of very fine cotton, for example cotton lawn, in a small embroidery hoop and, if necessary, colour a section of it using flesh-coloured watercolour pencil. Dampen the colour with water, then dry it with a hairdryer. Transfer the neck shape on the cross grain of the fabric, making it 4–5mm (¼in) larger all round than the template to allow for turnings.

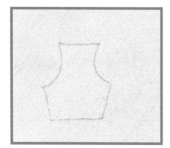

2 Cut out the shape and finger-press in the side seams (the top and bottom seams can be left as raw edges as they will be covered). Position the neck shape on the figure and stab stitch it in place using invisible thread or flesh-coloured fine polyester thread. Bring the needle through on the outline and pick up a tiny piece of cloth on the edge of the shape as you go back down.

Skirt

Next, mark out the area of embroidery for the skirt. The excess fabric on each side allows for gathering. The skirt will be embroidered as a slip in a separate ring frame, cut out a little larger and turned under before being stitched over the padding.

The area of the skirt marked out for embroidery.

Buttonhole shirt

Here is the final pattern for the buttonhole shirt. All the edges, apart from the neckline, have had an extra 2mm (⅛in) added to allow for the padding; the neckline is of a fixed size and not affected by padding.

Final pattern for the buttonhole shirt.

Top arm

The second layer of felt padding for the top arm is applied. The arm is stuffed at the same time as being stitched down.

Second layer of felt padding for top arm.

Buttonhole sleeves

Here are the final patterns for the buttonhole sleeves. All edges have had an extra 2mm (⅛in) added to allow for the padding, apart from where the sleeves meet the body; this is of a fixed size and not affected by padding.

Before stitching the sleeves down, hands are made and attached (see page 304).

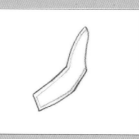

The final patterns for the buttonhole sleeves.

Making hands

Note
In order to shape the hand successfully, the wrapped wires should be longer than the finished fingers.

1 For the fingers, cut five lengths of very fine paper-covered wire, each approximately 9cm (3½in) long. Using a single strand of flesh-coloured cotton, wrap the middle 0.5cm (¼in) then fold the wire in half (see page 297).

2 Continue wrapping the doubled wire starting as close as possible to the folded end. Wrap the thread evenly, without overlaps. Knot the thread around the wire, leaving a long tail to finish.

3 Put a dab of water-based glue over the knot to secure it.

4 Make four fingers and a thumb, all following the same method.

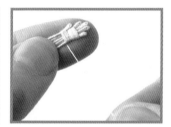

5 Group the four fingers together, arranged to resemble a real hand. Take another length of flesh-coloured cotton and bind them together, starting just below the nail of the little finger. Wrap down to where the base of the thumb will be.

6 Hold the fingers flat between a pair of tweezers and bring in the thumb.

7 Continue to bind the hand together down to the wrist, incorporating the thumb.

8 Hold the thread taut and press the fingers and thumb between a pair of tweezers. Pinch the wires together at the wrist.

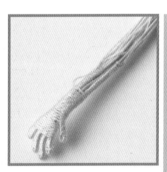

9 Continue to wrap the wires together along the arm, stopping just beyond the bottom of the sleeve. Secure the thread with a knot and manipulate the fingers into a realistic pose.

Attaching the hands

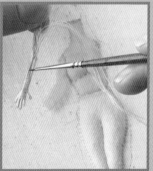

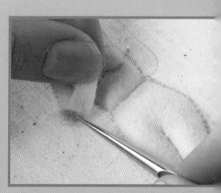

1 Decide where the hand will be positioned and locate the elbow. Apply a water-based glue using a small paintbrush to the unwrapped wires below the elbow.

2 Cut off the ends of the wires just below the elbow, leaving them sufficiently long to secure the arm to the embroidery.

3 Mark the position of the end of the wired hand on the fabric with a blue soluble pen. Stab stitch part of the way down the felt and stuff it lightly, up to the line, using small wads of fleece.

4 Position the hand on the fabric, making sure it is pushed firmly up against the stuffing. Hold back the felt using a needle and overstitch the arm in place using a waxed cotton thread. Make sure you pass the stitches in between the wires.

5 Stitch down towards the wrist, stopping just before you reach the part of the arm that will be visible beyond the sleeve. Once the arm is secure, stitch down the felt on either side (but not across the wrist) using stab stitch.

Attaching the sleeves

1 Lay the needlelace sleeve in position on top of the arm and stab stitch it in place. Bring the needle up through the needlelace and down through the background fabric. Start by securing the needlelace at the most important points and then fill the gaps in between with closer stitching.

2 Plunge the tail threads through to the back as you work around the arm and cast off.

Shoes

Draw shapes ready to be cut out of leather and stab stitched in place for the shoes. They are cut larger all round, apart from the top edge, to allow for padding.

Shapes ready to be cut out of leather for the shoes.

Making the face

Final shape of head.

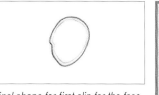

Final shape for first slip for the face.

1 Transfer the head shape to a small piece of very fine cotton, for example cotton lawn, using pricking and pouncing, then go round the outline using blue soluble pen. Work on the straight grain.

2 Make a slip to go over the face using the same cotton fabric, this time working on the cross grain. First colour the fabric as described on page 303. Transfer the head shape using pricking and pouncing, but do not mark the outline with a pen. Instead, work tiny running stitches, using white or flesh-coloured thread, just outside the outline, starting at the top of the head. Make the chin a little deeper.

3 When you have stitched all the way around the head, cut off the thread leaving a long tail. Do not cast off. Cut evenly around the stitched outline, leaving a 5mm (¼in) border, being careful not to cut the sewing thread.

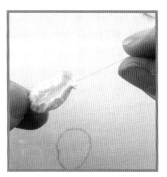

4 Pull the thread to gather up the fabric underneath the slip.

305

5 Use the gathering thread to secure the slip on the outline with stab stitches. Bring the needle up through the fabric on the line and take it down, catching the slip. Start at the top of the head and work down each side of the head as far as the ears.

6 Using small wads of fleece, stuff the top of the head with tweezers, a stiletto or a mellor.

Essential marks to achieve the facial features.

7 Mark the positions of the eyes in pencil using the template for guidance, and place three stab stitches in each eye – one in the middle and one in each corner – to create the indents for the eye sockets.

8 Stab stitch down the sides of the face to the start of the chin. Mark on in pencil the nose and the mouth.

9 Stuff the bottom half of the face and push a tiny ball of cotton wool into each cheek to make them more rounded. Hold down the chin with a pin and place two or three stab stitches into the mouth.

10 Work a few more stab stitches down towards the chin, then put in a final piece of stuffing – a tiny ball of cotton wool for the chin. Complete the stab stitching.

11 Cut a small sliver of softwood from the corner of a block to make the nose. Glue the softwood nose to the face.

12 Lay one or two stitches over the nose to hold it in place.

13 Apply diluted water-based glue using a paintbrush over the stitched edge on the front and the back of the embroidery. Dry the glue thoroughly with a hairdryer.

14 Cut out the slip, trimming right along the edge of the stitching.

15 Place the slip on another piece of fabric on the cross grain, coloured as before, and draw around it in pencil leaving a 5mm (¼in) border.

16 Work tiny running stitches on the pencil line around the drawn shape. Cut off the thread leaving a long tail as before, then cut out the shape 5mm (¼in) outside the stitched line. Lay the shape over the face and gather up the fabric underneath by pulling on the tail thread.

17 Use the same thread to lace across the back of the face to secure the fabric.

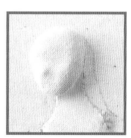

18 Attach the face to the embroidery using stab stitch worked in invisible thread or fine sewing thread. Start with three or four holding stitches placed evenly around the face, then work the rest of the stitches in between. Bring the needle up through the base fabric on the line and catch the edge of the face as you take it back down.

19 Mark in the eyes again with the blunt end of a stiletto or a pinhead, then place three tiny stitches in each one, as before. Reinstate the mouth in the same way, and come down the side and under the tip of the nose with a row of tiny stem stitches in invisible thread.

20 Draw on the outline for the hair in pencil or blue soluble pen. Use pricking and pouncing to transfer the outline for the hair from the template to a piece of felt and cut it out.

21 Position the padding for the hair on the figure and stab stitch it in place. Bring the needle through to the front of the fabric on the line and take it back down through the felt.

Hairline to be marked on the face.

Layer of felt padding for the hair.

22 Embroider the features using a very fine thread (fils à broder) or a single strand of stranded cotton. Begin with the eyebrows. Use either the template or the pricking to position the eyebrows and stitch them on using tiny stem stitches.

24 Define the shapes of the eyes by working some tiny stitches around each one, and work a few tiny straight stitches across the mouth using one or two strands of fine, dark pink silk thread.

25 Paint each cheek with a touch of pink watercolour.

23 Place a French knot in the centre of each eye.

Hair

1 Start to fill in the hair using straight stitches and silk shading, starting with the left-hand side. Use a variegated rayon thread.

2 Stitch the top part of the hair on the right-hand side of the head in the same way, then change to a brighter silk floss and work some longer stitches over the top.

3 Return to the rayon thread and work another row of long-and-short stitches further down, bringing the needle up in the stitches of the previous row and taking it back down at the edge of the felt.

4 Continue stitching in the same way, preparing a base for the ringlets that will be stitched on top.

5 To make the ringlets, fold a length of the rayon thread in half and wrap it around the end of a paintbrush, holding the loop in place with your left hand as you wind with your right.

6 Use a dilute water-based glue to paint over the coils, avoiding the loop at the end. Dry the glue thoroughly with a hairdryer.

7 Pull the ringlet off the paintbrush and make two or three more in the same way. Attach each one to the hair by stitching it in place through the loop and at a few other places along its length. Attach as many ringlets as you wish and trim to the required length.

WHITEWORK

Butterfly
See also pages 316 and 349.

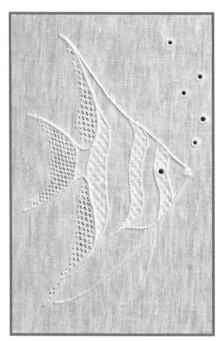

See also page 340.

See also page 332.

See also page 350.

FROM THE AUTHOR

The word 'whitework' is an umbrella term, meaning pretty much any piece of needlework comprising white embroidery on white fabric. This means that any surface stitches done with only white could be referred to as whitework; but there are also a number of techniques that are specific to whitework. These are pulled thread work, counted satin stitch, drawn thread work, eyelets and cutwork. These techniques are all used to bring texture and tone to the design.

Typically both threads and fabric used for whitework are made from either cotton or linen fibres. Usually the fabric is evenly woven so that counted stitches may be worked, and within these criteria there are many options.

I have been stitching in one way or another all my life, and discovered whitework for the first time while studying Art & Design at college. I wrote a detailed study of cutwork, and the ideas lingered in my mind until I started the 'Basic Whitework' module in my second year of training at the RSN.

Since then I have loved whitework because it is incredibly versatile. That might sound surprising since it has no colour, but in fact that gives you freedom to tackle all sorts of designs – even those you might usually rule out because you don't like the colour.

A good example of this is my Autumn Maple Leaves design on page 320. Orange and yellow are not really my colours, but the beautiful shapes lend themselves perfectly to whitework.

Whitework is all about the stitches – they have to do all the work, because there is no colour to distract the eye! For someone like me, who sees the world through a haze of stitches, this is perfect. I can take an image and translate it into a pattern of different stitches without concerning myself with colours. Unlike many other types of embroidery, whitework has almost unlimited stitches, which means you never get bored. Because the stitches are the stars, whitework really helps you to hone your needlework skills.

This is by no means an exhaustive list of stitches, but it will help you to understand the principles involved, and you will see how to combine any or all of the fantastic techniques to suit your own style.

I hope that you will discover the joy of whitework, and you will take the information and run with it in your own way.

Lizzy Lansberry

THE HISTORY OF WHITEWORK

The history of whitework is diverse and complicated, because there are so many techniques and cultures involved. In its many forms, it may be seen in historical textiles all over the world. In this book I have concentrated on the European traditions of whitework. The styles of whitework have seen external influences in design and technique, particularly from India since the 16th century, but trade within Europe seems to have had the greatest impact.

Pulled thread work means the use of counted stitches to pull apart the threads of the ground fabric, creating lace-like patterns. It can be found placed among surface stitches in many whitework pieces. There is speculation that it may have been used as early as 50BC on garments worn by Cleopatra of Egypt. Examples in Europe date from the 13th century and are most notably represented in Dresden work, a beautiful densely worked style of whitework developed in Germany, identified by the abundance of pulled thread fillings. This style gained popularity in the early 18th century as a substitute for lace. See examples on pages 315 and 334.

Surface stitches appear in combination with other techniques in every form of whitework and the most commonly used is satin stitch. Throughout its history, whitework designs have focused on natural forms such as flowers and leaves, for which surface stitches are perfect. In the early 19th century the local women of Ayrshire, Scotland, developed a highly skilled industry producing large volumes of a very detailed style of whitework known as Ayrshire work. It is known for its dense surface stitching on very fine fabrics and is most often seen on christening robes and bonnets.

Eyelets are most frequently seen in a style known as Broderie Anglaise (originally a French term literally translating to English Embroidery), which was at its height in the late 19th century. This style uses both round and shaped eyelets to create patterns, with no other stitches required. It is useful as a means of decorating textiles that must withstand a lot of washing, and still reappears in summer fashion.

Drawn thread work uses a two-stage process to achieve a lace effect, and is thus distinguished from pulled thread work. Threads are removed from the ground fabric, and then the remaining threads and spaces are embroidered or woven. The earliest known example of drawn thread work was discovered in the 9th century tomb of Saint Cuthbert when it was opened in the early 12th century.

Cutwork is the name for the removal of areas of fabric, after securing the edges with stitching. Cutwork developed in its various forms all over Europe, but the most accomplished work came from Italy. The most famous style, Richelieu embroidery, is named after Cardinal Richelieu, who introduced it to France from Italy in the 16th century. It is identified by small loops on the buttonhole bars, known as picots. Cutwork became so popular in England in the 16th and 17th centuries that a law was passed allowing only the noble classes to wear it.

Tablecloth

This is a charming example of intense stitching on a densely woven cloth. You can see that, because of the nature of the fabric, the pulled thread areas create a lovely waffle texture, rather than a lacy pattern. The majority of the design is worked with satin stitch and trailing to create highly raised areas. The design itself, a symmetrical foliage pattern extending from the corners, could be from the 18th century.

Whitework border

Whitework can be used to create pretty borders and hems for clothing and table linens. This example shows a scalloped edging in buttonhole stitch with a repeated pattern of satin-stitch flowers, eyelets and a little pulled thread work.

TOOLS AND MATERIALS

Threads

Whitework uses quite a variety of different threads. The type of thread used depends on the technique, and it is therefore useful to have a selection.

I recommend using a length of no more than 25cm (10in) for whitework. This may seem excessively short, but because the thread is white it is very easy for it to become dirty. We rely on the texture of the thread, so it would not look good for it to become thin or fluffy.

Many of these threads are available in both white and off-white, and you should choose what you prefer – but make sure they all match! For this reason I try to buy as many of my threads as possible from the same brand so that the tones of white match well. There is no reason to choose any one brand over another; again it should be your own preference.

Stranded cotton
This is the dominant thread in most whitework designs. It can be used for any of the surface stitches, and gives a beautiful shine.

Coton à broder
This is a thicker thread that is quite soft, and not divisible. I usually use size 16, but it is available in other thicknesses. It may be used for surface stitches in the same way as stranded cotton to give a heavier, matt look. It is also very useful as padding for satin stitch or trailing.

Floche (soft cotton)
Also known as tapestry cotton, this thread is very thick and is made from slightly twisted strands of very soft fibres. It may be used for surface stitching on coarser work, but it can take practice to keep it under control. Its primary use is as padding for satin stitch and trailing.

Perlé cotton
This thread is very shiny and has a visible twist. It is available in a range of thicknesses and is useful for creating varied texture in a design alongside the other threads. It is suitable for surface stitches, and can also be used for larger scale drawn thread work.

Lace thread
Lace thread is a tightly spun thread that is very fine and very strong. It comes in a variety of thicknesses that create different effects. It is a good idea to begin with one of the thicker ones, and progress to the finest. A number denotes the thickness of the thread: the higher the number, the finer the thread.

Cotton or polyester machine thread
This is useful for tacking out areas of your design. You may use either white or light blue (either way it should be removed either as you work or afterwards).

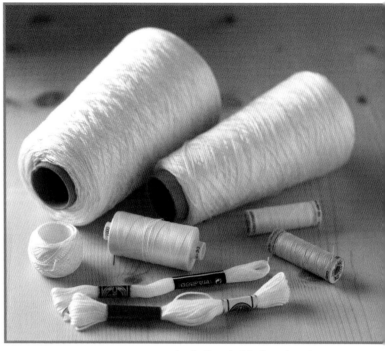

A selection of white threads and a blue thread for tacking.

Dragonfly

This design includes a number of surface stitches, including a counted satin stitch pattern in the lower wings. These are in contrast to the cutwork used in the upper wings; note where the buttonhole bars are placed to support the shapes. It is worked on 32TPI Belfast linen to allow the counted stitch pattern to be seen easily. Cutwork on this gauge of linen is quite tricky, but achievable if worked very carefully.

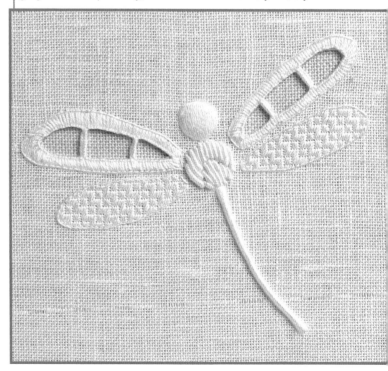

Needles

Three different types of needle are needed for whitework. They each have their own particular purpose, so it is helpful to have a selection handy.

Tapestry

These needles have blunt points, which makes them perfect for any stitch where you do not want to pierce the threads of the fabric – pulled thread work, counted satin stitch and drawn thread work. The size chosen depends on the thickness of the thread – a larger eye for a thicker thread.

Crewel

Otherwise known as 'embroidery needles' these are slender needles with sharp points. The eye of the needle fits within the line of the needle, allowing for accurate work. They are used when working surface stitches with stranded cotton, coton à broder or lace thread. Again, the size depends on the thickness of the thread.

Chenille

These very sharp needles have a larger eye than crewel needles and are therefore suitable for surface stitching with thicker threads. Their primary use in whitework is for padding with floche, or plunging thick threads when stitching trailing. I like to use a size 22, which is comfortable to thread and handle, as well as being accurate.

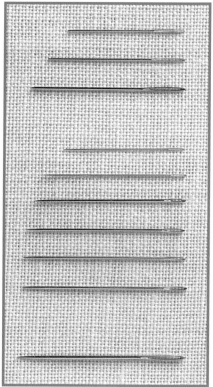

A selection of needles. From the top: tapestry needles sizes 28, 26 and 24; crewel needles sizes 12, 9, 8, 7, 6 and 5; chenille size 22.

Fabrics

Whitework is generally worked on an evenweave (or plain weave) fabric, where the number of threads per inch (TPI) is the same for both warp and weft. I always say you should buy the best you can afford, much as you might for clothing or furniture – after all, you are putting time and effort into your work, and you want it to be enjoyed long after you have finished it.

Evenweave linen is available in a range of TPI, from 20 to 55. It is also possible to get a cotton version in the heavier gauges. My preference for most of my projects is a 32TPI Belfast linen. Natural slubs may appear in this type of fabric, but it is easy to count the threads.

Cotton or linen batiste (or batist) is a very fine, soft evenweave fabric that is tricky to count, but is beautiful when used for surface stitches, cutwork and eyelets.

Cotton or linen lawn is similar to batiste, but finer and more sheer. Again it is lovely for surface stitches, cutwork and eyelets. It may also be used for pulled and drawn thread work, but this may be tricky unless you have very good eyesight.

Cotton or linen muslin is a sheer fabric with a lower thread count than lawn. It is therefore easier to stitch pulled or drawn thread work. It is suitable for surface stitching, but be wary of using too much weighty thread as it will alter the drape of the fabric.

Dressmakers' net or tulle is used for net darning embroidered lace, which we will look at on page 347.

Evenweave linen fabric.

312

Vogue

Worked by Helen Cox. This stunning contemporary piece shows the variation that can be achieved with whitework. It is perfectly suited to the defined straight lines in the text and border as well as the natural curves of the hair and flowers. The delicate drawn thread work in the background beautifully sets off the raised areas of satin and long-and-short stitch.

313

DESIGN

How do we design for whitework, with no colour to work with? Whitework is all about tonal and textural contrast, and it is amazing what can be achieved with these two basic elements. It is important to remember which techniques are suitable for the shapes of your design and the kind of texture they will achieve – think about which areas you want to be prominent.

   Also consider which techniques you can use together to be able to stitch most comfortably. For example, if you would like to include a lot of pulled thread work, you may wish to choose a coarser linen fabric, in which case cutwork would be difficult.

   The following elements are covered in detail. You may choose to use any combination of these techniques – as many or as few as you like.

Lovebirds

This design shows how the different elements can be combined. Note how the pulled thread, cutwork and eyelets really stand out when a dark backing is used. The birds' tails are both stitched in long-and-short stitch, but the two angles look totally different. The curled stem is a simple stem stitch line, but worked in coton à broder to make it more prominent. The small satin-stitch leaves catch the light at various angles.

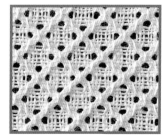

Open trellis filling (see page 327).

Pulled thread work

Pulled thread work involves pulling the threads of the fabric tightly together to make a lacy pattern. There are a wide variety of patterns, each giving a different effect. It is very good for covering large areas with texture and is usually worked within an outlined shape, though it can be worked without an outline in some designs. You are pulling little holes in the fabric, so this can be used to give a darker tone to an area. As a counted stitch, you may find this easier on coarser evenweave linen, but it may be stitched on any fabric, even fine cotton lawn.

Satin stitch

Satin stitch is often the most raised part of a design because it can be very highly padded. It gives the design an area of high shine. The direction of the stitches can be angled so as to catch the light differently in different places, such as turning around a curve, to emphasise shapes. Satin stitch is suitable for shapes up to about 8mm (¼in) wide. It is easier to achieve very smooth edges on finer fabric, but with a good split-stitch foundation, it may be worked on any fabric. See pages 330–331.

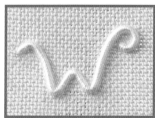

Trailing

Usually trailing creates fairly narrow lines. The width can be varied quite a lot by the number of core threads. It can be worked in stranded cotton or coton à broder and it picks up the light very well, giving a shiny surface. Use trailing for outlines and design elements such as tendrils. See pages 332–333.

Long-and-short stitch

Long-and-short can be worked in stranded cotton or silk, which give a smooth, blended appearance. Changing the angle of the stitches around a curve will emphasise the shape. Long-and-short is a good way of filling almost any shape, including ones with wobbly edges that would be tricky in satin stitch. For more on this stitch see pages 42 and 174.

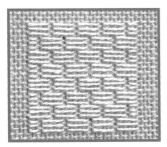

Counted satin stitch (see page 334).

Decorative stitches

These add texture and life to a design by reflecting the light in different directions; stitches such as fishbone (see page 54) are a simple but attractive way to fill a leaf shape, and French knots (see page 66) may be used to fill any shape or size of space.

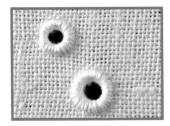

Eyelets

Eyelets are very useful design elements – a simple way to create high contrast. Worked in a variety of sizes and shapes, they can make a design in themselves, but they also combine very well with small satin-stitch elements and trailing. For more on eyelets, see pages 328, 335 and 336.

A woven wheel corner (see page 343).

Drawn thread work

Drawn thread work is most often seen in borders; used like this it can be a lovely way to finish off a design. You can also stitch drawn thread work within a design to create a striped pattern. Since this technique involves removing one thread at a time, it is easier on coarse linen, but it may be worked with care on any good, evenly woven fabric. See pages 336–343 for more information.

Cutwork with trailing (see page 345).

Cutwork

Cutwork is suitable for shapes up to about 8mm (¼in) wide, such as leaf shapes or bands. It may be used on wider and more complex shapes if several buttonhole bars are used as supports. Remember that completely removing part of the fabric means you can see through to whatever is behind it, so choose any backing colour wisely. Since cutwork involves cutting into the fabric, a firm, closely woven fabric will give a stronger result. It is not recommended to try this on coarse linen, as the stitching may not be enough to protect the edges.

Dresden Work

Detail of an embroidered border in the Dresden style. It features a variety of pulled-thread patterns combined with counted satin patterns and flat satin-stitch details, stitched on very fine cotton lawn.

Designing a piece

So now we know what we have to work with. Remember, you don't have to use all the different elements in one design – and most importantly, don't panic! If you are not used to designing your own work, start small. You will soon build the confidence to take on bigger projects. Try copying a historical piece – there is plenty out there to inspire you.

A good way to get started is to trace ideas on to paper, cut them out and rearrange them until you like the result. Begin by taking an image or pattern that inspires you, or simply doodle away until you come up with something you like. It is always handy to have a sketchbook around for those moments of inspiration when you are out and about, or in the middle of the night! I find the easiest way to design is to take a photograph, or a simple sketch, and work from there with tracing paper, or my trusty computer.

For this butterfly, I looked at a photograph my Dad took of a beautiful peacock butterfly (below). I first made a sketch of the butterfly, marking the placement of the details on the wings. I knew I wanted the wings to be relatively symmetrical so I dispensed with some of the perspective in the photograph to flatten out the image.

I scanned the image into my computer and used image-manipulation software to create a clear outline. I then created a simplified version by moving the elements around and evening out the curves. You can do the same thing by using tracing paper. Try tracing different elements separately and cutting them out. Then arrange them on a piece of paper until you are happy with the design, and retrace the final outline on a new sheet.

Once I have a clear outline to work with I create drawings of the design, trying out different stitch effects. Think about which areas would suit different stitches, and try to lightly sketch in a rough idea of the texture, for example cross-hatching gives the impression of pulled thread work. Colour any areas that are unstitched (including the background) with a very light tone, so that the white stitched areas stand out. If I am including satin stitch or long-and-short stitch in my design, I create another drawing showing the angle of the stitches. For cutwork areas I sketch in where I think any buttonhole bars will be needed for support.

When you are happy with the result, you are ready to transfer your design and frame up your fabric, and you can work out a stitch plan. Don't forget that as long as you have an outline you like, some elements of the design can change as you go along.

Lastly, think about a background colour. Whether it is a framed artwork or a draped tablecloth, the colour showing through makes a great difference to the overall effect. Throughout this book I have used blue backgrounds because blue makes the work look clean and white. Other colours may also work well – a cherry red can be beautiful for example. I would advise being wary of yellow, orange and yellow-greens as they are likely to make the work look discoloured. Hold various colours behind the work and see what you like best.

My sketch.

My computer drawing of the design, including ideas for stitching.

The finished embroidery.

Photograph by Peter Lansberry.

316

THE ORDER OF WORK

Before you start to stitch, it is important to plan the order of work. Although there is a degree of flexibility, particularly in the early stages, it is useful to have a guide so that you don't end up in a mess. With whitework there are some fairly clear guidelines, based on what effect each type of stitch has on the fabric. Some stitches add strength and some take it away; some stitches are flat, some are raised.

1. PULLED THREAD WORK

This comes first because it is flat, so it needs to be complete before any raised stitching is done.

2. CORE SURFACE STITCHES

Generally it is a good idea to work outlines first, and then any solid areas. This is also the time to work the stitching of cutwork (method 2 – see page 344), but do not cut them yet!

3. DECORATIVE SURFACE STITCHES

These are often used to fill an area so it is good to stitch these after any outlines are complete.

4. EYELETS

Eyelets create small details and the placement may be dependent on other parts of the design so you should work them after all the surface stitching is complete.

5. DRAWN THREAD WORK

This is a delicate process and should be worked after all the surface stitches and eyelets are finished. If it is used for a border, it is easier to position it at this stage. Stretch the fabric only once more after this to embroider on the remaining threads.

6. CUTWORK

This is the time to finish off the work by releasing the fabric from the frame and trimming any cutwork areas. After this is complete, it would not be a good idea to stretch the fabric in a frame.

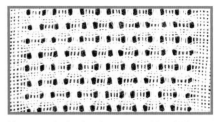

Honeycomb darning (see pages 320–321).

Turned satin stitch (see page 330).

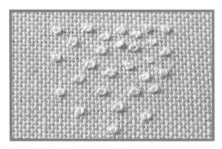

French knots (see page 66).

Shaped eyelets (see page 336).

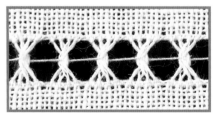

Double twist (see page 339).

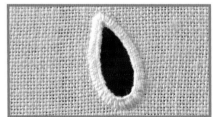

Cutwork with buttonhole stitch (see pages 344–345).

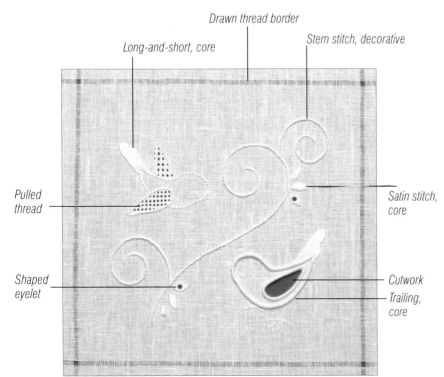

Long-and-short, core

Drawn thread border

Stem stitch, decorative

Pulled thread

Shaped eyelet

Satin stitch, core

Cutwork

Trailing, core

GETTING STARTED

Covering your work

It is always important to keep your embroidery clean, but especially so with whitework. With no colour to distract the eye, a small stain can be very obvious. While working, try to keep as much of the work covered as possible. For long-term storage and transport, I recommend wrapping the whole thing in tissue paper and an old (but clean) white sheet or cloth.

IN A HOOP FRAME

1 Frame up as on page 19, but with tissue paper between the fabric and the outer ring. Carefully make a hole in the tissue with a pin (this avoids getting sharp scissors near your fabric).

2 You can now tear away a piece of tissue paper to expose just the part of the design you are about to start stitching. As you work, either tear away a bit more tissue paper or simply reposition it when you take the fabric out of the frame. Remember to keep another piece of tissue paper handy to cover the whole thing when you take a tea break.

IN A SLATE FRAME

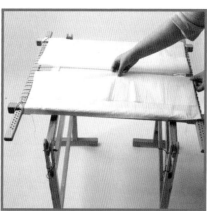

1 Use low-tack sticky tape to attach a double layer of tissue paper to each roller.

2 Fold back the sheets to expose a strip of fabric, including the area you are going to begin working.

3 Fold two more sheets of tissue paper into strips and slot them underneath the first two, leaving only a very small area exposed. Pin all the tissue paper in place. When you take a break, pin another double layer of tissue paper over the exposed area.

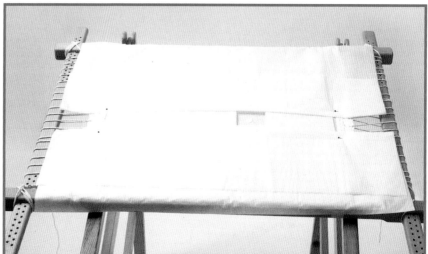

WHITEWORK STITCH FINDER

The following pages show the fundamental stitches of whitework. They are divided by technique, and displayed in the order they should be worked. Some are shown on blue fabric so that you can clearly see the threads. As for most types of embroidery, you should generally cast on with two little stitches in an area that will later be covered (see page 39).

Stitch	Type	Page
BASIC SATIN STITCH	CORE SURFACE STITCH	SEE PAGE 330
BUTTONHOLE BARS	CUTWORK	SEE PAGE 345
BUTTONHOLE STITCH	CUTWORK	SEE PAGE 344
CHAIN	DRAWN THREAD STITCH	SEE PAGE 341
COUNTED SATIN STITCH	CORE SURFACE STITCH	SEE PAGE 334
DIAGONAL CROSS FILLING	PULLED THREAD STITCH	SEE PAGE 326
DIAGONAL DRAWN FILLING	PULLED THREAD STITCH	SEE PAGE 325
DIAGONAL HEM STITCH	DRAWN THREAD STITCH	SEE PAGE 338
DOUBLE TWIST	DRAWN THREAD STITCH	SEE PAGE 339
DRAWN THREAD CORNERS	DRAWN THREAD STITCH	SEE PAGE 342
EYELETS	PULLED THREAD STITCH	SEE PAGE 328
FISHBONE STITCH	DECORATIVE STITCH	SEE PAGE 54
FOUR-SIDED STITCH	PULLED THREAD STITCH	SEE PAGE 323
FRENCH KNOTS	DECORATIVE STITCH	SEE PAGE 66
HEM STITCH	DRAWN THREAD STITCH	SEE PAGE 338
HONEYCOMB DARNING	PULLED THREAD STITCH	SEE PAGE 320

KNOTTED BORDER	DRAWN THREAD STITCH	SEE PAGE 340
LONG-AND-SHORT STITCH	CORE SURFACE STITCH	SEE PAGE 42
OPEN TRELLIS FILLING	PULLED THREAD STITCH	SEE PAGE 327
OVERCASTING	DRAWN THREAD STITCH	SEE PAGE 339
PADDED SATIN STITCH (SATIN STITCH VARIANT)	CORE SURFACE STITCH	SEE PAGE 331
PADDED SATIN STITCH (SPLIT STITCH VARIANT)	CORE SURFACE STITCH	SEE PAGE 331
ROUND EYELETS	EYELETS	SEE PAGE 335
SEEDING	DECORATIVE STITCH	SEE PAGE 49
SHAPED EYELETS	EYELETS	SEE PAGE 336
SINGLE FAGGOT STITCH	PULLED THREAD STITCH	SEE PAGE 324
SPLIT STITCH	CORE SURFACE STITCH	SEE PAGE 58
STEM STITCH	DECORATIVE STITCH	SEE PAGE 56
TAPERED TRAILING	CORE SURFACE STITCH	SEE PAGE 333
TRAILING	CORE SURFACE STITCH	SEE PAGE 332
TURNED SATIN STITCH	CORE SURFACE STITCH	SEE PAGE 330
WAVE STITCH	PULLED THREAD STITCH	SEE PAGE 322
WRAPPED BARS	DRAWN THREAD STITCH	SEE PAGE 341

PULLED THREAD STITCHES

Pulled thread work is used to create lacy patterns in the fabric, without removing any threads. The thread used should match the thickness of the grain of the fabric. The following pages take you through the steps of a few of the many patterns available.

   When the directions say to 'pull', this means that you need to give a short, sharp tug on the thread, in the direction of the stitch. This is generally each time you bring the needle up through the fabric. You will see that doing this creates little holes in the fabric, which will build into a lacy pattern. It is important to pull consistently on the fabric so that the pattern will be even; the best way to do this is to get into a rhythm.

   Try to begin an area across the widest point, considering which angle the pattern is worked at (some are straight across, others are diagonal). When working within an area, you will need to break up the pattern when you reach the edge. None of your stitches should go over the border, and the end of each row should be tied off with a couple of tiny holding stitches on the border. Sometimes it is helpful to put 'fake' stitches at the edge, which are not pulled tight but complete the look of the pattern.

   Note that these stitches are shown worked in one direction, but you may work them in whichever direction you find most comfortable, or which suits the shape.

Autumn Maple Leaves
This piece shows three pulled thread stitches: diagonal drawn filling, wave stitch and honeycomb darning (clockwise from top). The outline details are stitched with stem stitch and trailing.

Preparation

The shape should be outlined with double running stitch (see page 138) to firmly enclose the area. This helps to prevent the surrounding linen from being distorted.

1 Thread a length of lace thread into a small crewel needle and tie a knot in the end. Secure the thread with two little stitches on the line.

2 Make running stitches round the line. These should be around 2mm (1/8in) long, with gaps of the same length. Wherever possible, try to split the threads of the fabric rather than going through the holes.

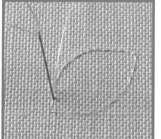

3 Go back around the line, filling in the gaps to make double running stitch.

The design prepared for pulled thread work, with a double running stitch outline.

Honeycomb darning

Honeycomb darning is a simple pulled thread pattern that is worked in horizontal rows. As the name suggests, it creates a honeycomb pattern. Try this with thicker lace thread for a raised effect.

1 Bring the needle up just inside your outline. Make a vertical stitch up over four threads.

2 Make a horizontal stitch under four threads, to the left.

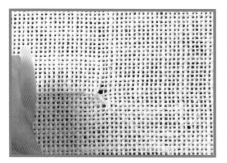

3 Pull to the left, against the last stitch.

4 Make a vertical stitch down over four threads.

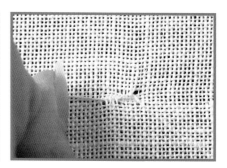

5 Make a horizontal stitch under four threads to the left, and pull again. Repeat to complete your first row.

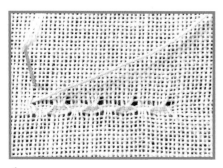

6 Make a holding stitch in the border and then bring the needle out of the first hole on the top of the previous row. Take a vertical stitch up over four threads to begin the new row.

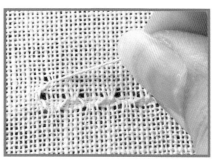

7 Make a horizontal stitch under four threads to the right, and pull.

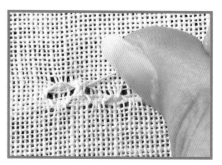

8 Make a vertical stitch down over four threads, taking the needle down through the hole of the previous row. Bring the needle up four threads to the right, through the next hole along, and pull again. Repeat to complete the row.

An example of honeycomb darning.

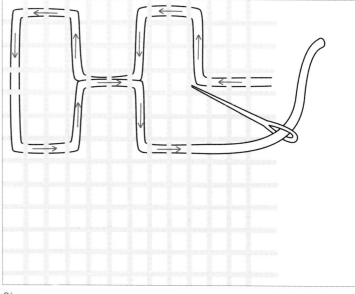

Diagram

Note

To make sure the pattern is correct, turn the embroidery over. On the back you will see that the horizontal stitches are doubled up.

321

Wave stitch

Like honeycomb darning, wave stitch is worked in horizontal rows. This one is a bit trickier to stitch evenly, but can be very useful and is good for small areas.

1 Bring the needle up two threads inside your outline. Count right two and down four and take the needle down.

2 Count left four, bring the needle up and pull to the left.

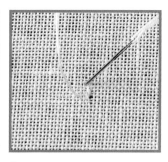

3 Take the needle back through the first hole (right two and up four).

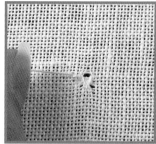

4 Count left four, bring the needle up and pull. Repeat to complete the first row.

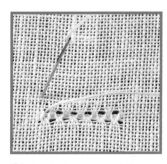

5 To begin the next row, bring the needle out of the first top hole of the previous row. Count left two and up four and take the needle down.

6 Count right four, bring the needle up and pull to the right.

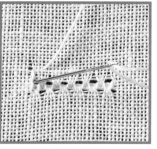

7 Count left two and down four and take the needle down in the hole of the previous row.

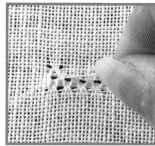

8 Count right four (to the next hole of the previous row), bring the needle up and pull. Repeat to complete each row.

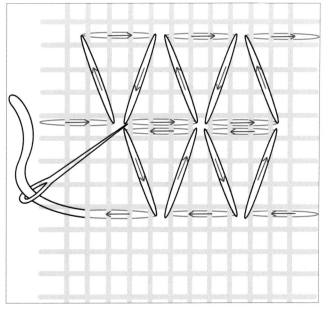

Diagram

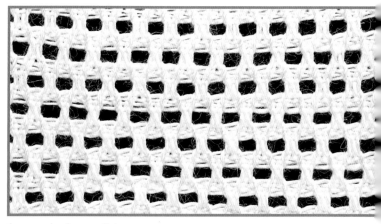

An example of wave stitch.

322

Four-sided stitch

Four-sided stitch looks as though it has a lot of steps, but it is really just a case of repeating squares. It creates a very even pattern of little holes, and is great for borders.

1 Bring the needle up just inside your outline. Make a vertical stitch up over four threads.

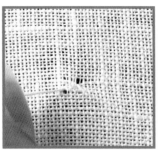

2 Count left four and down four and bring the needle up, making a diagonal stitch underneath. Pull to the left.

3 Make a horizontal stitch four to the right, taking the needle down in the first hole.

4 Count left four and up four and bring the needle up, making a diagonal stitch underneath, and pull.

5 Make a horizontal stitch four to the right, taking the needle down in the top right hole.

6 Count left four and down four, bring the needle up in the bottom left hole, and pull.

7 Make a vertical stitch up over four threads. This becomes the first stitch of the next square. Repeat to complete the row.

8 Count four threads up from the top left hole of the previous row and bring the needle up. Make a vertical stitch over four threads down to the hole to make the first stitch. Work the row in the same way as the first row, but in reverse.

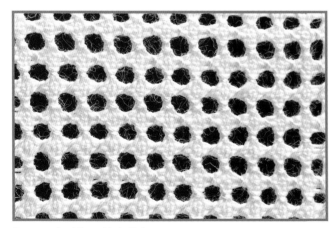

An example of four-sided stitch.

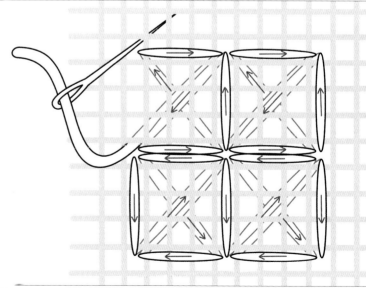

Diagram

Single faggot stitch

Single faggot stitch is a simple stitch worked on the diagonal.
It is the foundation for a variety of diagonal stitches.

1 Bring the needle up just inside your outline. Make a vertical stitch up over four threads.

2 Count left four and down four, bring the needle up and pull.

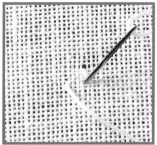

3 Make a horizontal stitch four to the right, back down into the first hole.

4 Count four left and four down, bring the needle up and pull.

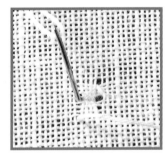

5 Make a vertical stitch up over four threads, into the previous hole. Repeat to complete the first row.

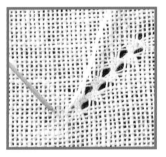

6 To begin the second row, bring the needle up through the first hole of the previous row and make a horizontal stitch over four threads to the left.

7 Count right four and up four, bring the needle up and pull.

8 Make a vertical stitch down over four threads, into the hole of the previous row. Repeat to complete the row.

Diagram

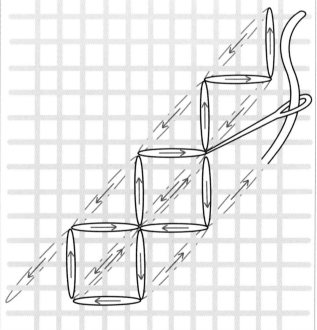

An example of single faggot stitch.

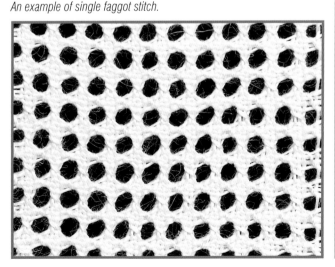

Diagonal drawn filling

Diagonal drawn filling is based on single faggot stitch, worked on the diagonal. The steps are the same as for single faggot stitch, but the rows are spaced one thread apart. It creates a pretty pattern that is one of my favourites.

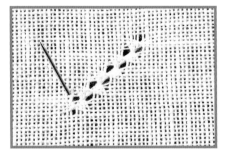

1 For the first row, follow the steps for single faggot stitch opposite. Instead of bringing the needle up in the first hole of the previous row, move it one thread up and one thread to the left.

2 Make a horizontal stitch over four threads to the left.

3 Count up four and right four, bring the needle up and pull.

4 Make a vertical stitch down over four threads, into the previous hole of this row.

5 Count right four and up four, bring the needle up and pull. Notice that when you pull this time, you open up a hole with a cross shape inside it (it looks a bit like a window).

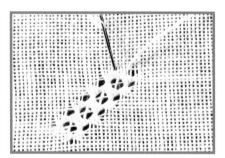

6 Repeat to complete the row.

An example of diagonal drawn filling.

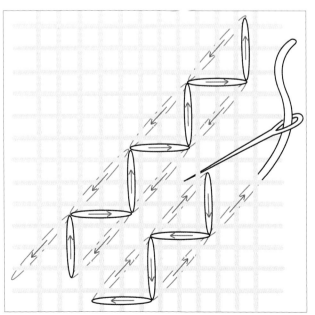

Diagram

Diagonal cross filling

Diagonal cross filling creates a neat pattern with raised stripes. Try stitching it with a thick lace thread to enhance the stripes, or with a fine thread to keep it flat.

1 Bring the needle up just inside your outline. Make a vertical stitch down over six threads.

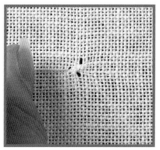

2 Count left three and up three, bring the needle up and pull. This makes a small diagonal stitch on the back.

3 Make a vertical stitch down over six threads. Repeat along the row.

4 At the end of the row, count left three and up three from the last hole and bring the needle up. Make a horizontal stitch to the right over six threads to form a cross.

5 Count left three and up three, bring the needle up in the next hole of the previous row and pull. Repeat to complete the row.

6 To start the next row, count up six threads from the first hole of the previous row and bring the needle up. Make a vertical stitch down over six threads into the first hole of the previous row.

7 Count left three and up three, bring the needle up and pull. Repeat along the row.

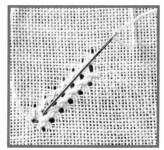

8 At the end of the row, repeat step 4 to complete the second row. Repeat to fill the shape.

An example of diagonal cross filling.

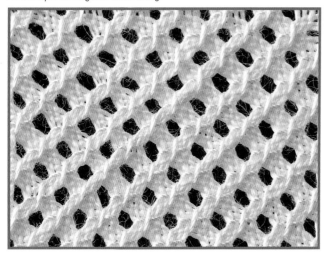

Diagram

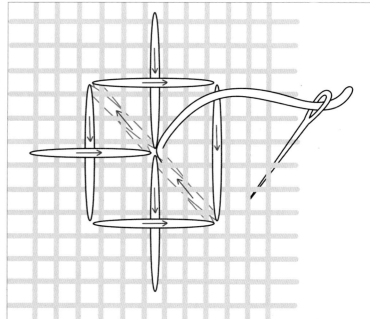

326

Open trellis filling

Open trellis filling is a lovely stitch based on diagonal cross filling. It is suitable for large areas.

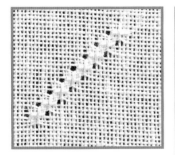

1 For the first row, follow the steps for diagonal cross filling, see opposite.

2 For the second row, again follow the steps for diagonal cross filling, but leave a space between the rows. From the first hole of the first row, count down six threads and begin the second row. Fill the shape with these evenly spaced rows.

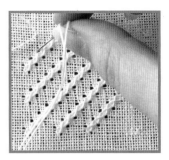

3 The next rows are worked in the same way, but from top left to bottom right, crossing the first rows. Bring the needle up in the top left corner, through the first hole of a row. Make a vertical stitch down over six threads, over the previous cross.

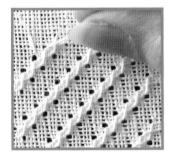

4 Count right three and up three, bring the needle up and pull.

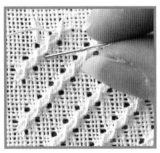

5 Make a vertical stitch down over six threads. Repeat along the row.

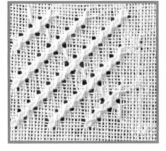

6 At the end of the row, count right three and up three from the last hole, and bring the needle up. Make a horizontal stitch to the left over six threads, down into the next hole, to form a cross. Repeat to complete the row.

7 Begin the next row, leaving a space between the rows. From the first hole, count down six threads and begin the next row. Fill the shape with these evenly spaced rows.

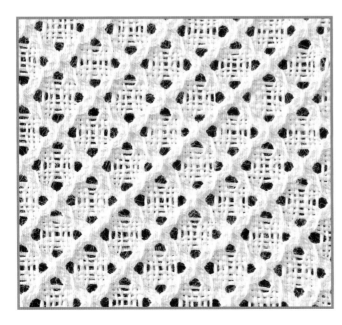

An example of open trellis filling.

327

Eyelets

Pulled work eyelets may be worked individually or combined to form a pattern. There are various different shapes to choose from. The method is the same for each, only the placement of the stitches changes (see diagrams). See pages 335–336 for more eyelet variations.

ROUND EYELETS

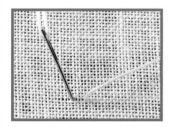

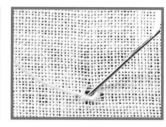

1 Bring the needle up and make a horizontal stitch four threads to the left (this is the position of the centre hole).

2 Bring the needle up one thread below the starting point and pull.

3 Take the needle down in the centre hole (four threads left and one up).

4 Follow the diagram for the placement of the stitches, and continue round the eyelet.

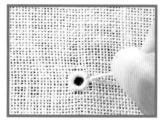

5 Pull the thread each time you bring the needle up through the fabric, to maintain a neat hole.

6 Pull the final stitch.

The finished eyelet.

Diagram

SMALL ROUND EYELET

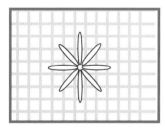

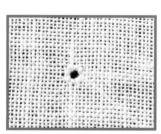

Diagram

The finished small round eyelet.

DIAMOND EYELET

The finished diamond eyelet.

SQUARE EYELET

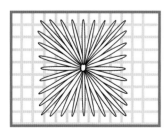

The finished square eyelet.

328

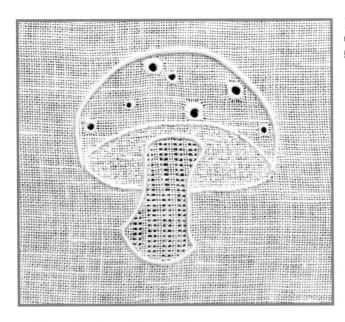

This toadstool design makes use of pulled work eyelets. Each eyelet is a different size and shape to give a natural appearance.

Combining pulled thread stitches

Many of the pulled thread stitches can be combined to create interesting patterns.
Try experimenting with the stitches to create your own patterns.

SINGLE FAGGOT STITCH WITH DIAGONAL CROSS FILLING

Both stitches are diagonal so they combine easily. To make the stitches fit neatly together, sometimes you need to change the count. Because the diagonal cross filling is counted over six threads, the single faggot stitch has been reduced to three instead of four: two times three makes six, so the two fit together.

FOUR-SIDED STITCH WITH SQUARE EYELETS

Square eyelets work well counted over eight threads, and four-sided stitch counted over four threads fits in well.

The pattern is worked as follows: two rows of single faggot stitch, a space of three threads, one row of diagonal cross filling, a space of three threads, one row of single faggot stitch, one row of diagonal cross filling, and so on.

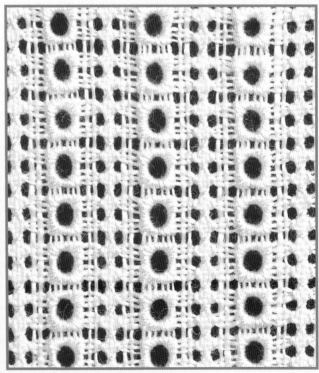

The pattern is worked as follows: one vertical row of four-sided stitch, a space of two threads, a vertical row of square eyelets (with no spaces in between), a space of two threads, and so on.

329

CORE SURFACE STITCHES

These stitches are essential to whitework. They give weight to the design by providing solid areas of stitch. They can be worked with stranded cotton, coton à broder or perlé cotton.

Basic satin stitch

Once you have mastered this simple stitch, you can tackle all sorts of designs. In some ways, although this is the most basic version, it can be the most difficult because you have to be very careful to keep the angle of the stitches consistent. Work split stitch around your shape first.

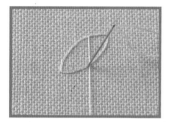  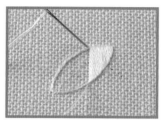 

1 Beginning halfway along one side, bring the needle up just outside the split-stitch outline. Hold the thread to set the angle of the first stitch, and take the needle down accordingly, just outside the split stitch.

2 Bring the needle up on the first side, very close to the first stitch, just outside the split stitch. Make a second stitch, angling the needle towards the previous stitch and towards the split stitch.

3 Work outwards towards the end of the shape, and then begin again in the middle. This time bring the needle up on the other side of the shape, and angle the needle towards the previous stitch as before.

The design worked in basic satin stitch.

Diagram of stitch direction.

Turned satin stitch

This is a very useful stitch because the changing angles reflect light in a very interesting way. The turned stitches allow for almost any shape to be worked.

1 Outline the shape with split stitch and fill with any padding required (see opposite). Bring the needle up just outside the split-stitch outline partway along the shape. Choose the required angle and take the needle down accordingly, just outside the split stitch.

2 Bring the needle up on the first side again, very close to the first stitch, just outside the split stitch. Make a second stitch, angling the needle towards the previous stitch and towards the split stitch.

3 Continue to stitch in this way to cover the shape. To change the angle gradually as you move along the shape, bring the needle up even closer to the previous stitch on the inside curve and take it down a little further away on the outside curve.

4 Complete the first half of the shape with a last neat stitch. Try to think about the angles in advance so that when you get to this stitch, it will easily cover the outline.

5 Begin again in the middle. As for basic satin stitch, you will reverse the direction of the stitches.

6 This time to change the angle, bring the needle up a little further away from the previous stitch on the outside curve and tuck it even closer on the inside curve.

The finished example of turned satin stitch. The angles will be different for each shape that you stitch, so try to have a rough plan of what you want it to look like before you start.

Padded satin stitch (satin stitch variant)

This version of padded satin stitch gives a smooth, rounded effect that is raised more in the centre of the shape and tapered towards the edges. Each layer of padding should be at a different angle, and the top layer should be at right angles to the satin stitch itself. There is no particular limit to the number of layers; it is determined by the size of the shape.

1 Outline the shape with split stitch first. Using a thick thread, bring the needle up a bit inside the split stitch outline. Make the first stitch across the longest part of the shape.

2 Bring the needle up close to the first stitch, at the same end, and make another stitch. Continue outwards to the edge.

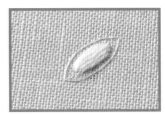

3 Start again in the middle and complete the layer.

4 Work the next layer of padding at a different angle to the first, starting in the middle and working outwards. Start again in the middle and work to the other end to complete the layer.

5 Stitch the third layer in the same way at another angle.

6 Work satin stitch with your chosen thread following the steps for basic satin stitch opposite.

The finished design in padded satin stitch.

Padded satin stitch (split stitch variant)

This version of padded satin stitch is a little more advanced. You need to be careful to keep a smooth surface on the padding to support the satin stitch. Because the layers are built up gradually, it allows for variation within one shape. You can work as many layers as you like, varying them according to the width of the shape and the desired height of the padding. Here I have worked a leaf shape in two halves, to demonstrate the different levels of padding.

1 Outline the left-hand side with split stitch first. Using a thick thread, stitch a line of split stitches just inside the split-stitch outline. The stitches should be 5–8mm (¼ –½in) long. Then continue the line around the shape, spiralling in towards the centre.

2 Add second and third layers of split stitch, continuing to spiral around the shape.

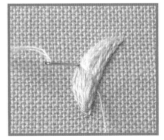

3 Work satin stitch over the padding, following the steps for turned satin stitch, opposite.

4 Outline the right-hand side with split stitch and then work split stitch padding inside it as before. This time stitch only one layer.

The finished design. The right-hand side is less padded than the left, giving it a flatter look.

White Peacock

Stitched by Sophie Long. This beautiful design of a stylised peacock makes brilliant use of long-and-short stitch – the whole body is filled with long-and-short, using the direction of the stitches to emphasise the shape. Swathes of satin stitch add highlights. Note the contrast between these shiny surface stitches and the patterned techniques in the peacock's tail.

Trailing

Trailing is a very useful stitch, brilliant for creating outlines. It has a lovely shiny surface that reflects a lot of light, and the width can be adjusted to give very fine or bold lines. Use stranded cotton for the stitching for accuracy. I suggest beginning with at least three floche or six coton à broder threads for the core while you practise, then progress to finer or bolder trailing.

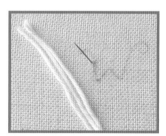 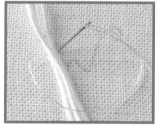  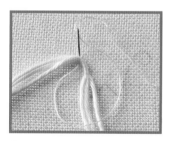

1 Begin partway along the line, preferably on quite a straight section. Decide how many threads to use as the core. Bring the needle up just to one side of the line.

2 Bring the needle over the core threads and take it down just on the other side of the line. The stitch should be at right angles to the line. Pull fairly tightly on the first stitch and maintain the tension as you work the next stitch (after this you can relax a bit).

3 For each subsequent stitch, bring the needle up from underneath the core threads and take it down underneath them. The stitches should be as close together as you can manage, so as not to let any of the core threads show through.

4 As you turn a corner, change the angle of the stitches so they stay at right angles to the line at all times. They will be spaced a little further apart on the outside curve and even closer together on the inside curve.

  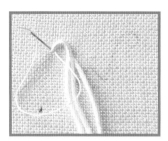 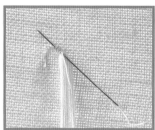

5 To finish a line, stop stitching just before the end of the line. Thread one of the core threads into a large chenille needle and take the needle down at the end of the line to plunge the thread through.

6 Repeat for the rest of the core threads and then continue to stitch, holding the core threads out of the way on the back.

7 Finish stitching to the end of the line, angling the needle out from under the core threads and back underneath them with each stitch.

8 If the trailing finishes away from any other stitching, turn to the back to cast off. Run the needle underneath the last few stitches, pull the thread through and trim.

9 On the back, trim the core threads as close as possible to the fabric so that no shadows will show on the front. Trim each thread individually for the neatest result.

 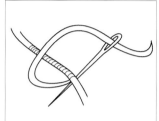

A finished example.

Diagram

Tapered trailing

Tapered trailing does exactly what it says on the tin: it is trailing, but tapered. With this method, you can go from any number of core threads down to nothing. In this leaf design I worked the outline with stem stitch and the stem with tapered trailing, starting with three floche threads.

1 Begin trailing as before. To gradually taper the line, separate the core threads (with floche you can divide the strands).

2 Lift the top threads out of the way and carefully snip a few of the strands closest to the fabric.

3 Continue to stitch over the remaining core threads, making sure no fluff shows where the threads were cut. Then repeat the trimming process as many times as necessary.

4 Finish the last few core threads as for trailing by taking them through to the back and finish off neatly.

The finished example of tapered trailing.

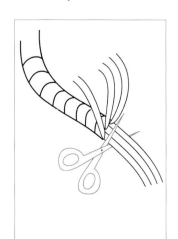

Diagram

Counted satin stitch

Counted satin stitch techniques will enable you to get an even pattern over a shape. These stitches contrast well with pulled thread work. There are endless patterns you can try; experiment with different threads and make up your own patterns. Use a tapestry needle so that it slides easily between the threads of the fabric.

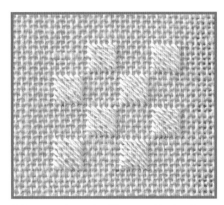

This pattern is made with square blocks of diagonal stitches, alternating with blank squares.

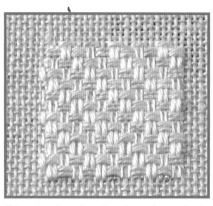

This pattern has alternating diagonal rows. Each row has pairs of either vertical or horizontal stitches. Two rows are worked with stranded cotton, then two with coton à broder and so on.

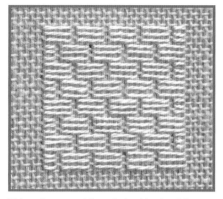

This pattern consists entirely of horizontal stitches over six threads. Blocks of three stitches are arranged in a bricked pattern.

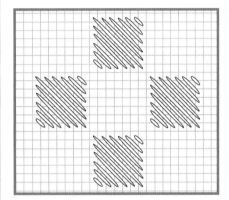

Diagram

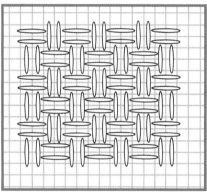

Diagram

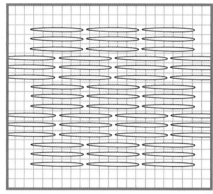

Diagram

Dresden Work, RSN Collection. This piece of fine cloth is edged with a deep border, densely worked with a wide variety of pulled thread patterns and counted satin stitches.

EYELETS

Eyelets can be used to make beautiful designs with no other stitching, or just with satin stitch. This style of whitework is commonly known as Broderie Anglaise. They are also a useful addition to other designs.

Round eyelets

Round eyelets are made by pushing the threads of the fabric apart, rather than cutting it, so they do not damage the fabric. They may be stitched with stranded cotton, coton à broder or perlé cotton.

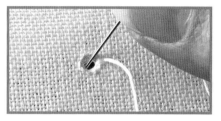

1 Work a ring of running stitch the desired size of the eyelet. The stitches should be about 2mm (1/8in) long. There is a limit to the size that can be made with this method – usually about 5mm (1/4in). A single line of running stitch may be enough on fine fabric, but on coarse fabric I like to work double running stitch; go back around the ring filling in the gaps.

2 Push the tip of a stiletto into the centre of the ring, twisting the stiletto to increase the size of the hole gradually. Then remove the stiletto from the hole while you stitch.

3 Bring the needle up about 2mm (1/8in) outside the ring, and then pass the needle down through the hole. Bring the needle up again next to the first stitch and back through the hole again.

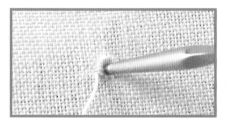

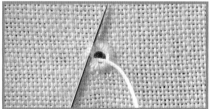

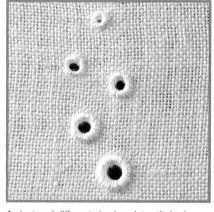

4 Repeat all the way around the eyelet, using the stiletto from time to time to neaten the hole.

5 Once complete, run the needle under a few stitches on the back to finish off tidily. Then use the stiletto to make sure the hole looks round.

A cluster of different sized eyelets stitched with this method. You can also make shaded eyelets by increasing the length of the stitches on one side.

Morris-inspired Cutwork

Worked by Jenny Adin-Christie. This piece of contemporary whitework demonstrates the versatility of the simple eyelet. The central flower motif is entirely separate from the fabric, simply supported by buttonhole bars.

Shaped eyelets

This method is used to create eyelets that are shaped (usually teardrop or leaf shaped) and may be used to create larger circular eyelets. They can be stitched with stranded cotton, coton à broder or perlé cotton.

1 Work a line of running stitch around the shape. The stitches should be about 2mm (1/8in) long. A single line of running stitch may be enough on fine fabric, but on coarse fabric I like to work double running stitch; go back around the shape filling in the gaps.

2 Insert the tip of a pair of very sharp embroidery scissors into the centre of the shape, and snip towards one end of the shape, being very careful not to cut your stitching.

3 Turn the scissors around and snip to the other end of the shape.

4 Carefully make two more cuts, from the middle to either side.

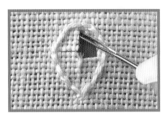 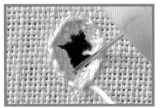  

5 Gently fold each quarter of the fabric back underneath the surrounding fabric.

6 Bring the needle up about 2mm (1/8in) outside the running stitch line, and then pass the needle through the hole.

7 Bring the needle up again next to the first stitch and then back through the hole again.

8 Continue all around the eyelet, trying to keep an even tension in the stitches and not distorting the fabric.

Try using a wider band of stitching for a bolder look.

DRAWN THREAD STITCHES

The essence of drawn thread work is the removal of threads from the fabric. This alone can create useful effects. Drawn thread stitches are perfect for borders, and also make pretty patterns that you can use to fill shapes. The following pages give you a step-by-step guide to drawn thread work.

Preparation

Before doing any drawn thread work, it is advisable to either remove your fabric from the frame entirely, or to loosen it so that it hangs slack in the frame. Then you can begin to remove threads. This method assumes that you are creating a border, or a line that does not meet any other stitching.

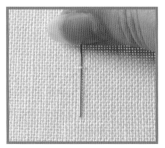

1 In the middle of the line you wish to remove, use a tapestry needle to hook up just one thread of the fabric and pull it up a little.

2 Slide the point of one blade of your embroidery scissors under the same thread, beside the needle, and snip the thread. It is very handy to have sharp-pointed curved scissors for this.

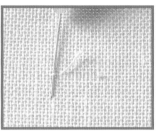

3 Move along the cut thread, using the needle to tease it free of the fabric. Continue this to the end of the line, and then do the same in the opposite direction.

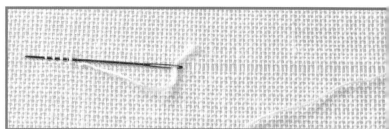

4 Thread the needle with the unpicked thread and weave it back into the fabric by four or five threads to secure the end. Do the same at the other end. Do not cut the thread until all the necessary threads are removed, in case you need to adjust the tension. Then trim away all the excess thread.

This sample shows five drawn threads.

Alternative preparation

This method assumes that you are working your drawn thread up to other stitching. It works for any reasonably solid stitching including buttonhole stitch, satin stitch, close clustered French knots and trailing.

1 Before working your chosen stitch, work a line of double running stitch with lace thread, just inside the outline (see page 138).

2 Work your chosen stitch along the line, covering the double running stitch. Here I have used buttonhole stitch (see page 52).

3 Remove the fabric from the frame and follow steps 1, 2 and 3 of the standard preparation as described above.

4 Once all the necessary threads are unpicked right up to the stitching, lift them all up, away from the fabric and slide one blade of your embroidery scissors underneath. Move the scissors so that the flat of the blade rests against the stitching and carefully snip the threads. By ensuring that the flat of the blade is against the stitching, you reduce the risk of cutting through your stitches.

The finished preparation using buttonhole stitch.

You can also prepare for drawn thread work using French knots, as shown here.

Alternative preparation for drawn thread work using satin stitch.

Hem stitch

Hem stitch is mostly used to create a foundation for decorative stitches, but is an attractive stitch in its own right. It is very useful for borders, and may be worked on both sides of drawn threads, or just on one side for different effects, as in the example on page 308. Vary the number of threads you gather together according to the look you want to achieve.

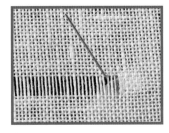

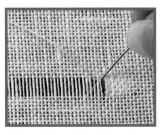

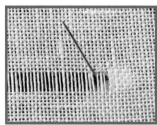

1 Cast on in the overwoven end, count three threads along and bring the needle up.

2 Go back over the same three threads and take the needle down.

3 Count three threads along and bring the needle up in the same place again.

4 Pull the thread tight to draw the threads together.

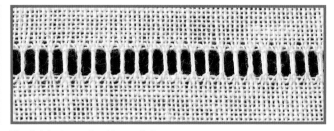

5 Count into the fabric by two threads and take the needle down, while holding the thread tight. This acts as a holding stitch to keep the threads gathered.

6 Go back to the drawn threads and count three threads along. Bring the needle up ready for the next stitch. Continue all along one edge, then repeat on the other edge.

The finished sample of hem stitch.

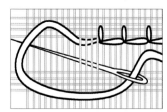

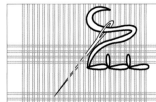

Diagram 1

Diagram 2

Diagonal hem stitch

Diagonal hem stitch is a variant of hem stitch, using the same method. It gives you a simple diagonal pattern. For this variant, you need to gather an even number of threads; this sample shows four.

Work the first edge following the directions for hem stitch above but gathering four threads together. Then work the other edge with the same stitch, but staggering the gathering stitch by bringing the needle out just two threads along for the first stitch, and from then on gathering four threads together.

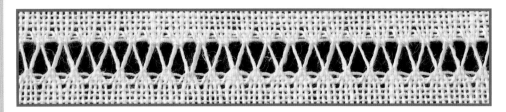

338

Overcasting

This is an alternative to hem stitch, giving a less dramatic effect. It is useful for very fine work where there may not be enough space for hem stitch, or as a quicker way to make a foundation for other stitches. It does not give quite such a strong edge as hem stitch, so it is not as practical for borders on household linens.

1 Cast on in the woven patch as before and come up in the first gap.

2 Take the needle down two threads along and two up into the linen.

3 Come up in the gap directly below.

The finished sample of overcasting. You need to pull fairly tightly to achieve the ladder effect.

Double twist

This is a great stitch for a reasonably wide border. For this sample, eight threads were removed, and then hem stitch was worked to gather the threads in bunches of two. This stitch can be tricky because it all relies on tension. Remember to keep holding the thread tightly all the way to the end and cast on and off very securely. Because it needs to be pulled so tight, it can be useful to work buttonhole stitch (page 52) over the overwoven ends before stitching.

1 Cast on in the overwoven end, count over four bunches and take the needle down.

2 Count back under two bunches and bring the needle up.

3 Count back over two bunches and take the needle down.

4 Count under four bunches and bring the needle up.

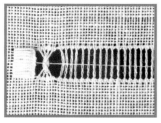

5 Pull the thread tight to twist the bunches together. Be careful to pull straight along the centre line so that the twist forms neatly.

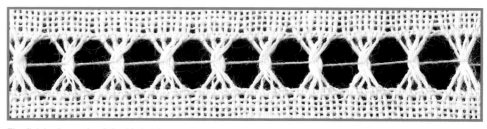

The finished sample of double twist.

Knotted border

This is a good stitch for almost any size of border. For this sample, eight threads were removed, and then hem stitch was worked to gather the threads in bunches of two. You could gather more threads, or stitch each knot over more bunches for different effects.

1 Bring the needle out in the first gap, loop the thread clockwise and take the needle back into the first gap.

2 Count under two bunches and bring the needle up inside the loop.

3 Close the loop to make a knot.

4 Pull tight. Continue in the same way.

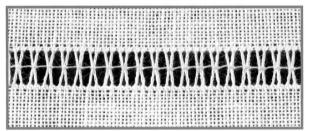

The finished sample.

Tulip
Worked by Lizzy Lansberry. The flower is stitched with pulled thread patterns. The background has a pattern of drawn threads throughout, and the piece is accented with trailing and padded satin stitch.

Chain

This is based on traditional chain stitch, but worked over drawn threads. It is lovely on narrow borders, but may also be repeated to fill a larger border. For this sample, five threads were removed.

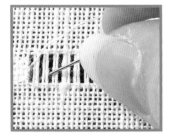

1 Cast on in the overwoven end, count over two bunches and take the needle down.

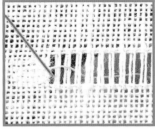

2 Bring the needle up again in the first gap, below the first stitch.

3 Take the needle down in the first gap, above the first stitch, leaving a loop.

4 Count under two bunches and bring the needle up, inside the loop.

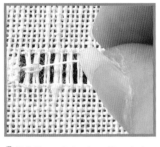

5 Pull through to close the chain. Remember this is a chain stitch rather than a knot, so do not pull too tight.

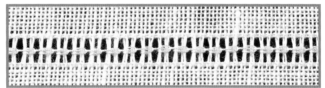

The finished sample.

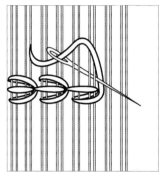

Diagram

Wrapped bars

Unusually for drawn thread work, this stitch uses stranded cotton. The idea is to create small bars of satin stitch, rather than pull the threads very tight.

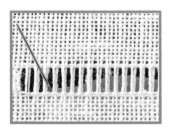

1 Cast on in the overwoven end, count under three bunches and bring the needle up.

2 Take the needle down in the first gap again.

3 Pull slightly to wrap the three bunches together, but not too tightly. Continue to wrap over the same bars, making sure that each wrap sits neatly next to the previous one. Count the wraps as you go. Push the wraps down with the needle to press them more tightly together.

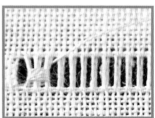

4 Continue to wrap the same way until you reach the other edge, then carry the thread under the next three bunches to start the next bar. Wrap each set of bunches the same number of times.

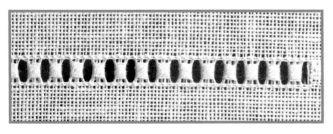

The finished sample.

Drawn thread corners

When working a border, you usually have a corner to fill. To prepare a corner, follow the preparation steps (see pages 336–337), making sure that the tension is even. For a large corner I advise working a line of buttonhole stitch along each edge.

BUTTONHOLE CORNER

1 Work your chosen stitch down the length of the vertical border and with the same thread, begin the corner stitch. Bring the needle up two bunches into the horizontal border.

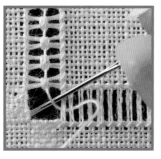

2 Take the needle down into the corner, catching the loop.

3 Bring the needle up two threads into the fabric.

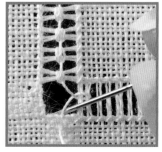

4 Take the needle down into the corner, catching the loop.

5 Bring the needle up two threads into the fabric.

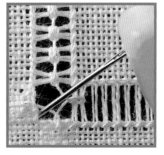

6 Take the needle down into the corner, catching the loop.

7 Bring the needle up in the corner through the first loop.

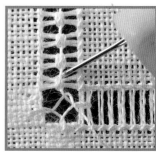

8 To finish off neatly, take the needle down two bunches into the vertical border and run the needle through the stitching so that you can cast off on the edge.

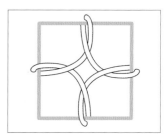

The finished buttonhole corner.

Diagram 1

Diagram 2. This stitch can be worked in either direction, so long as you catch each loop.

WOVEN-WHEEL CORNER

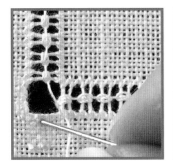

1 Work your chosen stitch down the length of the vertical border and then carry the thread across the corner square, taking the needle two threads into the fabric opposite.

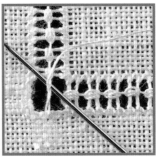

2 Use the needle to carefully wrap around the thread across the corner and then carefully run the needle through the stitching and cast off to the side. Repeat with the horizontal border.

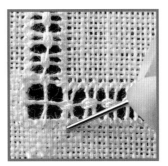

3 Bring the needle up two threads into the fabric in the top left and take it down at the bottom right to form a diagonal stitch, then wrap around this thread back to the start. Make a couple of small stitches to travel to the bottom left.

4 Bring the needle up two threads into the fabric in the bottom left and pass the needle through the crossed threads in the centre before taking it down at the top right.

5 Wrap along the thread as far as the centre to complete the spokes of the wheel. Then begin to weave through the spokes.

6 Weave over and under alternate spokes all round the wheel, keeping the thread fairly tight the first time.

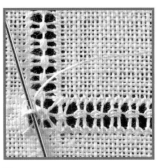

7 Weave round the wheel again, keeping the thread more relaxed for each subsequent circle so that it builds in size. Remember not to completely fill the corner.

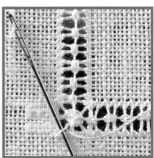

8 After a few circles the wheel is complete. To finish off, wrap around the last spoke back to the bottom left and cast off in the fabric.

The finished woven-wheel corner.

Diagram

CUTWORK

Cutwork removes part of the fabric, allowing the backing material to show through. Buttonhole stitch is the traditional stitch used for cutwork, and is the easiest way to get a neat finish because the stitch forms a corded edge. Stranded cotton and coton à broder work well for cutwork stitches. There are two methods to consider, depending on the shape you are stitching. For small, simple shapes such as circles, ovals or teardrops method 1 can be useful, because you trim the fabric first and fully encase the edge. For larger and more complex shapes method 2 gives a neat finish and can be used with buttonhole stitch, satin stitch or trailing. You can also use these methods to create a pretty hem for your work, for example a scalloped border. In this case, work the stitches the other way round so that the corded edge faces outwards.

Method 1, buttonhole stitch

This method must be worked after everything else is complete. It is worked on a still-tight frame, so you must be very careful with your tension. This method is best suited to very closely woven fabrics.

1 Work two lines of double running stitch around the shape and then begin to trim away the fabric by first cutting from the middle to each end, and then from the middle to each side.

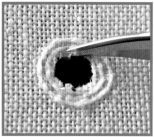

2 Carefully trim each tab away and gently remove any fluff.

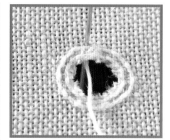

3 Cast on between the two running stitch lines. Bring the needle up through the hole and down just outside the outer line, leaving a loop.

4 Bring the needle up through the hole again, inside the loop. Pull through to complete the stitch and repeat all around the shape, making sure that the two ends match up neatly.

5 Cast off by running the needle under a few stitches on the back.

The finished example of cutwork with buttonhole stitch.

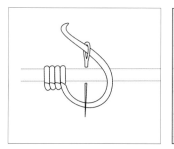

Diagram

Note

With this method you must be very careful with your tension. Pulling too tightly on the stitches can cause the fabric fibres to pull through the running stitch, ruining the shape.

Method 2

This may be worked with buttonhole stitch, satin stitch or trailing (see the examples opposite). Here it is shown with basic, narrow buttonhole stitch, but you could also try a wider line of buttonhole stitch, in which case you may find it useful to stitch a line of split stitch under the outer edge, just as you would for satin stitch (see page 330). The stitching may be worked at the same time as other core stitches, but the cutting away should be done at the very end.

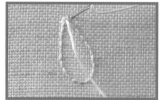

1 Work a line of double running stitch just outside the outline. To begin buttonhole stitch, bring the needle up just inside the line and take it down just outside the line, leaving a loop.

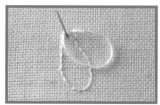

2 Bring the needle up just inside the line, right next to the first stitch, with the needle inside the loop.

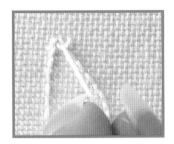  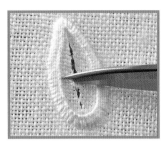 

3 Pull the excess thread to the back and then bring the needle and thread through to complete the stitch.

4 Repeat around the shape, placing the stitches as close together as you can. Make sure that the two ends match up neatly.

5 Begin to trim the fabric away by first cutting from the middle to each end, and then from the middle to each side.

6 Insert the scissors so that the flat of the blade rests against the stitches; this way the stitches will not be cut. Use small snipping movements to gradually trim away the fabric. Sometimes it is useful to turn to the back.

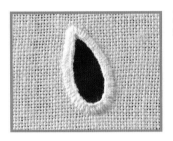

The finished example of cutwork with buttonhole stitch.

Note

To change thread while working, finish the last stitch by making a tiny stitch over the loop. Start a new thread and bring the needle up between the last two stitches to form the next loop.

Buttonhole bars

Buttonhole bars allow you to cut away larger shapes, by creating a network of supports. Consider whether you need these for support, and if they will add to the look of your design. Remember they really should be stitched before you do any cutting, not as an emergency fix afterwards!

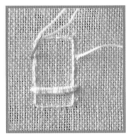 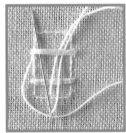 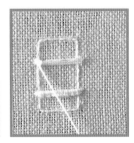  

1 Bring the needle up on the right, just outside the double running stitch, and down on the left. Make two more stitches: left to right, then right to left. The three threads across the gap should be taut, even a little too tight.

2 Bring the needle up on the left and begin to work buttonhole stitch across the three long stitches. Pass the needle eye-first under the threads from top to bottom, leaving a loop. Pass the needle over the loop.

3 Pull the thread tight to complete the stitch.

4 Repeat steps 2 and 3 across the bar, keeping the stitches close together and trying to keep an even tension. To finish the bar take the needle down outside the running stitch line. Work cutwork as before and be careful not to cut through the bars when you trim the fabric away.

The finished example of buttonhole bars.

Satin stitch

Work satin stitch in the same way as usual, following the steps on page 330. Remember to work a line of double running stitch first.

Trailing

Work trailing following the steps on pages 332–333. I would advise keeping the trailing quite wide because it will be stronger, but it is possible to do this with narrow trailing on fine fabrics.

FURTHER TECHNIQUES

Once you have mastered all the stitches, you might like to explore further.
The following pages give an introduction to layering fabrics and net embroidery.

Using layers

Layering is a kind of upside down appliqué, which allows you to use a combination of different fabrics within a design. You might use one simply to create a shadow, or to show off different techniques. When planning your stitching, you must think about where you would like to position any extra layers. A layer of linen may be secured by any dense surface stitch, for example satin stitch or French knots, but a layer of net must have at least two lines of stitching to hold it – for example trailing plus a line of double running stitch. Net should be applied directly after working any pulled work areas. Linen should be applied partway through the embroidery, so that it is not trapped anywhere that is not necessary to secure it.

Here I have shown how to apply another layer of linen and a layer of net, which can be useful in lending a little support to a large cut area (this is most suitable for embroidery that will not take any strain, such as artwork). The fabric should be loose or in a slack frame while applying layers. First, cut a square of linen or net large enough to cover the required area, plus an extra inch or so all around.

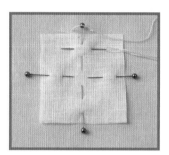
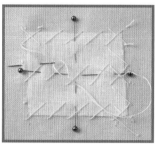
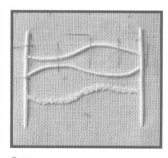

> **Note**
>
> It is really useful to have a pair of lace scissors for cutwork. They have a point on one blade and a ball on the other, so that you can slide them between two layers easily.

1 Turn to the back of the work. Pin the square to the main fabric as shown, lining up the straight grain. For a larger piece, use more pins, working from the centre out to the corners. With machine thread, use large basting stitches to secure the square, starting outside the square. Pass the needle through both layers, making a horizontal stitch underneath, and then repeat, leaving long diagonal stitches on the top.

2 Work a row of basting stitches through the middle, top and bottom. For a larger piece, more lines will be needed; work these from the centre out to the sides. At the sides, the stitches should overlap the edge of the square. Then rotate the fabric and work lines in the opposite direction.

3 Work any stitching required to trap the layers. As you work, cut any basting threads that are in the way – do not stitch over them. Once the stitching is complete, cut the remaining basting stitches and gently pull them away.

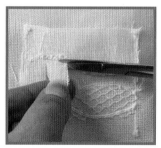
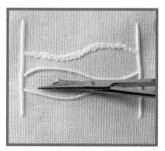
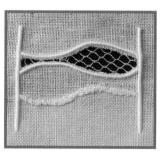

4 To trim the linen closely, first cut towards the stitching to create small tabs of fabric.

5 Carefully trim away each tab of fabric, keeping the flat of the blades against the stitches.

6 To remove the main linen over an area of net is a tricky task that really does require lace scissors. With a needle, make a small hole in the linen through which you can insert a scissor blade. Once the hole is large enough insert the lace scissors, using the blade with the ball against the net. Carefully snip towards each end, create tabs as before and gently trim away the linen.

The finished layered piece.

Net darning

There are various methods of net embroidery; we are going to look at the simplest one, needlerunning, meaning simply that a needle is used to weave a pattern on the net.

When including a net layer, you can achieve some very pretty results with net embroidery. I have included three patterns for you to try, but you can experiment with many more of your own. You should use a small tapestry needle for net embroidery but you may use any type of thread provided that it fits comfortably through the holes in the net. Traditionally lace thread would be used but in these samples I have used stranded cotton for clarity.

The net embroidery must be completed before adding the layer to your main fabric, so make sure you have worked out the size of area you need to stitch, with 1cm (⅜in) excess all around.

CASTING ON

Net darning is the only technique that has a different casting on method. Because there is no solid fabric, you must start with two half hitch knots.

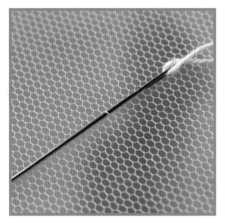 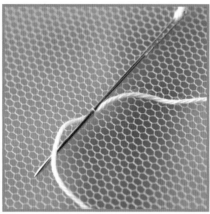 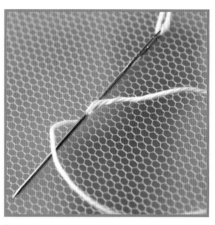

1 Pass the needle under one thread of the net, leaving a tail. Make sure it is a single thread rather than an intersection, so as not to distort the net.

2 Pass the needle under the same thread in the same direction as before, taking the needle through the loop of thread, and pull tight. It should catch in what is known as a half hitch knot.

3 Repeat step 2, making sure you catch the loop again to form a second half hitch knot.

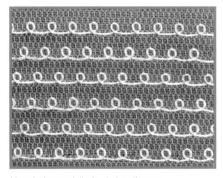 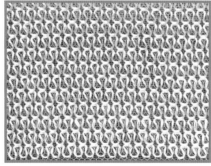 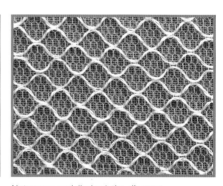

Net circles and (below) the diagram.

Net flowers and (below) the diagram.

Net waves and (below) the diagram.

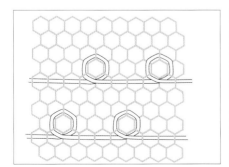 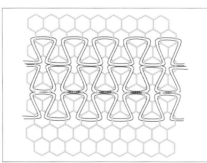 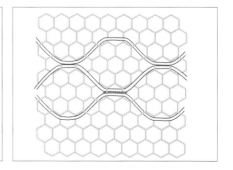

TAKING CARE OF YOUR EMBROIDERY

However you choose to display your embroidery, whether it is a functional item or a framed artwork, you want it to look its very best, so it is important to know how to clean and store it. The following method of cleaning is appropriate for any textile (unless the colours run) and is a good way to clean historical or delicate embroidery. I have used an antique handkerchief from my collection to demonstrate. Once your embroidery is clean and dry, the best way to store it is wrapped in acid-free tissue paper and/or a clean white cloth. If you are mounting your work for the wall, it will be best protected in a frame behind UV protective glass to prevent yellowing – and it really is best to wash the work before mounting.

Washing your whitework

1 Pour a little detergent into the bottom of a clean basin or container and fill with lukewarm water. Use detergent without optical brighteners if possible as these can leave residue. Place the embroidery on the surface, folded if necessary. Do not press down on the fabric.

2 Wait for the embroidery to sink naturally and leave for thirty minutes to one hour. If after this time any areas need particular attention, place the embroidery on a clean surface and use a very soft sponge to gently dab the area with the detergent solution.

3 Rinse the detergent out by soaking the embroidery the same way again in new, clean water. Repeat all steps if necessary.

4 Once you are happy the embroidery is clean, remove it from the water and place it on a clean towel. If possible, open it out flat, but fold it if it is too big. Blot the embroidery with another clean towel laid flat on top. To reduce the need for pressing, open the embroidery out flat and pin it carefully to a folded towel. Insert pins along the edge of the piece and stretch the fabric just a little (not so much that the edge is distorted).

Note

All embroidery looks darker when wet, so don't worry if it looks less than pristine during the cleaning process.

USING THE STITCHES

The following pages guide you through a few of my designs, with details of the stitches used to achieve the effects. Hopefully this will help you think about your own designs and how to use the stitches you have learned.

Butterfly

This design is based on a peacock butterfly (the design process is detailed on page 316). I love butterflies, and they work beautifully in all types of embroidery. They have a natural symmetry that is very appealing to the eye, but you can see that the design, like a real butterfly, is not perfectly symmetrical. The butterfly is stitched on 32TPI Edinburgh linen. The border has had a few threads drawn, and then hem stitch (see page 338) was worked along the inside edge only to achieve the pattern.

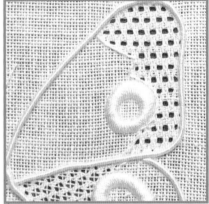

Detail of lower wing

Satin stitch is used here in two ways. The solid shape is worked with a single layer of satin stitch padding, then covered with basic satin stitch with stranded cotton. The circle is worked in turned satin stitch over varied depths of split-stitch padding, which is perfect for this sort of shape because it can be turned easily around curves.

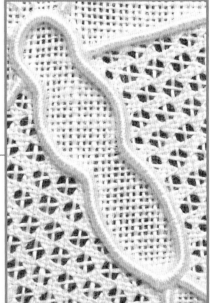

Detail of upper wing

The wings have three different pulled work patterns: diagonal drawn filling in the lower wings, wave stitch and honeycomb darning in the upper wings. The patterns were chosen to suit the shapes and to give a contrast. A fine lace thread was used so that it would almost disappear, emphasising the patterns.

Detail of body

The body and wing outlines are worked in trailing. For the body, the two ends of trailing are neatly joined. The trailing is worked, leaving both ends of the core thread free until there is only a small gap left. Then the core threads are divided and taken through to the back slightly overlapped. The gap is then carefully stitched over so that no join can be seen.

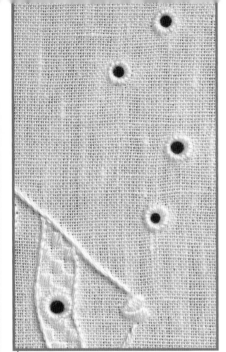

Detail of bubbles

The bubbles and the fish's eye are all created with round eyelets, using a stiletto (see page 335). The lips are two tiny shapes in satin stitch.

Angelfish

This contemporary design focuses on the use of simple methods to achieve results. Three main techniques are supplemented with outline stitches. The Angelfish is stitched on 55TPI Kingston linen.

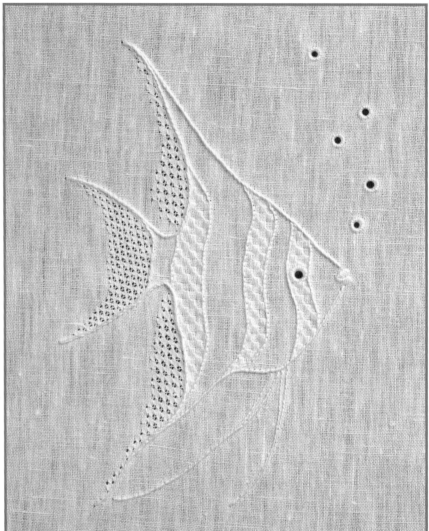

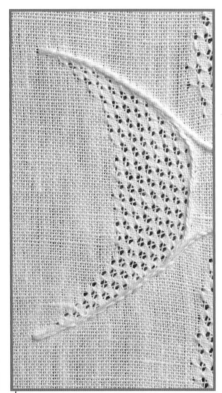

Detail of tail

The tail and fins are stitched with diagonal drawn filling in two different sizes to give a little variation. They are partly outlined with stem stitch so that they blend into the body of the fish. Where the stitches fade out into the background, they are not outlined with double running stitch – great care was taken to ensure the tension around these areas remained even.

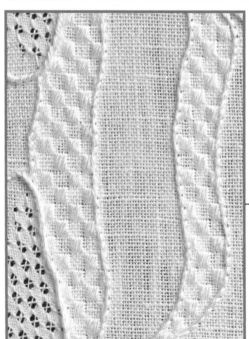

Detail of body

The stripes on the body are stitched with a counted satin stitch pattern, and further emphasised by outlines of double running stitch.

Japanese Garden

This design includes all the types of technique shown in this chapter.

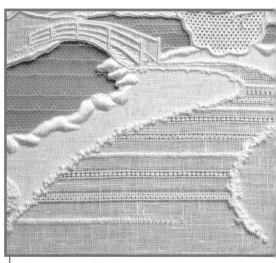

Detail 2

The pathway has been outlined with clustered French knots to represent pebbles, sealing the ends of the delicate drawn thread patterns. The boulders along the river's edge are individually worked in satin stitch at different angles to reflect the light. A very fine lace thread picks out movement in the river with a pattern of small circles.

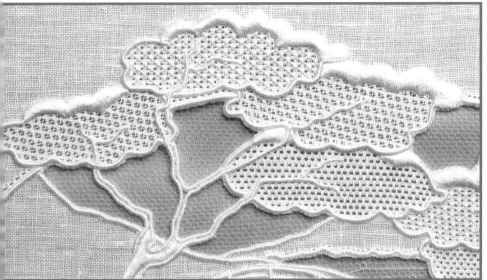

Detail 1

The treetops are worked in various pulled thread patterns, using different gauges of lace thread to give contrast. The shapes are then outlined with trailing, flowing into turned satin stitch. Trailing has also been carefully worked over the net areas to create the branches.

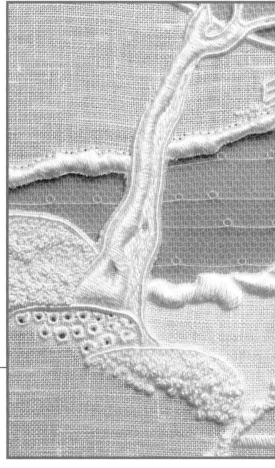

Detail 3

A combination of long-and-short stitch, satin stitch and trailing make up the tree trunk, giving a three-dimensional look. The shrubs are outlined with trailing and filled with French knots and random pulled thread eyelets.

MOVING ON

Reworking a traditional design

I love approaching a project from a historical perspective, and there is so much antique whitework to be seen that the only hard part is which one to choose. By reworking a traditional design, I don't necessarily mean copying it stitch for stitch, although that can be an enjoyable process. In the following pages you will see how I have looked at an antique textile from the RSN Collection and taken inspiration from it to design my own embroidery.

This historical whitework, RSN Collection 27, is a length of fine cotton lawn embroidered with a repeated pattern of floral sprays and a geometric border. Though we have no record of what this piece was used for, it seems likely that it was intended to be a skirt panel or similar. It may date from the early 19th century.

I focused on this large flower as the starting point of my design. The outer petals are worked with a combination of pulled thread techniques, with dense stitching in fine coton à broder for the outlines.

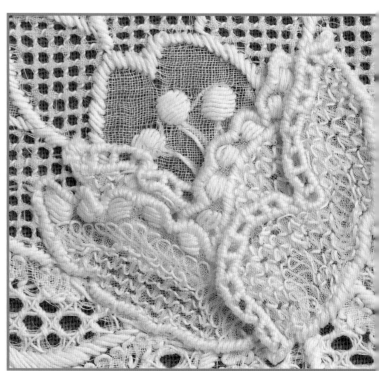

The central petals are worked on an even finer fabric, with each petal being stitched separately and then cut out and applied to give a three-dimensional effect.

352

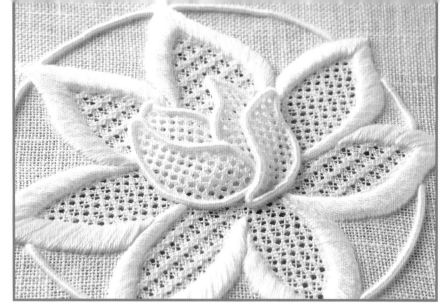

For this reworking I wanted to create a cleaner, modern and even more three-dimensional look while keeping the overall feel of the flower, so I decreased the number of petals and outlined each petal with turned, padded satin stitch using coton à broder. I added the circle border with trailing to ground the design.

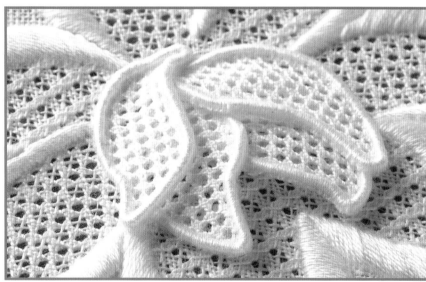

I used two different combinations of pulled thread patterns to get variation through the flower. The first is diagonal drawn filling with diagonal cross filling (left); the second is single faggot stitch with diagonal drawn filling (right).

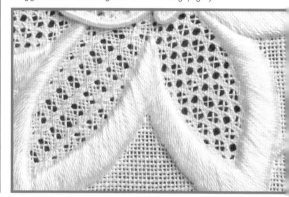

To create the central petals, I first drew each shape separately on a new piece of linen, and then filled each with single faggot stitch. I outlined them all with trailing, leaving the core threads trailing from the base of the petal. I then cut them out of the fabric, in the same way that you would for cutwork, and placed them on the design. I used the core threads to anchor the petals while stitching them in place, and then trimmed the excess away on the back.

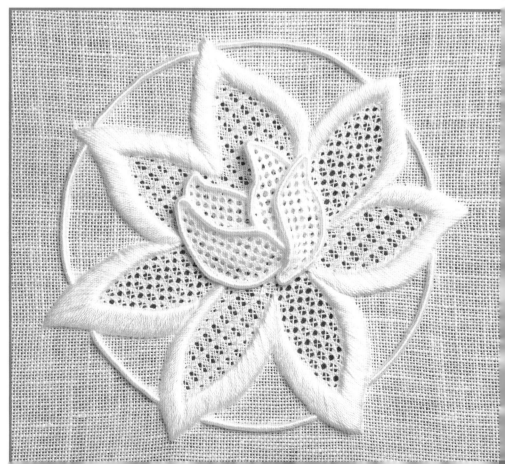

The complete embroidery.

BEAD EMBROIDERY

Snowflakes
21st century. (Shelley Cox's personal collection)

See also page 369.

Floral Romance
Part of an embroidered heart with a Victorian patchwork base featuring a variety of seed beads, sequins and buttons. 21st century. (Shelley Cox's personal collection)

Paisley Fantasy
A stunning combination of goldwork and bead embroidery. 21st century. (Shelley Cox's personal collection)

FROM THE AUTHOR

When I was three years old, a young cousin, cleaning out her bedroom, gave me a matchbox full of glass beads in various colours and sizes. They glowed and sparkled, and I was fascinated. So began my lifelong love affair with beads. To this day I still love to look at them, and run my fingers through and over them. They are amazingly diverse in material, colour, finish, size and texture, and there are so many ways in which you can use and enjoy them. I will share with you some of these ways and, in so doing, hope to inspire you to start your own love affair with beads, sequins, charms, shells and buttons.

Beadwork is such a large subject and I am, both at heart and by training, an embroiderer. As such, this section will cover embroidery with beads, that is, sewing beads to fabric with a needle and thread. This is still a broad subject! After a section on how to get started, including information about materials and which beads work well together and why, there is a stitch section that explains how beads can be attached to fabric in various ways and how they can be used to enhance counted thread and surface embroidery stitches, as well as fringing techniques.

Often the most difficult aspect of any piece of embroidery is the design phase. I find this is my own *bête noir*, but hope that the ideas in this chapter will help to make this process both exciting and less daunting for you.

One of the best things about bead embroidery and embellishment is that everyone, whatever their stitching ability, can enjoy it and create truly beautiful effects – the beads themselves ensure this. I have used commercially available beads and sequins in the samples as far as possible and stated when they cannot be substituted for alternative sizes. Otherwise, everything illustrated is interchangeable – sometimes this can create unusual and stunning results!

Whether you wish to embellish a collar, hide an adjusted seam on a cuff, add a fringe to a scarf, decorate a plain box lid or create a panel for a bag, cushion or quilt, you are limited only by your imagination and the beads at your disposal. I hope this acts as a starting point for you. Experiment, and indulge yourself in the colours and textures of these small pieces of glass, stone or plastic to create something amazing. Above all, have fun with it – beads are an embroiderer's way of laughing!

Shelley Cox

THE HISTORY OF BEAD EMBROIDERY

Beads, in one form or another, have been around since the time of Neanderthal man. Over the centuries they have been used as a form of currency; evidence of wealth and culture; and – in the act of embroidery – a means of education, relaxation and pleasure.

The earliest known beads, dating to 38,000BC, were discovered at La Quina in France. They were made from animal teeth and bones and worn as pendants. In fact, the archaeological evidence from the next 15–20,000 years tells us that all early beads were made from animal bones, shells, seeds and stone, and we can assume that they were used for both jewellery and clothing ornamentation. In 1964, a dig near Sungir, Russia, revealed the remains of a Cro-Magnon hunter, dating from 30,000BC. His clothing, boots and hat were decorated with horizontal rows of ivory beads.

Amber beads were produced in France and Spain from around 15,000BC, while beads made of precious metals, turquoise, lapis lazuli and other gems first appeared in Europe, Western Asia, India and Egypt from 10,000BC onwards. By 6,000BC a network of trade routes had been developed between Europe and Western Asia where beads and bead materials – being easily portable – became a major commodity for traders. In this way beads, patterns and techniques began to spread through the known world.

Glass beads were not produced until approximately 2,400BC in the Caucasus region and in 2,300BC in Korea and Japan. They were highly prized and frequently combined with beads of jade and other precious stones. China was also the source of silk, and many examples of thread embroidery incorporating beads have been discovered over the years. Over the centuries beads, along with fabrics and thread, patterns and techniques, gradually filtered around the world. Most indigenous peoples have their own form of native dress and often this incorporates some form of beadwork or bead embroidery. With the passage of time, people's increasing prosperity, and their increasing availability, beads of glass came to replace those of shell, seeds and bone.

By the Middle Ages, embroidery had become a status symbol in Europe; a privilege of the wealthy nobility and, in particular, the Church. Professional embroiderers worked with pearls and beads of semi-precious stones along with silk, gold and silver threads. Books, vestments and church furnishings were often decorated with pearls and beads. The development of steel needles in the 1500s, which replaced earlier clumsy iron needles, helped to encourage the fashion of clothing adornment.

From 1550 to 1700, expanding trade routes and new colonies resulted in large quantities of precious stones and pearls arriving in Europe from the Americas and the East. Portraits from this time illustrate elaborate court dresses, hats and headdresses, gloves, shoes and aprons. Also popular in England at this time were two other forms of embroidery – stumpwork and crewelwork. In stumpwork, pearls, beads and precious stones were often incorporated into embroideries for caskets and mirrors. In crewelwork, wool embroidery was worked on linen twill and made into hangings and furnishings. These occasionally incorporated beads, emphasising certain design features. The designs for these embroideries were created by professional embroiderers and sold as kits. These were worked by the lady of the house and young girls perfecting their stitching. Embroidery had largely become a domestic occupation.

Pouch

A buckskin pouch decorated with embroidered beads, from North America. 19th century. (Shelley Cox's personal collection)

During the 1700s, fashions became simpler and bead embroidery was largely limited to accessories, particularly beaded bags and purses. These were created both by embroidering beads on to fabric and also by stitching rows of beads on to fine canvas in various patterns and pictorial designs, often decorated with fringes and tassels.

By this point bead embroidery had become a suitable pastime for ladies. Beads were now being manufactured in England and not just being imported from Europe. Improved techniques in beadmaking after 1750 meant the production of much smaller beads as well as a bigger selection of colours being available. Some of the most delicate and beautiful bead embroidery belongs to this period. The beads were so fine that a needle could not be used. Instead, a fine silk thread was stiffened with shellac and the beads threaded on to it.

By 1830, many domestic items were being decorated with beads, including bell pulls, workboxes, wall tidies, spectacle cases and slippers. At this time a new craze swept Europe and America: Berlin woolwork. Developments in chemical dying meant a wide range of vibrant wools were now available for canvas embroidery, and charts were produced for the general populace in vast numbers. The designs were mostly floral, but geometric patterns, wildlife and pictorial charts were also available. The designs were worked in a mixture of either cross stitch or tent stitch, with beads picking out some elements, and sometimes plushwork as well. Many examples of this form of embroidery are still around today, although the colours of the wool have often faded.

The winning design from Suzy Amis Cameron's Eco-Fashion Campaign, Red Carpet Green Dress, unveiled on the Oscar Red Carpet on 24th February 2013 and worn by Naomie Harris (Miss Moneypenny in Skyfall). The dress was designed by Ghanaian fashion student Michael Badger, mentored by Dame Vivienne Westwood. The goldwork and bead embroidery was worked by a team of twenty-two from the Royal School of Needlework including Studio staff, tutors, volunteers, Certificate, Diploma and Degree students. The embroidery took 680 hours to work.

Face screens

Embroidered with the Prince of Wales' coat of arms, these Victorian face screens are worked in wool and embellished with metal and glass beads. 19th century. (Shelley Cox's personal collection)

Berlin woolwork was used for everything from stool and chair covers to pictures, face screens, banners and tea-cosies. It generated a great demand for beads of a consistent size and shape and the finest quality beads at that time were being imported from France. They were bought by weight, hence the term 'pound beads'.

The Industrial Revolution bought great changes to beadwork and embroidery generally. Machines were invented that could both embroider fabrics and add beads and sequins quickly and cheaply. Despite the efforts of designers such as William Morris and his compatriots in the Arts and Crafts Movement, all forms of hand embroidery declined.

Bead embroidery had a revival during the 1920s. The flirty flapper dresses and beaded bags then popular were often heavily embroidered with beads and bugles. Dress fabrics were usually lightweight silks, crepes or georgettes and have struggled to survive intact with the weight of beads attached. Since the 1920s, ornate handstitched beadwork on clothing has been largely restricted to high-end fashion and special occasion garments, although simple patterns of beads and sequins applied by machine are common.

Embroidering with beads for pleasure has had a resurgence in recent years. The availability of reasonably priced high-quality beads in a variety of consistent sizes and colours, as well as an increasing interest in crafts generally, has seen beads added to all sorts of embroidered items. There is a small cushion in the Victoria and Albert Museum in London, dated 1657, that reads: *'Natvrs Flowers Soon Doe Fade Ful Long We Last Cavse Art Vs Made'* – 'Nature's flowers soon do fade, full long we last 'cause art us made'.

Watch pocket

Hung from a bedpost, a watch pocket allowed the owner to keep his timepiece close by through the night. This Victorian example is made from velvet embroidered with pearls and beads. 19th century. (Shelley Cox's personal collection)

TOOLS AND MATERIALS

Fabric

The variety of fabrics available nowadays is as exciting and diverse as the threads and beads you can use to embellish it. I prefer to use natural fabrics such as silk, cotton, linen and wool rather than manmade fibres, but the decision of which fabric to use for your bead embroidery should be a personal choice. The selection of a fabric will largely depend on the look and purpose of the finished embroidery.

SURFACE STITCH FABRICS

Bead embroidery and embellishment can be done on almost any type of fabric, from lightweight sheers and silks to heavy velvets, upholstery fabrics and even clothing such as knitted sweaters. There are three things to consider when choosing your fabric:

- Is the fabric strong enough to support the weight of beads you intend to apply?
- Is the weave of the fabric close enough that the thread is secure and the beads sit comfortably on its surface without wobbling about or sliding through?
- What is the purpose of the finished embroidery?

You should also remember that the beadwork is the focus. Be careful if you choose a printed, patterned, textured or vividly coloured fabric that it does not overpower your embroidery. The embroidery samples in this book have all been worked on medium-weight natural fabrics – cotton, duchess satin, silk dupion and linen. If you wish to use a lightweight fabric, try ironing interfacing to the reverse or backing it with calico or cotton to give it more body and a firmer surface on which to work.

COUNTED-THREAD FABRICS

Counted-thread beadwork can be done on canvas, Aida and evenweave linens. All are suitable in general but you will need to match the gauge of fabric to the size of bead you wish to use or vice versa.

Heavy beading, such as Victorian canvas beadwork or a cross-stitch design worked largely in beads will require very careful matching. It is sensible to work a small sample, perhaps 2.5cm (1in) square, to check the sizes are compatible before you begin.

All of the samples below are worked in size 11 seed beads, to demonstrate how the fabric gauge can alter the design.

From left to right: two examples of Aida, two examples of evenweave, and three examples of canvas.

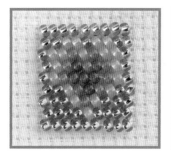

This design is worked on 14 count Aida.

This design is worked on 28 count evenweave.

This design is worked on 14 count double canvas.

Note

The Victorian canvas samples in this section have been worked on 18TPI (threads per inch) single canvas with size 15 seed beads and 14TPI Aida with size 11 seed beads. The canvas combination stitch samples have been worked on 18TPI interlock canvas with a mixture of bead sizes.

358

BEADS

Beads come in a vast variety of materials, shapes, sizes and finishes. Of all the many and varied beading techniques, stitching on to fabrics allows you to use the widest variety of beads and also to include other items such as sequins, buttons and stones. For me, this is one of its greatest attractions. If it looks good, and it fits, use it! The following are the types of beads and other items I find most useful.

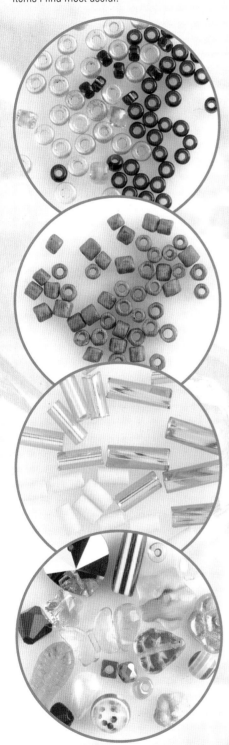

SEED BEADS

Seed beads are so-called because they look like seeds. They are also sometimes called rocailles. These small glass beads are the workhorses of the beading world. Reheated to round off their edges, they are shaped a little like a doughnut. The quality and consistency of size varies with the country of production, and it is generally accepted that the Japanese-produced beads are the best.

They come in sizes 6–16 (although antique beads are often as small as 24), with lower numbers indicating larger beads. Size 11 is the most commonly used size, and this size is what is generally meant by the term seed beads. Sizes 14 and 15 are known as petite seed beads. Sizes 5, 6 and 8 are commonly referred to as pony beads because they are similar in size and shape to beads traditionally used to decorate the manes and tails of horse. Seed beads may also be triangular, square or faceted.

DELICAS

These are small tubular beads similar in size to seed beads. They are as long as they are round, with a larger and more consistently shaped hole than seed beads. This makes them particularly good for weaving and embroidering with different weights of thread. They tend to be more expensive than regular seed beads.

BUGLE BEADS

These are tubular beads, made in the same way as seed beads, but have not had their ends rounded off, so you need to be wary of sharp edges when using them. Bugle beads come in lengths from 2–40mm ($^1/_{16}$–$1^1/_2$in). The most readily available sizes are:

- 3mm ($^1/_8$in), referred to as short.
- 6mm ($^1/_4$in), referred to as regular.
- 9mm ($^3/_8$in), referred to as long.
- 12mm ($^1/_2$in), referred to as extra long.

Bugles can be smoothly cylindrical or twisted. They are very useful for fringing, as one bugle bead can take the place of several seed beads.

FEATURE AND DROP BEADS

A single exotic bead or novelty shape can often be a focal point within a design, adding interest and humour.

Drop bead is a collective term for oval, teardrop or dagger shapes with a sideways hole at the top so they dangle, or for large circular, petal, leaf or novelty shapes with central holes that can be used as a weight at the bottom of fringes and edgings.

BEAD FINISHES

Glass beads are described in different finishes:

Opaque Solid colours, often used for ethnic-style embroidery.
Transparent Made of clear or coloured glass, which allows light through.
Lustre Beads with a transparent coating which gives them a sheen.
Frosted Transparent beads that have been tumbled in acid.
Matte These are beads with a dull finish.
Metallic or **galvanised** These are beads coated in metallic particles for a metal finish.
Colourlined Either clear or coloured beads, with the hole lined in another colour.
Silverlined Similar to colourlined beads, with the hole lined in silver.
AB (Aurora Borealis), **iris** or **rainbow** These have a coating of metal salts which give the beads a rainbow appearance.

Embellishments

SEQUINS

These are discs with central holes made from metal or plastic. They can be flat or cupped and come in a variety of shapes and sizes. Paillettes are similar to sequins but the securing holes are punched on the edges.

Sequins come in a variety of finishes, including bright and shiny, matte, pearlised or holographic. They are a natural complement to beads in your embroidery.

IMITATION GEMSTONES

The use of diamantes, rhinestones and similar sparkly items gives a wonderful sense of luxury and light to a design.

These can be flat backed with holes on the edges or attached with a claw setting. They are available in various shapes and sizes and are often used as a focal point in a design.

OTHER EMBELLISHMENTS

Silver and gold charms, semi-precious stone chips and shells that have been drilled with a hole, as well as jewellery findings such as filigree and bell caps which have been flattened, are just some of the items that can be added to an embroidery for special effects and added texture. They come in many different sizes, finishes and colours, adding interest and texture.

For embroidery, the most effective buttons are those that are flat-backed and without shanks that will cause them to move about. Buttons can be sewn down with beads to disguise the holes, be worked over and around, or simply added because they are beautiful and appropriate.

Sequins can be bought separately or on strings.

Like beads, buttons and imitation gemstones are available in a huge array of types, colours and styles.

Threads

Your choice of thread, like your choice of fabric, is personal. You may like to try several different sorts before deciding on what suits you. The thread you choose needs to be fine enough to travel through the bead at least twice. It should also be strong enough to hold the beads in place according to the purpose of the embroidery. For example, thread for beading on to a wearable or washable garment would need to be significantly more robust than that used for a small motif or panel destined to be framed. Here are some of the choices available to you.

SYNTHETIC BEADING THREADS

Specialist threads such as Nymo and C-Lon are made of nylon and preconditioned with wax. They are strong, fine, available in various thicknesses and colours and will not rot away.

Nymo is probably the most readily available and comes in sizes 00, 0, A, B, D, F (smallest to largest). I find size D is generally a good choice for most work and will fit into a size 12 embroidery or larger beading needle. Nymo needs to be gently stretched prior to use to straighten it and to remove any give that can make the stitch tension loosen over time.

Do not moisten the end of any preconditioned thread, as this will cause it to fray. Instead, cut the thread at an angle and moisten the eye of the needle.

EMBROIDERY THREAD

I sometimes use embroidery threads when incorporating beads into surface embroidery stitches where part of the stitch remains visible. Fine perlé thread, stranded silk and twisted cottons work well, but if the embroidery will be exposed to wear I often add an additional fine nylon thread for strength.

SYNTHETIC MACHINE THREADS

These are also useful for beading, being both fine and strong. They are readily available in many colours.

SILK, POLYCOTTON AND LINEN THREADS

These can also be used to sew beads down. Silk and polycotton are both strong and very pliable. Linen, if you can find one fine enough, is also a viable thread.

Thread conditioning

All threads (except embroidery threads) not already treated should be run through a thread conditioner or good-quality beeswax prior to use. This prevents any sharp bead edges from fraying the thread. Keep the lengths of the thread shorter when working on fabrics that have been backed with fusible interfacing or a second support fabric, as they will wear more quickly.

Thread colour

When choosing the colour of your thread it is most common to match the thread to the fabric. However, when working with one colour of bead only I generally match the thread to the bead. Mostly I work with whichever colour seems to be the least obvious, especially when working on a multicoloured surface with different coloured beads. Using transparent beads and a contrasting coloured thread can achieve some wonderful effects, so do not be afraid to experiment!

Needles

There is a variety of needles available to use. The choice you make will largely depend on three things: the size of the beads, the thickness of the thread and the type of bead embroidery you will be stitching.

Needles are available in different types – which indicate the shape and length of their eye and point – and different sizes, with higher numbers indicating finer needles. Not all needles are suitable for beading, so here are the types that I recommend, having found them more useful.

EMBROIDERY NEEDLES

Also known as crewel needles, embroidery needles have a long eye designed specifically for embroidery threads. They are available in sizes running from 3–12. I use these needles for surface embroidery stitches and work mostly with sizes 10 and 12 when adding beads. Size 11 needles are also useful but not as readily available as 10 and 12.

Sharps These needles use the same size system as the crewel needles, but they are designed with small round eyes for general sewing. They are meant for a single sewing thread. I occasionally use a size 12 sharps when I want a needle with less flexibility but more strength than a short beading needle.

TAPESTRY NEEDLES

Tapestry needles range in size from 18–28. They have a blunt point enabling them to slide through canvas and evenweave fabrics without splitting the threads. I use sizes 22 and 24 for working counted embroidery stitches and sizes 26 and 28 for adding beads. The smaller sizes are often difficult to find, so small sharps or beading needles are often a good substitute. Work with the smallest needle you can manage that will do the job. When choosing a needle, remember to try it in your beads with your chosen thread before anchoring it to your work!

BEADING NEEDLES

These very flexible needles have long, thin eyes and are available in sizes 10–13. They fall into two types: long and short. Long beading needles are most often used for loom work, but I have found them useful for long fringes.

Short beading needles are more suited to embroidery. I use sizes 10 and 11 needles for size 11 seed beads and bugle beads and finer sizes 12 and 13 needles for size 15 petite seed beads.

Embroidery needles from top to bottom: size 10 crewel, size 10 sharps, size 12 crewel, size 12 sharps.

Tapestry needles from top to bottom: size 20, size 28.

Beading needles from top to bottom: short size 11, long size 11, extra long size 12.

Other materials

In addition to your fabric, frame, needles and thread, some other items you will find useful in your sewing kit for bead embroidery are the following:

Beading mat A beading mat will let you lay out your bead selection and compose combinations easily without them rolling away. You can also use a piece of suede or velvet; or glue suede or velvet into a tray, which will give the mat stability and save you losing any beads if it is bumped.

Wax or **thread conditioner** Keeping your thread in good condition and preventing it from fraying and knotting is essential. Beeswax is both excellent and traditional, but nowadays it is also possible to get commercially made thread conditioners and paraffin-based wax that will also do the job.

Bead scoop These are really useful when moving your beads from container to the work surface and back again.

Bead reamer This is a small tool, with a tapering cylindrical file surface, used to smooth rough or irregular bead holes or to enlarge the holes when necessary.

Pliers or **crimpers** A pair of needle-nosed pliers are useful for carefully crushing beads that have become stuck or are incorrectly positioned. However, as beads are usually made of glass, this can cut through the thread. Crimpers are a jewellery maker's tool that will crush the bead like pliers but not so strongly, which means the thread will likely be left intact.

Thread-laying tool If you intend to combine your beading with counted thread and surface stitches it is useful to have a small tool called a mellor, or laying tool, to help your threads lie smoothly.

Glass-headed pins These are useful for holding beads and sequins in place while stitching and also for measuring spaces.

Pincushion Beading needles are very fine and easily lost. Always have a pincushion or needlecase to keep them in between uses. A pincushion is also useful for holding pins, of course.

BEAD EMBROIDERY STITCH FINDER

This chapter contains instructions for four different types of surface stitching that incorporate beads. Each section starts with a design and information page relevant to that technique then the stitches follow in alphabetical order.

Counted-thread beadwork stitches These are essentially canvas stitches, which may be worked on any counted-thread fabric. Parts of the stitch patterns are removed and substituted for beads or the beads are stitched on top of the patterns to embellish them.

Bead embroidery stitches These are the standard stitch techniques for applying beads to fabric. You should not see the threads at all, as the beads are the focal point.

Surface embroidery stitches These are traditional embroidery stitches adapted to incorporate beads. The threads are an integral part of these stitches and the beads complement them.

Edging and fringing stitches No beaded article is entirely finished without some sort of edging or fringing! The stitches cover simple picots to more complicated loops and netted fringes, which will enable you to create those edgings.

For advice on threading a needle and starting and finishing stitches on canvas, Aida, evenweave and open linens see page 365; for all other fabrics see page 39.

Stitch	Type	Page
ALTERNATING LOOPED FRINGE	EDGING AND FRINGING	SEE PAGE 396
ALTERNATING PICOT EDGE	EDGING AND FRINGING	SEE PAGE 393
ALTERNATING STRAIGHT FRINGE WITH A BACK STITCH BASE	EDGING AND FRINGING	SEE PAGE 395
BACK STITCH	BEAD EMBROIDERY	SEE PAGE 377
BACK STITCH, THREADED AND WHIPPED	SURFACE EMBROIDERY	SEE PAGE 386
BUTTONHOLE STITCH	SURFACE EMBROIDERY	SEE PAGE 386
BYZANTINE STITCH	COUNTED THREAD	SEE PAGE 366
CHAIN STITCH	SURFACE EMBROIDERY	SEE PAGE 387
CHEVRON STITCH	SURFACE EMBROIDERY	SEE PAGE 387
CIRCLETS	BEAD EMBROIDERY	SEE PAGE 378
CORAL STITCH	SURFACE EMBROIDERY	SEE PAGE 388
COUCHING WITH A SINGLE NEEDLE	BEAD EMBROIDERY	SEE PAGE 378
COUCHING WITH TWO THREADS	BEAD EMBROIDERY	SEE PAGE 379
CRETAN STITCH	SURFACE EMBROIDERY	SEE PAGE 388
CUSHION STITCH	COUNTED THREAD	SEE PAGE 366
DIAGONAL STITCH	COUNTED THREAD	SEE PAGE 367
FEATHER STITCH	SURFACE EMBROIDERY	SEE PAGE 389
FLY STITCH	SURFACE EMBROIDERY	SEE PAGE 389

HERRINGBONE STITCH	SURFACE EMBROIDERY	SEE PAGE 390	SIMPLE PICOT EDGE	EDGING AND FRINGING	SEE PAGE 393
HORIZONTAL NETTED FRINGE	EDGING AND FRINGING	SEE PAGE 397	SMYRNA STITCH	COUNTED THREAD	SEE PAGE 373
HUNGARIAN STITCH	COUNTED THREAD	SEE PAGE 367	SPACED PICOT EDGE	EDGING AND FRINGING	SEE PAGE 393
HUNGARIAN GROUND STITCH VARIATION	COUNTED THREAD	SEE PAGE 368	SPACED PICOT EDGE WITH DROPS	EDGING AND FRINGING	SEE PAGE 394
JACQUARD STITCH	COUNTED THREAD	SEE PAGE 368	STAB STITCH	BEAD EMBROIDERY	SEE PAGE 385
LINKS AND CROSSES	BEAD EMBROIDERY	SEE PAGE 380	STAGGERED FRINGE WITH A BACK STITCH BASE	EDGING AND FRINGING	SEE PAGE 395
LOOPS	BEAD EMBROIDERY	SEE PAGE 381	STAIRCASE STITCH VARIATION	COUNTED THREAD	SEE PAGE 373
MOORISH STITCH	COUNTED THREAD	SEE PAGE 369	STEM STITCH	SURFACE EMBROIDERY	SEE PAGE 391
MOSAIC STITCH	COUNTED THREAD	SEE PAGE 370	STRAIGHT FRINGE	EDGING AND FRINGING	SEE PAGE 394
NORWICH STITCH	COUNTED THREAD	SEE PAGE 370	TENT STITCH	COUNTED THREAD	SEE PAGE 365
OVERLAPPING LOOPED FRINGE	EDGING AND FRINGING	SEE PAGE 396	TWILL STITCH	COUNTED THREAD	SEE PAGE 374
PARISIAN STITCH	COUNTED THREAD	SEE PAGE 371	TWISTED LOOPED FRINGE	EDGING AND FRINGING	SEE PAGE 396
RHODES STITCH	COUNTED THREAD	SEE PAGE 371	VERTICAL MILANESE STITCH	COUNTED THREAD	SEE PAGE 374
RICE STITCH	COUNTED THREAD	SEE PAGE 372	VERTICAL NETTED FRINGE	EDGING AND FRINGING	SEE PAGE 397
RUNNING STITCH	BEAD EMBROIDERY	SEE PAGE 381	VICTORIAN STEP STITCH	COUNTED THREAD	SEE PAGE 375
SATIN STITCH	BEAD EMBROIDERY	SEE PAGE 382	WHIP STITCH	SURFACE EMBROIDERY	SEE PAGE 391
SEEDING STITCH	SURFACE EMBROIDERY	SEE PAGE 390	WILD GOOSE CHASE STITCH	COUNTED THREAD	SEE PAGE 375
SEQUIN LINES	BEAD EMBROIDERY	SEE PAGE 382			
SEQUIN ROSETTES	BEAD EMBROIDERY	SEE PAGE 384			
SHAPED FRINGE	EDGING AND FRINGING	SEE PAGE 394			
SIMPLE LOOPED FRINGE	EDGING AND FRINGING	SEE PAGE 395			

COUNTED-THREAD BEADWORK

Counted-thread beadwork is practical, decorative and can be very hardy. Canvas stitches can be adapted to incorporate beads and these patterns can be combined with Victorian beadwork (see below) on any counted thread fabric to create panels or pictures.

Your choice of fabric will be related to the purpose of the finished product and how pliable it needs to be. Canvas is more hardwearing than an evenweave or Aida, but it is also stiffer and less flexible. Using evenweave or Aida means that not all the fabric needs to be covered, which gives more freedom for stitching. Canvas can be left uncovered, but is not as appealing. Many people prefer to cover it completely or to paint, dye or appliqué the exposed areas if working a creative design.

Designing counted-thread beadwork

VICTORIAN BEADWORK

Victorian beadwork is the easiest form of bead embroidery with which to start out, as it is based on a chart similar to those used for needlepoint and cross stitch. It is very important with this technique that all the beads are the same shape and size and the correct size for the count of the fabric or they will not sit neatly.

Try substituting some or all of the stitches in your tapestry pattern or cross-stitch design by matching the colours to beads and following the trammed tent stitch instructions opposite to attach them. If working the whole design in beads you will not be able to use a design that includes quarter stitches, half stitches or back stitches.

CANVAS STITCHES

This technique lends itself wonderfully to geometric designs, both symmetrical and non-symmetrical. Draw the outline of the finished panel on to canvas using a waterproof pen or HB pencil, then divide it up as you wish and work a different stitch pattern in each area. You can also incorporate an area of Victorian beadwork into the panel.

If you do not want a geometric design, you could try looking through design books or colouring books for bold outline drawings. A flower design with enough space in each petal or leaf for a repeat pattern will be very effective, for example. Balance the pattern sizes and bead density on each petal so they look even.

If working on canvas, complete the background with a simple cross or tent stitch for contrast. If working on evenweave fabric or Aida you may choose to leave the background unstitched.

An antique Berlin woolwork pattern, suitable for use in needlepoint, cross stitch and Victorian beadwork.

Tip
If adding borders to your design, count your border stitch out first, making sure you have the correct number of threads so the repeats fit, then divide the resulting interior space.

Butterfly

This example of Victorian-style beadwork is worked in trammed tent stitch on 18-count single canvas (see opposite). 21st century. (Shelley Cox's personal collection)

PICKING UP A BEAD

1 Carefully pour your beads out on to a beading mat or other suitable surface.

2 With your threaded needle, tap the inside of a bead.

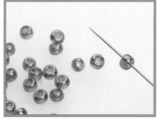

3 Lift the needle and let the bead slide down it.

You can pick up a sequin from a beading mat in much the same way. Note that many sequins are shaped. Depending on your design, you may need to pick them up from a specific side.

Starting your thread

One of the most important things in beadwork is starting, or anchoring, your thread correctly and securely. There is nothing more soul destroying than having beads work their way free after so many hours of careful stitching! The following techniques should be followed for all embroidery on the following fabrics: canvas, Aida, evenweave and open linens. For other fabrics, see page 39.

1 Thread your needle and tie a large knot in the end. Take the needle down a dozen or so holes away from your intended starting point (as shown in this example).

2 Bring your needle up approximately three holes to the left of your knot and draw the thread through.

3 Take the needle back down one hole to the right.

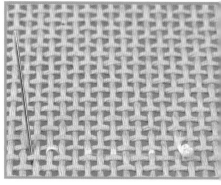

4 Repeat three or four times every two to three holes, aiming to split your working thread underneath to prevent the thread running free if pulled, until you reach your starting point.

Finishing your thread

While working, finish your old thread by bringing it back to the surface where you will place your knot for your new thread (as above).

To secure your thread once you have finished working, turn the work over and slide the needle underneath the stitches on the reverse (see right) then pull it through. Trim away any excess using sharp embroidery scissors.

Counted-thread beadwork techniques

TENT STITCH – TRAMMED

Victorian beadwork commonly involved attaching beads with a tent stitch in pictorial designs, and this stitch is a fundamental part of adding beadwork to counted-thread fabrics.

When working this stitch it is important to note that the rows are always worked from left to right and usually from top to bottom, as you would read a book.

> ### Note
> The pictures show the stitch worked on single canvas, over one thread. If working on evenweave or linen fabric, work over two threads, as you would in cross stitch.
>
> When tramming Aida, evenweave, linen or a double canvas (known sometimes as Penelope), bring the needle up through the fabric between the threads at the end of the row and go back down between the threads at the beginning of the row.

1 Start your thread with an anchoring knot at one end of your design line. Work at least three securing stitches along the line back to the beginning before bringing your needle up and threading your first bead. Take the needle down one hole diagonally left and below.

2 Draw the thread through and bring it up one hole to the right of the starting point. Pick up another bead and take the needle down one hole diagonally left and below.

3 Repeat the sequence to the end of the line, then trim away your anchoring knot with embroidery scissors.

4 Bring your needle back up through the top right hole that is holding your final bead.

5 Take the needle straight through the holes in all of the beads (see inset), draw it through, then take the thread down through the lower left hole that is holding the first bead.

6 Repeat the process for any further rows. To finish your thread, turn over and darn through the stitches on the reverse, knotting at least three times as for surface stitching (see above).

Counted-thread stitches

Byzantine stitch

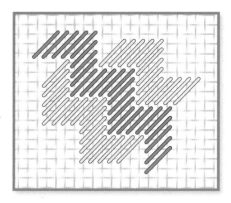

This is a diagonal, stepped stitch worked over three by three threads in groups of five stitches. The fifth horizontal stitch becomes the first vertical stitch of the next group, then the fifth vertical becomes the first horizontal of the next group and so on.

Each band of the pattern is worked in turn, usually from top to bottom, and the diagonal lines can go from top right to bottom left (as shown) or the opposite way if desired.

You can vary both the length of the stitch and the number within each group to create different effects or accommodate the beads you wish to add to the pattern. This stitch is best worked in a multistranded thread for a smooth satin appearance.

Tip
For the best results, always separate the threads when using multiple strands in the needle and use a laying tool or large darning needle to ensure the strands lay flat and do not twist as you sew.

The sample shows bands of the pattern worked in thread alternating with bands in which some of the stitches have been replaced by bugles or seed beads. An area in the bottom left corner shows a band that has been worked entirely in petite seed beads.

Cushion stitch

This stitch is a satin-stitch square block over a regular number of threads; the sample consists of five stitches and is worked over three by three threads. Each stitch runs from bottom left to top right.

REVERSED CUSHION STITCH

This is the same basic stitch as regular cushion, but each alternate square is stitched in the opposite direction: from bottom right to top left. Again, both of these patterns may be worked with stitches substituted for beads – the longest stitch being substituted for a bugle bead or a mixture of seed beads, for example. Alternatively both cushion and reversed cushion can become a base for bead patterns based on links, crosses, loops and circlets (see pages 378 and pages 380–381). With a smooth finish, both cushion and reversed cushion suit a multistranded thread best.

CROSSED CUSHION STITCH

This stitch is an extension of cushion and reversed cushion. Having worked one of the former patterns, diagonally crossing stitches can be added on the top. These can be a combination of thread stitches and beads, or just beads. You can add all of the crossing stitches, or just the longest one for a variety of different effects.

If you are making some of the crossed stitches in threads, try using a perlé or other single, twisted thread for a different texture.

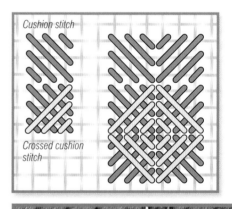

Cushion stitch

Crossed cushion stitch

Tip
Cushion and reversed cushion squares can be worked over any number of threads (e.g. seven stitches over four by four threads, or nine stitches over five by five threads). The larger the number of threads, the longer and more unwieldy the middle stitch becomes. If adding beads do not go larger than five by five threads.

The sample shows regular cushion, reversed cushion and crossed cushion in thread on the left-hand side. On the right-hand side is a variety of patterns in beads using seed beads, petite seed beads and bugle beads. The size of your beads will often dictate the scale of your initial cushion squares.

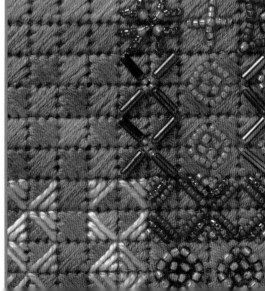

Diagonal stitch

This stitch is a diagonal pattern based on joined squares. Five stitches are worked diagonally over three by three threads, and the fifth stitch becomes the first stitch of the following square.

The pattern can be worked with the diagonal lines running top right to bottom left, as in the sample, or be reversed and run from bottom left to top right. If you wish to reverse the direction of the rows, you can turn the pattern through 90°. Stranded cottons or silks will give the smoothest finish.

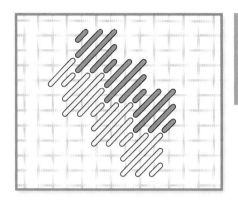

Tip
Try using different shades of plain colours for a dip-dyed effect in the thread rows. Alternatively, the use of variegated or space-dyed threads can create wonderful colour variety with very little time and effort.

The sample is worked with every alternate line of the pattern in a combination of stitch and beads, with the beads substituting for different stitches in the pattern. The bottom left corner shows the pattern entirely worked in petite seed beads.

Hungarian stitch

This stitch is composed of horizontal rows of vertical stitches that form small diamond tile shapes and are separated by two threads. The tile is formed of three vertical stitches in a pattern over two, four, two threads. In each subsequent row the long stitch slots into the gap between the previous row's tiles. As a result, the odd-numbered rows sit directly underneath one another and the even rows do likewise.

Substituting alternate rows of stitches for beads is very effective and the pattern lends itself to a variety of bead combinations, using both seed beads and bugle beads in various sizes.

For a smooth effect that completely covers the fabric, you can use a stranded cotton or silk thread.

It is important when working this pattern to use enough threads and to separate them before threading the needle, as they must spread and cover the canvas on either side of the stitch for the pattern to look really good.

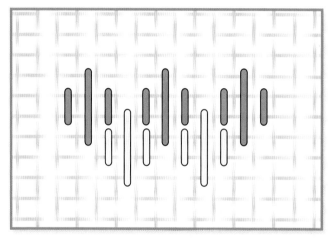

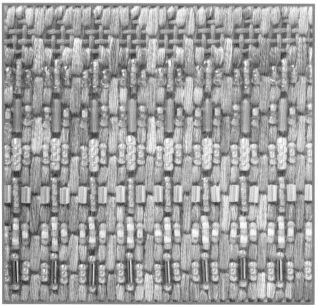

The sample shows alternating rows of the pattern in beads. Combinations of seed beads and petite seed beads, and also bugles and petite seed beads, show that many variations are possible.

Hungarian ground stitch variation

This stitch consists of two differently patterned horizontal rows made up of vertical stitches that slot together. The first row is worked in vertical stitches, each over four threads. With the first vertical stitch worked, the second stitch is started one thread higher and one along. The third stitch is likewise another thread higher and along. The fourth stitch then moves one thread back down again. The fifth stitch becomes the first stitch of the next group and the pattern continues along the row, moving up and down in a wave pattern.

The second part of the pattern is the same as a single row of Hungarian stitch (see page 367). The tiles slot into the spaces left under the second, third and fourth stitches of the repeated pattern. Work the first pattern row again around the tile pattern – it will result in a mirror image of the first line. As with Hungarian stitch, a multistranded thread works best to ensure that all of the threads are covered.

With two different patterns in this stitch there is a choice as to which line you work in beads. The sample shows the tile patterns in beads in the top half and the wave pattern in beads in the lower half.

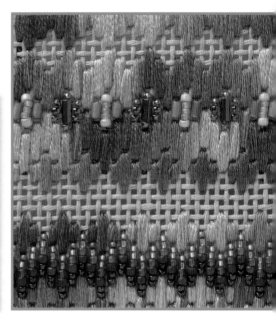

Jacquard stitch

This stitch is worked diagonally in a stepped pattern with two distinctly different alternating rows.

The first row makes a step, with each stitch worked diagonally over two by two threads. Each step is formed of six stitches that run in alternate horizontal and vertical groups. The last horizontal stitch of the initial group becomes the first vertical stitch of the next group, and the last vertical stitch becomes the first horizontal stitch of the following group.

The alternate rows are formed of tent stitches (see page 365) that follow the steps formed in the first row. This stitch can be altered by working the wide rows over a different number of threads (try three by three or four by four) and in different size steps – in groups of four, five or seven, for example. You can also work it in the opposite direction.

Try working the wide row in stranded threads and the tent stitches in a single twisted thread, perlé or similar.

With two patterns it is possible to replace either row with beads or a combination of beads and thread stitches. The sample is worked with the tent stitches replaced by beads in different combinations (top right-hand corner) and the wide rows worked in beads (bottom left-hand corner).

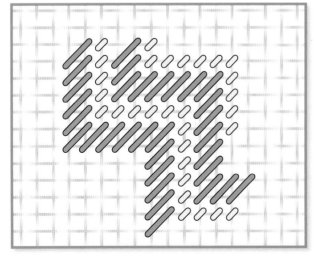

Moorish stitch

This is another combination stitch. It is a mixture of diagonal stitch (see page 367) and steps of tent stitch (see page 365).

Work a single row of diagonal stitch: linked satin squares over three by three threads, with the fifth stitch becoming the first stitch of the next satin square.

Alternating rows are made of tent stitches following the stepped pattern formed by the squares. Three stitches across and three down, the third horizontal stitch becoming the first vertical stitch and so on.

This pattern can also be worked in the opposite direction if desired, with the rows running from bottom left to top right.

Work the diagonal stitch rows in stranded thread and the tent stitches in a single twisted thread for contrast. You can also reverse this combination, but make sure the canvas is covered.

Tip
Work all the thread stitches within a pattern first before adding the beads. It is easier to see the potential overall effect and to make sure the bead shapes and colours are spread evenly across the pattern.

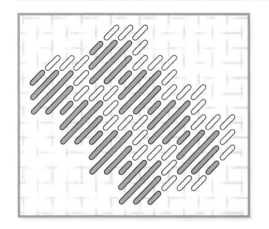

The sample shows the tent stitches replaced by beads towards the top right-hand corner. The bottom left-hand corner shows the alternate row of linked squares replaced by combinations of beads and stitches.

Box with embroidered panel

The lid of this oak box has an inset embroidered panel that incorporates beaded canvaswork stitches including Milanese, cushion, Hungarian and Norwich stitches (see pages 374, 366, 367 and 370 respectively), among others. It is worked in a mixture of perle and stranded cottons, seed beads, petite seed beads and bugles. 21st century. (Shelley Cox's personal collection)

Mosaic stitch

This two-row pattern is worked diagonally in straight rows. The first is tent stitch (see page 365) alternating with a row of diagonal stitch (see page 367) over two by two threads. The next row is made up of tent stitches that slot in between the longer stitches of the previous (diagonal stitch) row.

Continue to alternate the two rows and you will see that the longer stitches always lie diagonally underneath one another and all of the tent stitches in both rows also lie diagonally underneath one another.

For the rows in this pattern to retain their distinctive straight look it is not possible to alter the stitch length combinations. However, you can work the pattern in the opposite direction for variety.

Try the wide row in a multistranded thread so it looks smooth and the tent stitch row in a single, twisted thread for a different texture.

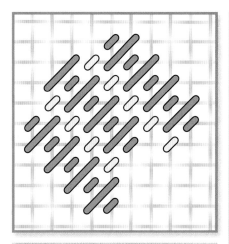

Tip
To see how to work the patterns in the opposite direction turn the stitch diagram through 90°.

This sample shows various combinations of beads replacing the stitches in the different rows.

Norwich stitch

This stitch is sometimes known as waffle stitch and is usually stitched over an odd number of threads, (the example in the diagram to the right is worked over nine by nine threads). It has a wonderful woven appearance that makes a striking feature in a design when worked on a large scale. Norwich stitch is useful for texture and as a base for beads rather than as a pattern where the beads replace stitches.

It is worked by starting in the bottom left corner at number 1, taking the needle back down at number 2 in the top right corner. Continue to follow the numbers until you reach the last stitch (35–36), then slide the needle under the stitch 29–30 before going down into the fabric to secure.

If you have an even number of threads available in your design you can still work this stitch, but the last circuit of stitches will go down into the central hole in each side and not cross at the edges (see the large Norwich stitches on the right-hand side of the sample).

This stitch looks particularly good when worked in a single twisted thread, such as a perlé thread, as it makes the pattern nice and clear.

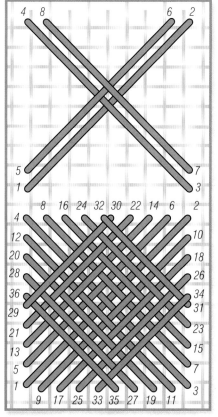

The sample shows circlets (see page 378) worked in the centre of a group of four small Norwich stitches. You can cross the corners with different bead combinations, work crosses across the centres or links into the corners of the larger patterns (see page 380 for information and instructions on working links and crosses).

Parisian stitch

This is a very simple pattern of vertical stitches worked in horizontal rows, which can nevertheless be very effective.

The first row starts with a short vertical stitch over two threads followed by a long vertical stitch over four threads that sit one thread higher and lower than the first stitch. Work these two stitches alternately across the row. The second row is exactly the same pattern but it starts with the long stitch over four threads and is followed by the short stitch.

Variations of this stitch can be tried by doubling or tripling the stitches – two short stitches side by side followed by two long stitches, for example. Try also turning the pattern on its side and working horizontal stitches in vertical rows.

The most effective thread for this pattern is a multistranded cotton or silk to give good coverage and a smooth finish.

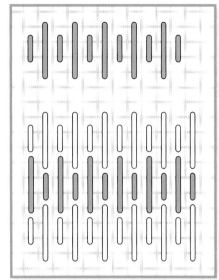

Various thread and bead combinations replace alternate rows in the pattern here.

Rhodes stitch

This is a wonderful stitch for adding texture to a design. It is also very effective as a border stitch. Rhodes stitch can be worked over any number of threads and also as a rectangle.

The diagram shows the stitch worked over six by six threads. Find the bottom-left corner and bring the needle up one thread further over on the bottom line. Take the needle down on the top line one thread in from the right-hand corner. Come up again on the bottom line one thread to the right of the first stitch and go down on the top line one thread to the left of the first stitch. Continue to work in an anticlockwise direction, fanning the stitches around the square until the last stitch is reached (bottom left-hand corner to top right-hand corner). It is important to always work this stitch in the same way so that the last stitch is always the same.

This stitch is easy to check: when you come up in a corner you must go down in the opposite corner. If you do not, double-check that you have not missed a hole or put two stitches into the same hole.

Like other crossed patterns, this stitch looks best when worked in a single twisted thread. It can be very bulky if worked in a thick thread because of the build up in the centre where the stitches cross. This also occurs on the reverse.

Tip
Draw out the square shapes on your fabric or canvas with a pencil before you begin, as it makes the Rhodes stitch pattern shape easier to see.

The sample shows Rhodes stitch worked over different numbers of threads. It is a stitch that can be decorated with beads rather than one in which stitches within the pattern are replaced by beads.

Rice stitch

This pattern is a large cross stitch, traditionally worked over any even number of threads to form a square, with the corners crossed by small diagonal stitches. The diagram shows this stitch worked over four threads. When working the cross over a large number of threads (six or eight), it is possible to work two or even three small diagonal stitches across the corners.

When beads are added instead of the small corner stitches the central cross can often be completely disguised and the stitch looks entirely different. Try some very large crosses and experiment with two or three stitches in each corner of different bead combinations.

This stitch can also be used over an uneven number of threads, but you will always end with a thread exposed in the centre of each side. Luckily, this just adds more opportunity to experiment with your beads!

This stitch will give different effects in different threads. Try using a single twisted thread for smaller crosses and a multistranded thread for larger crosses, as the coverage is better.

The sample above shows this stitch worked over both two and four threads with various bead combinations crossing the corners.

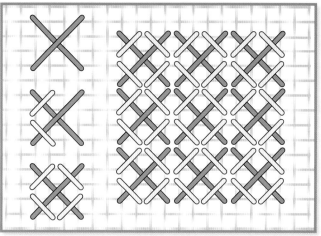

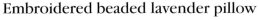

Embroidered beaded lavender pillow

The Hardanger embroidery on this lavender pillow incorporates pearl beads, variegated thread and handmade lace for a textured, contemporary look. 21st century.
(Shelley Cox's personal collection)

Autumn Glory
The beaded embroidery on this jewellery box incorporates beads and canvas stitches. 21st century.
(Shelley Cox's personal collection)

Smyrna stitch

This stitch is also known as double cross stitch. It must always be worked over an even number of threads, usually four (as in the diagram). The sample also includes a variation over two threads.

First work a diagonal cross, then work an upright cross over the top. It is not critical whether the vertical or the horizontal cross stitch is uppermost, but do be consistent with your choice as this will give your embroidery a neater look.

It is also possible to work the stitch in reverse for a different effect by working the upright cross before the diagonal cross.

Like rice stitch (see opposite), using a multistranded thread gives better coverage for this pattern when worked over four or more threads. A single twisted thread is often better for smaller patterns as the definition of the stitch will be clearer.

This stitch lends itself particularly well to beading. Try adding beads to the top stitch using the links and crosses technique on page 380. You might also stitch beads along the sides or across the corners as in rice stitch.

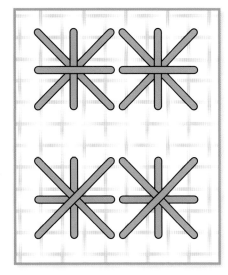

Tip
Any stitch based on a square – such as crossed cushion, Norwich, Rhodes, rice and Smyrna – can be worked as a pattern together over the same number of threads or worked freely in different sizes to create wonderful textures. They all make very effective border stitches.

The sample shows the two component cross stitches (top left), as well as various combinations of stitch and bead. The lower part shows Smyrna stitch combinations worked across only two threads.

Staircase stitch variation

This is a diagonally worked stitch similar to Moorish stitch (see page 369), except the step row is wider and the squares are smaller.

Instead of a step of three tent stitches (as in Moorish stitch), work a step of three stitches over two by two threads. Start with three horizontal stitches, then work three vertical stitches; the third horizontal stitch becoming the first vertical stitch and the third vertical stitch becoming the first horizontal stitch.

Next, below and above the steps, work the three small diagonal stitches in the following sequence: one by one thread, two by two threads, one by one thread.

Like Moorish stitch, this stitch can also be worked in the opposite direction with the rows running from the bottom left-hand side to the top right-hand side.

For a nice satin-smooth look, this stitch looks best in a multistranded thread.

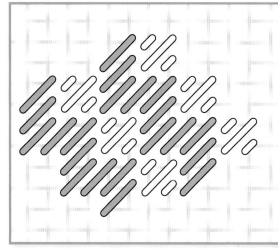

The sample shows the pattern worked with the small squares replaced with beads of various combinations or with stitches and beads.

Twill stitch

Most twill fabrics are used with the grain running from the bottom left-hand corner to the top right-hand corner, hence the direction of this pattern. Technically you could reverse the direction and work the rows running bottom right to top left but this would not, strictly speaking, be twill.

Start the pattern by making a vertical stitch over four threads. Follow this with subsequent vertical stitches all over four threads but starting a thread higher than the previous stitch each time.

Follow this row with another row worked the same way but this time over two threads. Continue to alternate the two rows. For a different look you could try working this pattern as horizontal stitches instead of vertical stitches. This stitch should be worked in a stranded cotton or silk thread for the best finish.

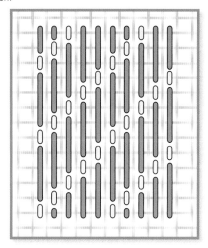

The sample shows the narrow rows replaced by beads at the top left and the wider rows being replaced by beads at the bottom right.

Vertical Milanese stitch

This two-row repeating pattern is worked in horizontal rows. The first row starts with a vertical stitch over six threads followed by another vertical stitch over four threads then another over two threads. Each stitch starts one thread lower and finishes one thread higher than the previous one. Continue repeating this sequence of three stitches across the row.

In the second row, work a vertical stitch over two threads below the four-thread stitch in the first row, followed by a vertical stitch over four threads below the two-thread stitch in the first row. Continue along the row repeating this sequence of two stitches.

For a smooth finish and good coverage of the fabric this stitch works best in a multistranded thread.

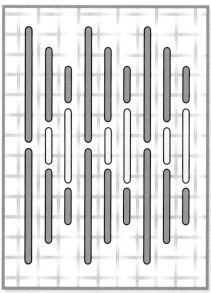

The sample shows the second row of the pattern in various bead combinations. Replacing the first row can also be very effective.

Victorian step stitch

This pattern is composed of vertical stitches worked diagonally in a series of shallow steps. Begin by working a vertical stitch over four threads. Follow this with three smaller vertical stitches, each over two threads. These begin two threads down from the top of the longer stitch and finish level with its base.

After the three small stitches, work another long vertical stitch over four threads, starting level with the three short stitches and finishing two threads below them. Follow this with another three smaller stitches.

Continue to repeat this pattern across the row. The second row slots into the gaps of the first row. Start with the first of the three small stitches immediately under the first long stitch of the previous row. The third row will start with the second of the short stitches underneath the first short stitch of the second row.

This pattern can be altered by changing the number of short stitches to make the 'steps' shallower or steeper. Use a multistranded thread for the best results.

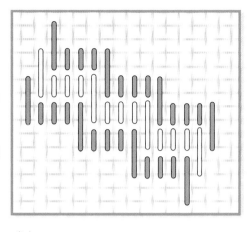

The sample shows the pattern worked with alternating rows in beads. The long stitch has been replaced by a bugle bead and the small stitches with seed beads.

Wild goose chase stitch

This stitch is worked in horizontal bands over an even number of threads. There are four rows to the pattern. Start by working a small vertical stitch over one thread. Follow this with stitches over two, three and four threads. The stitches will all be level at the top and get longer at the bottom. Repeat this pattern of four stitches across the row.

The second row begins with a stitch over four threads, which is directly below the small stitch over one thread in the first row. This is followed by stitches over three, two and one threads. The lower edge should remain level so that the top edge fits into the stitches above. Continue to repeat this pattern across the row.

The third and fourth rows follow the same pattern of stitches but are a mirror image of the first two rows. The third row begins with stitches over four, three, two and one threads and the fourth row begins with stitches over one, two, three and four threads.

When the pattern is complete you should be able to see the wings of the geese formed by the middle two rows following one another towards the right. Replacing the middle two rows of the 'flying geese' with beads is very effective. This pattern works best when stitched in a multistranded thread for a satin effect.

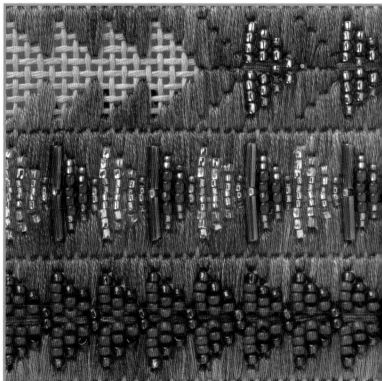

The sample shows the top pattern worked in a combination of thread and beads and the lower two patterns in various bead combinations of bugle, seed and petite seed beads.

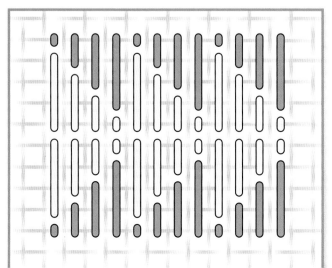

BEAD EMBROIDERY

This section covers the various beading stitches used to attach beads to fabric. The stitches will enable you to create different beaded shapes and motifs that stand alone without the thread being visible or to enhance existing motifs and patterns within the fabric.

Beading stitches can be worked on virtually any fabric but, because the threads travel across the back between beads, they may not always be suitable for sheer fabrics.

These stitches are used for beading on to clothing and bags in particular. They have a distinctly decorative purpose, but can also be used for practical reasons, such as their use in beaded motifs to cover damaged areas or new seams when altering an item of clothing. The stitches are hardwearing and very secure, so will not break when the items are used or washed.

Designing bead embroidery

First of all you must decide on the purpose of the finished embroidery, as this will usually point to which fabric to use. Once this is decided, inspiration for the design can often be taken from the fabric itself.

USING PATTERNED FABRIC

Enhancing an existing pattern, whether woven into or printed on to the fabric, is an easy way to start your bead embellishment journey. You can start by outlining an element or two and then see where that takes you. The first few stitches are daunting, but they usually lead to more exciting ideas!

STARTING FROM SCRATCH

If you are looking to create a design from scratch, inspiration can come from many sources, such as photographs, design books, shopping catalogues, vintage items or current fashionable items.

This design relies on the motifs within the cream damask. It is almost entirely worked in back stitch with a few loop and couching stitches in the centre, in a mixture of seed beads (size 11) and petite seed beads (size 15).

OTHER DESIGNS

A bold outline design will give you plenty of space to experiment with couching stitches, and also mixing different bead finishes and textures as you fill the spaces. Combining these will create a rich, heavy embroidery.

Lighter, scrolling, floral designs are perfect for enhancing dresses and other wearable items. I often take designs of this sort from pieces of lace. Photocopy the lace and draw a design from the paper image, adapting the size and removing or repeating elements until it fits the space intended.

Whether you use watersoluble pens and pencils for the design lines or tack them out with pins, they are removable, as are any beads you apply. Do not be afraid to experiment with different combinations – if you do not like them, you can take them off.

Take the plunge and stitch – sometimes not quite knowing where a design is going can be both liberating and exciting, and the results truly beautiful. The beads and sequins themselves almost guarantee this.

The inspiration for the design and colour scheme of this piece came from a piece of lace.

Bead-embroidery stitches

Back stitch in bead embroidery

This is one of the staple bead embroidery stitches. It has the advantage of added security as each bead is sewn individually and the beads can be stitched very close together or spaced apart at regular or varying intervals as required.

The pictures show back stitch being worked from right to left, but it can be worked in either direction.

Note

This is the same basic technique as back stitch in fringing (see page 392), the difference is simply in the spacing – in bead embroidery, the beads will usually sit very close together, whereas in fringing, they may be spaced further apart.

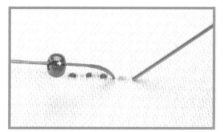

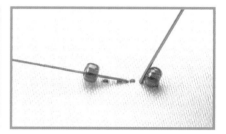

1 Bring the needle up a bead's width forward of your starting point (if you are using multiple beads, increase the distance accordingly). Draw the thread through and pick up a bead. Take the needle back down at the starting point.

2 Draw the thread through, trapping the bead. Bring the needle back up a bead's width forward along the design line.

3 Draw the thread through, pick up a second bead and take the needle back through the fabric immediately to the left of the previous bead.

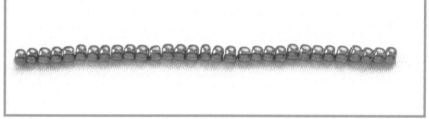

4 Pull the thread through to the back, trapping the second bead next to the first.

5 Bring the needle up a bead's width forward along the design line, thread a bead and repeat for the length of the design.

Fringed pincushion

This piece is worked on suedette with size 11 seed beads and pearls. The fringe has been worked with a spaced picot edge and drops (see page 394). 21st century. (Shelley Cox's personal collection)

Circlets

These little bead motifs can be worked in different sizes, as part of larger designs – flower centres or berries, for example – or as stand-alone shapes. They can enclose any shape, it need not be circular. Try them around an oval- or teardrop-shaped jewel, or a pretty shell or stone.

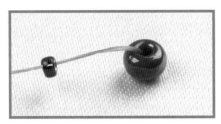

1 Mark a dot for the position of the centre of the circlet. Start your thread in this spot, then bring the needle up in the same spot. Pick up a large central bead and slide it down to the surface, then pick up a smaller bead to act as a stopper.

2 Take the needle back through the central bead, then draw the thread through so the stopper sits securely on the central bead.

3 Bring the needle up a small bead's width away at the 6 o'clock position (directly below the bead).

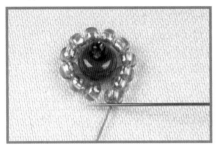

4 Pick up enough beads to encircle the central bead.

5 Take the needle back down at the point where you came through. Draw the thread through.

6 Couch the encircling thread (see couching, below) at the 12 o'clock, 3 o'clock and 9 o'clock positions to finish. For larger circles, you may wish to couch further points.

SMALLER CIRCLETS

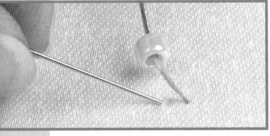

1 Mark a dot for the position of the centre of the circlet. Start your thread just to the side of this spot. Pick up your central bead and take the needle back through the spot.

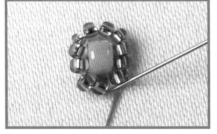

2 Bring the needle up at the 6 o'clock position and thread on enough petite beads to encircle the central bead. Take the needle back down at the 6 o'clock position.

3 Couch the encircling thread at the 12 o'clock, 3 o'clock and 9 o'clock positions to finish.

Couching with a single needle

This version of couching should be used with short lengths of beads, no longer than 5cm (2in), and preferably on straight lines. The thread becomes unwieldy with a large number of beads. The beads themselves can then appear crowded because the longer the length, the more couching stitches are required for it to sit securely on the design line.

1 Bring the needle up at the start of the design line, draw the thread through and pick up as many beads as required to cover the design line.

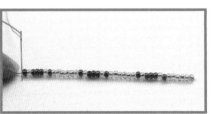

2 Use the needle to push the beads up to ensure that they fill the line, then take it down at the end of the line.

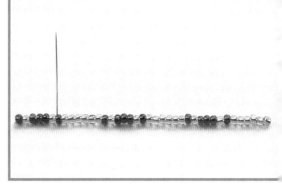

3 Draw the needle and thread through. Ensure that no thread can be seen between the beads and that the beads are not pushing each other out of shape. Bring the needle up on the far side of the thread, two or three beads back from the end.

4 Draw the thread through and take the needle back down into the fabric on the near side of the thread between the same two beads. Pull the thread to the back to trap (i.e. couch) the long thread at this point.

5 Bring the thread up on the far side of the thread, two or three beads further back along the line.

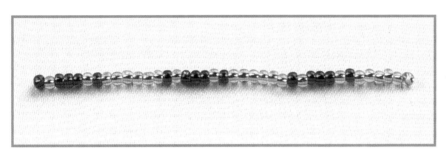

6 Take the needle back down on the near side of the thread to couch at this point, then continue along the line back to the start. Continue to couch the long thread every three to four beads, gradually working along the line of beads back to the start.

Couching with two threads

This technique is very versatile and can be used for designs where long lines of beads need to be stitched in waves or swirls. Using two threads makes it easy to add or change the bead combinations as you stitch. Working with a separate couching thread makes it easy to keep the tension and spacing between the beads constant with no bunching or crowding.

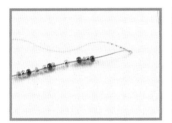

1 Secure two threads at the start of your design line. The first is your couching thread and the second your stringing thread. Take the couching thread through to the back. Pick up a dozen or so beads on your stringing thread.

2 Push the beads down to the beginning and hold them in place with your thumb. Bring your needle with the couching thread up on the far side of the stringing thread, two or three beads from the start.

3 Take the needle down on the near side of the stringing thread to couch the thread. When you draw the thread through, the couching thread will slide between the beads and disappear.

4 Ensure the stringing thread is sitting on the design line, then couch it again two or three beads further along. You are aiming to ensure that the beads stay on the design line, so you may need to couch more frequently than with single couching (see opposite) particularly on tight curves and turns.

5 Continue couching until you run out of beads, then pick up a dozen or so more on the needle and continue.

6 Continue to the end of the design line to finish. Secure both of your threads in the usual way.

Links and crosses

These stitches are very useful and have many adaptations. They can be worked in a variety of bead combinations; over other stitches, sequins and beads for texture or worked corner to corner for a diamond trellis appearance.

 The most important bead is the linking bead and making this a different colour or size, so it is easily recognisable as the stitches are worked, will help.

LINKS

These three-pointed shapes can be evenly spaced or have two legs closer together. The legs can be all the same length with the same bead combination or all be different.

 The bead that will end up in the centre is the linking bead. Make this stand out by choosing a different size or colour bead. You can have as many as four threads going through this bead (depending on the number of legs), so make sure it is large enough to handle this.

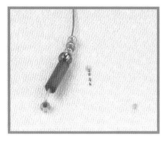

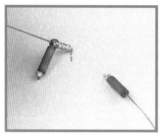

1 Mark the three points of your link on the surface. Start your thread where it will be covered by the beads. Bring your needle up at one of the side points and pick up enough beads to reach the next point while covering the centre point.

2 Take the needle down at the next point, then up at the third.

3 Draw the thread through and thread on beads to match the other side. Pass the needle through the central bead and along the beads to point number two and down into the fabric.

4 Draw the thread through to tighten the link to finish.

CROSSES

These are worked similarly to links but have four legs. If the central bead is large enough, by placing the first two legs closely and the second pair symmetrically opposite, it is possible to use this stitch and add more legs between the two original pairs.

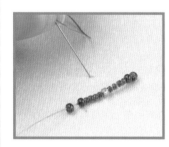

1 Mark four points on your surface. Start your thread where it will later be covered by beads. Bring your needle up at the top right and thread on enough beads to take you to the top left point while crossing the centre. Take the needle down at the top left.

2 Bring the needle up at the lower right point and thread on enough beads to take you to the central point.

3 Pass the needles through the central bead of the first strand, then pick up enough beads to take the needle to the lower left point to finish the cross.

Loops

These loop motifs make wonderful petals for flower motifs. Usually they are only anchored at the points and the tips but if the finished article is likely to be worn or used extensively, extra couching stitches can be made along the sides of the petals to prevent them catching and breaking.

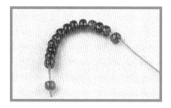

1 Mark a central point. Start your threads where the stitches will be hidden by beads in the finished loop. Thread on a base bead then an odd number of other beads.

2 Bring the beads around in a curve and take the needle back through the base bead and into the fabric. Draw the thread through to create a loop that stands up from the surface.

3 Keeping tension on the thread, push the loop back against the fabric and work it into an attractive shape on the surface. Bring the needle up to the right of the bead in the middle of the loop.

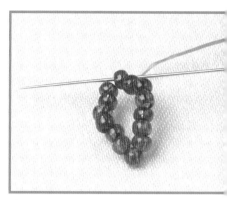

4 Pass the needle through this central bead and take it back down into the fabric immediately after to anchor the top of the loop to the fabric.

5 Draw the thread through and take it down just to the left of the bead. For very large petals work several couching stitches between beads along the sides to keep the loop the shape you want.

Tip
Loops can also be worked with a base bead and an even number of extra beads to give a more rounded top. In these instances, use a couching stitch over the thread between the two middle beads to anchor the top of the loop.

FILLED LOOPS

Adding beads to the centre of a loop can help to maintain its shape.

1 Prepare a loop as above, then bring the needle up immediately beneath the central bead.

2 Thread on enough beads to reach the base bead.

3 Take the needle down through the base bead, then draw the thread through to finish. The newly added beads will be raised towards the loop's point.

Running stitch

This is the simplest of all beading embroidery stitches. It can be worked with the beads close together or spaced apart. It is important to note that beads cannot be sewn as close together with this stitch as with back stitch. If working along a design line, be aware that the line will be visible between the beads and mark it appropriately with a removable pen, pencil or tack line.

Tip
It is sensible with most of these beading stitches, but particularly for running stitch to knot your thread securely around a stitch on the reverse every few beads. This is a safety precaution in case the thread breaks and will prevent all of the beads coming adrift.

1 Bring the needle up and thread on a single bead. Take the needle down into the fabric the width of the bead going forwards.

2 Draw the thread through to secure the bead, then bring the thread up a small distance further along the fabric.

3 Continue to repeat steps 1 and 2. This stitch can also be used for small multiples of beads.

Satin stitch

This stitch is useful for filling in solid areas of beads. It can make geometric shapes or be free flowing. It is also possible to work this stitch over padding – for raised areas and flower stems, for example.

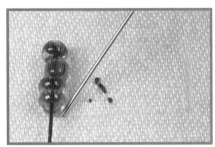  

1 Start your thread within your design and bring the needle up at the edge (top left in this example). Thread on enough beads to take you to the other side of the design, then take the needle down into the fabric.

2 Draw the thread through and bring the needle up next to the starting point (see inset), close enough that the beads will not leave a gap, but not so close that they crowd the previous row. Thread on enough beads to take you to the other side and take the needle down as before.

3 Continue in the same way to fill the shape. You can add different types of beads – simply ensure you bring the needle up a suitable distance from the previous row.

Sequin lines

Sequins are a natural accompaniment to beads and the two are often embroidered together. Here are a few ways to use sequins in your designs to further enhance your bead embroidery.

SEQUIN LINES USING RUNNING STITCH

1 Secure your thread near the start of the design line. Bring the needle up half a sequin width from the starting point. Pick up a sequin from the convex side (i.e. cup side down).

2 Push the sequin down the thread so that it sits cup side up on the fabric, then pick up beads equal to the radius of the sequin (i.e. half the width of the sequin).

3 Take the needle down into the fabric just past the edge of the sequin.

4 Draw the thread through, then bring the needle up half a sequin's width ahead (see inset) and repeat the process.

5 For a different effect, bring the needle up quarter of the sequin's width ahead (see inset) and take the needle down directly next to the sequin. The sequins will tilt up rather than lying flat on the fabric.

6 Repeat the technique to the end of the design line. In this example I have created a pattern of two sequins lying flat and two held up.

SEQUIN LINES USING BACK STITCH

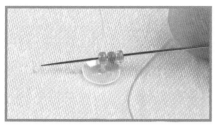

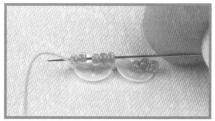

1 Secure your thread near the start of the design line and bring the needle up half a sequin's width from the starting point on the line. Pick up a sequin from the convex side and sufficient beads to cover half of the sequin.

2 Take the needle down behind the sequin, draw it through and bring it up half a sequin's width along the line. Pick up another sequin and enough beads to cover the entire sequin.

3 Take the needle down through the centre of the previous sequin (see inset) and draw it through. Come back up half a sequin width further along the line again.

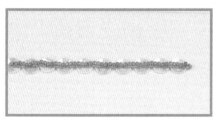

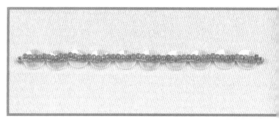

4 Continue to place sequins along the line, with sufficient beads to cover each sequin, until you reach the end of the design line.

5 Bring the needle up at the edge of the final sequin, pick up sufficient beads to cover half the sequin's width, then take the needle back down through the final sequin.

6 Draw the thread through to finish.

SEQUIN LINES USING STEM STITCH

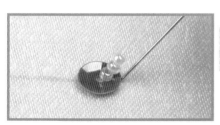

1 Secure your thread near the start of the design line, then bring your needle up half a sequin's width from the start of the design line. Pick up a sequin from the convex side and enough beads to cover half the sequin's width. Take the needle down directly behind the sequin.

2 Draw the thread through and bring the needle up immediately beside the sequin (see inset). Pick up a second sequin and sufficient beads to cover the whole width of the sequin. Take the needle down by the edge of the preceding sequin directly below the beads on the preceding sequin.

3 Bring the needle up in front of the second sequin, pick up another sequin and sufficient beads to span it, then take it down into the hole of the first sequin. Make sure you work beneath the beads on the previous sequin.

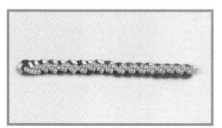

4 Repeat this technique to the end of the design line. You can use tweezers to tidy the line as you go.

5 At the end of the line, bring the needle up in front of the final sequin and pick up just enough beads to span half the width of the sequin. Take the needle down through the hole of the final sequin.

383

Sequin rosettes

These little motifs can add an extra sparkle and wow factor to any embroidery. Try alternating the colours of the sequins and the size of the centres for different effects.

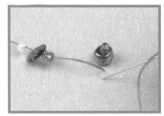

1 Mark the centre of the rosette with a dot and secure your thread here. Bring the needle up in the centre and secure a central bead. You can use any method of securing this bead. Here I am using stab stitch (see opposite).

2 Bring the needle up at the 6 o'clock position, a small distance away. Pick up two beads and then a sequin, cup side up as shown.

3 Pick up a seed bead that matches the colour of the fabric and take the needle down half a sequin's width further out from the 6 o'clock position.

4 Draw the thread through and the sequin will sit upright at an angle, then bring the needle up half a sequin width from the 6 o'clock position and repeat the process. The new sequin should slightly overlap the previous one.

5 Work clockwise around the central bead in the same way, overlapping each previous sequin.

6 For the final part, ensure the last sequin sits over the previous one and under the very first sequin to finish.

FLAT HALF CIRCLE SEQUIN ROSETTES

These motifs can be as varied as your imagination and the selection of beads and sequins at your disposal.

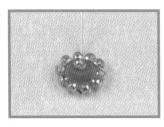

1 Make a circlet (see page 378) and bring the needle up at the 12 o'clock position, immediately above the circlet.

2 Thread on any combination of beads, then a sequin (cup side up). Take the needle down a distance equal to the lengths of the beads used. Ignore the sequin for the purposes of working this distance out.

3 Draw the thread through so that the sequin lies flat, then repeat at the 3 o'clock and 9 o'clock positions and in between, as shown.

4 Starting in any of the gaps, bring the needle up near the circlet and pick up a new sequence of beads, a sequin (cup side up) and, finally, a bead that matches the colour of your fabric.

5 Take the needle down a distance equal to the lengths of the beads used. Ignore both the sequin and the surface-coloured bead when working out this distance so that the sequin sits up.

6 Fill the remaining gaps in the same way to finish.

Stab stitch

This simple stitch is really useful for securing a single bead and works well as the centre of a circular motif. For height and variety in a design try using a bugle bead for the base bead, or adding three small beads to act as stopper beads instead of just one.

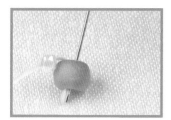

1 Bring the needle up and thread on your chosen base bead. Now thread on a smaller bead to act as a stopper and take the needle back through the base bead but not the stopper bead.

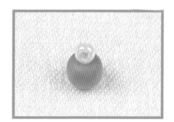

2 Draw the thread through to secure the beads; the stopper bead sits in the top of the base bead.

BEADED SURFACE EMBROIDERY

This section explores the use of traditional embroidery stitches and how you can use them as a base for embellishment with beads and sequins. Each stitch is shown with various bead treatments from adding a single bead to adding many beads so that the stitch appears to be worked entirely in beads.

If you intend the embroidery stitch to be visible and embellished with beads then the needle needs to be suitable for the size of the beads used (usually size 9 or 11 seed beads). The thread also needs to be a suitable thickness to thread into the chosen needle. If you intend to work the entire stitch in beads then you can use beading thread in a beading needle and whatever size of bead you wish.

These stitches can be worked on any fabric that you choose to use for surface embroidery.

Designing beaded surface embroidery

Most of the stitches in this section have either a horizontal or vertical linear orientation in the samples but they can be adapted as filling stitches in the same way the stitches would be adapted for surface embroidery generally.

Similarly the designs suitable for surface embroidery should also work for these stitches so look around for embroidery templates, crewel designs and even sampler patterns where you can incorporate some of these stitches enhanced with beads and sequins. Transfer the images to your fabric with removable lines – watersoluble pens or pencils or tack lines.

If you want a bit more freedom to experiment with your stitches and beads then a very effective base, with little need for an overall plan, is a panel of patchwork with irregular patches as in Victorian crazy patchwork. Work these stitches along the seams, then try other ideas from the previous section within the patches, or add lace motifs and embellish them with buttons and other items.

These stitches can also be used on clothing to hide a hemline that has been let down or a tear that has been repaired.

Using patterned fabrics can also be a good design beginning. The embellishment of existing lines and patterns with embroidery stitches enhanced with different beads can be very rich, colourful and striking and make wonderful cushion or bag panels.

Note

Back stitch, running stitch and satin stitch, as used in the bead embroidery section (pages 377–385), are also embroidery stitches and can be worked in embroidery thread and partially embellished in a way similar to those in this section.

Fantasia

This spectacles case is worked on silk dupion in perlé and stranded cotton threads with a mixture of seed beads, petite seed beads, bugle beads and sequins. 21st century. (Shelley Cox's personal collection)

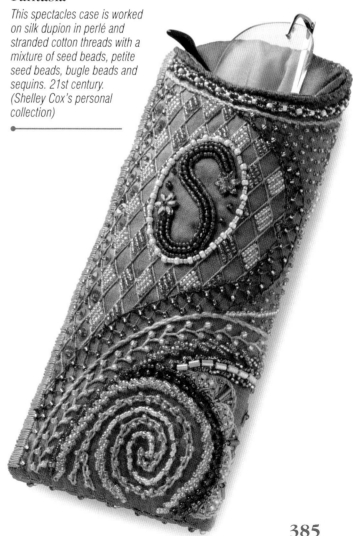

Surface-embroidery stitches
Back stitch, threaded and whipped

To work either of these stitches, first work a row of back stitch (see page 57) in thread, as in examples 1–4; or in beads, as in examples 5–8 (see page 377).

For threaded back stitch, slide the needle under the stitches from each alternate side without penetrating the fabric.

If the back stitch is worked in beads it is sometimes more secure to stitch underneath the back-stitched bead.

Whipped back stitch is worked by threading under the back stitches from the same side each time. Again a better (more secure) finish can be achieved by stitching under the back-stitched bead.

1 Whipped back stitch.
2 Threaded back stitch.
3 Back stitch in thread, whipped in petite seed beads.
4 Back stitch in thread, threaded with seed beads.
5 Back stitch in seed bead, whipped with petite seed beads.
6 Back stitch in bugles, whipped with seed beads.
7 Back stitch in seed beads, threaded with petite seed beads.
8 Back stitch in bugles, threaded with a mix of petite seed beads and seed beads.

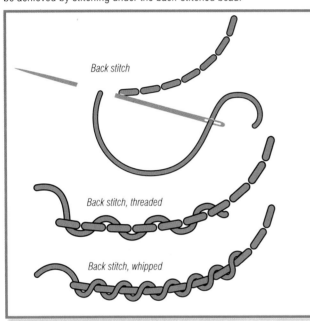

Back stitch

Back stitch, threaded

Back stitch, whipped

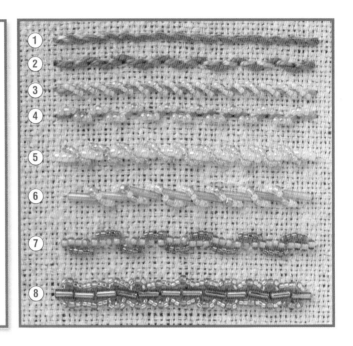

Buttonhole stitch

In this stitch the beads are added as you work the stitch. When working with an embroidery thread that will leave part of the stitch visible, the beads will be limited to the size of the needle used: see examples 1–3.

If the whole stitch is worked in beads you can use a beading thread and needle as in examples 4–6.

The variety of effects are unlimited with this stitch and it incorporates sequins very easily as well (see example 6).

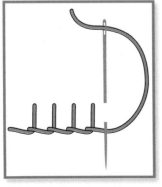

1 Regular buttonhole stitch.
2 Regular buttonhole with a single seed bead in the loop.
3 Regular buttonhole with petite seed beads and seed beads, plus varied lengths on the straights.
4 Alternate buttonhole with petite seed beads and seed beads.
5 Regular buttonhole with bugle beads and seed beads.
6 Regular buttonhole with bugle beads, seed beads and sequins.

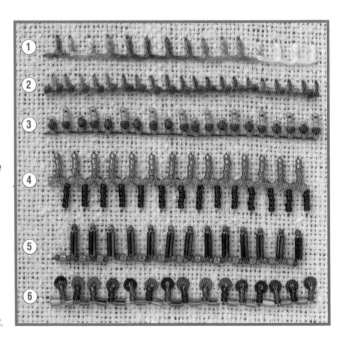

Chain stitch

Beads can be added to this stitch as it is worked in embroidery thread, as in examples 2–3, or the stitch can be worked entirely in beads, as in examples 4–8.

It can also be worked in a series of linked loops (see page 381). Altering the number and size of beads within each loop creates different effects. In example 5, the loops are first worked in linked pairs, then filled.

In example 6, linked chain stitch is worked as normal loops with three base beads instead of only one.

Example 7 is worked the same as example 4, but the link is started deeper inside the previous loop and more beads are used, so the effect is raised and more ornate.

Example 8 shows single detached chain stitches, a variation commonly known as lazy daisy (see page 71).

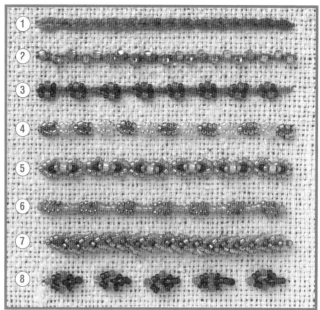

1 Chain stitch.
2 Chain stitch with single seed beads.
3 Chain stitch in alternating thread and seed beads.
4 Chain stitch in seed beads.
5 Filled chain stitch in seed beads and petite seed beads.
6 Linked chain stitch in petite seed beads and seed beads.
7 Chain stitch in seed beads.
8 Detached chain stitch in seed beads; also known as 'lazy daisy'.

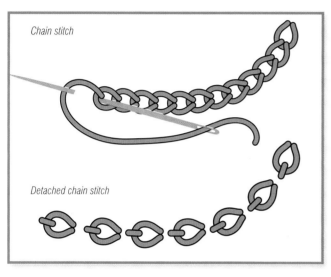

Chain stitch

Detached chain stitch

Chevron stitch

A combination of horizontal and diagonal stitches, this is a relatively difficult stitch as the regular spacing is very important. Fortunately, the addition of beads actually helps with this.

The length of the horizontal stitches and the angle and length of the diagonals can be varied to create different effects with the various bead combinations used – compare example 3 with 5 for an illustration.

This stitch is also useful as a base for adding other stitches to it to create wider, more decorative, borders. Try adding little flowers of lazy-daisy loops (see above) and bugles on top of the horizontal stitches.

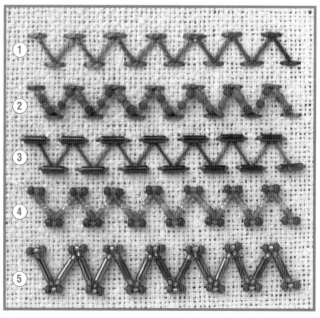

1 Chevron stitch in thread.
2 Chevron stitch with diagonals in seed beads.
3 Chevron stitch with horizontals in bugle beads.
4 Chevron stitch in seed beads and petite seed beads.
5 Chevron stitch with bugle beads and seed beads.

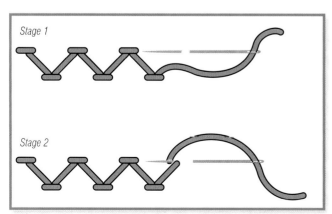

Stage 1

Stage 2

Coral stitch

This stitch incorporates a knot, which is necessary to anchor the thread and beads, but which is also decorative. It is therefore only possible in embroidery thread.

The distance between the knots and the combination of beads is directly related to the line on which the stitch will be worked. The curvier it is, the shorter the distance between the knots and the fewer beads you will need. Controlling the knot with tension as it is pulled down will give the best result and prevent the thread between the knots from coming loose.

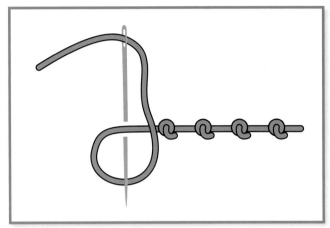

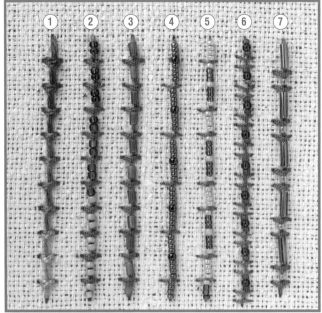

1 Coral stitch in thread.
2 Coral stitch in thread with seed beads.
3 Coral stitch in thread with short bugles.
4 Spaced coral stitch with seed beads and petite seed beads.
5 Alternating spaced coral stitch in thread with seed beads.
6 Alternating spaced coral stitch in thread with seed beads and petite seed beads.
7 Alternating spaced coral stitch in thread with seed beads and bugles.

Cretan stitch

This stitch is worked in such a way that the beads can be situated at the centre of the stitch or towards the edges and are locked in place with each succeeding stitch.

It can be worked in embroidery thread with beads added, as in examples 2–3; or entirely in beads on a beading thread, as in examples 4 and 5.

The spacing and width of this stitch can be altered to accommodate different sizes and combinations of beads, and sequins can also be added at the edges for additional effect.

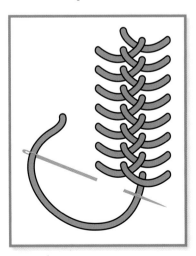

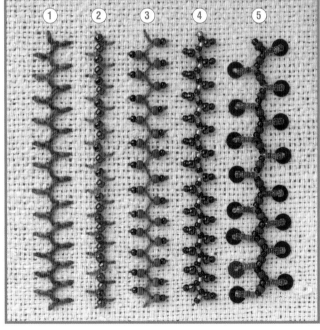

1 Cretan stitch in thread.
2 Cretan stitch in thread and central seed beads.
3 Cretan stitch with side seed beads and petite seed beads.
4 Cretan stitch in seed beads and petite seed beads.
5 Cretan stitch in seed beads, petite seed beads and sequins.

Feather stitch

This stitch has a similar feel to Cretan stitch (see opposite), but the loop depth is deeper and the spacing is different. Like Cretan stitch, it can be worked in embroidery thread with a single bead added to the outside edges or the inside, as in examples 2–3; or it can be worked entirely in beads, with or without sequins, as in examples 4 and 5.

Examples 1–4 show single feather stitch, while example 5 shows double feather stitch. Instead of working a single stitch to each side, two stitches are worked.

Triple feather stitch is worked in a similar manner to double but with three stitches to each side. This stitch can also be worked as free feather stitch where the number of stitches to each side can vary as desired. The addition of different numbers and sizes of beads can create endless variations.

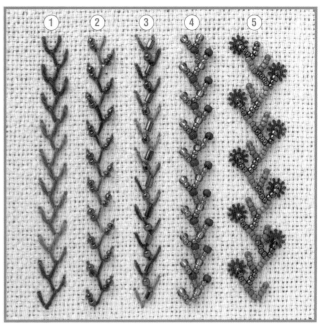

1 Feather stitch in thread.
2 Feather stitch in thread with seed beads and petite seed beads.
3 Feather stitch in thread with central seed and short bugle beads.
4 Feather stitch in seed beads and petite seed beads.
5 Double feather stitch in seed beads and sequins.

Fly stitch

This stitch can be worked as a single detached stitch or in a continuous line, as the examples show.

If worked in embroidery thread, beads can be added to the sides or down the centre, as in examples 2–3.

If worked entirely in beads, as in examples 4–6, the spacing can be altered, bead combinations varied, and sequins added as desired.

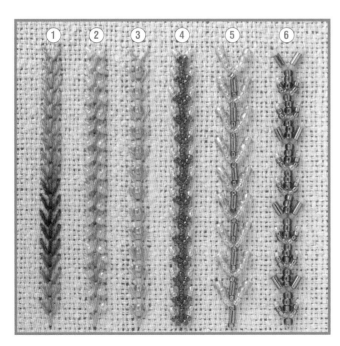

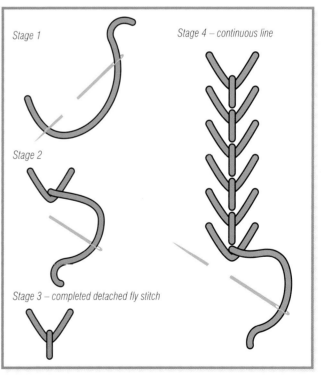

Stage 1

Stage 2

Stage 3 – completed detached fly stitch

Stage 4 – continuous line

1 Fly stitch in thread.
2 Fly stitch in thread with side seed beads.
3 Fly stitch in thread with central seed and petite seed beads.
4 Fly stitch in petite seed beads.
5 Fly stitch in seed, petite seed and bugle beads.
6 Fly stitch in seed beads and bugles (alternative arrangement).

Herringbone stitch

This stitch, a series of overlapping crosses, depends on its regular spacing to look good. When worked in embroidery thread with a single bead added (as in example 2), it is necessary to pass the needle through each bead twice to stabilise its position.

Example 3 shows the pattern in embroidery thread with each successive stitch holding the previous set of beads in place.

Examples 4 and 5 are worked entirely in beads, although example 5 has been stitched as if it had no beads. The beads therefore overlap giving a raised and textured effect.

Like chevron stitch (see page 387), herringbone is a good base stitch for further embellishment to create wider, more decorative, borders.

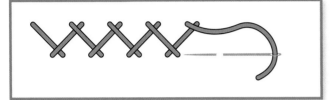

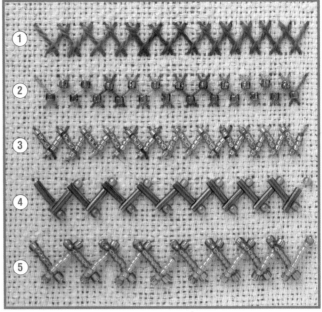

1 Herringbone stitch in thread.
2 Herringbone stitch in thread and seed beads.
3 Herringbone stitch in petite seed beads.
4 Herringbone stitch in bugles and seed beads.
5 Herringbone stitch in seed beads and petite seed beads.

Seeding stitch

This stitch is very simple and consists of small, evenly worked, stitches in random directions. It is great for providing an area with background colour.

It can be worked in a mixture of thread and beads, similar single beads of different colours (shaded) or similar colours but various sizes and shapes (textured).

Example 5 shows beads secured with stab stitches (see page 385).

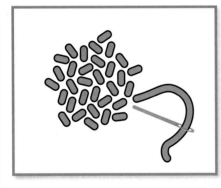

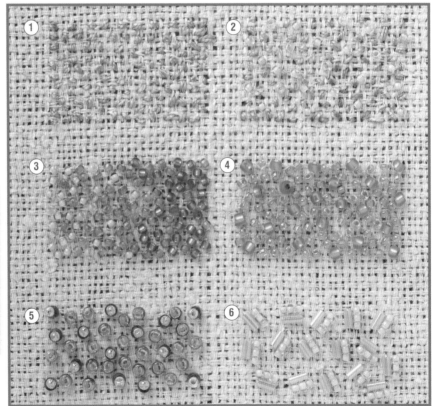

1 Seeding stitch in thread.
2 Seeding stitch in mix of thread and petite seed beads.
3 Shaded seeding stitch in petite seed beads.
4 Seeding stitch in petite and regular seed beads.
5 Seeding stitch in sequins and petite seed beads.
6 Double seeding stitch with short bugles and petite seed beads.

Stem stitch

This stitch creates a wonderful rope effect. When the twist runs from bottom left to top right it is called stem stitch, when it runs from bottom right to top left it is called outline stitch. The examples below show stem stitch.

Altering the stitch length or combination of beads creates a variety of effects and changes the width of the finished stitch.

The stitch is worked in the same way when adding sequins except that a sequin is added after each bead combination before the needle is taken down into the fabric. The needle then comes up in the hole of the previous sequin. The number of beads must be equal to the width of the sequin for the stitch to work because the sequins overlap by half their width.

This stitch, while worked differently, looks the same as the sequin line using stem stitch shown on page 383.

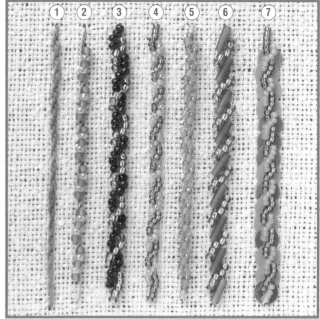

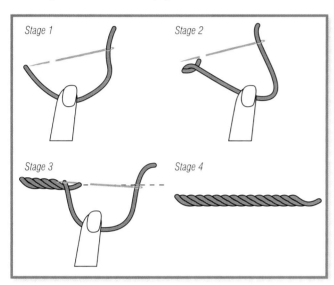

1 Stem stitch in thread.
2 Stem stitch in alternating thread and seed beads.
3 Stem stitch in seed beads (alternating colours).
4 Stem stitch in alternating seed beads and petite seed beads.
5 Stem stitch in mixed seed beads and petite seed beads.
6 Stem stitch in alternating seed beads and regular bugles.
7 Stem stitch in petite seed beads with sequins.

Whip stitch

This stitch is a very simple, effective, alternative to stem stitch. When worked in embroidery thread and beads, as in examples 2–3, it is quite open. Worked in different bead, or bead and sequin combinations it becomes more linear and closed.

Interesting effects can be achieved by varying the lengths of the stitches, or by alternating between different beads, or combinations of beads and sequins.

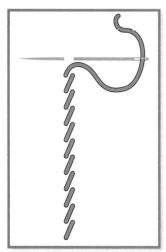

1 Whip stitch in thread.
2 Whip stitch in alternating thread and regular bugles.
3 Whip stitch in thread, petite seed beads and seed beads.
4 Whip stitch in seed beads.
5 Whip stitch in alternating lengths of petite seed beads and seed beads.
6 Whip stitch in regular bugles.
7 Whip stitch in sequins, seed beads and petite seed beads.

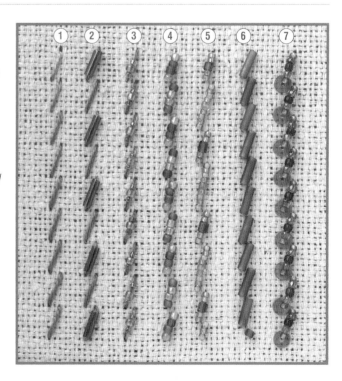

FRINGES

Edging and fringes can be very simple, long and complex, straight, staggered, twisted, netted or looped. The one thing they all have in common is the ability to enhance and 'finish' a textile item. An edging is generally narrow, short and relatively simple, while a fringe is longer, fluid and usually more complex.

This chapter covers the basic construction of different types of edgings and fringes. All look different when worked in varying bead sizes and combinations.

Designing beaded edges and fringes

In most cases it is advisable to complete the article to be fringed before deciding on the type of edging or fringe and combination of beads to be included. Designing your fringe is largely based on personal preference but some points do need to be considered before starting:

- What type of item is it? Small items like pincushions, box edges, cuffs or collars will be best enhanced with a short fringe or small loops. A fringe that will move and give weight to an edge works well on the edges of scarves, shawls, hemlines, tablecloths and wall hangings.
- What fabric is it made of? Few fabrics are completely unsuitable for edgings and fringes but it is essential that the fabric to which the fringe is attached is suitable for the weight and type of fringe.
- Do you have enough beads to complete the fringe? This sounds basic but I have been caught out with this! Before you begin, measure the item carefully and work out your spacing and the number of drops required to ensure you have sufficient beads for the edge or fringe.

THREADS, NEEDLES AND TENSION

Generally the thread you use for edges and fringes should be matched to the colour of the fabric. The examples in this section have all been worked on nylon-coated beading thread for its strength and fineness. The edgings, being shorter in depth, can be stitched easily with a small beading or fine embroidery needle, but I often use a long beading needle for the fringes because of the long drops.

The stitch tension for a fringe is looser than that for an edging so that the fringe swings nicely. If pulled too tightly, the fringe will not dangle fluidly and drops will stick out at strange angles.

Victorian needlepoint bag
19th century.
(Shelley Cox's personal collection)

MARKERS

Once you have measured your item and decided on the type and combination of beads for your edging or fringe, use a ruler and fine pins to mark the intervals along the edge where the base beads will be attached. This is particularly important for spaced, looped and netted fringes.

BACK STITCH FOR FRINGES AND EDGINGS

This stitch is often used as a foundation or base row for further embellishment. While the technique is slightly different, owing to working along an edge, back stitch for fringing is worked in a similar way as for back stitch in bead embroidery (see page 377).

Note

It is very important to finish the thread securely with several back stitches and a couple of knots in the fabric as fringes are very tactile and often handled a lot.

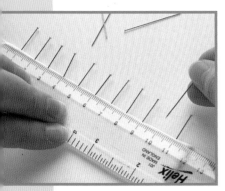

1 When using markers, bring the needle out just after the marker pin.

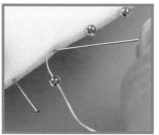

2 Pull out the marker pin, pick up a bead and take the needle back in, just behind where the thread emerges.

3 Take the needle through and bring it out just in front of the next marker, then continue to the end. Finish the thread with several back stitches.

Edging and fringing stitches

Simple picot edge

This is a basic, commonly used edging, as it fits any shape and measurement. The spacing of the base beads may vary depending on the size and shape of the picot bead (shown in green in the diagram).

Come out of the fabric and thread on three beads, go down into the fabric making a small 2mm ($^1/_{16}$in) stitch, leaving enough space for the first and third bead to sit beside one another and the middle bead to be comfortably situated below them. Come back down the third bead and thread on another two beads before making another small 2mm ($^1/_{16}$in) stitch in the fabric and repeating.

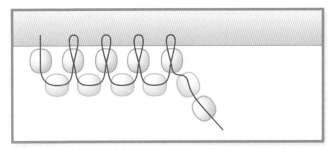

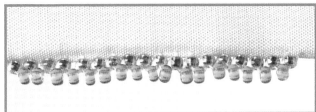

Alternating picot edge

This is worked in the same way as the simple picot edge but every other stitch the picot bead (shown in green in the diagram) is omitted. It is not quite as easy to fit to any measurement as the alternative nature of the pattern needs to be maintained along each edge.

Tip
Lay out the beads in order and with the correct amount of spacing on a beading mat to try out various patterns before stitching.

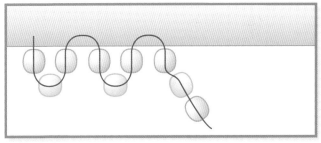

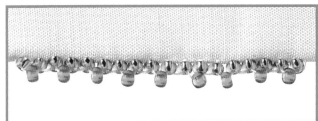

Spaced picot edge

Stitch this as for the simple picot edge (see above), allowing enough space between the base beads (those touching the fabric) to accommodate the number of beads in the loops. Use markers to work out the spacing before starting this edging stitch.

Adding larger or heavier beads in the centres of the loops will give a different effect and add weight to the edging while maintaining the curved outline.

This edging can be extended in length to create another version of a looped fringe (see page 395).

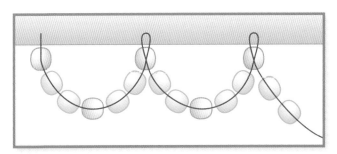

Spaced picot edge with drops

This pattern gives a pointed, rather than curved, shape to the edging. It is worked similarly to the spaced picot edge (see page 393) with a drop in the centre of each loop.

Start by coming out of the fabric and adding all the beads up to and including the small seed bead following the drop bead. Miss out the small seed bead and pass the needle back up the drop bead, then add the rest of the beads to the base bead, make the small 2mm (¹/₁₆in) holding stitch and repeat.

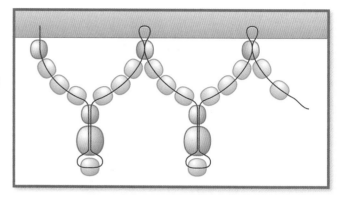

Straight fringe

This is the basic dangle fringe and the variations of this are unlimited depending on the number and size of beads used. All of the dangles are the same length.

Come out of the fabric and thread on all the beads in the dangle. Miss the final bead and pass the needle back up through all the beads to the top and into the fabric, then bring the needle out in position of the next dangle. Pull the first drop up firmly, but not tightly.

If using a shaped drop bead on the end, space the dangles to accommodate the extra width, in order to ensure the drop beads do not crowd one another.

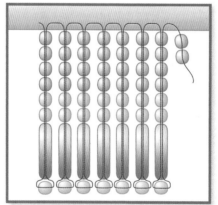

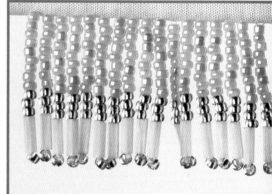

Shaped fringe

This is worked in the same way as the straight fringe (see above), but the number of beads change with each dangle to create a fringe with a specific repeating shape.

The shapes you can produce with this technique include scalloped, pointed and saw-toothed, wide and shallow, and narrow and deep. Shaped fringes are most effective when the dangles are placed close together.

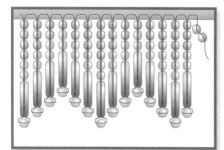

Alternating straight fringe with a back-stitch base

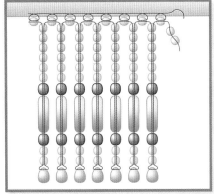

This is a simple straight fringe hanging from a row of back stitched beads.

Start by using back stitch to secure a base row of beads, each a bead's width apart from each other. The dangles are then suspended from these beads rather than the fabric.

The dangles tend to move more freely with this method but the fringe is not as robust. It works well on wall hangings but is not suitable for items that will have a lot of handling.

Staggered fringe with a back-stitch base

This is worked in the same way as the alternating straight fringe with a back stitch base (see above). In this fringe the dangles alternate between two different lengths. Shaped fringes of various types can also be suspended from a back stitch base in this way.

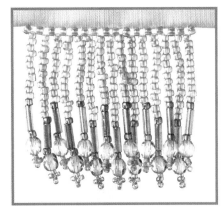

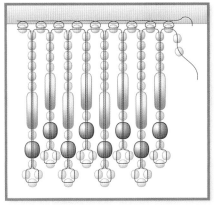

Simple looped fringe

This fringe is a series of side-by-side loops, worked individually. Joined loops should be worked like the spaced picot edge on page 393.

Use marker pins to work the spacing out so that the loops fit the edge to be worked. Next, bring the needle out of the fabric, string on all the beads for the loop and make a short stitch going into the fabric just before the next marker pin and coming back out just after it to make a second loop.

A simple looped fringe can also be worked suspended from a row of spaced back-stitched beads.

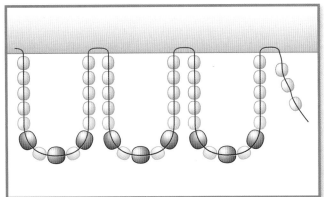

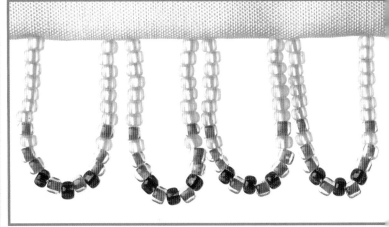

Alternating looped fringe

This fringe is worked in the same way as the simple looped fringe (see page 395) but the individual loops are in two alternating lengths. This fringe is particularly attractive when the two loops are worked in different combinations of beads, as in the example below. Heavy beads placed in the centre of each loop will give weight and interest to the fringe. Again, this fringe can be suspended from a row of spaced, back-stitched beads.

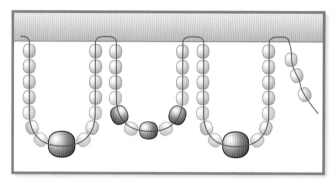 

Overlapping looped fringe

This fringe can be very heavy and dramatic and has a wonderful layered effect. It works best in a circle, around a tablecloth or cushion, for example, as the beginning needs to be overlapped by the end for a consistent look.

Mark the edge at regular intervals – the example was marked at 1cm (½in) intervals – then make the first loop from point 1 to just before point 4. Make the second loop from point 2 to just before point 5, the third loop from point 3 to just before point 6, the fourth loop from point 4 (after the end of the first loop) to just before point 7, and so on.

Make sure the pattern continues when the end reaches the beginning again.

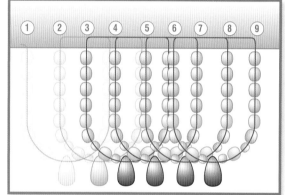 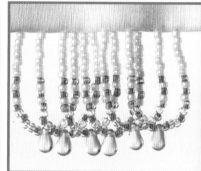

Twisted looped fringe

This is a simple fringe that looks more complicated than it is. It is worked in the same way as the simple looped fringe (see page 395) for the first loop. The second loop is started in the same way, but before anchoring the loop in the fabric wrap the needle (once, twice or more, as desired), around the previous loop. For the sample below, the needle was wrapped twice. The length of each loop needs to be long enough to accommodate the twists. This is one of the few fringes that do not take bugle beads well.

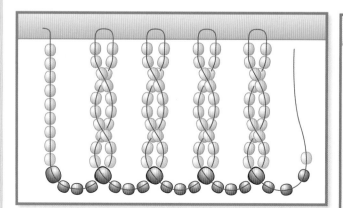 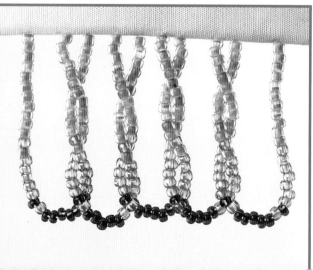

Horizontal netted fringe

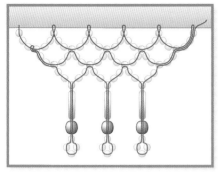

Tip
Make the central linking bead in each loop a different size or colour so it is obvious when working each subsequent row.

This is a dramatic fringe, worked in horizontal rows. It can be worked to a point and finished with a tassel drop if required. The sample is worked in three rows with drops.

Work the first row as a spaced picot edge (see page 393) with an uneven number of beads between each base bead. On completing this edge, take a stitch in the fabric and thread the needle back down the last loop to emerge from the central bead. Work another row of loops off the central bead of each first-row loop.

On completing the second row, make a slip knot around the thread in the last loop and pass the needle back down the last loop of the second row, emerging from the central bead. The third row is worked like the second, incorporating a decorative drop. Thread the needle back to the fabric at the end of the row and finish as normal. It is important to note that the width of the fringe decreases by one loop with each row. Therefore, depending on the width of the original row, there will always be a finite number of rows to this pattern.

Vertical netted fringe

This fringe is also netted but, as it is worked in vertical rows, it can be any width and any length.

Each dangle is worked in turn and linked to the following one at specific points within the pattern.

This form of netting is very versatile and particularly impressive on shawls, wall hangings and bags. Unlike the horizontal netting it does not decrease or taper. It falls well because it can be made quite weighty.

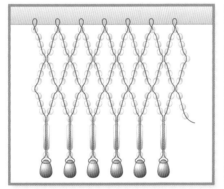

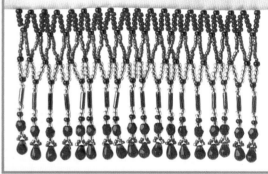

Detail of antique fringe
A typical example of a Victorian fringe, showing a 15cm (6in) scalloped shape with a rose design depicted within the drops. 21st century. (Shelley Cox's personal collection)

INDEX